The People along the Sand

THE SPURN PENINSULA & KILNSEA
A History, 1800-2000

Coxswain Robertson Buchan ringing the call-out bell.

The People along the Sand

THE SPURN PENINSULA & KILNSEA
A History, 1800-2000

Jan Crowther

Phillimore

2006, reprinted 2010

Published by
PHILLIMORE & CO. LTD
Healey House, Andover, Hampshire
www.phillimore.co.uk

ISBN 13   978-1-86077-654-0

Printed in England

The People along the Sand

The people along the sand
All turn and look one way.
They turn their back on the land.
They look at the sea all day.

As long as it takes to pass
A ship keeps raising its hull;
The wetter ground like glass
Reflects a standing gull.

The land may vary more;
But wherever the truth may be—
The water comes ashore,
And the people look at the sea.

They cannot look out far.
They cannot look in deep.
But when was that ever a bar
To any watch they keep?

Robert Frost

Contents

List of Illustrations

Frontispiece: Coxswain Robertson Buchan ringing the call-out bell

Preface

This social history of Spurn and Kilnsea covers the period from the opening of the 19th century until the end of the 20th. The emphasis is upon how the landscape of this very unusual area has impacted upon the people who have lived there or been associated with it. The book has been written in a broadly chronological form, but within each chapter an attempt has been made to collect the material together thematically. Running through the narrative is the story of the farmers, the tradespeople and the ordinary villagers of Kilnsea, and how they have coped with the challenges that have come their way, notably from the sea and the Humber, which enclose them on either side. Over the years their land has been utilised by the military, and more recently they have found themselves living close to a nature reserve, visited by numerous bird-watchers, sightseers and holidaymakers. Every year they lose land to the sea. Every year their village becomes more vulnerable to gales and floods.

On Spurn itself the last 200 years have been a time of great change. The coming of the lifeboat, the great breach in the peninsula in the middle of the 19th century, the building and rebuilding of lighthouses, the enormous changes brought about during two World Wars by the military presence on the peninsula, the withdrawal of the army in the late 1950s and the purchase of the peninsula as a nature reserve by the Yorkshire Wildlife Trust, the establishment of Spurn Bird Observatory, the usage of Spurn by pilots and for navigational technology on the Humber, the regular crises brought about by the sea's encroachment upon the peninsula – all these factors and many more contribute to Spurn's unique and exciting story.

I have known the area since the early 1980s, and have been collecting material and talking to people who have lived there or visited it ever since. The result is this book, which I hope will be enjoyed by all those who love the area, and will serve to introduce new enthusiasts. I am aware that my version of the history of Spurn and Kilnsea can only be partial. The last chapter, which covers the period from 1970 until the millennium, could have been as long as the book itself. Hard choices have had to be made, and the chapter is much shorter than the amount of material relating to it merits. Spurn Bird Observatory, the Yorkshire Wildlife Trust, the Humber Lifeboat, the Humber and its maritime services, Kilnsea and Spurn's history, geology and geomorphology – all now figure on regularly updated websites, which include much information about topics of interest. A group called the Spurn, Kilnsea and Easington Area Local Studies Group (SKEALS) has been created in association with this book, and a website has been launched which contains more information on the area, and for people to contribute their own memories, photographs and comments. The URL is http://www.skeals.co.uk. I hope that this book will inspire people to visit the website and add more to what is already known about this beautiful and fascinating area.

Acknowledgements

Many people have helped me with this work and it is impossible to acknowledge all of them. The book is truly the tip of the iceberg as I have accumulated many audio tapes, notes and photographs in the course of its preparation as a result of my contacts with people who have been associated with Spurn and Kilnsea over the years. Although all their reminiscences and photographs could not appear in the book, I can assure them that they will be preserved and may well appear in a different form in the future. I owe a special debt to Howard Frost for his meticulous reading and commentary on the text. I am also grateful to John Cudworth, George de Boer, Jeffrey Dorman, Barry Spence and Alan Williamson, who have read certain sections and helped me with information. Needless to say any mistakes are my own. The following people and institutions have also helped me in various ways and I apologise for any omissions: Cyd and Win Barker, Brian Bevan, Beverley Local Studies Library, Sybil Blewett (née Cheverton), Gwen Bousfield, Brynmor Jones Library of the University of Hull, Robertson Buchan, Henry Bunce, Louise Clarke, Albert Clubley, Gordon Clubley, June Collins (née Hopper), Tim Collins, Peter Cook, Audrey and Roland Cooper, Mike Coverdale, Eva Crackles, Martin Craven, Arthur Credland, Vera Cross, East Riding of Yorkshire Archives, East Riding of Yorkshire Council, Anne Eldon, David Erving, Andrew Gibson, Tom Graham, Gillian Granger, Brian Heckford, Robina Herrington, Denis Hopper, Diane Horncastle, Carrie Leonard, Richard Loughlin, Arrol McInnes, Alan McKinstrie, Larry Malkin, Liz and Peter Martin, Joyce and Colin Massingham, Stella Morris, Wendy Munday, Susan and David Neave, Shirley Pashby, Peter Pearson, Arthur Piggott, Hilda Reed (née Sparrow), Tony Regan, Rosie Robertson, Richard and Terri Robinson, Brian Rushworth, Sandra Shann, Martin and Miriam Shead, Alf Shearsmith, Liz and Peter Simmonds, Roy Skelton, Dorothy Smith, Spurn Bird Observatory Trust, Spurn Heritage Coast Project, Dave Steenvoorden, Pat Stevenson, Marjorie Tillott, Nick Tindall, Trinity House (Hull), Christine Wainwright, David Webster, Dorothy Webster, Mike Welton, Edith Wheeler-Osman, Roland Wheeler-Osman, Karen Wood, Donald Woodward, and the Yorkshire Wildlife Trust.

This book contains over 200 illustrations which I have gathered from a variety of sources which are listed below. I would like to specially thank all those individuals and institutions included in this list who have allowed me to use their photographs or permitted me to reproduce illustrations in their possession. I am grateful to Wendy Munday whose skilfully drawn maps succeed in conveying a complex situation in a most succinct and straightforward way. I am also grateful to Nick Tindall for permission to use his painting of the *Crown and Anchor*. The maps and black and white illustrations are referred to by their number in the general sequence of illustrations and the coloured plates by their plate number in **bold**, as follows: R. Barratt (R. & R. Studio) **pl. 31-2**; M. Batchelor (H.M. Frost Coll.) 138, 140-1; B. Bevan **pl. 20**; S. Blewett 129; Brynmor Jones Library Archives 135, 142; J. Child **pl. 1-2**; L. Clarke 124; J. Collins 28, 43-4, 46-8, 64-5; A. Cooper 15, 106; R. Cooper 151; M. Craven 10, 56-60, 79; V. Cross 49, 51, 88, 93-9, 109, 111, 114, 116-17, 122-3, 127; Crown Copyright (RCHM) 90, 118,

121; J.E. Crowther 76, 160-1, 166-9, 193, **pl. 5-6, pl. 12, pl. 30**; P.A. Crowther 4, 7, 9, 17, 86, 194, **pl. 15-19, pl. 22-8**; G. de Boer 2; E.R. Yorks. Archives Office (DDCC 89/11) 18; E.R Yorks. Archives Office (Spurn Heritage Coast Coll.) 11, 23, 70-5, 80-1, 84, 126; E.R. Yorks. Council 186-7, 192; A. Eldon 21-2, 24, 31, 37, 77, 92; H.M. Frost 66, 115, 180; H. Gastineau (engrav. by J. Rogers) **pl. 3-4**; T. Graham 39, 105, 153-4; G. Granger 178; J. Hagan (H.M. Frost Coll.) 146; B. Heckford 76; T. Hildred 83, 101, 103; Hull Daily Mail (R. Buchan Coll.) frontispiece, 147-9, 157-8, 172, 174-5; Hull Maritime Museum 85; C. Leonard 102, 104, 107-8, 112, 128, 130, 155; J. & C. Massingham **pl. 13**; H. & K. Morris 6, 52, 55, 66-7; W. Munday (maps) 1, 3, 19, 69; J. Nicholson 14; S. Pashby 181, 188, 189-90, **pl. 14**; A. Piggott 53-4, 132; G. Poulson 5, 20; R. & T. Robinson 26-7, 30, 32-6, 38, 40, 45, 62-3, 87, **pl. 7-9**; A. Shearsmith 119, 131; T. Sheppard 8; D. Smith Coll. 12-13, 16, 25, 29, 41, 61, 68, 78, 82, 120, 125, 184; B.R. Spence 162-3, **pl. 10-11, pl. 29**; Spurn Bird Observatory Trust 133-4, 136-7, 139, 145, 150, 159, 176-7, 182-3, 185,191; P. Stevenson 152; The Sun (R. Buchan Coll.) 144, 173; M. Tillott 42, 50; N.J. Tindall **pl. 30**; C. Wainright 100; I. Walker **pl. 21**; D. Webster 113; E. Wheeler-Osman 89, 91, 110; R. Wheeler-Osman 164-5, 171; Yorkshire Post (R. Buchan Coll.) 143, 156, 170, 179.

I would like to express my thanks to the staff of Phillimore's for their help and expertise in preparing this book for the press, especially Noel Osborne, Anthony Lovell, and Peter Cook. In addition I must thank the Easington Enhancement Fund, the Langeled Fund, and British Petroleum (Easington) for generously supporting the publication costs of the book. All profits that arise from it will go towards new projects in the local area.

Finally I wish to thank the person who has helped me most of all in the preparation of this book, my husband, Pete, who has sub-edited the text, compiled the index, taken many of the photos, and above all remained patient and supportive throughout the years. I know that he loves the place as much as I do, and I should like to dedicate this book to him.

Introduction

This history of Spurn peninsula and Kilnsea village starts at the beginning of the 19th century, so it is necessary to say a little about their earlier history. The first peninsula at the south-east tip of Holderness probably developed after the retreat of the last Ice Age, when Holderness, which has one of the fastest eroding coasts in the world, was formed. As the ice retreated it left behind a blanket of boulder clay between 20 to 50 metres deep. The peninsula or peninsulas at the tip of Holderness were formed from material transported southwards, and their alignment must have changed considerably over time. Historical records suggest that at least parts of them have periodically been washed away and have subsequently regrown, but whether they have been subject to a regular cycle, as suggested by George de Boer, formerly Reader in Geography at the University of Hull, cannot be proved. What is certain is that for most of recorded history there has been a promontory or spit of land attached to Holderness: we know the one that exists today by the name of Spurn Head or Spurn Point.

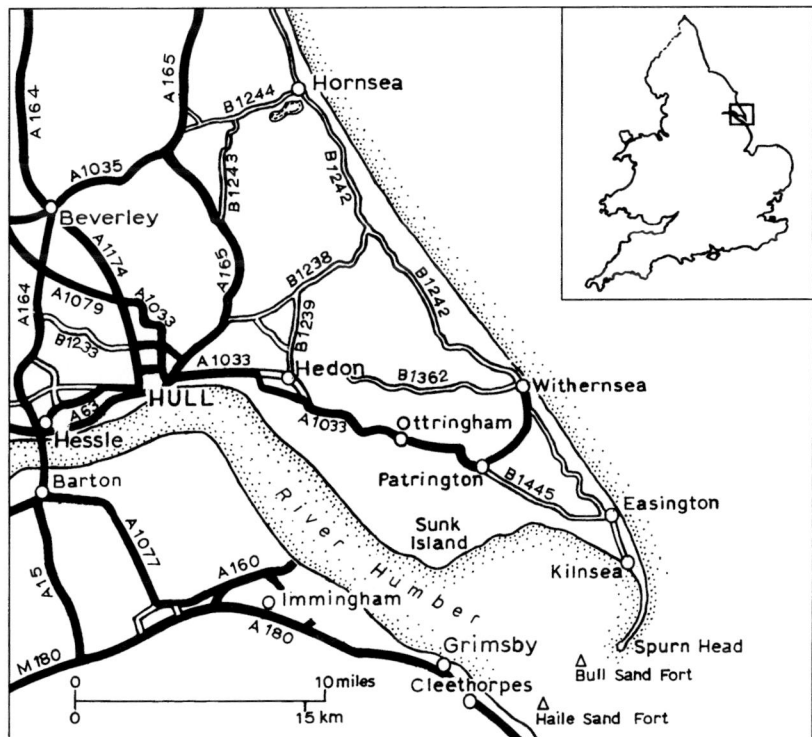

1   *England with East Yorkshire inset.*

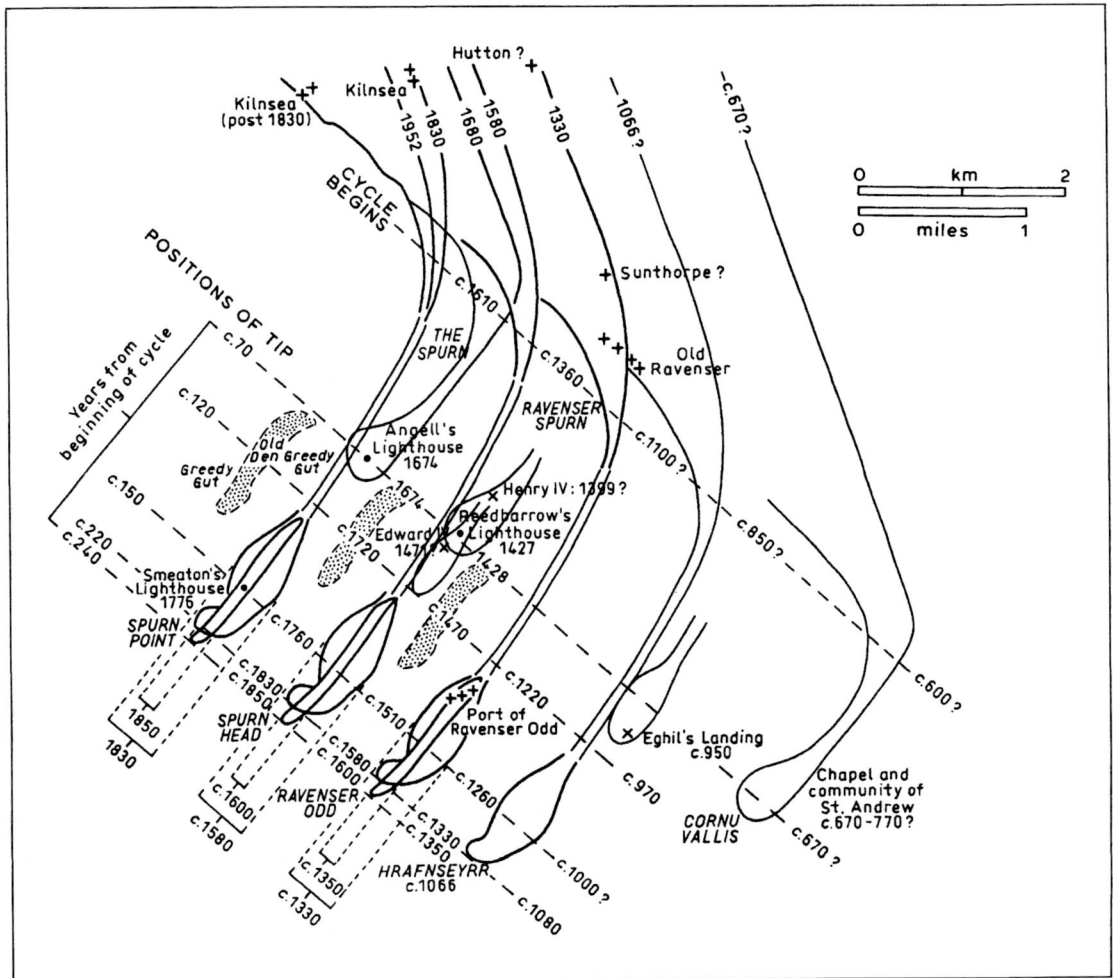

2 *Spurn cyclical theory.*

It has been estimated that when the Romans were in Britain the coastline of Holderness was about three and a half miles further east than it is now, whilst when the Domesday Book of 1086 gave us our first full list of settlements the coastline was probably about two miles further east. Villages such as Auburn, Hartburn, Northorpe, Monkwell, Monkwike, Waxholme, Dimlington, Turmarr, Owthorne, Hoton, old Kilnsea, Ravenser and Ravenser Odd all lie under the sea off the Holderness coast. In their time they had churches, fields, farmhouses and cottages, mills and ponds, but they were established on the boulder-clay coast of Holderness, and their downfall was inevitable as the cliffs crumbled into the sea. Some of their names are perpetuated in existing village street names or houses. Otherwise they are lost indeed.

The earliest reference to a headland at the mouth of the Humber is in the seventh century AD. Wilgils, the father of the apostle to the Frisians, Willibrord, is said to have settled there as a hermit. The headland was known in Wilgils's time as *Cornu Vallis* (the horn of the valley). The sandbank makes its next appearance in historical records in an Icelandic saga, recording when Egil was wrecked *c.*950 upon a spit at the Humber mouth. That may be the feature later known as 'Hrafn's Eyr' or 'Hrafn's Sandbank' (Ravens' beach or sandbank), which was the embarkation point for the defeated Norwegian army after the Battle of Stamford Bridge in 1066. Ravenser was the name of a village at the tip of Holderness, which seems to have been located somewhere near the base of the headland a mile or two south-east of old Kilnsea. Never itself a settlement of major importance, and predominantly rural in character, Ravenser was to be completely overshadowed by what may be described as a medieval 'new town', its near-neighbour, Ravenser Odd. At the height of its fortunes in the early years of the 14th century, Ravenser Odd was a town of national importance, regularly supplying the king with two fully equipped ships and armed men for his wars with the Scots. At the same time it had achieved borough status and was receiving harbour and other dues from more than 100 merchant ships a year. Benefiting from a Royal charter, it had its own market and annual fair, a town mayor, customs officers and other officials, and was furnished with cargo ships, fishing boats, wharves, warehouses, customs sheds, a tanhouse and windmills as well as boasting a court, prison and chapel. By about 1340, however, the town was being threatened by the inroads of the sea. Sea levels were rising at that time and, if the cyclical theory of the peninsulas at the end of Holderness is correct, that particular spit was coming to the end of its life. By 1346 two-thirds of the town and its buildings had been lost to the sea by erosion, and its residents were no longer able to make a living by trade, or to pay the tolls and tithes that had been levied upon them. Between 1349 and 1360, the sea completed its destruction of Ravenser Odd. The chronicler of Meaux Abbey described how the erosion exposed the bodies buried in the chapel's graveyard, much as it was to do some 450 years later at nearby Kilnsea and Owthorne: 'The inundations of the sea and the Humber had destroyed to its foundations the chapel of Ravenser Odd, built in honour of the Blessed Virgin Mary, so that the bodies and bones of the dead were horribly apparent.' As was to happen later at Kilnsea, the bodies were reburied in the churchyard at Easington.

The next recorded reference to a peninsula at the mouth of the Humber comes in 1399, when Henry Bolingbroke, who was to become Henry IV, landed on a spit called Ravenser Spurn or Ravenserspurn. (The spur of land near Ravenser.) The Kilnsea Cross, which now stands in Hedon, was reputed to have been erected on the peninsula to commemorate that historic event. Another royal visitor, Edward IV, returning from exile in the Netherlands, landed on the spit in March 1471 on his way to depose Henry VI. By that time the first lighthouse had been built on the peninsula. William Reedbarrow, a hermit, was in 1427 granted dues from passing ships to complete a lighthouse, which he had already begun to build there. Little is known about that lighthouse, and it was to be another 250 years before Justinian Angell, a London merchant, received a patent from Charles II in 1676, to 'continue, renew, and maintain' two lights at Spurn Point. The peninsula on which Angell built his lighthouses is the present one, though it was much shorter than the one we know today.

Angell's high lighthouse was built near the then tip of the peninsula, on a site in the vicinity of the feature known as 'Chalk Bank' today. It lasted over 100 years, but various low lights, which were more temporary constructions, were washed away by the sea and rebuilt. The sea coast of the peninsula was retreating westwards, and it continued to elongate in a south-westerly direction between the late 17th and the late 18th century. In 1776 John Smeaton was commissioned by Hull Trinity House to build a new lighthouse on Spurn (chapter two). His lighthouse lasted until 1895, when it was replaced by the present one. That shone out over the peninsula until 1985.

By the end of the 18th century the village of Kilnsea was very close to the cliff edge, and had lost many acres of land to the east. Between 1800 and 1850, old Kilnsea crumbled into the sea and joined the list of lost villages, but the village that was recreated on the western side of the parish from 1840 still remains. The spit that we call Spurn has also managed to survive into a new millennium. Whatever its future may be, its past is a fascinating one, which it is hoped the following pages will demonstrate.

EASINGTON

NORTH MARSHES

Beacon Cottage

COMMON ROAD

SEA

NORTH FIELD

WEST MARSHES

Long Bank

the Year 1818

THE GERMAN OCEAN

the sea since

Grange Farm

Westmere Farm

Rosabel Terrace

Blackmoor Farm

Primitive Methodist Chapel

Humber View

Crown & Anchor

St Helen's Church

Cliff Farm

Coastguard Cottages

Southfield Farm

WEST FIELD

Northfield Farm

EASINGTON ROAD

Blue Bell Inn

Blue Bell Cottage

Church

Cross

SEE INSET

ROAD

KILNSEA

THE RIVER HUMBER

SOUTH FIELD

Land taken by

Warren Cottage

KILNSEA WARREN

0   0·5 mile
0   1 km

0   250 yards
0   250 metres

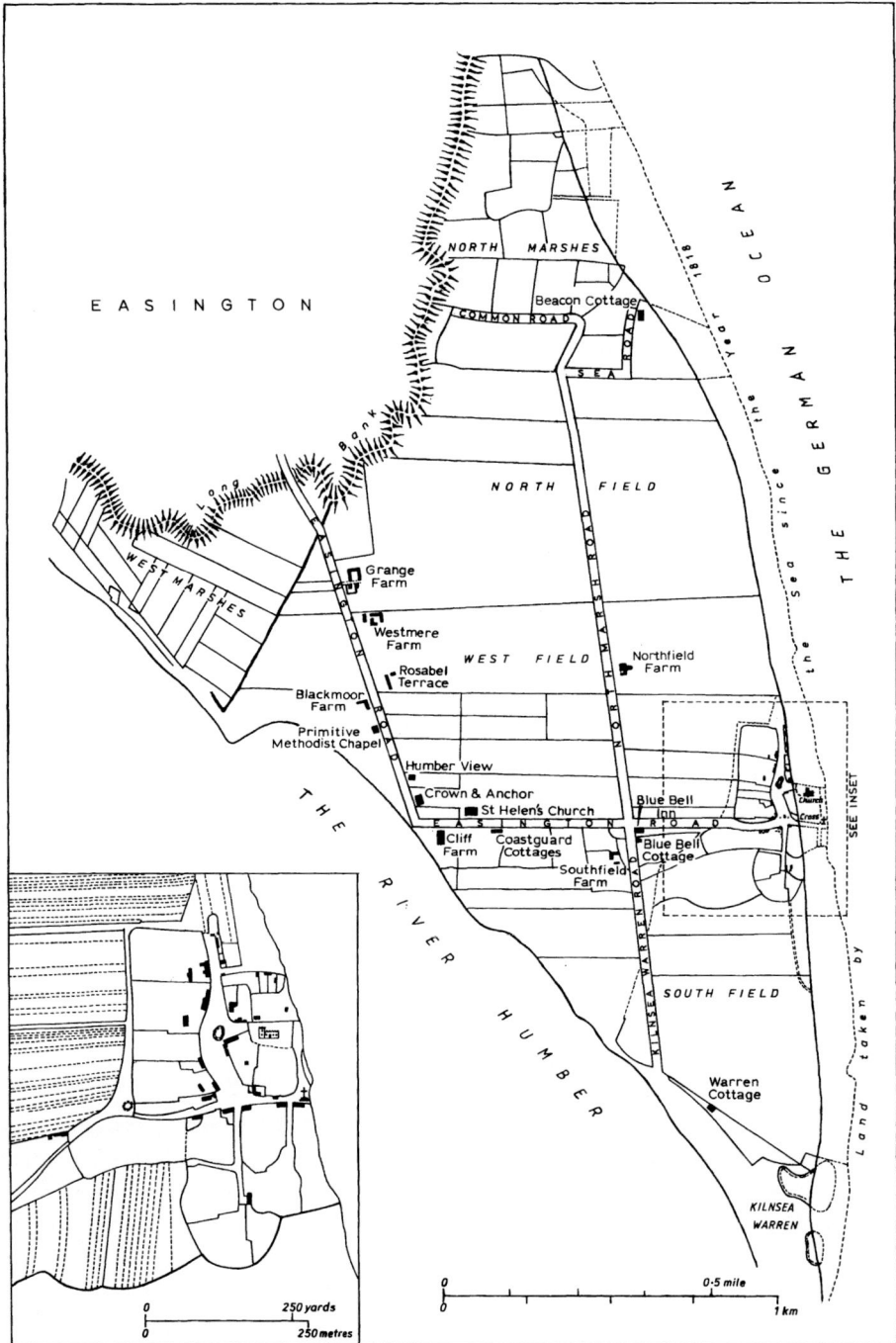

3   *Kilnsea in the 19th century. This map aims to show the changes in Kilnsea between 1800 and 1900. The inset map, based upon a map of 1818 (East Riding of Yorkshire Archives Office, DDX/127), shows the centre of the village when the church still stood and when the cross was still on the village green. The strips of the open fields near the village are also shown. After the enclosure of 1840 the new roads and fields were laid out, and a new village was created nearer to the River Humber.*

One

Kilnsea Reborn, 1800-79

The first half of the 19th century was a crucial period for the southern tip of Holderness. In the 1820s and 1830s the inhabitants of Kilnsea watched their little settlement toppling into the sea as the clay cliffs on which their homes were built crumbled. The bodies of their ancestors were exposed as first the churchyard and then the medieval church slipped over the cliff. A little further south, on Spurn itself, the sea was turning the spit into a string of islands, cutting off the small community of lifeboatmen from the mainland. Kilnsea village was about to join the list of lost Holderness villages and, if the cyclical theory was correct, the peninsula of Spurn was in danger of washing away, before slowly rebuilding further inland. Actions that were taken in the 1840s and 1850s prevented, or at least delayed, such catastrophes.

The Enclosure

The approach to Kilnsea and Spurn is through the village of Easington. As one gets nearer to Kilnsea the land narrows until it turns into the peninsula of Spurn Head. The parish boundary between Easington and Kilnsea was formed by Long Bank, a sinuously winding dike and raised bank. The dike was once a natural watercourse. Over many centuries the bank had been raised and the dike deepened to facilitate drainage and prevent flooding. In the early 19th century a traveller crossing Long Bank into Kilnsea would have seen a farming pattern that had not changed since medieval times. The parish was shaped like an elongated triangle. On the southern side of Long Bank was a low-lying area consisting chiefly of marshes and small meres. Further to the south lay the open arable fields. Until

1840 Kilnsea was cultivated under the open-field system – with the arable land divided into strips and pasture land held in common. Kilnsea had once had four open arable fields, named after the points of the compass. By the early 19th century East Field had been entirely washed away, but there were still 220 acres in North Field, 217 acres in West Field, and 124 acres in South Field. Adjacent to the Humber lay a common pasture called Walker Butts, and adjoining Spurn Head was Kilnsea Warren, an extensive rough common, low-lying and full of small meres, with a rabbit warren, which at one time had been farmed commercially. In the northernmost part of the parish were the North and West Marshes, which were also pastureland.

The movement to enclose open fields by Act of Parliament began in the East Riding in the 1740s, and by 1820 very little open-field land remained, so that Kilnsea's open fields at that late date were exceptional. Indeed, Kilnsea was one of the very last parishes in the East Riding to lose its open-field system. The reason for its late enclosure was directly related to its geographical position on an ever-decreasing narrow neck of land. Even in a good year about a yard of land was lost annually to the sea. Any reallocation of the land in such a position was bound to be contentious. Who would want all their land adjacent to the cliff edge? Inevitably the decision was put off, until it was forced upon the landowners, when not just the land but also the village itself began to fall into the sea. Whilst the land was farmed under the open-field system there was no prospect of building elsewhere in the parish, because land had to be left available for grazing communally after the crops had been

4 *Kilnsea Cross at Holyrood House, Hedon, c.1995. Much weathered, the cross now stands in the garden of a residential home.*

harvested. An Act of Parliament was required to redistribute the strips and commons, so that each landowner could hold his own land separately from that of his neighbours, hedge and fence it and, if he wished, build a new farmhouse further away from the devouring sea. New roads and ditches could also then be built. Until the enclosure the only road from Easington went along the cliff top, and straight into the old village of Kilnsea. By the early 19th century that, like the village itself, was right on the edge of the cliffs. There was an urgent need for a new road to link Kilnsea and Spurn with the rest of Holderness.

Once the decision to enclose had been made all those changes could be set in hand. A commissioner-cum-surveyor, Richard Fowler of Keyingham, was chosen to reallot the land. At a meeting of interested parties, which took place in October 1838, it was recorded that 'due regard be paid by the

Commissioner to each and every allotment so that it have its just portion of frontage next the sea'. As the strip map shows, by 1840 the village was right on the eastern boundary of the parish, and several houses and cottages had already been lost. Many centuries earlier the village had been in the centre of the parish, situated upon a small hill. Indeed further east there had been other villages, such as Hoton and Northorp. But by 1835 a visitor, George Head, said that he had never seen human dwellings so critically placed, 'the houses huddled together … on a crumbling foundation, against which the waves continually beat'. Despite the inevitability of destruction the villagers insisted on remaining 'till the ground was almost torn from under their very beds'.

Old Kilnsea

Only about 15 farmhouses and cottages still remained in the old village in 1840. Around those houses and cottages were little gardens and small fields, with a village pond and a green, a church and, until it was removed in 1818, a large ornate stone cross. Before enclosure, all the buildings in the parish were located within the confines of the village itself with the single exception of an isolated farmhouse, later known as Southfield Farm or Southfield House, which, together with its associated farm buildings, was built in 1811 by Thomas Suggitt, of Kilnsea, and was sold the same year to Leonard Thompson, of Sheriff Hutton. The Thompson family had for many years owned an estate in Kilnsea, comprising land and a house that stood in the old village but was lost to the sea in the early 19th century. It was presumably as a replacement for the old house that Leonard Thompson purchased Southfield House, which was tenanted by the Clubley family from the 1840s.

An enclosure had to take place fairly rapidly, so as not to disrupt the farming programme, and in the course of a year or two Fowler's actions had transformed the landscape of Kilnsea. Having ascertained the number and dimensions of the strips that each person owned, and their share of the commons, the commissioner divided the land into rectangular blocks, drew up a map, which he made available for everyone to consult, and staked out the boundaries of the new fields. The new owners and their tenants were required to provide hawthorn hedges, and dig out dykes for drainage. There were 12 new owners, with plots varying from one and a half acres to 154 acres. The new rectangular fields were very different to the long narrow strips of an open-field village, and it must have taken some time for the farmers to become used to a new landscape, especially at a time when their very houses were falling from under them!

New Kilnsea

Establishing a new village was a priority for the residents once the land had been released for building. The precarious state of the old village is well exemplified by the situation of the church. A church existed at Kilnsea by the beginning of the 12th century, but little is known about its fabric. The building that still stood in the old village of Kilnsea in the early 19th century was certainly medieval in origin. St Helen's was stone-built and had a nave flanked by aisles as well as a chancel, a clerestory, and a three-storey tower. In 1766 the church was 95 yards from the sea, but by the early 19th century it found itself, in company with many other buildings in Kilnsea, teetering on the very edge of the cliff. The churchwardens carried on using the building until the very last moment. When, in 1824, the chancel fell over the cliff, a wall was built at the east end of the remaining part of the church so that services could still be held inside. Only a year or so later another large landslide took the partition, with the north wall, its pillars, pointed arches and pulpit, down the cliff 'with a tremendous crash'. The fact that the building still contained the reading desk and service books suggested that the churchwardens must have been taken by surprise. The south wall of the church, a solitary window and the ruins on the western side, continued to stand 'in a threatening state', but soon they too succumbed. The tower remained for only a year or two, before finally falling over the cliff in 1831.

That was not the end of the drama. Hundreds of parishioners, and untold numbers of mariners who had been washed up on the beaches of Kilnsea and Spurn over the centuries, lay in the graveyard. As the cliff crumbled, the contents of the graveyard became shockingly exposed. In 1835 George Head was walking back from Spurn towards Kilnsea when he saw a skull on the beach. Distressed by the sight, he hastened into the village to tell someone of his find, only to learn that 'human bones at the village of Kilnsea were as coals to Newcastle'. He was taken to look on the shore just below the village, where he saw the ruins of the church and 'avalanches of earth, consisting of rich churchyard mould, in which were profusely scattered bones, skulls, fragments of coffins, remnants of garments, buttons, &c, heaped, in some places under the edge of the cliff, in height almost level with the summit'. Those distressing

5   *St Helen's Church, c.1826. This drawing in George Poulson's* History of the Seigniory of Holderness *(published 1840) shows that the church was stone-built and had a nave flanked by aisles as well as a chancel, a clerestory, and a three-storey tower. The chancel was built with stone from a limestone quarry, near Roche Abbey, on the border of Yorkshire and Nottinghamshire.*

6   *The stone pillar outside Tower House, Easington, c.1900. It seems probable that this was made from pieces of dressed stone rescued from St Helen's Church, Kilnsea. When this photograph was taken the pillar was surmounted by a bust of Queen Victoria to commemorate her Jubilee (60 years) in 1897. It was later topped by an eagle, which was removed during the First World War because it was regarded as a German symbol.*

sights were of more than passing concern to the inhabitants of Kilnsea. Many of the bodies were those of their relations or friends. Apparently some people attempted to collect the remains for reburial at Easington. One man called Medforth placed his father's bones in a granary and when his sister died asked the vicar for permission to bury them with her body. The vicar asked for double fees, to which Medforth retorted that he would not pay twice, his father already having been buried once: the undertaker surreptitiously placed the bones in the coffin. As this southern tip of Holderness was so hazardous for shipping, many of the graveyard's occupants were strangers to Kilnsea. The burial register for the period 1790-1810 shows that 32 people were buried in Kilnsea churchyard in those years, of which no less than 15 were shipwrecked mariners.

Various parts of the church were rescued when it toppled over the cliff. Stones from the chancel were stored with a view to their being used in a future church. The font was taken to a garden in Skeffling, where it remained for many years. A large holy water stoup and two sanctuary chairs were preserved, and eventually found their way to the *Crown & Anchor*. Portions of stone pillars, lintels and so on, were removed to gardens in Kilnsea and Easington. The dressed stone was used in the cobble walls of outbuildings of nearby Cliff Farm and as the cornerstones of Warren Cottage. In Easington it is probable that the stone pillar outside Tower House is made from stones from Kilnsea Church. In Hedon, in the garden of Ivy House, the home of James Iveson, an avid collector of antiquities, are some remains of Kilnsea Church, though they are difficult to identify, being intermixed with fragments that Iveson had collected from other churches.

The practical villagers of Kilnsea dismantled their houses and cottages before they fell over the cliffs. Building materials were precious and were saved from the sea where possible. Soon after the enclosure award had been signed in 1843 the new village of Kilnsea began to appear, mainly built on the Humber side of the parish, as far away from the sea as possible. The houses may have been new but, as well as the fabric of some old houses, many of the families maintained continuity, as the Clubleys, the Tennisons, the Hodgsons and the Medforths moved from the old into the new village. Those same families, almost clans, especially the Clubleys and the Tennisons, are inextricably linked with the history of the area and some remain to the present day.

The Medforths were in Kilnsea in the 18th century and in the early years of the 19th century. Robert Medforth (c.1755-1827) was a fairly substantial owner-occupier. His house, however, was in an increasingly precarious position as it was next to the church, which was teetering on the edge of the cliff. Services were held here for a while after the church was gone, and in the fold-yard the bell was hung, being struck with a stone to let villagers know of services. Robert drowned, aged 72, when crossing floodwater on horseback, while returning from Patrington market one Saturday night. A stone in Easington churchyard records the accident:

> Bewildered in the dead of night
> upon a dangerous shore
> Not knowing where to tread aright
> I fell to rise no more
> On every side the waters flowed
> In vain I strove to save
> my life: Alas, compelled I bowed
> And found a watery grave

One of Robert's sons, John (1785-1865) was recorded in the 1820s as being the landlord of the *Ship*, one of the pubs in the old village. By the 1840s and 1850s, having lost the pub, he was working as an agricultural labourer. When he died in 1865, his daughter Elizabeth (c.1796-1881), who recorded herself in the 1851 census as 'old maid', went to live with her nephew Medforth Tennison, when he took over the newly built *Crown & Anchor*. After her death no more Medforths lived in Kilnsea, but the name was perpetuated as a first name in the village, by Medforth Tennison and Medforth Hodgson, who were both known as 'Meddy'.

7 *The porch of the new St Helen's Church, with a stone inset from the old church.*

The Tennisons (some branches by the 20th century favoured the spelling Tennyson) were also a long-established Holderness family. The branch that came to Kilnsea was from Burstwick, where they had lived since the 17th century. Edward Tennison (1783-1872) married Mary Medforth, daughter of Robert Medforth, in 1808 and the couple moved into Kilnsea, where Edward is variously recorded as carpenter and wheelwright, labourer and shopkeeper in parish records of the early 19th century. By the 1840s he was running a beerhouse in the old village. Like the Medforths the Tennisons combined farming with innkeeping. At the enclosure Edward was allotted a key plot overlooking the Humber and there he had the *Crown & Anchor* built (see below). His son, Robert, was a lifeboatman on Spurn for many years. Other Tennisons became important tenant farmers in Kilnsea in the later 19th and 20th

8   Blue Bell Inn, *cobble wall with plaque, pre-1880. No illustration has been found of the* Blue Bell Inn *before it was re-modelled, but this picture shows the plaque in situ set into a cobble wall. The probability is that the inn, when built, faced towards the old village, rather than, as now, towards the new.*

centuries, being associated with Grange Farm and Northfield Farm for lengthy periods. The Tennisons flourished and were only outnumbered by the other major farming family in Kilnsea – the Clubleys.

The Clubleys' connection with Kilnsea originated with John Smith Clubley of Welwick (1769-1839), who married Sarah, the daughter of a large farmer in the village, John Hunton, in 1793. John Clubley remained at Welwick, but his younger son, also John (1795-1857), was a beneficiary of his grandfather John Hunton's will and inherited Buck Farm, in old Kilnsea. As well as owning a large estate himself John was a tenant of Leonard Thompson, and by 1841 (probably earlier) he was at Southfield Farm, with his wife Nancy (née Fenwick), son John (later of Cliff Farm), son Robert Hunton (later of Firtholme between Kilnsea and Easington), son Francis John (later landlord of the new *Blue Bell*) and daughter Sarah, and a large living-in labour force. John himself retired to Easington where he died, but the association of Clubleys with farms in Kilnsea continued. At some periods in the 20th century it seemed that every farmhouse, cottage or pub had either a Clubley or Tennison association!

Both families were allotted some land at the enclosure in 1840, but the largest holding at that time, about 200 acres, belonged to an absentee owner, Henry Burgh. One of his new fields stretched from the new road from Easington across to the sea, and on that allotment he soon erected the first building one sees on entering Kilnsea – Grange Farm, also known as Kilnsea Grange – a somewhat dour house of grey brick standing four-square and facing west, with its outbuildings partly made of cobble, a traditional building material in South Holderness. Between the 1840s and the 1870s Burgh had a fairly rapid turnover of tenants but, by the later 19th century the Charlton family, formerly of Easington, worked and lived at Grange Farm and remained there for several decades. As was customary at that time, the Charltons employed living-in farm servants, drawn from local families.

The next house on the left was Westmere Farm, built on 44 acres of land allotted to John Clubley in the enclosure award and sold to John Ombler, a Welwick builder and farmer, in 1858. By 1861

9 Cobble barn at Cliff Farm, c.1990. The cobble barns of Cliff Farm are a fine example of the many cobble buildings in South Holderness. Several churches, notably Skeffling church, and parts of Easington church, are partly made of cobble from Holderness beaches.

Ombler had built the farmhouse and was living there with his wife and family. He was variously described as dairy farmer, builder, contractor, inspector and superintendent of Spurn beach works under the Board of Trade. He apparently gave up active farming in favour of his work for the Board of Trade some time in the 1860s, though he remained at Westmere Farm until his death in 1895. John Ombler was a staunch Anglican, and it was largely due to him that Kilnsea was provided with a new church in 1865 (see below). His wife Jane died in 1879 and his daughter Rosabel remained as housekeeper. When John Ombler built the three cottages a little further along the road he called them after her – Rosabel Terrace. In the 1860s and 1870s, William Hodgson, an agricultural labourer, and his wife Kezia, formerly Tennison, were living at Rosabel Terrace. When Kezia was later widowed she took over the *Crown & Anchor* from her father, Medforth Tennison. William Hodgson was related to the family of the same name who lived almost opposite Rosabel Terrace in another newly built farmhouse and smallholding – Blackmoor House, also called Click'em or Clickham Farm in some sources. That farm overlooking the Humber was about 30 acres in size when first established and, throughout the latter part of the 19th century remained in the hands of the Hodgson family.

However by 1881 most of its land had been sold off and it had shrunk to nine acres.

At the time of the enclosure there were two alehouses in old Kilnsea – the *Ship* (renamed the *Blue Bell*) run by Robert Medforth, and Edward Tennison's beerhouse. The new village clearly needed new licensed premises to replace them and so the *Crown & Anchor* was built, on a prime site overlooking the Humber estuary, in the late 1850s. The first publican was Edward Tennison's son, Medforth Tennison, a widower, who was helped in the pub by his aunt Elizabeth Medforth (whose brother John had run the *Ship* in the old village), and his married daughter, Kezia Hodgson and her husband William. Such links between pubs were common in the area. Medforth Tennison's sister, Mary Ann Tennison, ran the *Life Boat Inn* on the Point for a time in the 1850s. Medforth Tennison remained as landlord of the *Crown* for 40 years. On his death in 1893 his daughter Kezia Hodgson became landlady of the pub.

The enclosure plan of 1840 shows the road from the sea to the *Crown & Anchor* as newly laid out. However, the river frontage had always been an important part of the economy of Kilnsea. Old maps indicate that a lane from the old village ran just to the south of Southfield Farm and led to the Humber. Moreover, since at least the early

18th century and probably much earlier, a jetty had stood on the foreshore in front of what was to be the site of the *Crown & Anchor*. There were other landing places further up the Humber, at Easington and at Skeffling. As late as the early part of the 20th century vessels used to anchor off Kilnsea jetty and provide the *Crown* with custom.

Almost opposite the *Crown* another new farmhouse was built, on land that had been in the Medforth family but was sold in 1834 to Henry Sykes, and then sold on to the Constable family who owned Spurn peninsula. That farmhouse, variously called Cliff Farm, Cliff Cottage or Cliff House, was built by 1852. At first that holding of just over 100 acres was farmed by the Robinson family from Out Newton but, by 1871, the Clubley family had taken it over, and various members of that family were to be associated with Cliff Farm until the 1930s.

Coastguards

Along the road towards the sea, on land belonging to the Constable family, two small cottages were built in the later 1850s for the newly formed Admiralty-controlled Coastguard Service. The Humber is one of the most important rivers in the country and provides a channel of navigation that leads into the heart of England. For centuries smuggling was an important part of the local economy of those who lived around the Humber and the North Sea. Most people did not regard it as a crime, and those of the highest and lowest social status were actively involved, or were happy to accept smuggled goods. Indeed Adam Smith, the economist, writing in the 18th century, described the smuggler as 'a person who … would have been in every respect an excellent citizen had not the laws of his country made that a crime which nature never meant to be so'. As a result the government lost an enormous amount of revenue, and made great efforts to catch smugglers. In the early 19th century, under the auspices of the Board of Customs and of the Board of Excise, a number of different bodies were responsible for watching the coast. Revenue Cruisers operated at sea, whilst to prevent the inland movement of smuggled goods, mounted Riding Officers patrolled day and night up to 10 miles inland, although they were never allowed to stay in one place very long for fear that they might become too close to the local inhabitants.

10 *The coastguard cottages, late 19th century. This is the only known photograph of the cottages when they were used by the coastguards. When they moved out the cottages were converted into one dwelling, and renamed Rose Cottage.*

Another branch of the coastal service was the Preventive Water Guard, established in 1809 during the Napoleonic Wars. They operated in coastal waters to tackle smugglers who had evaded the Revenue Cruisers further out to sea, and cruised up and down the coast checking on ships. The Water Guard also had a life-saving role, being issued with Manby's Mortar, which fired shot with a line to a ship in distress. A watch-house was set up at Spurn Head for the use of that group in 1822. Demobilised sailors manned the Water Guard, which was responsible to the Treasury, whilst the Revenue Cruisers were the responsibility of the Admiralty, and the Riding Officers were responsible to the Board of Customs. All three groups worked together, but confusion was inevitable. By 1820 the preventative forces were in danger of duplicating each other's work, and were costly to maintain. Accordingly a Select Committee of 1821 recommended that the Board of Customs form a new body to be called the Coastguard, comprising the Water Guard, the Revenue Cruisers and the Riding Officers. Coastguards generally worked at night. They wore a uniform, drilled regularly and were strictly disciplined. To prevent conflict of interests they were forbidden to engage in trade or possess a shop or a pub. The stations set up around the coast were each manned by a chief officer, a chief boatman and several ordinary boatmen, and provided with a four-oared gig or six-oared galley.

The reduction of duties from the 1830s led to a diminution of smuggling, with the single exception of tobacco, still being brought into the Humber in large quantities throughout the 19th century (indeed even to the present day!). The duties of those watching the coast changed as a result of this decline in smuggling, and safety at sea became a greater priority for them. At the end of the Crimean War in 1856 the Coastguard Service Act transferred the Coastguards from the control of the Board of Customs to the Admiralty. Their duties were said to be the defence of the coasts of the Realm and the ready manning of the Navy, whilst the protection of the revenue, that is the control of smuggling, became only a minor part of their duties. Coastguards were also required to go to the assistance of vessels in distress, take charge of wrecks, operate life-saving apparatus and where necessary man lifeboats. They were issued with arms, comprising a bayonet, musket, two pistols, sword, powder and ammunition. The Admiralty redivided the coast into new districts, Spurn being placed in the Eastern District. It was at that point that Coastguard cottages were built in suitable locations, including Kilnsea, though those in Easington were not built until about 1900.

The census shows that between 1861 and 1891 the Kilnsea team consisted of four boatmen and a chief boatman, originating from many parts of Britain. The first documented inhabitants of Coastguard cottages as listed in the 1861 census were George Crowley, Coastguard boatman, born in Gosport, with wife and family, and his neighbour John Carthy, born in Ireland, with his wife Eliza. The Chief Boatman was a Scot, Peter Flucker, who lived with his family on the road to the sea, past the *Blue Bell*, with a Cornishman George Goodman, the third boatman, next door with his wife and family. Peter Flucker remained in Kilnsea after his retirement in 1880 when he was sixty. His replacement was James Prout, a Devon man, whose two daughters both married local men.

Old and New

At the crossroads another new pub was built soon after the enclosure. That was the *Blue Bell*, built in 1847, perpetuating an earlier pub with the same name in the old village. In order to record future erosion a plaque was placed on the newly built pub, stating that it was 534 yards from the sea. In 1994, when the building was restored, another plaque recorded that it was 190 yards from the sea, a loss of about two yards annually. In 1847 the *Blue Bell*, partly built of cobble, apparently faced towards the old village. In the late 19th century it was enlarged, and its main façade was turned to face the new village on the west. William Westerdale, the first licensee of the new *Blue Bell*, was succeeded by his son, Benjamin, who remained as landlord until about 1870. As was common the Westerdales combined their roles as licensees with farming. When they left, Robert Snowden, a Hull man, took over. He soon sold the pub to yet another member of the Clubley clan, Francis John Clubley, a farmer from Easington.

11   Blue Bell Inn, c.1900. *Members of the Clubley family standing outside the inn.*

Whilst these new farms and pubs were be-ing built some families were still able to live in old Kilnsea. The 1841 census, taken just before the enclosure was finalised, and before any new houses had been built, shows that there were 17 households in the village, including six headed by farmers, and six headed by agricultural labour-ers. Many of those households were not entirely dependent on farming. At that time the gravelling trade on Spurn was providing locals with another source of income, though it was soon to be under threat as its deleterious effect on the peninsula became apparent, not to speak of its divisive effect upon relationships between the two communities of Kilnsea and Spurn.

As a result of the rebuilding of the village, Kilnsea experienced a rise in its population and the 1851 census records 26 houses and cottages with another three in the process of being built. Farmers headed five households, and men described as either labourer or farm labourer headed twelve. By that date it was a depressing experience to walk past the *Blue Bell* on the road leading to the sea, both for locals and visitors. What had once been a thriving little settlement, centred around a village green, with its ponds, small cottages and larger farmhouses, stone-built church and graveyard, was almost gone.

The enclosure gave everyone hope of a new beginning as the landscape was remade. The road north from the old village had fallen into the sea, and from the *Blue Bell* crossroads a new lane leading northwards was made at the enclosure. It gave access to the marshes, which provided the farmers with rough pasture for their stock, and to the newly enclosed arable fields lying to the south of them. Hawthorn hedges were planted on either side of the new lanes, whilst around the perimeter of the newly enclosed fields new hedges were also planted. The hawthorn hedges of the present day, some of them still quite bushy and healthy, are those same enclosure hedges, now over 150 years old.

North Marsh Lane or Road is also known as Beacon Lane. A beacon had existed near Long Bank since Elizabethan times, when the threat from the Spanish Armada caused a series of signals to be erected in order to warn inland areas of possible invasion. When the threat was renewed during the period of the French Revolutionary and Napoleonic Wars – 1794 to 1815 – the beacons were refurbished, but after the war they became disused. By that time a different form of beacon was required: seafarers needed landmarks to steer by and they usually used prominent buildings, especially church towers. When Kilnsea church fell into the sea, a new landmark was needed, and Trinity House decided to erect a navigational beacon as a replacement. A 67-foot-high triangular beacon was therefore erected in 1840, and lasted until 1895, when it was so close to the cliff edge and so dilapidated that it was replaced by another, 95 feet high. That in its turn was removed in 1940, because it was felt that it provided too obvious a landmark for enemy aircraft. However, the area immediately to the north-east of Kilnsea is still called 'the Beacon area' to this day.

A few hundred yards along North Marsh Lane, on the right, a new farmhouse was erected on 25 acres of land allotted to John Clubley but later sold to John Tennison. John Tennison died in 1894, aged 71, and his wife, Maria, died in 1906 aged 77, but Northfield Farm remained with the Tennison family until the late 1960s, when much of its land had been lost to erosion and it was pulled down. Further along North Marsh Lane another farmhouse was built soon after the enclosure. It was known as Eddowes or Beacon Cottage, and was a substantial brick-built house, with a pan-tiled roof and cobbled barns. The Clubleys lived there from the 1890s. Judging from its appearance the house had been built to last, but by the early 20th century it was uncomfortably close to the beach.

The remaining holdings were in the hands of men whose families had been in the area for many years. The Longhorns were small farmers – Samuel Longhorn and family were living at so-called 'Stone Walls', in the old village, in 1841, and he and his brother William received small allotments in the

12 Crown & Anchor Inn, c.1900. *Kezia Hodgson and family standing in the doorway of the inn.*

13   *Eddowes, also known as Beacon Cottage. This farmhouse, situated at the end of North Marsh Lane/Road, was washed away by the sea, c.1916.*

enclosure award in 1843. The Brantons were another family that had been in Kilnsea for many years: after the enclosure Francis Branton lived in a new house on the eastern side of North Marsh Lane, farming about nine acres, and also working as a graveller. When he died in 1874 most of the land was sold to John Peacock Crawforth, an Easington man who was amassing quite a lot of land at the end of the 19th century.

Southfield Farm (sometimes called Walker Butts Farm) had been in Clubley hands in the 1840s but, by 1851, the Sharp family, who were to remain for a century, were the tenants. Walter Sharp (1819-89) and his wife Mary (née Eddom) originated from Welwick. When Walter died his brother William took over the farm. William Sharp, a widower, farmed the land with his son John until well into the next century. The continuity of that farm in the same ownership was reflected in the name of 'Sharp's Bay' for that part of the Humber adjacent to Southfield Farm.

Kilnsea Warren

Past Southfield Farm the land narrows on the approach to Spurn peninsula itself. From the *Blue Bell* crossroads a new straight road, called 'rough lane' in the late 19th century, was made by the enclosure commissioner, ending at what is now the entrance to the nature reserve. From that point southwards the Constable family of Burton Constable owned all the land. From the entrance to Spurn to where the land narrows was Kilnsea Warren, an uncultivated common, which had been the site of a rabbit warren since at least the 15th century. Commercial rabbit warrens had once been quite prevalent in the East Riding. Most of them were on higher ground, mainly on the Wolds, but they were also established on sandy soil, though the quality of those rabbits was somewhat inferior. The animals were farmed for both their flesh and their fur, and were usually kept confined by turf walls. At the head of Spurn peninsula there would have been little problem containing them, with the river Humber acting as a barrier on one side and the sea on the other.

Looking at this area now it is difficult to imagine it as it was in the middle of the 19th century, when it was well over a quarter of a mile wide, with an open mere called Great Pit Marsh and smaller meres. Though the land was unsuited to arable farming, it nevertheless formed an important part of the local economy as its natural assets could

PLATE 1 *Kilnsea Cross from the west, 1818. Drawn by John Child. Apart from the church itself, this cross was the most prominent landmark in the parish. Originally erected on the peninsula to commemorate the landing of Henry IV at Ravenser in 1399, it was subsequently removed to Kilnsea in the early 16th century when the peninsula had become eroded, and then to Burton Constable in the early 19th century when once again it was threatened by the sea. This picture was drawn just before the cross was dismantled and removed from Kilnsea village green to Burton Constable. Note the donkey on the beach below.*

PLATE 2 *Kilnsea Cross from the east, dismantled, 1818. Drawn by John Child. The house shown is presumably that of Robert Medforth, in whose foldyard the church bell was hung for a time.*

PLATE 3   *St Helen's Church, 1829. The village stood on a small hill, as clearly shown by the height of the cliffs in this picture. The tower finally collapsed in 1831. When Walter White visited in 1858 he spoke to Medforth Tennison's wife, who said that she remembered Kilnsea Church standing 'at the seaward end of the village, with as broad a road between it and the edge of the cliff. But year by year, as from time immemorial the sea advanced, the road, fields, pastures, and cottages, were undermined and melted away'.*

PLATE 4   *The low and high lighthouses looking south-west, 1829. This shows Smeaton's lighthouse, which was built in 1776, and one of the low lighthouses, built in 1816. Until the low lighthouse built in 1852 all low lighthouses at Spurn were on the seaward side of the peninsula. The group of houses between the two lighthouses is presumably the barracks, which were built during the Napoleonic Wars, and from c.1810 utilised as accommodation for the coxswain of the lifeboat and for the first Lifeboat Inn.*

PLATE 5 *Spurn Point from the top of the lighthouse, c.1905. This view shows the mortuary within what appear to be allotments or gardens. In this coloured postcard hedges appear to surround it, which is very unlikely given the nature of Spurn's 'soil'. Most probably they are wooden fences. Note the cart track leading to the cottages, and the lifeboatmen's look-out hut.*

PLATE 6 *Spurn Point, c.1905. Note the large group of visitors on the platform surrounding the lifeboatmen's look-out hut. The postcard is franked as from Cleethorpes, so was probably bought by one of the trippers who went over in a steamer.*

PLATE 7 *Painting, by Arthur Hoskins, of Spurn during the First World War. The painting is in one of the autograph albums kept by the Hopper daughters during the First World War. It shows the low lighthouse before the water tank was placed upon the top, the Lifeboat Inn, the lifeboatmen's cottages and the school.*

PLATE 8 *U-boat cartoon. One of the sketches from the Hopper girls' autograph albums.*

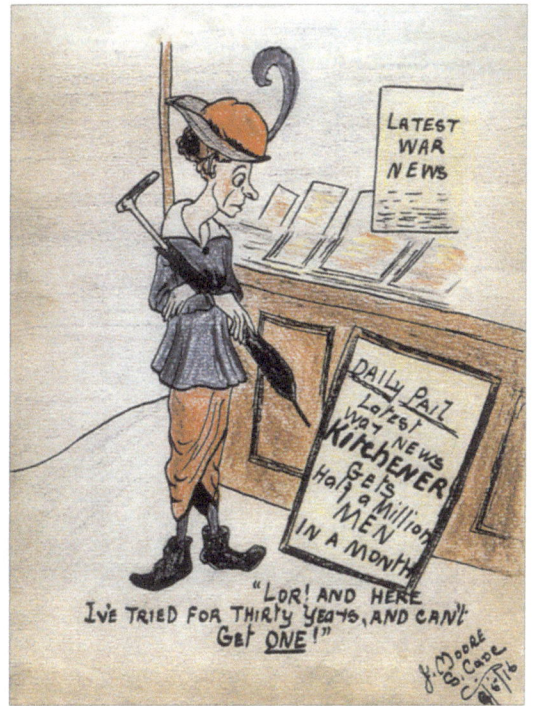

PLATE 9   *Cartoon from autograph album. One of the sketches from the Hopper girls' autograph albums.*

PLATE 10   *Looking north towards the lighthouses, October 1964. Many substantial military buildings still remained at this time. The brick buildings to the left of the road are on the site of what is now the new lifeboat houses. The anti-submarine boom can be seen stretching into the Humber beyond the 19th-century cottages.*

PLATE 11   *The sea breaking over the sea wall at Kilnsea, 1964. The two battery observation posts on Godwin Battery (now Sandy Beaches Caravan Park) show well on this photograph. The anti-tank blocks were still in situ at this date. The sea wall was not to last long under this onslaught from the sea.*

PLATE 12   *Sandy Beaches, 1964. The large building in the bottom right-hand corner of the photograph is the former officers' quarters. Most of the military buildings still remained in 1964. Near the cliff stands the new coastguard tower. The building between the two gun emplacements is now (2006) teetering on the cliff edge and the gun emplacements themselves lie on the beach.*

PLATE 13 *Looking towards Kilnsea, 1974. The eroding sea wall is just visible near the cliff. The anti-tank blocks can also be seen.*

PLATE 14 *Chalk Bank/Wire Dump area flooded, November 1977. At that time spring tides flooded the area frequently via a channel in the salt marsh open to the Humber. By 1986 this channel had closed up and the nature of the vegetation changed as a result.*

PLATE 15 *The coastguard tower on Sandy Beaches Caravan Park and one of the gun emplacements, 1988. This tower was used by the coastguards for a time in the 1960s, after they left the Port War Signal Station.*

PLATE 16 *Southfield Farm, 1990. This farmhouse was the first to be built outside old Kilnsea. Built about 1811, it has a large barn to the north, which has now been converted to a residence.*

PLATE 17   *Gun emplacement on Spurn Point, May 1991.*

PLATE 18   *The Blue Bell café and information centre, 1996. Built in 1847, this building has undergone many changes over the years. From the late 1950s when it closed as a public house, the Blue Bell was run as a café and later as a shop. In 1996 it was refurbished as an information centre, café and the Yorkshire Wildlife Trust warden's flat.*

PLATE 19 *The lifeboat house and the end of the railway pier, June 1995. Soon after this photograph was taken both these features were demolished.*

PLATE 20 *Brian Bevan and crew, June 1995. Left to right: Bob White (later from 2001 to 2003 Superintendent Coxswain), Chris Barnes, Brian Bevan (Superintendent Coxswain), Dave Steenvoorden (Superintendent Coxswain from 2004 to date), Les Roberts.*

PLATE 21   Barbecue to celebrate the 50th anniversary of Spurn Bird Observatory, 1996. The barbecue took place alongside the 'annexe' within clear view of the beach. Fifty years earlier the beach and the sea were many yards further away.

PLATE 22   Part of the collapsed concrete road near Chalk Bank, 1996. In 1996 several sections of the road were washed away. However, thanks to co-operation between all interested parties, new sections to the west were soon in place.

PLATE 23 *Sea holly on the Narrows, July 2000. Sea holly is one of the most attractive plants characteristic of Spurn. It grows most profusely on the Narrows. In the 19th and early 20th centuries Spurn children used to gather it and sell bunches to visitors. Now, of course, it is an offence to pick it.*

PLATE 24 *Warren Cottage, 2000. Built in the 1850s for Mr Constable's bailiff, this cottage is still (2006) in use by Spurn Bird Observatory Trust.*

PLATE 25 *The* Pride of the Humber *greeting the replica of the Endeavour, May 2003. The replica of Captain Cook's Endeavour was on a round-the-world voyage at the time.*

PLATE 26 *Concrete sea wall at the Narrows viewed through a collapsing groyne, 2003. After the peninsula was bought by the Yorkshire Wildlife Trust in 1960 the sea defences were no longer maintained.*

PLATE 27 *Spurn lightship in Hull Marina, 2003.*

PLATE 28 *The lighthouse, 2004. The lighthouse's paintwork is badly in need of attention.*

PLATE 29 *Flood tide at the Narrows, early April 2005. On this occasion the sea met the Humber.*

PLATE 30   *The Crown & Anchor pub, painted by N.J. Tindall. The Crown and Anchor has been Kilnsea's social centre for over 150 years.*

PLATE 31   *Aerial view of Spurn peninsula, 1993. This photo shows the old lifeboat house and the railway jetty still in situ. A pilot boat approaches the pilots' jetty. Three of the searchlight emplacements can be seen in the dunes near the tip of the Point, as can other former military buildings.*

PLATE 32 *Aerial view of the Point, 1998. This an unusual aerial view of the Point. The old lifeboat house and the railway jetty have been removed. Part of the Stony Binks can be seen just off the tip. To the left of the low lighthouse is the car park, which is the site of the Victorian lifeboatmen's cottages. It is still protected by the crumbling zig-zag revetment. Similar defences protect the area below, where stood the old Lifeboat Inn and the first cottages. On the seaward side opposite, the site of the Port War Signal Station can easily be seen. At the bottom of the photo the peninsula broadens out where two chalk banks were constructed to seal the mid-19th-century breach.*

be used by the villagers. Besides the rabbits, there were wild fowl and fish, brambles and elderberries for food, and gorse for fuel and animal bedding. When Kilnsea was enclosed the warren area remained untouched, though in the late 1840s Warren Cottage, an attractive cobble single-storey cottage, was built by the Constable family. Around that time relations between the people on the Point and those at Kilnsea were at a very low ebb and Warren Cottage may be seen almost as a frontier post between the two areas. Constable's first tenants were James and Jemima Watson. James's father and mother had been lighthouse-keepers at Spurn, and he followed them in that role in the 1830s and 1840s. When he lived at Warren Cottage, although described as an agricultural labourer in the censuses of 1851 and 1861, he was there to collect the dues from the gravelling ships and pass them on to Mr Child, Constable's agent, who lived in Easington. Watson was also Constable's representative on Spurn and

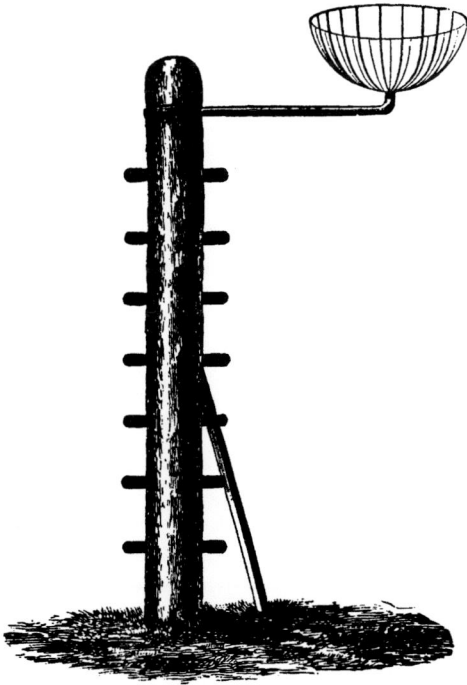

14   *Kilnsea Beacon, c.1830. The beacon used at Kilnsea during the Napoleonic Wars to warn of invasion by the French was of this design.*

could report back on the many disputes that took place between the villagers of Kilnsea and Easington and the lifeboatmen (see chapter two). In the late 1850s Walter White visited Spurn and wrote in *A Month in Yorkshire* (1858):

> A short distance from the Crown & Anchor stands a small lone cottage built of sea-cobbles, with a sandy garden and potato plot in front, and a sandy field in which a thin, stunted crop of rye was making believe to grow. Once past this cottage, and all is a wild waste of sand, covered here and there with reedy grass, among which you now and then see a dusty pink convolvulus, struggling, as it were, to keep alive a speck of beauty amid the barrenness. ... Presently there is the wide open sea on your left, and you can mark the waves rushing up on either side, hissing and thundering against the low bank that keeps them apart.

Local Services

Records show that old Kilnsea had all the services expected in a village – not only a church and public houses, but also several shops. In 1838, for example, Medforth Tennison ran a grocery shop, Edward Tennison had a general shop, Thomas Hodgson also had a general shop, and John Hodgson had a beer shop. As the village gradually toppled over the cliff and its residents relocated, some services had to be recreated. The public houses were clearly regarded as a priority, but censuses and directories show no-one keeping a shop in the new village. Fortunately, in the second half of the 19th century Easington, Kilnsea's northern neighbour, had several general stores, and could provide specialist services, such as blacksmiths, joiners, wheelwrights and coal merchants. It was near enough for Kilnsea people to travel there on foot or by cart, carriage or on horseback. Moreover the traders of Easington were happy to bring their services to Kilnsea and further south to Spurn itself. A general stores-cum-post office, which was established by the Websters in the 1870s, is still being run by that same family today. From the late 19th century the Websters ran a regular weekly horse and cart to Kilnsea and Spurn, a service that they continued for several generations. (See chapter three.)

15 *The former 'iron chapel' after conversion to private house. This photograph shows Ernest Tennison standing outside the cottage, c.1928. He died, aged three. Note that the chapel windows are still in situ. This building, called Hodge Villa by the Tennisons, is now Chapel Cottage*

16 *St Helen's Church, early 20th century.*

Church

There seemed to be no immediate rush to build a new church in Kilnsea after the old one fell over the cliff. Parish records show that a baptismal register was still kept, indicating that the vicar came through to the village for that ceremony, though marriages took place at Easington, and of course people had to be interred there. However, in 1864 the decision was finally made to provide the village with a new church, apparently to a large extent due to the efforts of the Board of Trade superintendent of the Spurn beach and sea defence works, Mr John Ombler. At that time he was working closely with Alfred Burges, a partner in the firm of Walker & Burges, who were responsible for the sea defences programme after the 1849 breach. Subscriptions to fund the building of the church were raised locally, and Alfred Burges contributed £150 whilst the Diocesan Society contributed £102. Burges's son, William, the celebrated high Victorian architect, designed the building of red and yellow brick, which was erected at a cost of £500 about three-quarters of a mile west of the former site, which by that time was on the beach. Superficially the new church bore no resemblance to the old, but Burges, with a proper respect for continuity, used stones from that church for the foundations, the buttresses and the coping. Furnishings and fittings from the old St Helen's soon began to find their way back. The medieval font was rescued from Skeffling, the holy water stoup from the *Crown & Anchor*, the church registers were brought back from Easington, and services resumed on a regular basis. When Ombler died in 1895 at the age of 84, a plaque was placed in the new church to record his services as a churchwarden for 35 years.

Chapel

The Church of England was not the only religious body to build in Kilnsea in the 19th century. Methodism was generally more popular than Anglicanism amongst the labouring classes at that time, being more informal in its approach, and less élitist than the Established Church was perceived to be. In the 1820s the Wesleyan Methodists were being challenged in popularity by an offshoot group,

the Primitive Methodists, founded to revert back to the simplicity and plainness of the early followers of John Wesley. One of their leaders was William Clowes. In 1820 he went on a mission into Holderness, then, according to a history of the sect, 'a benighted part of the country'. Clowes reached Kilnsea, where, he wrote, 'I preached in the house of Mr W. Hodge, who had a large family of children, of whom many were converted.' He also visited one of the lighthouses at the Point, and on return noticed the church of St Helen's falling over the cliff, with the bones and coffins of parishioners visible. Rather than being impressed by the power of the sea, he concluded that that was the result of the wickedness of the inhabitants. 'What an awful sight! What hath sin done!' A Primitive Methodist chapel was built in Easington soon after Clowes's visit in 1823. The Wesleyans were somewhat later, building in 1850 when the Primitives refurbished theirs, but Kilnsea and Spurn were only served by itinerant preachers. However, William Hodge's four sons, John, Samuel, William and Henry, had moved to Hull, and established a seed-pressing firm there, which became very successful indeed. Henry Hodge realised that the village of his birth was without a place of worship and, in 1885, built a chapel, constructed of corrugated iron, on the edge of the Humber, near Blackmoor Farm. This so-called 'iron chapel' remained in use as a place of worship until it was converted into a cottage about 1917.

Education

Even though it was a very small village, old Kilnsea had a school in the early 19th century. Little is known about it apart from the name of the schoolmaster – Henry Hildyard. He was there in the early 1820s, and apparently remained until the late 1830s, though a different person, Elizabeth Thompson, aged 63 is recorded as schoolmistress in the 1841 census. The cottage where she taught must have been lost to the sea. Records also show a little school for younger children in Kilnsea in the 1860s. Nearby Easington had a school throughout the 19th century, which several Kilnsea children attended. By the end of the century, when education was compulsory, they were all taken to school by one of the farmers in his wagon.

17   Plaque to John Ombler inside St Helen's Church. John Ombler was primarily responsible for a new church being built at Kilnsea. St Helen's Church is now (2006) being converted to a private residence, but the plaque will remain in situ.

Nostalgia

Establishing a virtually new village of Kilnsea cannot have been without trauma for the residents. New beginnings usually arouse positive feelings, but older inhabitants of Kilnsea mourned their old village. An insight into how they felt is provided by an account related to John Cordeaux the naturalist, writing in *The Field*:

> Often in long winter evenings I have sat for hours hearing stories and traditions connected with this desolate coast ... Not the least interesting are the reminiscences of lost lands. How old Kilnsea was the prettiest village in all Holderness, standing on a hill with a wide prospect over sea and land, and a noble old church, pleasant gardens sloping down the hillside and a fine spring of bright water surrounded by willows, eastward of all this was the road and fruitful fields down to the beach; ... Those were the days when Kilnsea and Easington Commons were quite uninclosed, with many small ponds or sykes, and birch trees.

Two

Living on Spurn Island:
Life on the Peninsula, 1800-79

Whilst the village of Kilnsea was falling over the cliff and being relocated, the peninsula to its south was also under attack from the sea and, after many small breaks in the neck, in the middle of the century a massive breach occurred, which was only repaired with the expenditure of much money and effort. At the beginning of the 19th century only a few people were living on Spurn but during the Napoleonic Wars, when there was a threat of invasion, measures were put in hand to defend the East Yorkshire coast, and batteries of 24-pounder guns were established at Paull and on Spurn Point. The men who manned the Spurn battery thus joined the little community of lighthouse keepers who constituted the only permanent residents on the Spurn Peninsula until the arrival of the lifeboat crew in 1819. As the century progressed, however, the community that was able to call Spurn its home gradually expanded.

The Shape of the Peninsula

What sort of a place was Spurn in the 19th century? It seems to have been a very shifting and fluctuating environment indeed. By that period good evidence of changes in the shape of the peninsula can be derived from accurate maps, and more personal accounts, taking us back to the end of the 18th century, have survived in the Constable papers. In 1850 Robert Bird, then aged 74, remembered Spurn 50 years previously. He described how, about 1800, the Humber and the sea began to meet across the spit from time to time, and said that such 'meetings of the sea and Humber' had increased gradually ever since and 'the spoon', or what is called the Spurn

Island, had diminished to two-thirds the size it was when he first knew it.

Samuel Hodgson, aged 77, also speaking in 1850, said that he remembered that about 52 years before (*c*.1798) there was:

> a great storm wind north east in February. The sea broke over all the way from Kilnsea warren to near Spurn opposite to the south of Den and past it a good bit swept all the bents [marram grass] entirely away over to the Humber shore and there laid in lumps till they grew again and gathered the sand and progressively became bent hills thus shifting the point and neck from the east to the west. Spurn island now is not so big by a third as it was before that storm or as it was 50 years ago.

He was also recorded as saying that 'the sea always has in his time kept the Spurn even with the land and he believes it always will that is to say as the land is taken away the sea will continue to drive the Spurn westward'. He had lived at Kilnsea 57 years and 'knew Kilnsea and Spurn well before'.

Thomas Carrick of Easington, a labourer aged 77 in that same year, was born at Easington and lived there all his life. When he was about 17 (i.e. *c*.1790) he went to work at Spurn and had worked there off and on since at gravel vessels. In his youth:

> The sea beach was then much further eastward and beyond what was then the low light and a house called Mr Constable's house north of the low light and the site of it is now far in the sea ... The south end of the point was then where the house now the public house occupied by Welburn is – that house was first built as barracks for soldiers during the war and two batteries were formed but no guns

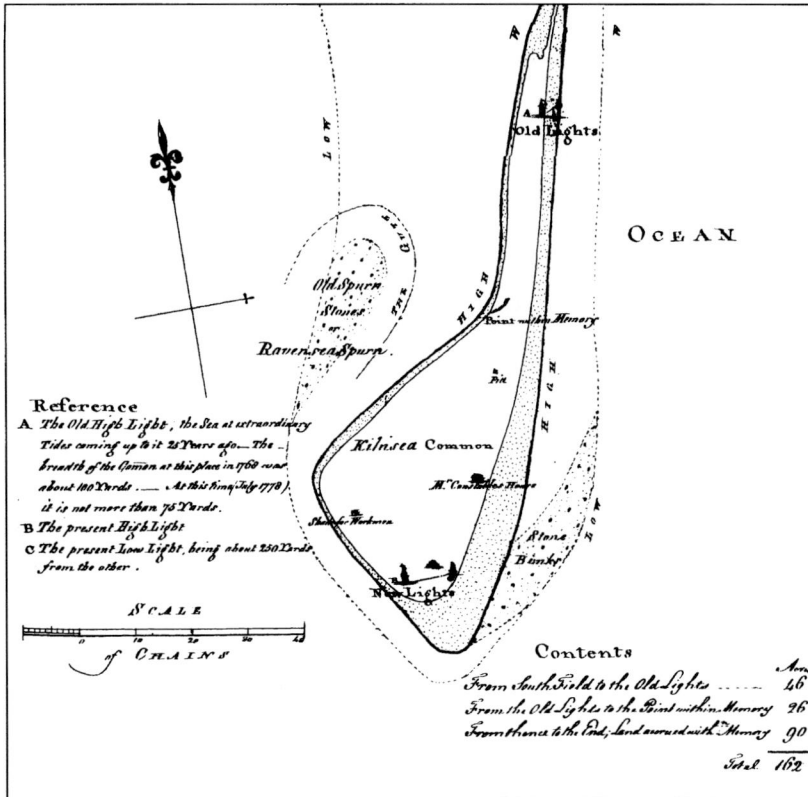

18 *1778 map of the Point. Depicted as 'A' is Angell's 16th-century lighthouse. 'B' is the lighthouse built by John Smeaton in 1776. The compound surrounding it is adjacent to the present lighthouse, but is now almost entirely covered by sand.*

mounted. The warren [Spurn warren] was then twice as large as it is now both the sea and Humber having encroached upon it. Then the bent hills extended from the warren [Kilnsea warren] about a mile then an opening of sand and no bent hill about a mile and then began the Spurn warren. The beach then laid high and tho' the sea and the Humber did sometimes meet there it was only in storms or high tides. The stony binches then laid north of the low light but now they are half a mile to the southward of that place. About 50 years ago the sea threw up a sand bank which immediately became bent hills to the south of the low light to the extent of about 10 acres and this laid about 9 or 10 years and then the sea took it all away again.

Maps of the 1820s and 1830s show the neck of the peninsula as extremely narrow. At very high tides it was regularly washed over by the sea. The usual name at that time was Spurn Island, demonstrating how it was perceived by the people who lived there. Most people came by the river or the sea because the journey by road was so difficult. Travellers on land had to take the road from Easington east to the sea (still called Ten Chains Road) and then go south towards Kilnsea along the cliff top. George Head visited the area in 1835, when access to Kilnsea and Spurn was at its most challenging, because the coastal road to old Kilnsea village had fallen over the cliff and there was no proper inland road. He wrote:

> The distance from Patrington to Spurn Point … is little more than twelve miles. Six miles of very good road, as far as Easington, are in an easterly direction; the same line leads to the coast, half a mile farther, whence, turning to the south, it extends a mile and a half over deep heavy sand along the sea shore. Here the traveller leaves the circuitous bend of the coast, and taking a direct course across a few spacious arable fields, again arrives on the sea-shore at Kilnsea. Spurn lighthouse is four miles beyond Kilnsea, the intervening land being a narrow barren ridge, a few hundred yards in breadth, and bounded by the sea on one side and the river Humber on the other.

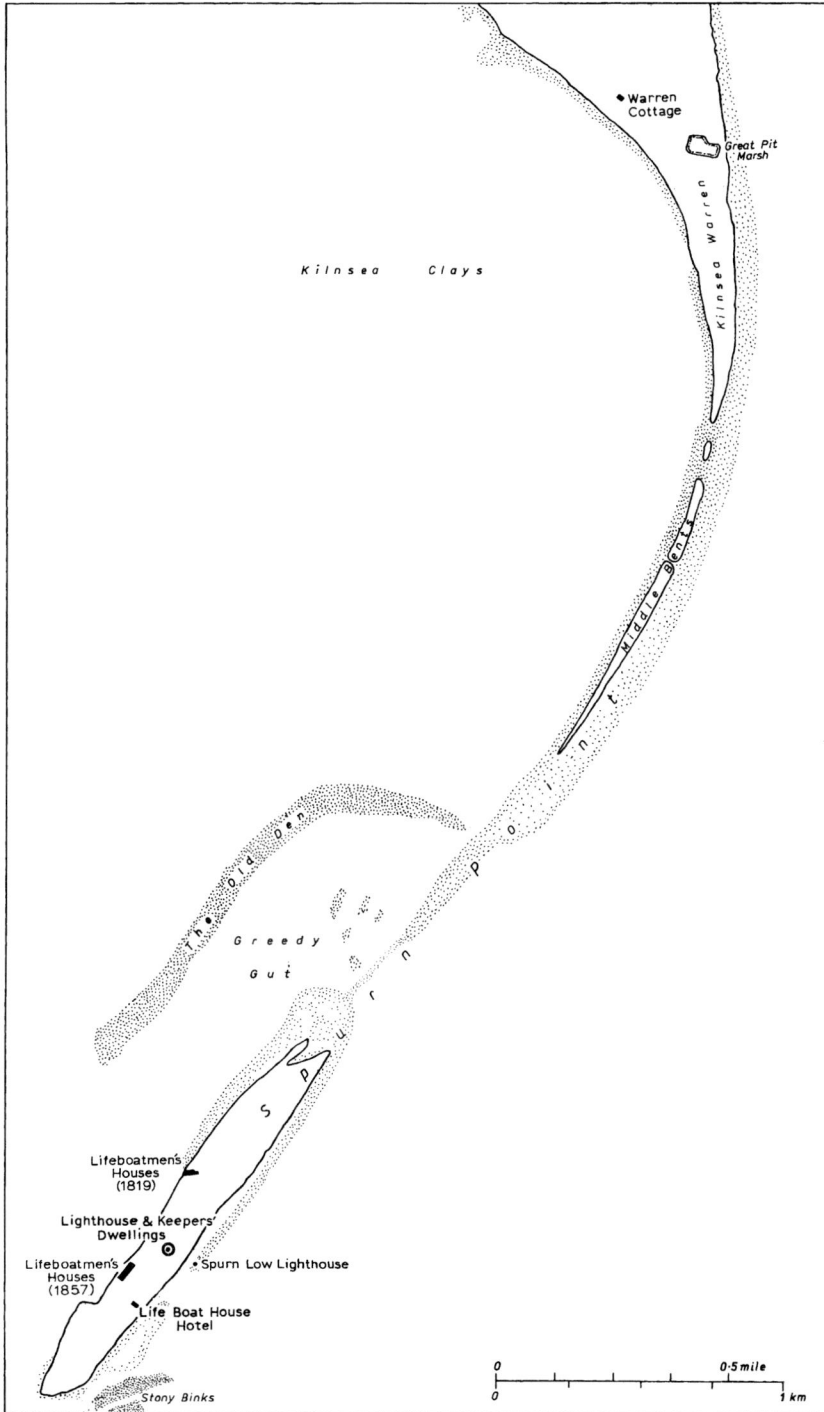

19 *The Spurn peninsula in the middle of the 19th century. Based upon the 1854 Ordnance Survey, this map shows Spurn when it was breached. Both the old lifeboat cottages (1819) and the replacement cottages (1857) are shown.*

The narrow ridge described by Head was a hard journey on foot or on horseback. Any wheeled vehicle found it awkward in the extreme. The narrow neck was covered by sands and marram grass (the bents), and by the sea when there were exceptionally high tides. Most carts and carriages found it impossible, and usually travelled part of the way on the Humber clays. Little wonder that few came by land until the later 19th century.

The traveller approaching the Point would have seen two lighthouses – the low and the high lights. In the first half of the 19th century the low light was almost on the beach, with the high light a little to its western side. In 1835 George Head wrote:

> The approach to the lighthouse is across a sand-bank, covered with hard turf, barely covered with herbage, and perforated with rabbit burrows in every direction. … the site of the lighthouse, for the present, seems quite secure, though as a place of habitation, in dreary winter weather, at the end of a narrow spit of land, and menaced on three sides by the tumultuous ocean, the prospect must be dreary and awful. The lighthouse is a circular brick building a hundred feet high, and contains a stationary light of eighteen Argand lamps [lamps admitting air to both the inside and the outside of a flame], and one of coloured glass, all with plated reflectors. The low light is contained in a wooden building, about a hundred yards from the other; the lantern, containing the lamps, moveable, so as to be let down or drawn up to the top. A little distance to sea is the Bull-sand floating light, which shows eight Argand lamps, and is moored by mushroom anchors.

The Lighthouses

Lighthouses had been present on Spurn for at least 500 years. Indeed it was recorded that in 1427 a hermit, William Reedbarrow, was granted dues from passing ships to complete a lighthouse that he had begun to build there, though little further is known of it. In the late 16th century a high and a low light was erected on the peninsula by Justinian Angell. The lighthouses were erected at what was then the tip of the spit, probably somewhere to the north of Chalk Bank. The low light had to be rebuilt several times owing to its proximity to the sea, but the high light lasted until the late 18th century, when John Smeaton, the celebrated engineer who had built the third Eddystone lighthouse in 1759, designed two new lighthouses, which were erected under the direction of the Hull and London Trinity Houses. In Poulson's *History of the Seigniory of Holderness* (1840) Smeaton's high lighthouse is described as:

> a noble circular building, comprising several stories, and the lantern is accounted one of the best arranged in the kingdom. In the centre is a tripod of bronze, supporting two circles, containing in each tier ten Argand lamps, with large silver reflectors behind

20 *The high and low lighthouses looking north-east, c.1840. The low lighthouse shown in Colour Plate 4 was undermined by the sea in 1829 and abandoned in 1830, being replaced by the temporary wooden light shown in this engraving.*

each light; the windows of the lantern are plate glass, and the frames of a curious metallic composition. ... There are three or four other cottages about the high light, [which] has also dwelling-rooms; it is walled around, with a paved court-yard, having cisterns either for water or oil. ... The low light [is] ... in a perilous situation on the very verge of the sand hills.

That lighthouse, completed in 1776, was the immediate predecessor of the present lighthouse. It was 90 feet high and built of bricks on an artificial foundation consisting of four circles of thick wooden poles rammed down into the sand and surmounted by a platform of stone about 12 inches deep. The lighthouse was lit by coal until 1819, when a lantern was erected and an oil light substituted for the smoky flames of the open fire. The keepers lived within the compound and in separate buildings. The site of the circular compound in which it stood, although now covered in sand and with the walls almost entirely eroded, can still (2006) just be seen a few yards to the south of the present building.

The lighthouses were owned by the Angell family, though from the 18th century they were actually under the management of Hull Trinity House, which appointed the keepers and inspected them regularly. The keepers were generally local men and most of them stayed for many years. Manning the lighthouses did not take up all their time and, in the 18th and early 19th centuries, they ran licensed premises to supply both residents and visitors to the Point with liquor. The first recorded licensee, Patrick Newmarch, was the lighthouse-keeper from 1736 to 1767. He applied for a license to run a public house every year from at least 1754, and probably before. Visiting ships apparently furnished him with most of his business, and when he lacked customers he seems to have been an enthusiastic partaker of his own liquor. In 1765 Newmarch was replaced as keeper by Audas Milner, who applied for a licence to sell liquor himself, though Newmarch remained for another two years, still running his own hostelry.

The building of new lighthouses, from 1767 to 1776, had brought many strangers to Spurn. William Taylor, the contractor, leased a house, which had been originally built for shipwrecked seamen, and applied in his turn for a licence to sell liquor. In 1771 Angell's agent, Worth, brought 'a gang of

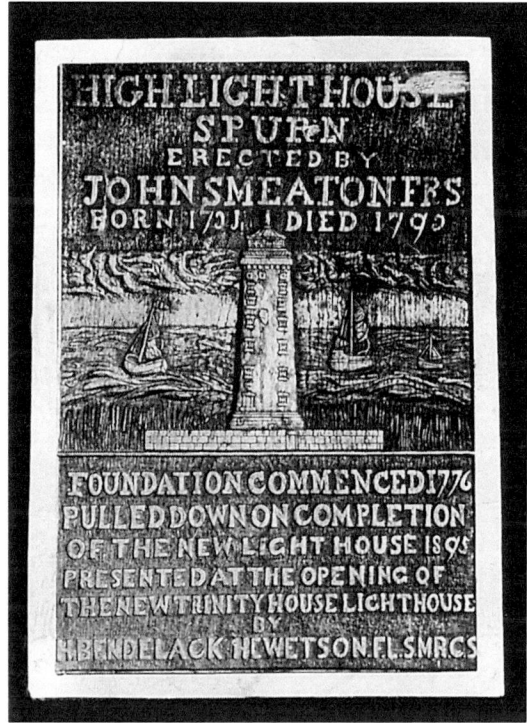

21 *Plaque to commemorate Smeaton's lighthouse. Henry Bendelack Hewetson lived at Tower House, Easington. He was a keen archaeologist and took a close interest in the lighthouses on Spurn. Until recently the entrance hall of Tower House had a decorative frieze made of pieces of glass from Smeaton's lighthouse embedded in plaster. The present whereabouts of the plaque is not known. Possibly it was placed in the new lighthouse for a time.*

unruly labourers to Spurn, [and] kept them well supplied with liquor'. By that time Taylor's rival licensee was another lighthouse-keeper, John Foster, with whom he was constantly at odds. Foster was dismissed in November of that year, but Taylor remained on Spurn, continuing to run a licensed public house, until at least 1780. Records show that between 1780 and 1788 there were no less than three licensed hostelries on Spurn, though their names, if they had any, are not recorded. One pub, which was recorded on the Point from the 1820s to the 1840s was the *Tiger*, which in the 1841 census John Thompson was described as running in conjunction with his lighthouse duties. Thompson was the last keeper to combine the job of licensee with that of lighthouse-keeper.

In the late 18th and early 19th centuries the Watson family had a long association with the lighthouse on Spurn, beginning with John Watson, a Kilnsea man, who was recorded as a keeper there in 1798. When he died in 1807 his wife, Mary, then took over as one of the keepers in order to support her young family. When she died in 1824, her youngest son, James, succeeded. He stayed at Spurn until about 1846, moving in the late 1840s to Warren Cottage, where he collected the gravelling dues for Mr Constable. (See chapter one.)

The normal complement of personnel required to manage the Spurn lighthouses was three keepers, who, with their families, lived in the dwellings situated within the circular lighthouse compound surrounding Smeaton's lighthouse. Keeping the lights in good order was a time-consuming task in the early 19th century. A survey done in 1808 recorded that 'in windy weather the light required trimming every quarter of an hour or twenty minutes, for doing which took them about five minutes'. In 1836 an Act of Parliament placed all English lighthouses under the control of London Trinity House, and the management of Spurn lighthouse changed when in 1841 it was sold to that body. The change in management at Spurn is reflected in the changes of personnel who took care of the lighthouse. The job became 'professionalised' under the management of London Trinity House, and keepers moved frequently from one lighthouse to another, both to gain experience on different types of lighthouses, and to improve their position from supernumerary assistant keeper, to assistant keeper, through to principal keeper.

The Lifeboat

The lighthouses, and the people associated with them, always excited the interest of visitors, but even more interesting to most of them was the

22   *The low lighthouse of 1852. This lighthouse remained in use until 1895.*

lifeboat and her crew. The establishment of a lifeboat owed much to the Constable family who owned the peninsula, though the original suggestion appears to have been made about 1800 by Henry Greathead of South Shields, who had recently established a lifeboat in that town, and wrote to Trinity House offering to supply them with a lifeboat built to the same design – a boat that could be rowed in either direction without being turned around. Mr Iveson, steward to Francis Constable of Burton Constable, who owned Spurn, agreed to the establishment of a lifeboat station, though matters were left for a year or two, until in April 1810 another letter came to the house from Iveson stressing Francis Constable's 'great desire and enthusiasm for a lifeboat, for humanitarian reasons alone', and saying that he had obtained the shell of a building, previously used as a barracks, to convert to the residence of the lifeboat master and with suitable temporary accommodation to lodge shipwrecked mariners. Mr Constable also offered to erect a boathouse, and said that he would provide 'twelve able men to be always ready as the crew and will also provide a means of livelihood for the master of the boat and for the mate if it was thought necessary that provision should be made for him'. The means of livelihood for the master was to be the managing of a tavern to be constructed in part of the building, and the selling of poultry, vegetables and provisions to vessels (numbering about 500 a year) that stopped at Spurn to ballast with cobbles and gravel, to labourers who worked on the vessels and to visitors. Mr Iveson also stated that the 12 men to crew the lifeboat could be obtained from nearby villages. A subscription was started by Trinity House to buy a lifeboat and pay for the establishment of a station at Spurn. The house subsequently ordered a strong 10-oar boat for £200. By 20 June 1810, £300 had been subscribed, including £50 from Trinity House, £50 from Hull Corporation, and £50 from Lloyds of London.

By agreement with Francis Constable:

the lifeboat master was to have a residence fitted up, management of the public house, and to be supplied with coals, candles, a spy-glass, a flag staff and flag and six casks for the storing of fresh water. For these supplies and concessions, £47 10s. 0d. was to be deducted from the master's earnings per year,

and should his earnings not reach £100 per year, then they were to be made up to that figure by Mr. Constable. The use of the flag was to assemble the people in the neighbourhood so that speedy help could be given to the rescued.

By 15 August 1810 Robert Richardson had been appointed the first lifeboat master, and the new lifeboat arrived in Hull on 2 October of the same year.

The original plan was for the master to live at Spurn, and the crew to be drawn from Kilnsea and Easington. Records show that this was indeed at first the case, with Hodgsons, Longhorns and Tennisons being included in the first crew. In order that they should be given some means of support, they were allowed to have 'full preference and priority' over the other locals in loading the vessels that came to Spurn for gravel and cobbles. At that time the trade was flourishing. Giving the crew special priority on Spurn ensured that they were on the peninsula for

23   *The low lighthouse of 1852.*

much of their time, but a considerable amount of time might elapse before they could man the lifeboat if they were not already training or otherwise working on the peninsula. To solve that problem, in 1819 Trinity House suggested that cottages should be built at Spurn to house the crew. Mr Constable signified he would be very willing to lease as much land as required for the purpose at a 'peppercorn' rent, and a further subscription was raised by Trinity House, netting £800. A row of cottages was built just south of the lighthouse, on the Humber side of the peninsula.

With the arrival of the lifeboatmen and their families the population of the peninsula almost trebled. It could now merit the name 'Spurn village', a description often used in the 19th century. The first coxswain, Robert Richardson, remained until he retired in 1841 aged 60, having served for a total of 31 years. The master had considerable power over appointments, and by 1822 five of the lifeboatmen appointed in 1819 had been discharged, having failed to give satisfaction. Robert Branton returned to Kilnsea and resumed his work as an agricultural labourer and no doubt the others did likewise, probably becoming rivals on the gravelling trade. Four more men were discharged after serving for only a few months, in November 1822. However, several men who stayed many decades were taken on in 1819 or soon after, and they all retired round about the same time as did Robert Richardson.

The records available as to the number of rescues carried out in those early decades are not complete, but they show that the presence of the lifeboat at Spurn made an enormous difference to those who risked their lives at sea, and several hundred sailors were saved from drowning. Many if not most of the ships that got into difficulties were stranded on the Stony Binks, a sandy and pebbly bank or rather series of banks, which ran down the eastern side of Spurn Point. Those mariners not familiar with the Binks had a tendency to think that when the tide changed they would just float gently off. Owing to the ferocity of the tides on the tip of Spurn, that was far from the case. When the coxswain of the lifeboat approached the ships stranded on the sandbank he often got short shrift from their

masters, who were suspicious that the lifeboat crew was only concerned about salvage. There are many stories of the lifeboat being told to go away – it was not needed. Often the coxswain just stood by, knowing that the ship was likely to get into trouble. Of course, that often resulted in greater danger for his crew once the emergency unfolded.

A constant watch was kept by the crew, following a rota system. The nightwatchman's task can easily be imagined – alone on the beach in all weathers looking over the sea and the Humber. Unsurprisingly, wrecks mainly took place in darkness in the winter months. Ships that got into distress would show lights, fire signal guns or even light tar barrels. Having seen a ship in distress the watchman had to alert the coxswain and crew and make ready to launch the tender from the shore.

The first lifeboat stationed at Spurn, to Henry Greathead's design, was 10-oared and 30 feet long and very heavy. It had a launching carriage with wheels 16 feet in diameter, and horses were kept at Spurn to pull it over the sands. However, that was soon found to be impractical: it was far too heavy to be pulled across the sand when the tide was out. The horses were dismissed and it was decided to keep the lifeboat afloat and maintain a tender in the boatshed instead. Keeping the lifeboat afloat meant that in stormy weather it was liable to break from its mooring and drift off. Usually it came to no harm, but in 1823 it overturned and was badly damaged. The new boat, which arrived in June 1824, was a little lighter than the first and could sometimes be kept in the boatshed. In 1838 it was modified, being given improved buoyancy and a mast and sail, which made it more versatile. The tender being used in 1847 was in a poor state, and when the *Cumberland* got into difficulties off Kilnsea she overturned and a crew member, John Branton, was lost. By that time the lifeboat itself was over 20 years old and, as the coxswain pointed out, keeping it afloat meant that it suffered more wear and tear than if kept in the boathouse. In 1853 a new lifeboat, which was to give good service for 30 years, was built by Hallet & Company of Hull.

John Branton was the first crew member to lose his life whilst on service. In the early years the crew went out on missions wearing oilskins but no buoyancy aids. In 1841 four members of the Whitby lifeboat crew lost their lives and Mr A.G. Carte, who was the ordnance store keeper at the Citadel in Hull, wrote to Trinity House to tell them about lifebelts that he had designed. Accordingly 12 of those belts, costing 12 shillings each, were sent to Spurn. In 1847 the coxswain told Carte that he thought the belts were not buoyant enough and Carte sent five more and suggested that crew members should wear two. In 1850, when the brig *Cumberland* got into difficulties off Kilnsea, Carte suggested in a letter to the Trinity House Brethren that had Branton been wearing the lifebelts he might not have been drowned. Two years after that disaster, another crew member, John Welburn, died, having never really recovered from injuries sustained in that rescue. In 1855 two more crew members, John Combs and Henry Holmes, were lost during the rescue of the schooner *Zabina*. When a crew member died in the 19th century, there was no pension or other provision made for his widow and children. Indeed the family had to vacate the house more or less at once. When Branton died in 1847 a public subscription raised £42 11s. 6d. That must have helped his family, who would otherwise have had to apply to the overseers of the poor for help.

Life on the Point for the Coxswain and Crew, the Lighthouse-keepers and their Families

When Robert Richardson came to Spurn in 1810, he was 25, his wife, Elizabeth, was 20, and they had one infant son. Elizabeth Richardson's new home was a former barracks, built during the Napoleonic Wars to house soldiers stationed at Spurn to protect the country from invasion by the French. A room within it was made into a tavern, which also served as accommodation for 'the reception of ship-wrecked persons'. The inn was intended to supply the Richardsons with an income. They were also to run a shop, selling 'ships stores … groceries … bread, pork living and dead, poultry, potatoes, peas'. The wives of lifeboatmen were (and still are) crucial to their husbands' ability to carry out their job, most especially at a place like Spurn. Richardson was well supported by his wife, Elizabeth, who was kept very busy, writing all Robert's letters, working

24 *Smeaton's lighthouse shored up, early 1890s. In 1892 cracks were discovered in the tower of Smeaton's lighthouse, and further examination revealed that the building was settling, probably because the wooden piles on which it had been built were decaying.*

with him in the public house and carrying out her family duties, which were considerable. During the time that they lived at Spurn she produced 16 children, including one set of twins. Sadly seven of them died. The nearest medical support was the doctor at Patrington, or across the Humber at Grimsby, so during childbirth and bereavement the help and support of the other women must have been particularly important. Very large families were not uncommon in the 19th century, but Elizabeth's situation, in such a relatively isolated spot, makes her family life of particular interest. The years 1814 and 1815 were very difficult ones: she lost an infant boy in 1814, and then in 1815 their eldest son, aged six, and second son, aged four and a half, died. Only a two-year-old was left. However, Elizabeth went on to give birth to another 12 children. Although the coxswain's family had fairly capacious living accommodation in the converted barracks, the crew's cottages were more cramped; they were described in 1837 as 'ten very small cottages ... the[ir] gardens ... instead of embellishing, add to the desolate appearance of the spot'. Domestic life must have been difficult for the lifeboatmen's wives, living so far from their families and menaced by the elements in stormy weather. Those living in the first cottages have left no accounts of their lives, but the 1841 census and a list drawn up in 1846 by the vicar, the Reverend Inman, gives a few details of who was there in the 1840s. From Inman's informal census we know that quite a number of children lived on the Point: in 1846 there were 15 boys and 21 girls under 14. Presumably those of their parents who were literate tried to teach them to read and write.

There is much to learn from the correspondence between the coxswain and Hull Trinity House about life on the Point. The first cottages gave their occupants cause for concern at times. In October 1836, when the crew had been reduced from 12 to 10 men, the oven ranges and fireplaces needed repairing and new windows were required. Probably the extreme weather on Spurn had taken its toll. In February 1845 a high tide filled the houses:

> halfway up the ovens etc. brake away part of the fencing and washed away our coals and left the houses in a very wretched state for we expected every wave to burst the doors in for it came with such fury that we had no time to secure anything having to attend the crews of the stranded vessels to get on shore with their boats our wives and infants having to be upstairs about four hours without any fire on account of the chimneys smoking so bad and when they came down the house floors was near an inch thick with mud that the water brought in and left.

The coxswain's pub was usually called the *Life Boat Inn*, or the *Lifeboat Hotel*, a name that it retained after it moved into the first cottages on the Humber side, where it remained until just after the First World War. In the early years there seems to have been no lack of business, for the labourers at the gravel trade were thirsty souls who were given an allowance of 6d. per day that had to be spent at the inn. The *Lifeboat Inn's* beer was two-pence half-penny a pint, whereas the *Tiger's* beer was only two pence, though of apparently inferior quality. Constable's agent advised Richardson to lower the quality of his beer as 'the labourers at Spurn are no judge of quality and their heads and stomachs can bear anything'.

When Robert Richardson retired in 1841 he wrote that he had saved 304 lives, that the lifeboat had never been afloat without him in all his years of service and he had never lost a crew member. A testimony to his good management may be the fact that four of his crew served with him for 20 years or more. He was replaced by Joseph Davey. Under Davey's management the Spurn station declined in efficiency, and he was replaced in 1843 by Robert Brown, who entered into the trade of licensee with enthusiasm. However, he found that the decline in the gravel trade as a result of the new regulations had led to a considerable loss of income, and he wrote to Trinity House in 1846 that he wished to 'erect a Tenement for the accommodation of visitors, a considerable number of whom have been down, and across the Humber from Cleethorpes, during the late summer, but for whom we have no accommodation'. Brown obtained permission from Sir Clifford Constable, the owner of Spurn, to erect such a building but, only two years later, having been refused an outdoor licence, he resigned, asserting that he could not make a living unless allowed to take beer and other drinks out onto the beach. Apparently visiting parties such as that of Captain Bell of the pilot ship *Neptune*, who, in 1846, gave 'a select party' a trip to Spurn and back, were not enough to make a living. Brown was succeeded as coxswain and innkeeper by Michael Welbourn, who remained in the post until his death in 1853.

Erosion

The little community of lifeboatmen and lighthouse-keepers and their wives and families became well used to the difficulties in adapting to life on a peninsula that turned into an island periodically. Maps from the early 19th century are fairly accurate and show that the point changed its shape in those years considerably. Spurn may have been reaching the end of its natural life by that time. There are currently two theories to explain the geographical

25 *Rear of the lifeboat cottages. The new school can be seen on the extreme left of the photograph.*

development of Spurn. One of them, making use of historical records and maps and charts, postulates the periodic destruction and washing away by erosion of the peninsula, followed by its re-formation further westward within a cycle of approximately 250 years. Such a theory accords with data from the early 17th century suggesting a breach in an earlier peninsula and subsequent regrowth of what is in fact the present spit. It also accords with the evidence from the 14th century when the important port of Ravenser Odd was inundated by the sea and entirely destroyed between 1360 and 1370. An alternative and more recent theory asserts that the tip or head of the peninsula, resting on a foundation of glacial till, has remained in a relatively constant and stationary position centred approximately on the area known at the present day as Chalk Bank, whilst the narrow sand spit linking it to the mainland has moved progressively westwards as the mainland coast to the north has eroded and itself retreated westwards. The historical evidence of earlier breaches cannot be ignored, however, and it is indisputable that in the 18th century the spit reached a greater length than the present position of the chalk bank, and that breaches occurred in the 14th and 17th centuries, when the head was destroyed. Of course the position of the neck has shifted as the coast of Holderness has retreated.

How could it be otherwise? At the present time the early history of Spurn must remain open to debate.

When one reaches the 19th century theories can be replaced by facts. Since Angell built his lighthouse in the late 17th century, the peninsula had lengthened considerably. The testimony of local people such as Thomas Carrick (quoted above) and evidence from maps, shows a very changeable peninsula with a narrow neck, which was overflowed by the sea at the highest tides. The sand dunes that composed the neck were quite low, and shifted considerably. Spurn is 'fed' by the movement of material down the Holderness coast. Sand, gravel and cobbles form the beaches of Spurn on both the eastern (sea) and western (estuary) sides of the peninsula. However, by the later 18th century the natural processes that made the spit were being affected by man's activities. The improvement of the roads of the East Riding meant that there was increasing demand for gravel for road-making. Growing towns needed cobbles for paving the streets, and places like Beverley imported cobbles from Spurn on a large scale. Accordingly, there developed a thriving trade in those raw materials from the east coast, and especially from the vicinity of Kilnsea and Spurn. The trade grew up rapidly and by the early 19th century it was said that several vessels daily would lie off the Binks to

26 *The Hopper family outside the* Lifeboat Inn, *1880s. This photograph shows that the two-storey* Lifeboat Inn *was inserted into the original row of one-storey cottages soon after the lifeboat crew moved into the new terrace of cottages in 1857. Some time between 1895 and c.1900 the small cottage on the Humber side of the inn was demolished.*

be loaded with gravel and cobbles by local men. The owner of the peninsula, Mr Constable, employed a coastal bailiff, who collected £1 per load from the ships' masters. In 1815 the Constable family's account book shows that they received £223 11s. for gravel, and £39 2s. 6d. for cobbles, whilst in 1836 the total was £479 12s. 4d. Giving the lifeboat men priority for the gravelling on Spurn caused great offence to the 'countrymen', as the local men from Easington and Kilnsea were called. Many heated disputes ensued, some ending in violence.

Of more lasting consequence was the effect of the gravelling on the peninsula itself. The removal of such large quantities of its fabric inevitably led to a weakening of the neck, and its obvious fragility in the early 19th century can certainly be connected to the trade. Another factor that probably led to a narrowing of the neck was the changes to Sunk Island further up the Humber. Until the 19th century Sunk was actually an island separated from the mainland by North Channel. It had emerged by natural processes of accretion and was composed of very rich alluvial soil. Active reclamation meant an increase in its size, until by about 1800 it had virtually ceased to be an island. The silting up of the North Channel changed the tidal flows in the Humber, and Spurn

Peninsula lost an important source of sandy sediments on its western side. Whatever the causes, it is undeniable that the peninsula in the first half of the 19th century was becoming increasingly vulnerable. Whilst the neck was regularly over-washed by high tides, the head, or Point, was being eroded on both the sea and river sides and it began to dwindle in size markedly after 1825.

At that time (as indeed again today) Spurn was not protected by any system of sea defences, and the practice of collecting shingle on a large scale for commercial purposes was accelerating the process of erosion, making a catastrophic breach much more likely whenever the conditions most favourable to it – a high spring tide and prolonged north-westerly gales – should coincide. In the last week of December 1849, several days of gale-force north-westerlies in the north Atlantic, pushing masses of water around Scotland into the North Sea, built up a huge tidal surge, which was to cause flooding and damage down the whole of the eastern coast of England from the Humber to the Thames. The crisis at Spurn came on 28 December during an exceptionally high spring tide, when the sea tore through the peninsula at a point about three-quarters of a mile north of the compound enclosing

Smeaton's lighthouse, in the area now known as Chalk Bank. The gap deepened and widened in the ensuing weeks as the bad weather and strong winds continued, and fishing vessels and other small craft soon began to use it as a short cut from the sea to the Humber at high tide.

The lifeboat is recorded as having first passed through the breach on 29 February 1850. Later in the year, Captain James Vetch, the Admiralty engineer, reported that 'on the 23rd July, I found that the sea had made a breach or gap … about 320 yards wide at [the] time of ordinary high water, and then it is about 12 feet deep, allowing a vessel of 60 tons and drawing 10 feet of water, to pass through, and as many as seven vessels have been observed to sail through in one tide'. Although the gap itself was then measured at only 320 yards, as Captain Vetch pointed out, the dunes at either end of it had been washed away, so that at high spring tides as much as three-quarters of a mile of the peninsula was underwater.

The breach became known locally as 'Chance Bay' and probably got that name on account of the dangers involved in attempting to ford it. At the wrong state of the tide such attempts could prove fatal on account of the strong current produced by the tide flowing through the gap at an estimated speed of six or seven knots. At least one man was drowned here, and possibly more.

Towards the end of the year, a second breach occurred, some 500 yards to the north of the main breach. The lighthouse-keeper, reporting on the state of the peninsula on 28 February 1851, mentioned that breach as having been present for 'some four or five months'. He estimated it as being four and a half feet deep at spring tide, and stated his belief that, at the next occurrence of a north-westerly gale and a spring tide, the 500 yards of spit separating the two breaches would very likely be washed away. At that time the main breach had both widened and deepened. It is noticeable when looking at the Ordnance Survey map of 1852 (surveyed in 1851) that the tip of the peninsula or 'Spurn Island' does not show the characteristic 'spoon' shape that appears on both later maps and earlier charts. It is shown as narrow and elongated, which suggests that it had become considerably eroded since George Head

described it as a secure site 'receiving augmentation, rather than sustaining diminution'. It is very probable that the erosion of the Point had begun when the peninsula was breached, and that the flow of material that had previously been carried southwards to 'augment' it was now being interrupted at the breach and diverted into the Humber. From the reports of contemporary witnesses, it appears that if nothing had been done to effect repairs, the breaches would have continued to expand, and without its usual 'augmentation', the Point on which the lighthouse stood would have continued to erode rapidly until it was completely washed away, along with much of the peninsula.

Another concern was the potential danger to shipping if the shelter provided to the west of the Point by Hawke Roads, the only safe anchorage in an easterly gale between Harwich and the Forth, were to be lost, and the deep-water channel made to shift. Accordingly the Admiralty began to take steps to protect Spurn from further loss and destruction. Its engineer, Captain Vetch, had recommended a four-point plan: a ban on taking shingle from the beaches, the closing of the breach, the installation of groynes, and land reclamation between Spurn and Sunk Island. In the event only the last point was not adopted and put in hand.

A ban on the removal of shingle for ballast had in fact already been decreed soon after the breach was made and, although it had been relaxed to the extent of allowing the lifeboatmen to load gravel from the extreme tip of the peninsula, elsewhere the practice had been effectively stopped by the autumn of 1850. Of more immediate importance was the closing of the breaches in the peninsula. James Walker, another engineer, was given responsibility for this task, and in March 1851 he asked his employers for a sum of £10,000 to carry out the necessary work. The money was granted by Parliament in July and Walker set about his task. He first tackled the smaller breach and, by installing groynes to build up the beaches and erecting a fence of stakes and wattles, backed up by a rampart of chalk to trap floating debris and other material brought by the sea, he succeeded in effectively closing the gap, and was able to report that this smaller breach had been sealed by May the following year. Unfortunately the main gap proved more recalcitrant and was still unsealed in 1854, when the grant of £10,000 had been exhausted. Although partly closed at the northern end the strong current was still carrying beach material through the remaining gap at its southern end, and the Point was still continuing to erode at a rapid rate. A further grant of £6,000 was obtained and, by 1855, after a great deal of difficulty and effort, including the dumping of bargeloads of chalk from the quarry at Barton, the breach was finally closed. No sooner had that breach been sealed, however, when a third breach was made the following year. Fortunately this breach was much smaller than the two previous ones, being only 80 yards in width although 13 feet deep at high water. After further expense and effort, it was sealed the following year, in 1857.

Thus, eight years after the original great breach of 1849, Spurn was no longer an island. The traveller Walter White has left a description of what Spurn was like soon after the breaches had been sealed, and it is very clear that the peninsula must have still looked very fragile, despite all the work of reclamation and sea defence. Describing his walk along the peninsula southwards, he wrote:

> Presently, there is the wide open sea on your left, and you can mark the waves rushing up on either side, hissing and thundering against the low bank that keeps them apart. A broad long sand in the shape of a spoon, is the description given of Spurn in a petition presented to parliament nearly two hundred years ago; and, if we suppose the spoon turned upside down, it still answers. It narrows and sinks as it projects from the main shore for about two miles and this part being the weakest, and most easily shifted by the rapid currents, is strengthened every few yards by rows of stakes driven deeply in, and hurdle work. You see the effect in the smooth drifts accumulated in the spaces between the barriers which only require to be planted with grass to become fixed. As it is, the walking is laborious: you sink ankle-deep and slide back at every step, unless you accept the alternative of walking within the wash of the advancing wave. For a long while the lighthouse appears to be as far out as ever. A little farther, and we are on a rugged embankment of chalk: the ground is low on each side, and a large pond rests in the hollow between us and the sea on the left marking the spot where, a few years ago, the

sea broke through and made a clean sweep all across the bank. Every tide washed it wider and deeper, until at last the fishing-vessels used it as a short cut in entering or departing from the river. The effect of the breach would, in time, had a low-water channel been established have seriously endangered the shore of the estuary, besides threatening destruction to the site of the lighthouse. As speedily, therefore, as wind and weather would permit, piles and stakes were driven in, and the gap was filled up with big lumps of chalk brought from the quarry at Barton, forming an embankment sloped on both sides, to render the shock of the waves as harmless as possible. The trucks, rails, and sleepers with which the work had been accomplished were still lying on the sand awaiting removal. Henceforth measures of precaution will be taken in time, for a conservator of the river has been appointed.

The 'rugged embankment of chalk', along which White walked, is not the same ridge of chalk that now leads in a straight line from near the hide overlooking the Humber south-west towards a Heligoland Trap. That 'chalk bank' was constructed in 1870 as part of a later programme of defence works. Walker's 'chalk bank' of 1855 was curved and followed the present shoreline of the Humber, where traces of it can be seen in the scattering of chalk boulders on the river beach.

Problems for Inhabitants

The storms of the 1849 to 1851 period not only made a massive breach in the spit, they also caused great damage to several of the buildings on the Point. The last low lighthouse on the seaward side of the peninsula was washed away at that time. Erosion on the Humber side as well as on the sea side had become severe. Loads of chalk from Hessle had been laid down by the edge of the river after the 1836 flooding of the cottages, but it now had little effect. Other inundations followed, but the most serious occurred as the result of a violent storm on 5 and 6 March 1851. When the cottages were built they had been well within the land, but by the 1850s they projected out into the Humber. The coxswain asked for more protective chalk to save them from being inundated.

A storm in early January 1852 resulted in severe damage. The coxswain wrote:

27 *Customers, chickens and dog outside the* Lifeboat Inn.

Spurn Point is a miserable place this morning, last night the storm and sea very high swept away the low light tower and cottage at half past 7 pm – a great quantity of the cliff and ramparting also about 30 feet of the bents all along the beach. At half 6 am this morning [it] swept every thing away from the Low Light many of the heavy piles the pump against our house the tide in our yard and stable and about 3 feet high in the cottages and most of the island covered … It requires immediate protection to the High Light and our property if it continues.

Recognising the problem, in 1853 Trinity House decided to pull down the three cottages nearest the Humber and build three new ones at the other end. At that time the coxswain still lived separately from his men, a little further south in the old *Lifeboat Inn*, so close to the sea that 'when it blows it is almost fit to blow one out of the house'. Walter White on his visit to Spurn in the 1850s observed the situation of the inn, standing:

in what seems a dangerous situation, close to the water. There was once a garden between it and the sea; now the spray dashes into the rear of the house; for the wall and one-half of the hindmost room have disappeared along with the garden, and the hostess contents herself with the rooms in front, fondly hoping they will last her time. She has but few guests now, and talks with regret of the change since the digging of ballast was forbidden on the Spurn.

In 1852 the coxswain asked Trinity House for a new room to be built on the north-western end of his house as the tide might take the south-eastern end off at any time. In such dire circumstances evacuation would seem to have been more advisable! The brethren were becoming convinced by the middle of the century that the old houses would need too much money expended upon them, and the decision was taken to build new cottages on land a little to the south. The Constable family agreed to release more land for the purpose, and plans were made for a terrace of 10 new houses, with the coxswain's larger house at one end, and the mate's at the other. It was only just in time for the coxswain and his family. By January 1855, though the inn still remained, it was only four yards from high water and 'if it continues blowing we expect the house end going every tide'.

The late 1840s and early 1850s must have been one of the most difficult in the lifeboat's history for coxswain and crew, and that is reflected in the many comings and goings of that period. A period of instability followed Robertson's departure in 1841, both for the lifeboat crew and for Spurn itself. Between 1841 and 1857 six coxswains served. Spurn was turned into a line of islands. The work of loading gravel and cobbles was stopped, except upon the Binks, because it appeared to be accelerating the

28   *The lifeboat cottages from the Humber.*

erosion of the peninsula, and the men lost their main source of income. Between 1850 and 1859, 30 of the 52 men who were appointed to the 10-man crew served for one year or less, and another eight served less than two.

William Davey, Robertson's successor, started badly by dismissing three crew members, Ezard, Whitehouse and Laycock, who wrote to Trinity House on 23 December 1841 to complain of their treatment:

we have been discharged suddenly and we are quite unprepared for it and in debt for last 3 month for we have not earned 30s per month and we have had a bad year altogether then to have to leave in the middle of winter when we have lade all our money out in stocks for our asses and selves which we have to sell for nothing almost, gents [.] It is really cruel to turn us out with our families at this season of the year some of us have children sucking at the mothers breasts and with 8 days weaning and we do not know what for it cannot be our age as there is a man to be kept in the boat turned 62 and what Mr Davey has heard to our disadvantage we are confident it is the effect of malice ...

The correspondence demonstrates the importance of crew members' wives. Davey's own wife had found the coxswain's accommodation uncomfortable, and had been unwell since she arrived in a house that 'when it blows it is almost fit to blow one out of the house'. In February Davey told Trinity House that another man wished to leave, as his wife had not settled, and in March a second man was leaving whose wife 'has made more disturbance on the island than anyone'. Quarrels between families were not uncommon, and were hardly surprising when they were in such close proximity to one another. The

Trinity House records include many complaints about the coxswain by the crew and vice versa. In the late 1850s, Fewson Hopper, who was later to be another long-serving coxswain, joined the crew at a time when a relatively stable period had arrived for Spurn. The new defences were fairly effective, modern houses had been built, and between 1860 and 1869 few men left. Hopper, the son of a Patrington corn miller, brought a family of two girls and four boys to the peninsula, and whilst at Spurn he and his wife produced two more girls and two boys. In 1858 Hopper and two other crew members had a dispute, and their wives, who became involved, were described by Willis the coxswain as 'three viragos of the first class, a disgrace to their sex'. However, the quarrel must have soon been forgotten, for Hopper was appointed mate in 1861 and, when William Willis left, aged 65, to take over Killingholme lighthouse (no retirement at 55 in the 19th century!), Hopper was promoted to coxswain.

Hopper served until 1877 when, at 55, he left to become keeper of Saltend lighthouse – at that period lifeboatmen often became lighthouse-keepers and vice versa. Several Hopper children stayed on at Spurn, including James, who at 15 became a telegraph clerk on Spurn, and then went on to run the *Lifeboat Inn* (now established in an extended two-storey building incorporated in the row of 1819 cottages, and no longer the province of the coxswain) in the later 1870s, remaining as the licensee until just before the First World War. James's brother, Consitt Hopper, became the Lloyd's Agent at Spurn, remaining until the First World War (see chapter three), and another brother, William Fewson Hopper, followed his father as a lifeboat man, serving from 1879 to 1883, and again between 1894 and 1911, being appointed as mate in 1897. William's cousins James and Frederick were also crew members in the latter years of the 19th century, and William's son, George, followed his father as a crew member from 1931 until 1940.

The new houses, which were built in the second half of 1857, cost £1,350. By January 1858 some of the crew had already moved in, though they

29　*People on the Binks with gravel sloops.*

30 *Making crab pots. This is an occupation of lifeboatmen on the Point to this day.*

were still being painted. The new houses were also close to the estuary, which meant that they too were under attack at high tides, and in 1863 they were protected by a bank of chalk. In 1875 revetments made of planking filled with chalkstone were placed in front of the cottages. By contemporary standards the cottages were constructed to quite a high standard, and were to last for 120 years. Their alignment, with their 'front doors' looking over the Humber, rather emphasises the fact that access by water was far more important than that by land. Each two houses shared a porch, and to help avoid flooding the porch was entered by climbing two steps and going through a double door. From there a further two steps and a door led straight to the front room. The crews' houses were 'two up and two down'. One of the downstairs rooms was a living room, which could be used for sleeping if necessary, and the other was the kitchen. Two bedrooms were upstairs. Each cottage had an outside yard with an earth closet at one side and a wash-house at the other. The cottages at each end, occupied by the coxswain and mate, were larger.

Their only neighbours were the lighthouse-keepers, still living in houses that were situated within the lighthouse compound. When Walter White visited Spurn in the late 1850s he noted that Smeaton's lighthouse had been given further protection after the breaches that had just occurred in the spit. He wrote:

> At the time of my visit, rows of piles were being driven in and barriers of chalk erected, to secure the ground on the outer side between the tower and the sea ... The paved enclosure around the tower is kept scrupulously clean for the rain which falls thereon and flows into the cistern beneath is the only drinkable water to be had. The lesser tower stands at the foot of the inner slope, where its base is covered by every tide. Its height is fifty feet, and the entrance, approached by a long wooden bridge, is far above reach of the water. This is the third tower erected on the same spot; the two which preceded it suffered so much damage from the sea that they had to be rebuilt.

The three keepers had two lights to maintain. The low tower mentioned by White was newly built. The great storm of 1849 and subsequent gales had swept away the low light on the beach on the seaward side of the spit, and in 1852 a new tower was built on the beach on the Humber side, being lit for the first time in June of that year. It still remains.

Life on the Point later in the 19th Century

As the above quotation shows, water was at a premium on Spurn. There were no wells, and the rain that filled the gutters had to provide all the cottages with water. Mr George Jarratt was brought up in one of the lifeboat cottages, and remembered:

> When there was a westerly gale blowing, the spume and spray would come over the rooftops of the cottages and the shutters had to be put in front of the windows. The spouts had to be diverted, so that the sea water did not get mixed up with the rain water, as this was the only water we had to drink. It was collected in an underground cistern close to our back door and each week the Coxswain came and allotted to each house so many bucketfuls for the week. In dry weather water was brought in barrels by the Trinity House yacht, which were dropped on the Humber foreshore and rolled up the beach to the houses when the tide went down. (*Memories of Spurn in the 1880s.*)

Fuel was abundant, as timber was washed up onto the beaches at almost every tide. An even more effective fuel was sea coal, which was often deposited from wrecked colliers. The coal was collected into wicker baskets, which allowed sand to fall through, leaving the coal behind. It produced very hot fires and was highly valued by the people living on Spurn.

Provisions were not easily obtainable. Most of them had to come in by boat from Grimsby or Cleethorpes, especially in the first half of the century when the peninsula was broken through. In 1839 a letter from some of the crew mentioned the 'privation having to pay almost double for every little thing we want'. The wives of the crew had to plan carefully in advance. No fresh milk was available, so any milk was tinned. Both the old and new cottages apparently had little plots around them, but they can hardly be called gardens. They were described in 1835 as 'a square patch of barren land for a garden

in front … but half cultivated. The gardens are of sterile soil, and fenced with dry sticks and old barrel staves.' Since the soil on Spurn is composed mostly of sand it is surprising that the lifeboatmen even attempted cultivation, but photographs and maps from the early 19th century show allotments near the lighthouse and, later, plots further north near Chalk Bank were established. Potatoes were grown, and Jarratt mentions seaweed being used as a fertiliser. When Spurn was an island, tradesmen could not get through, but once the breach in the peninsula had been mended they began to travel to Spurn by land from Easington or even further afield. Jarratt mentions a greengrocer coming from Welwick and a butcher from Easington in the 1880s. By then a cart track ran along the southern part of the peninsula, though the journey by wheeled vehicle was not an easy one. From the Warren area as far as the High Bents the Humber clays were used, because when the tide was out it was far easier to use the Humber beach than struggle over the dunes.

Some families kept chickens or even a pig, which could be fed on kitchen waste. Rabbits were plentiful and provided a regular source of meat, as did wildfowl. Fish, crabs and lobsters were abundant. For a time in the 1850s the lifeboatmen actually tried to make a living through fishing. Throughout the first half of the 19th century the lifeboatmen were poorly paid. They were dependent in the early years on gravelling, which provided a fluctuating income. When the money coming in from gravelling went down because of the restrictions placed by the Board of Trade on taking material from the beaches, times were very hard indeed. The men received a share of the salvage on ships, but that too was only intermittent. The attempt to earn a living by fishing was not a success, because the men could not fish too far distant from Spurn. Rather surprisingly, in 1855, they were given permission to take a boat to fish as far away as Flamborough Head and southwards from Spurn 'as far as the light on Spurn could be seen'. But they were impinging upon the areas where established fishermen were working and as a commercial undertaking that was apparently not successful. An important step was taken in 1855, when Trinity House agreed to pay the men – initially £10 per annum, out of which they had to pay 1s. per month for the rent of a house. In 1856, having found great difficulty in attracting crews, Trinity House raised the wages to £2 10s. per month. Though the breach caused difficulties in getting work gravelling, it brought new opportunities to earn money from unloading chalk for the defences, and later driving piles for the new groynes. A combination of all those sources of income meant that the families were comparatively well off in the second half of the 19th century.

Medical support was not readily available. The wives of the lifeboatmen helped each other in childbirth, and employed folk remedies for ordinary ailments. Jarrett wrote in the 1880s of brimstone and treacle and Parrish's Blood Mixture as being common remedies, and the old folk cure for whooping cough of a roasted mouse was being administered to his sister. The nearest doctor was at Patrington or over the water at Grimsby, and to the normal fees charged by a doctor at that time would be added the cost of travel.

The comforts of religion were more accessible. They were not so far away from the services of church and chapel, which at times came to them despite the difficulties of access. In October 1846 the vicar of Kilnsea, the Reverend Inman, wrote to Trinity House that he now had a curate and could therefore conduct 'divine service at Spurn to the 72 souls there'. He offered two services every three weeks in summer, and one every other week in winter. However, he said that the curate would need a horse and he (the vicar) would require a small two-wheeled carriage for his conveyance to Spurn, apparently expecting Trinity House to help with his expenses. They did not oblige, and it was not long before others, who were anyway more to the taste of the lifeboat families, filled the gap. Edward Thring, a chaplain to Missions to Seamen from Grimsby, went across to Spurn in 1858-9, where 'the master of the lighthouse had made a chapel for a local population of about sixty persons. The master conducted weekly services which Thring promised to supplement. It would be their first regular preaching since 1841.'

31 *Loading gravel on the Binks, c.1900.*

32   *Loading gravel on the Binks, c.1900.*

(A.R.B. Robinson. *Chaplain on the Mersey 1859-1867*, privately printed, 1987.)

From the late 1850s the Primitive Methodists sent a preacher almost weekly to Spurn. The Church of England eventually responded to the competition and, from 1869, they too sent a minister. In January 1874 the Reverend John Escreet, who had been taking services in the lighthouse for keepers and crew for five years, wrote to Trinity House that he was about to move and wished to repay the gentleman whose horse he has been borrowing with the gift of a Bible. George Jarratt, in his reminiscences of living at Spurn in the 1880s, says that a preacher sent by the Patrington Primitive Methodist Circuit came for an afternoon service, left his horse and trap at Southfield Farm, and walked to the Point, where the service was held in the lighthouse, one storey up. That was Smeaton's lighthouse, and Jarratt describes his frightening experience as a small child of walking up stone steps with no guard rail. Apparently

the lifeboat families were always lukewarm about any Anglican services, and in the early 1880s they refused to attend their services at all. The Anglicans appear to have withdrawn completely following that disagreement, and services were only resumed after a visit from the Archbishop of York in 1893. Thereafter a fortnightly service was held, though the number of worshippers was always considerably lower than at the Primitive Methodist service, which still took place weekly.

Until the passing of the 1870 Education Act the government did not involve itself actively in providing schools. What schools there were tended to be provided by the Church or private individuals. So it was not surprising that the Spurn children were without educational provision. Nevertheless, their parents wished them to attend school. Many of the lifeboat families were large; indeed throughout the 19th century between 45 and 50 per cent of the people on the Point were aged 19 and under.

33   *Sloops on the Binks.*

In 1839, in a letter to Trinity House about their dissatisfaction with their conditions, the crew wrote that 'we are in danger of being washed away every high tide there is no place of worship nor a school for our children within 7 miles of Spurn'. In 1865 Thomas Winson, a Derbyshire man, joined the Spurn lifeboat, later becoming coxswain. The Winsons had a large family, 10 in all, eight of them born at Spurn. When Winson's wife, Eliza, arrived she realised that the 20 to 30 children under 12 needed to be educated. She began a school in her own house in 1867 and, when she left in 1869 to go to Grimsby, Eliza Hopper, daughter of Fewson Hopper, took over. As Eliza later became postmistress and telegraph clerk that was not an entirely satisfactory arrangement.

The recreational possibilities at Spurn must have been very limited. Gardening, snaring rabbits, wildfowling and other outdoor pursuits for the men were available in daytime hours. In the winter, however, when daylight hours were short, the time may have passed rather slowly, apart from those dramatic punctuations when ships were in danger. As seamen,

the lifeboatmen no doubt had the practical skills to make things, and would be able to fill their time with various hobbies. Making crab and lobster pots was certainly one of the spare-time activities. Social interaction between the small group of families on the Point must have been highly valued, though their close proximity to one another must have meant also that squabbles became more important and long-lasting. The role of the coxswain in preserving social harmony cannot be overstated.

The Lifeboats

Whatever was happening domestically the lifeboat coxswain and crew continued to give good service and to save many lives. Their success depended upon their being alerted as soon as possible when a ship was in distress in the neighbourhood. Throughout most of the 19th century no coastguards were actually stationed at Spurn. About 1855 the Coastguard Service wrote to Trinity House requesting that there should be a station at Spurn but, because of the difficulties of accommodating the men, it was decided that they should be stationed at Kilnsea instead. The lifeboatmen got their first look-out post in 1858 after having drawn the attention of Trinity House to the difficulty of keeping watch in gales, heavy rain and high seas. Accordingly, a strong wooden hut was built on top of the dune ridge. The watchman was given an old ship's bell to summon the crew. The hut lasted until 1884 when a storm washed it down the cliff, and a new larger one set on piles replaced it. Another hut housed the Lloyd's agent, and the coastguards later had a substantial watch-house too.

The third Spurn lifeboat, which had given service for almost 30 years, was becoming unseaworthy and the fourth Spurn lifeboat was delivered in 1881. She had 30 copper airtight tanks and cost £195. Unfortunately, in 1883 she broke away from her moorings in a storm, was driven out to sea, and eventually turned up in Holland! Stronger moorings were then put in place, and the old lifeboat was patched up and reused until the new boat was back on station in January 1884. In 1888 disaster struck again when the lifeboat tender was swept away whilst

assisting the Bull lightship and had to be replaced. The main power for the lifeboat at that time was still oars, but in 1897 the RNLI were making plans for a steam lifeboat for the mouth of the Humber. It was decided that such a boat would not be suitable for the conditions off Spurn and so it was located at Grimsby as an experiment. By 1901 the Spurn lifeboat was leaking badly. It had to be taken away for repairs and the Grimsby sailing boat was sent to Spurn as a stop-gap. Trinity House decided that a fifth lifeboat was needed and Earle's shipyard in Hull was asked to build it. David Pye, who was coxswain at that time, made several suggestions as to the dimensions and specifications of the new boat, and also asked for a light carriage to run the tender down the beach because his men were finding themselves exhausted before they even got to sea in the lifeboat. The experiment of having a steam lifeboat at Grimsby was judged to be unsuccessful, and it was again suggested placing it at Spurn, but the coxswain and crew let it be known that rescuing ships from the Binks would be impossible with a steam-driven boat. The new lifeboat was delivered in

34 *Gravel sloops at Spurn.*

1903 but was beset by problems, and the old lifeboat often had to replace her in her first year of service.

Continued Protection of the Point

Work to protect the peninsula and prevent another breach continued throughout the 19th century. James Walker's measures had largely succeeded and, on his death in 1863, Messrs Coode took over, operating under the Board of Trade rather than the Admiralty. Between 1864 and 1870 11 groynes were erected on the seaward side of the peninsula, and a straight line of chalk embankment (the one today known as 'Chalk Bank') was built where the main breach had occurred. Walker's earlier chalk embankment, although immediately effective, had not been successful in the long term since it projected too far into the Humber. It was being washed away and also had the unfortunate effect of hindering the movement of beach material northwards. Its legacy remains apparent, however, in the bulge of the peninsula on the Humber side, and in the chalk stones still remaining on the beach there. The breach was healed further by the marram grass that Walker had planted as an efficient binder of sand

dunes. Stakes and wattling had also been effective in encouraging the accumulation of sand, and by the later 1860s the breach was being colonised by a plant very characteristic of the present peninsula – sea buckthorn.

Most of the neck of the peninsula at that time was low and during the highest tides the sand was washed over it. However, by the later 19th century that section called the High Bents was in need of extra protection and, in 1883-4, a length of timber revetment was put in on the seaward side. That was an area that was to receive much more attention in the following century. The lines of groynes that stretched down the peninsula required regular maintenance, and so Spurn began to receive much more attention from the government than had formerly been the case. The Humber was an increasingly busy waterway and it was realised officially that the shipping lanes needed to be protected. Any further breach would bring unpredictable results to the flow of the estuary. The protection of Spurn was to last for another century, give it a renewed lease of life and, though that could not have been predicted, allow it to become a military base in the two world wars of the next century.

Three

Opening Up to the Outside World: Spurn and Kilnsea, 1880-1913

The closing years of the 19th and the early part of the 20th centuries witnessed a number of important changes and significant events in the history of Kilnsea and particularly Spurn. Many of the changes at Spurn reflected the growing awareness of the importance of the area with regard to shipping. The mid-century breach had made the authorities aware of the threat that such an occurrence might pose to the Humber's main navigational channels and the disruption of trade that would ensue to the Humber's busy and thriving ports if the free passage of shipping should thereby be disrupted. One consequence of this was the decision to inaugurate and maintain effective sea defences against erosion and so consolidate the good work that had been done in healing the breach.

35 *The Hopper family and friends outside the Lifeboat Inn. The Hoppers were all descended from Fewson Hopper, the coxswain of the lifeboat in the 1860s and 1870s. His son James ran the Lifeboat Inn (1877-1913), and brought up a large family there. His brother Consitt worked as Lloyd's agent (1880-1919), whilst their sister Eliza ran the post office over the same period. Brother William Fewson was a member of the lifeboat crew (1879-1883, 1891, and 1894-1911). Cousin Frederick served on the lifeboat crew from 1891 to about 1916. His brother James was a member of the crew from 1873 to 1883, and 1891. This photograph shows Consitt Hopper on the extreme left, with Eliza seated. James Hopper is seated on the ground, and his wife, Martha Ellen, is second from the right, with daughters Ada, Agatha and Annie and unidentified girls at the back.*

Still connected with the interests of shipping was the establishment of an efficient system of communications of shipping movements in and out of the Humber. The building of a new lighthouse to replace the old one was one of the main events of that period, which also saw major changes in the organisation and management of the lifeboat service on Spurn. In addition, partly as a result of those developments, the number of people living and working on Spurn increased and that had consequences for such matters as the provision of more effective schooling, and the organization of religious worship, as well as additional trade for local suppliers of goods and provisions. The period saw too a marked increase in the number of visitors, some of them day-trippers, but also naturalists and wildfowlers, as the area had become more accessible when rail and road facilities improved both regionally and nationally. Kilnsea, too, was affected by those developments but more significant to its inhabitants were the serious floods that took place

36   *Barney Coy, Spurn postman.*

37   *Coastguards and visitors, c.1900. The chimneys on the right belong to the lighthouse keepers' cottages in the compound.*

38 *Consitt Hopper, Lloyd's agent, and Coastguards, at flag practice. Note the cradle halfway down the lighthouse, which is being painted.*

between 1900 and 1908 and resulted in improved banks to protect the village.

Communications

Connected to the south-east corner of South Holderness by only a tenuous thread, Spurn Head always had poor communications with the outside world. Naturally there was much coming and going via the sea and via the Humber, but land communications were bad and to this day remain difficult and liable to disruption by incursions of the sea. The passage of shipping up and down the Humber estuary is vital to the trade and commerce of the ports that it serves. Nowadays the Vessel Traffic Service (chapter nine), which is located on the Point, gives instant information on the river traffic, but it is often forgotten that a direct forerunner of this service was established between Spurn and Hull as early as 1839. During the Napoleonic Wars (c.1791) two French brothers called Chappe had invented a mechanical (sometimes called an optical) system of long-distance communication. The system used a line of towers or high points upon which were built posts with extending arms, which could be moved into a variety of positions to convey messages. Observers were placed at each tower with telescopes, and they could interpret the signals and pass them on to the next tower. In

April 1838 Hull Chamber of Commerce decided to set up such a system between Hull and Spurn. With the co-operation of Trinity House of Hull and the Commissioners of Pilots, Lieutenant Watson of Liverpool, a man experienced in the establishment of telegraphs, surveyed and then set up the line of signals, which was opened in September 1839. From Hull it followed the Yorkshire shore of the Humber to Paull and then crossed to Killingholme and Grimsby on the Lincolnshire side, terminating at Spurn. By means of that new system it was said that 'vessels with the necessary signals, at a distance from two to twenty miles from Spurn, will ... be reported at Hull two minutes after arriving in sight'. In 1857 Cleethorpes took over Spurn's role of notifying shipping movements.

Whilst the mechanical telegraph line was being constructed between Hull and Spurn, the electric telegraph was being developed by William Fothergill Cooke and Charles Wheatstone. The world's first commercial electric telegraph line was built in 1839 between Paddington and West Drayton – the first of many. The first public telegraph line was opened by Queen Victoria in 1845. The private companies that were formed subsequently were taken over by the Post Office in 1870 and in the following year Spurn got its own telegraph office. In fact a post office at Spurn had predated this by three years, when in 1868 one was set up in the coxswain's house.

Two telegraph clerks are listed in the 1871 census: James Hopper, aged 15, son of the coxswain, and Henry Shaw, aged 16, a boarder in the same house. Eliza Hopper, James's sister, who was schoolmistress at that time, was aged 21 in 1871 and, though not named as postmistress in the census, she soon took on that role too, combining it with telegraph clerk and conducting all her work in the parlour of the coxswain's house. Not finding it easy to combine all her various jobs, she eventually resigned as schoolmistress (see below) and was left to concentrate upon the postmistress and telegraphing duties. Her father, Fewson Hopper, had left Spurn by that time, but Eliza remained as postmistress and was still performing that task during the First World War. She worked closely with her brother Consitt, who was also a central figure in the communication network at Spurn, being the Lloyd's agent.

The Lloyd's Agency System had been established in 1811, when the company was given the power to appoint agents whose job it was to notify the movement of ships around the seas and ports. Lloyd's agents had to be resident and well-established at the place concerned and be of 'high commercial status and integrity' in their local community. Under an Act of 1888, Lloyd's was given the powers to establish signal stations with telegraphic equipment in key locations. Spurn was in an obvious place for such a station and Consitt remained as Lloyd's agent at Spurn for over 30 years. Another big step forward in improving communications on Spurn came in 1893, when a telephone was installed in the coxswain's house connecting it to the coastguard stations at Easington and Kilnsea 'for rapid communication if a vessel should run ashore on the nearby coast'.

The telegraph and telephone brought striking changes to the landscape of Spurn. A line of telegraph posts with the wires now stretching down the peninsula provided a vertical element to what had been hitherto a uniformly flat vista. Unfortunately, these wires proved to be a hazard to birds passing along the peninsula. There are several references in the *Naturalist* to birds being killed by flying into the wires. If in good condition, they were taken to Philip Loten, the Easington taxidermist (see below) for stuffing. The electric wires were later to become a similar hazard for birds in the 20th century.

Eliza Hopper was the only holder of the office of postmistress, and her tenure lasted over 50 years. Directories show that letter and parcels arrived at the Point in the late morning, and were sent off at about two o'clock in the afternoon. They were taken by Barnard (Barney) Coy of Easington, who was the Spurn postman from 1871 (soon after the opening of the post office in 1868), until his retirement aged 68 in 1906. He served as the postman for 35 years and the it was calculated that in that time he had walked 165,000 miles – the equivalent of circumnavigating the globe six and a half times! This was no ordinary postal round. The first part of the journey from Easington to Kilnsea was on a public road, but in the late 19th century it would not have been a particularly good one, being described in 1878 by a traveller as 'becoming always more sandy and more disorganised'. Coy made the journey six times a week in all weathers. He sometimes had quite a heavy load: he recalled that when the new lighthouse was being planned he carried sample bricks and sand for the architects and builders!

The New Lighthouse

Smeaton's lighthouse had been standing for over a century by the 1890s. It had been well built, on a foundation consisting of four circles of thick wooden poles rammed down into the sand and surmounted by a platform of stone about 12 inches deep. However, in 1892 cracks were discovered in the brickwork and the lighthouse keepers complained that the tower swayed and rocked in high winds. Further examination showed evidence of settlement caused, it was believed, by the rotting of the timber piles in the foundation. The tower had to be supported by wooden scaffolds whilst a new one was built. Thomas Matthews was the engineer employed by Trinity House to design a new lighthouse, and he decided that as it could not be built on a rock, then he would have to create an artificial rock as a foundation. Smeaton's timber piles had been only 10 feet deep. Matthews planned to have a much deeper base. His design incorporated 21 concrete cylinders, each 22 feet in depth and seven feet in diameter. These were positioned vertically and sunk below the level

39 *Building the lighthouse, showing the concrete foundations.*

40 *The high lighthouse and the mortuary, with workmen, c.1900.*

of the sand down to hard, compacted gravel. The cylinders themselves and the spaces between them were then filled with concrete, and covered by an additional layer of yet more concrete to the depth of several feet, to make a solid impermeable mass. The work itself was contracted out to Messrs Stratton of Edinburgh, the same firm who had just recently completed the building of Withernsea lighthouse. Due to its comparatively isolated position, Spurn lighthouse was a more arduous undertaking than its Withernsea counterpart. Apart from the usual building materials, all the water used in making the cement had to be brought to the site in carts, because seawater was not suitable. The lighthouse took one year and 11 months to construct. When finished, it stood 128 feet high from base to vane, one foot higher than Withernsea lighthouse. Its base is 40 feet in diameter and the walls are five feet six inches thick at the base and almost three feet thick at the top. The tower is brick-built throughout, being constructed of more than 300,000 Staffordshire blue vitrified bricks, and it weighs 3,020 tons.

When first built, the lighthouse was fitted with an eight-wick, oil-burning lantern built by Chance Brothers of Smethwick. The basement of the tower was designed to hold 8,000 gallons of heavy mineral oil in lead-lined tanks, the oil being pumped up to the service room at the top of the tower when required. The main light, which was an occulting one, flashing on and off, had a flash equal to 120,000 candle power, but it could be increased to 180,000 when the visibility was especially poor. Its focal plane was 120 feet above mean high water (as at Withernsea) and it could be seen from a distance of 17 miles. Apart from the main flashing light at the top of the tower, there were three steady subsidiary lights shining from lower down the tower: one covered an arc over the Humber, the other two, one of them red, shone out to sea over the Chequer shoal and Haile Sand buoy respectively.

41 *The new lighthouse and the old lighthouse compound, c.1900.*

That new arrangement of lights made the low light redundant and it ceased to be used for navigational purposes. Its lantern was removed and the tower was subsequently utilised first as an explosive store and finally as a water tower providing the lifeboat cottages with a regular water supply. (See chapter five.) The new light was put into operation for the first time on the night of 12 September 1895.

The Lifeboat

Hull Trinity House had been established as a medieval guild, but from the 16th century onwards it became more and more powerful, so that it eventually controlled the navigation of the Humber, installed beacons, buoys and lightships, licensed pilots, oversaw the management of Spurn lighthouse and managed the Spurn lifeboat. It was, too, immensely influential in the civic and economic life of Hull. The 18th century probably saw the apogee of its power and influence.

Until the 19th century Hull Trinity House had exercised a monopoly upon the licensing of pilots on the river Humber. When the master of a ship requested a pilot to navigate the dangerous sandbanks of the river, only Trinity House Brethren were allowed to operate. This monopoly lasted until 1800 when the Humber was made 'pilot water' – that is all vessels over a certain tonnage were obliged to have a qualified pilot on board. That move was supported by Trinity House, but the house lost much of its powers as a result of the Act that no longer required a Humber pilot to be a Brother of Trinity House. The Humber Pilot Commission, set up under the Act, was closely associated with Trinity House and many pilots were still Brethren, but this weakening of its powers was a sign of things to come.

In 1836 the powers that Hull Trinity House had over the Spurn lighthouse were removed by an Act that vested all lighthouses under London Trinity House. That did not end Hull Trinity House's interest in Spurn, however, because it still maintained the Spurn lifeboat. Most other lifeboat stations (and by the late 19th century there were 240 lifeboat stations in operation around the coasts of Britain and Ireland) were affiliated to the Royal National Lifeboat Institution. Spurn had remained an exception because the crew were full-time life-

42   *The lifeboat crew, c.1894. Robert Little, crew member from 1894 to 1898, is on the left of the second row.*

43   *The lifeboat crew in front of the look-out hut, c.1900. The first wooden hut, which was built on top of the dune ridge and equipped with a bell for the watchman to summon the crew, lasted until 1884, when a storm washed it down the cliff, and this new larger one set on piles replaced it. In this photograph George (Dod) Hopper is second from the right. His grandfather, Fewson Hopper, and father, William Fewson Hopper, were lifeboatmen on Spurn, and in his turn he became a member of the crew in the 1930s.*

44   *The lifeboat crew with the lifeboat, c.1900.*

45   *Consitt, James, and Martha Ellen Hopper outside the Lifeboat Inn, c.1890.*

boat men and the lifeboat was operated by Hull Trinity House. After 97 years the latter was about to change.

In 1852 a Humber Conservancy Act had been passed, which established a new authority for the river Humber – the Humber Conservancy Board – and removed control over the shipping in the Humber from Hull Trinity House. In 1907 a second Act transferred the remainder of the House's responsibilities for navigation, and that included the Spurn lifeboat. On 1 January 1908 the lifeboat became the responsibility of the Humber Conservancy

Board and three unhappy years began for the lifeboat crew. The Board's correspondence demonstrates clearly that it had no desire to support the lifeboat – 'as this Board is practically a commercial body, it scarcely falls within their province to maintain the Lifeboat'. The problem was the unique nature of this lifeboat service. Being full-time it needed considerable financial support. Trinity House had recognised that need, and had been paying the crew's wages since the 1850s, albeit very modestly. In 1908 the Board entered into negotiations with the RNLI, but problems soon arose because of the high cost of supporting the station. The RNLI offered £150 per annum but, as running costs, mainly crew's wages, were over £450 per annum that was far too little. Many letters went backwards and forwards and the Constable family, who had leased the land used by the lifeboat to Trinity House since 1810, began to interest themselves in the case. They pointed out that not only the lifeboat but also the coastguards and Lloyd's signalling station were established on the Point, all at a nominal rent. Given the uncertainty about the future of the station the Constable family felt that notice to quit in twelve months' time should be served on the Humber Conservancy Board, which could apply for a new lease if it wished to do so. That seems to have been regarded by the Conservancy Board as an opportunity to rid itself of the burden of the lifeboat. In June 1910 the Board played their ace – unless the RNLI agreed to take on the station it would be closed. Up to that point negotiations had been kept secret, but by now the press became involved, and there was much interest in the case. Despite public support for the lifeboat, in August 1910 letters were sent out to the crew informing them that at the beginning of August

they would receive dismissal notices to terminate their employment on 2 September. The Secretary of the Board of Trade, recognising the importance of the Spurn station for the safety of shipping, wrote to the Conservancy Board urging it to reconsider and asking for a delay in dismissing the crew, and offering to make an annual contribution of £100 per annum. In December the Board of Trade asked the Conservancy Board if it would be prepared to make a contribution of £200 per annum towards the cost of the lifeboat. That was agreed, it being apparent that the bad publicity that they would attract if they failed to do so would be harmful in the extreme. In February 1911 the RNLI agreed to take over the Spurn lifeboat station and in May the crew signed new contracts.

David Pye was the coxswain of the lifeboat from 1894 until 1912. His time coincided with what was one of the most stressful periods in the history of the lifeboat to date. The uncertainty experienced by the crew between 1908 and 1911 made it very difficult for them and their families to continue doing their duty, and it says much for Pye's management skills that he retained most of his crew over that period.

46   *A picnic at the back of the* Lifeboat Inn, *c.1910.*

When Pye resigned he was replaced by Robert Cross, a Flamborough man who had served as a crew member from 1902 until 1908. In that year he returned to Flamborough and bought a share in a herring boat. In 1909 he was a member of the lifeboat crew that went out to help several cobles caught in a severe gale. Two of the cobles were lost, one being *The Three Brothers* in which Robert Cross's brother and two nephews were drowned. After that tragedy Cross resolved to dedicate himself to saving lives, and when Pye retired Cross applied for the job. He was to become one of the most celebrated coxswains Spurn has ever had.

The Spurn Community

Linkages by marriage between lifeboat and lighthouse were very common, and numerous examples could be given. The Cross family was no exception. Robert Cross had met his wife, Sarah Hood, at Flamborough, where she was the principal lighthouse-keeper's daughter. They married in 1902, and came to Spurn that same year. They soon had a son but sadly he died aged four months, and they had to wait until 1918 before their daughter, Vera, was born. From 1912, when Cross became coxswain, until 1943, when he retired, Robert Cross and his wife nurtured the little settlement on Spurn. She delivered babies, gave medical aid, and generally supported the wives of the crew, their husbands

and families for three decades. Cross had a policy, followed by coxswains since, that wives of his crew must be as enthusiastic about living on the Point as were their husbands. Cross was a staunch Methodist and teetotaller, as were several of his crew. During his years at Spurn he was society steward of the small Methodist Society, which met fortnightly in the little school. After cycling many miles, often in inclement weather, visiting preachers faced a long trudge over the sand dunes, but were welcomed by Sarah Cross with refreshments and hospitality.

By the late 19th century the first photographs of Spurn become available, and they show the Point positively bristling with huts and watch-houses. The lifeboatmen had got their first lookout post in 1858. Another hut, which housed the Lloyd's agent, was apparently shared with the coastguards, who in the late 19th century lived at Kilnsea (see chapter one) but also monitored Spurn Head. Apart from these huts and the crew's cottages, the *Lifeboat Inn* and the two lighthouses, photographs show little shacks scattered everywhere. And by that time a new and rather attractive building, usually known as the mortuary, had appeared near the lighthouse. This little chapel-like building, with round windows, was apparently built to shelter the bodies of people washed onto the beach from wrecked ships or taken off by the lifeboat crew. Early views of the Point show it within a fenced area, which appears to contain allotments.

47   *George (Dod) Hopper and fishermen at Spurn, c.1905.*

48   *A group of residents at Spurn, c.1905. They are standing near the coxswain's house. The iron tank shown held rainwater, which was used for both washing and drinking.*

The pub on the Point must have been a welcome sight for visitors but the first inn, established in the old barracks, was, by the middle of the century, according to Walter White's description, in 'a dangerous situation, close to the water' with the spray dashing into the rear of the house. Michael Welburn, who was described in directories of 1851 and 1858 as licensee of the *Lifeboat Inn*, master, and general shopkeeper, was to be the last coxswain to run the pub, as the building itself was fast succumbing to the ravages of the sea. When the new cottages were built in 1857 the old ones further north were partly refurbished, and one was enlarged, and provided with a second storey. Sir Clifford Constable allowed the new *Lifeboat Inn* to be established there, and apparently the coxswain, William Fewson Hopper, arranged the building work. Mary Ann Tennison, whose father had been an innkeeper in old Kilnsea, and whose brother Medforth was running the newly opened *Crown & Anchor* in Kilnsea, took over the pub on its new site, until the late 1860s when the Quinton family of Easington replaced her. John

Quinton and his father Thomas ran the *Lifeboat Inn* until Thomas died in 1877, when James Hopper, the son of Fewson Hopper, the coxswain, took it on whilst still only in his early twenties. He was to remain as landlord for 40 years, until the First World War.

The School

From at least 1871 until 1890, Miss Eliza Hopper served as the schoolmistress in the school on the Point but, since she combined that role with that of postmistress and helping her brother who acted as Lloyd's agent, the situation was far from satisfactory – 'She always seemed to be sending messages for her brother, who was Lloyd's agent' said Jarratt of his time at Spurn in the 1880s. According to Jarratt the unsatisfactory arrangements in the school caused five families, including his own, to leave Spurn in the 1880s. In 1890 Miss Hopper resigned as teacher and Mrs Winson, who had returned to Spurn, was appointed as official teacher by Trinity House.

By 1890 it was the duty of the government to provide board schools in those places without other provision. Pressed by the lifeboatmen, Trinity House had agreed to build a schoolhouse when Mrs Winson was appointed. In January 1891 the school was completed, and opened with 20 children attending. It was situated just west of the cottages and cost £170, being a one-roomed rectangular brick building, measuring 26 feet by 20 feet, and heated by a stove standing near the middle of the room. Although the school was at first for the children of the lifeboatmen, when in 1893 the Trinity House Brethren applied for a certificated teacher, it became an elementary school under the Education Authority, with the Brethren subscribing £10 per year. That change of status opened the school to all children in the area, including those of the lighthouse-keepers. The first certificated teacher was Mary Atkinson, who took charge of the school on 5 April 1893, after being introduced the previous evening with a church service in the schoolroom. James Hopper, the innkeeper of the *Lifeboat Inn* was a school manager and kept a close eye on the school, which was attended by his own children. Mary Atkinson recorded in the school logbook that 23 children attended at first, but she decided to dismiss five because they were too young,

49 *Harvest festival in Spurn school, c.1905. Spurn must have been an unusual place to hold a harvest festival!*

50 *Spurn children with teacher, Mary Atkinson, c.1894. Reuben Little is in the centre of the back row (he later became chairman of the Bridlington Harbour Commissioners), his brother Edward is in the centre of the second row, their sister Margaret (Maggie) is in front of Edward at the end of the third row, and their youngest sister Ada (with mouth pursed trying to whistle) is at the front.*

OPENING UP TO THE OUTSIDE WORLD / 57

three being under four and two under five. The hours of attendance were 9 a.m. until 11 a.m and 1 p.m. until 4 p.m, but in the summer months they finished at 3 p.m. on Mondays and Thursdays, since boats with excursionists from the south bank of the Humber came on those days, and the girls were needed to help their mothers cater for the visitors. Other problems of attendance were recorded by Miss Atkinson. 'Coaling' was a constant source of irregularity – 'When coal or wreckage etc. is on the beach away go all the elder children to help.' When Miss Atkinson left in 1895 she was replaced by Joseph Webster, a widower aged about 50, who was to become Spurn's longest-serving teacher, retiring in 1914 at the age of 67.

Visitors: The Naturalists

In the 19th century, especially during the second half, Spurn began to attract people interested in its unusual landscape, its flora and its fauna. Travel had become somewhat easier, with railways linking East Yorkshire with the wider world. Geographers, geologists and natural historians became aware that the Spurn peninsula was a fruitful area to study. With its long coastline and low-lying, poorly drained soils and many meres and streams Holderness had much to offer those interested in birds, plants and topography. Geologists found its clay soils and low cliffs of limited interest, but fossils could be found on the beaches and in the submerged meres. Holderness was an area that provided good sport for wildfowlers, though by the second half of the 19th century much of the land had been drained and the meres dried up. By the end of the 19th century the subject of erosion on the East Coast was also beginning to attract much attention. Many naturalists were also interested in geology, archaeology and other similar subjects. Those who came tended to base themselves at Easington, with its good inns and other services, and explore the area south from there. The 'Beacon area' south of Long Bank was of interest both ornithologically and for its flora and insect life. The northernmost fields of Kilnsea were generally pasture, but owing to the primitive sea defences of the time they were often inundated by the sea.

The landscape of Holderness had changed quite markedly in the 19th century as a result of large-scale drainage. As early as 1796 an observer of the harvest near Patrington could write of 'the former watery plains and furzy heaths' of the area having changed to arable fields 'shining with the well-ripened fruits of Ceres'. Certainly by the 1850s when under-draining with tiles and pipes was common, the many meres for which Holderness was well known had mostly disappeared. Such a development, whilst popular with farmers, was less welcome to wildfowlers. The habitats of wildfowl were inevitably diminished, and several writers on the wildlife of the area remarked on the losses. As J.J. Briggs wrote in the *Zoologist* in 1845:

> Wild fowl are said to be far less abundant about Spern [sic] Head than formerly. About sixty years ago it was not unusual to find them in such multitudes, that when they rose in the air, the rush of their wings might be heard a mile away, or sometimes even more. Now they are fewer in number, owing to the drainage of the marshes and swamps which they haunted.

A diminution there may have been, but nevertheless Spurn and South Holderness, with its long seacoast on the east and the rich muddy estuary on the south and west, was still an area abundant with bird life. The rural economy was linked with the sea. Most of the farmers near the coast had boats and went inshore fishing; they were keen shooters and their tables were frequently augmented with wildfowl, rabbits and hares.

The landscape that Briggs described in 1845 emphasised the isolation of Spurn:

> When you pass the village of Kilnsea ... the land assumes a desolate appearance. The sand of the shore has been drifted by high winds into large heaps, and these are covered with coarse herbage and rank grass, but the surface abounds with curious wild plants ... On one hand stretches a boundless ocean, covered with ships and cobbles [boats, i.e. cobles], with the waves rolling at your feet; and on the other the magnificent river Humber, with its curiously ribbed sands, and still waters dotted with vessels; whilst the ground upon which you tread is like an arid waste, its dreary surface only enlivened by sea-fowl and plover, which start from their haunts in amazement at your approach.

51 *The Cross family's holiday home on Spurn, c.1909. Robert Cross, having been a member of the crew from 1901 to 1908, left Spurn to go back to Flamborough, but liked the Point so much he built a little holiday home there. This shows Robert, Sarah, his wife, and her brother, Walter Hood. The Crosses returned in 1912, when Robert became coxswain.*

52 *Inside Philip Loten's museum, Easington, c.1890.*

Southern Holderness became less isolated when the Hull to Withernsea line was constructed in 1854. The original plans were to terminate the line further south, possibly at Easington. Withernsea would then have remained a tiny hamlet and it would have been Easington that filled with new houses, hotels and all the trappings of a Victorian seaside resort, and Spurn might well have been very different in the second half of the 19th century. In the event, the promoters of the new railway decided that Withernsea was more suitable as a terminus. The new line meant that people wishing to visit Spurn could make part of the journey by train. At Patrington they transferred to horses and traps for the remaining 10 miles or so. Richard Stead, a visitor in 1878, described his party arriving at Patrington only to find that the Easington carrier insisted upon waiting for the next train, to make his journey more lucrative. Stead looked around Patrington and then:

we mounted up into [a] vehicle of the most wondrous kind. It was of the dog-cart build, but constructed to carry apparently any number of passengers required. At any rate the owner couldn't tell how many it would hold. He had seen "fowerteen" in it, but evidently thought it far from full on that occasion. We had a delightful drive to Easington … the last village of any consequence on the rapidly narrowing headland. Here our postman-carrier – for he combined the two offices – stopped, but he offered to drive us to Kilnsea, the next village, or even to Spurn itself, if we wished. As, however, we found that the distance to the Head was barely six miles, we decided to walk.

By the 1880s many people were making that journey, and the local inhabitants become quite used to outsiders. Most visitors stayed several days, and local hostelries benefited from the income that they brought. The *Neptune* at Easington was a favourite inn at which to board. The Reverend Henry Slater stayed there in the autumn in the 1880s and 1890s, often bringing his wife and young family with him. He commented in 1891, having stayed at the *Neptune* for ten days: 'Our bill came to £14. 18s.!! this includes horse hire, drinks and everything! they charge 5/- a day for us, 3/- for nurse and 2/- each for the kids, and do us well.'

Slater (1851-1934), a keen naturalist and wild-fowler, met other ornithologists who were staying in Easington or Kilnsea. They were all professional men, and included the celebrated John Cordeaux, William Eagle Clarke, the Reverend Edward Pon-sonby Knubley, the vicar of Staveley, near Harrogate and later of Steeple Ashton in Wiltshire, and Francis Boyes, a Beverley banker. Cordeaux, Slater and Eagle Clarke have left several descriptions of their stays

in the area. John Cordeaux (1831-99), whose name is still associated with Spurn, lived on the opposite bank of the Humber, at Great Coates, near Grimsby. He was a land agent and farmer who became very interested in all aspects of natural history, but particularly birds. He began visiting Spurn in the later 1860s, usually arriving by boat.

One family headed by a naturalist was semi-resident: Henry Bendelack Hewetson (1851-99) had been born in Beverley. He became a surgeon at Leeds General Infirmary, but retained a link with the East Riding by leasing Mount Pleasant (later Tower House) in Easington. Hewetson was an early photographer of wildlife. He was typical of several of the people who began visiting the area in the second half of the 19th century, being interested in archaeology, as well as in history, geology and natural history.

Another family that spent considerable time at Spurn, were the Whites. Major, later Colonel, William Lambert White (1849-1929) was the head of an important Hedon family, which had made its money from fruit-importing in Hull, and later moved into sugar and subsequently deep-sea trawling. Colonel White was a keen sportsman, and he rented Warren Cottage at the entrance to Spurn, 'as a shooting-box', from the Constable family, from at least 1880 until *c*.1910. The White family

53 *Craggs Clubley duck-shooting on Kilnsea Clays. Wildfowlers dug out a hole in the clays, filled it with straw and hid themselves in it, waiting until the tide advanced and with it the birds.*

54 *Craggs and Lambert Clubley (his eldest son) fishing. Craggs Clubley and his large family were the first to live in Rose Cottage, after it had been converted from two coastguard cottages at the end of the 19th century.*

spent much time at Spurn, erecting several further buildings at the Warren, so that it became a little community at the entrance to the peninsula. White's wildfowling interests are demonstrated by the fact that from the end of the 19th century until he left Warren Cottage, he employed a gamekeeper who lived at the Warren, presumably in the cottage, when the Whites were not in residence. In the 1901 census Samuel Robinson, gamekeeper, and his wife were in residence, and they remained there for some years.

The majority of those visitors were drawn as much by the sporting opportunities as by the chance to observe birds. Wildfowling was ridden with class prejudice. Before 1831 only those who owned land worth £100 per annum were allowed to kill game, or indeed rabbits and other animals. Essentially that meant that only the landed classes were entitled to shoot, either for sport or for the table, though poaching was widespread. From 1831, with the Game Act of that year, anyone could kill game if they purchased a game licence. Cordeaux's description in 1877 of the 'loafer ... with rusty fowling-piece and villainous cur at his heels' shows how the traditionalists viewed this new breed of licensed shooters.

For much of the 19th century, shooting birds was considered to be the only sure way of identifying them. Nor did a bird's rarity preserve it from death

by the gun; indeed, it made that death more likely. Poor identification in the field meant that the body needed to be procured. Slater wrote in September 1884 'Day fine and very hot. Yorkshire Naturalists' Union at Spurn. Went down at 9, shooting a Lesser Whitethroat in the Buckthorn and found Winson [the coxswain] had shot me a young Nightjar.' The hoopoe shot in 1891 'by one Biglin, a farmer with No. 4 shot at 20 yards', was presumably taken straight to Philip Loten, the local taxidermist, and set up for one of the ornithologists.

Philip Warrener Loten (1845-1908) was the son of the landlord of the *Neptune*, one of the Easington inns. Having been apprenticed to his father who was also a tailor, Philip the younger put his skill with the needle to good effect by turning his attention to taxidermy. In the second half of the 19th century, as the desire amongst naturalists for their own private collections grew, the technology of stuffing and preserving birds improved. Thomas Sheppard, the curator of the Hull Museums, wrote in the *Naturalist*:

> 'Philip', as he was generally known, had lived all his life in the vicinity of Spurn peninsula, where the flotsam and jetsam provided many treasures, and where he had early acquired his father's taste for natural history ... His skill as a taxidermist was widely known and many important museums and private collections are enriched by his handiwork.

Loten was also an experienced observer of wildlife, and wrote several articles for the *Naturalist*. He is mentioned several times in Slater's diary and in Cordeaux's articles and notebooks. The separation of classes is apparent, however, for Loten is referred to as Philip, whilst fellow professionals are invariably given their surnames.

Loten at first prepared the skins of birds for people to take away, but soon realised that there was an opportunity for displaying his skills to a wider public. He set up a small museum in his house and filled it with exhibits. As Sheppard recalled:

> For years Loten's Museum has been a calling place for the scores of people who daily visit the Spurn district in the summer months. His specimens of rare birds were a source of attraction to the naturalist, his cases arranged to illustrate 'Who killed Cock Robin?' and other stories were a delight to children … all and sundry admired his beautiful garden – a miniature paradise of blooms of all kinds.

Many of the distinguished visiting naturalists to Spurn were concerned to protect the eggs of the colony of Little Terns that nested on its beaches. The birds mainly nested near the lighthouse in the 19th century, and in 1861 between 40 and 50 pairs were recorded. At that time their greatest enemy was people. In the 1880s there are numerous references in the *Naturalist* to the parties of excursionists who visited Spurn by water from Grimsby and Cleethorpes, and took many Little Tern eggs. Cordeaux remarked in 1890 that 'It is surprising that the Spurn colony continues to exist considering the ceaseless plundering of the nests that goes on year after year.' The day-trippers from Cleethorpes were not the only hazard: Slater recorded in his diary for 6 September 1882, 'Clarke, who was on the clays, saw two Lesser Terns and knowing I wanted some, he fired two ineffectual shots.' Fortunately not all ornithologists were so inclined: Cordeaux was an early advocate of setting up protection for the Little Terns. Owing to his efforts, and those of others, the Yorkshire Naturalists' Union in 1891 set up a committee dedicated to bird protection. It was initially called the Wild Birds and Eggs Protection Committee, and had an early success in persuading the East Riding County Council to apply a protection order to Spurn Point in 1895, and employ a local man to implement it. The protection scheme was only a limited success, for several reasons. In 1897 the whole colony was washed out by very high spring tides and the 1899 season was a bad one, with '30-40 eggs taken by a single individual'. Petch, writing in 1900, said that 'Spurn presents more difficulties than any other protected area I know of.' He cited the length of the colony, the children living there, the Grimsby trippers and the gravel diggers who walk from Kilnsea to Spurn daily. Also,

55 Neptune Inn, *Easington*.

local people were encouraged by so-called 'naturalists' to collect as the eggs had a ready market. It was even asserted that the watcher connived with those naturalists who were also still collectors. In 1900 several YNU members collected a small fund to pay a watcher, and Colonel White's gamekeeper, Samuel Robinson, took on the task of protection. Robinson achieved some success (at least 100 pairs hatched), helped by the local policeman, a lighthouse keeper and 'inhabitants'. Despite setbacks the protection scheme continued. Moreover, the 1906 floods in Kilnsea produced a good beach, and some of the colony established itself there.

In 1906 Spurn Point was declared a sanctuary by the East Riding County Council, though Fortunes, writing in the *Naturalist* said that 'there is no-one to see these orders carried out'. Fortunately in 1907 the YNU Bird Protection Committee took over responsibility for protection of the colony. It was agreed that a subscription fund should be opened to pay the wages of a warden. The first report of that committee to be published in the *Naturalist* was for the 1909 season, when it was reported that the season was late and at the usual time for the watcher to cease there were still 'lots of helpless terns', so the season was extended by two weeks. The warden's job was made more difficult, because there were now two main colonies, one near the lighthouse and one near Kilnsea Beacon. In 1910 the 224th YNU meeting was held at Spurn where:

> recent ravages of the sea in the low-lying flooded land … floods so serious as to have interfered with the character of the tongue of land at two or three points. In one place near Kilnsea Beacon the sand which has washed over the fields has resulted in a new colony of Lesser Tern.

In 1914 despite the Sunday excursion steamers from Hull and Grimsby bringing excursionists 'who wander promiscuously about the Point, sometimes bringing dogs and causing the watcher a good deal of anxiety', the season was a good one.

Other Visitors

The naturalists were by no means the only visitors to the area in the second half of the 19th century. Geographically Spurn Head might appear to be isolated, indeed cut off, from contact with the outside world. In reality Grimsby and Cleethorpes were within easy reach by water and the lifeboat families made regular shopping trips over the Humber. With the expansion of seaside resorts as a result of transport improvements, notably the railways, and the introduction of bank holidays and annual holidays, people began to visit resorts like Withernsea and Cleethorpes. Paddle steamers began to take parties across the Humber to Spurn from Grimsby and Cleethorpes in the summer, and they also came from Hull. Some of those who arrived from Hull had travelled from the Midlands and the West Riding by rail on huge excursion trains, and were delighted to have the chance of a 'sea' trip down the Humber.

The visitors to Spurn sometimes came in huge numbers, either landing on the beach or by fishing boats from the paddle-steamers. In 1852 the coxswain wrote of a 'tea party of 1,500' arriving. One such visit led to tragedy for a member of the crew. In July 1865 a works party of 300 men was expected and two lifeboat men and a wife set out to buy new provisions from Grimsby with which to cater for the party. A thunderstorm overtook them and one, John Marshall, was killed, leaving four children, the eldest being only eight years old. Undoubtedly the crew's wives found these influxes of visitors provided a welcome extra income, and they baked cakes and provided teas in their houses for those who did not wish for alcoholic refreshment at the pub. By the summer of 1893 the excursion boats were coming on Mondays and Thursdays, and the school logbook records that the girls were wanted at home to help their mothers, to the displeasure of the schoolmistress. Embarking from the steamers was no easy task as, at that time, there was no jetty at Spurn, and at certain times of the tide the boats could only get so close to the shore. The lifeboat-men earned themselves a few pence by carrying the holidaymakers, especially the ladies, across the water. The children also earned pocket money by picking wild flowers to sell to the day-trippers, as they were still doing in the 1930s. The lifeboat men also made some money selling fish and shellfish to the tourists. Visitors were not always a blessing, however: Jarratt records that a fire was started

56 *The White family near Warren Cottage. Note the rough fence around the cottage. There is no sign in this photograph of what must be a later addition, the brick building at the rear, but it was certainly built by 1906.*

57 *Building 'The Rest' near Warren Cottage. The cottage itself was very small and it seems that, when the White family used it as a holiday home, they extended the accommodation in several ways, including this small wooden bungalow, called 'The Rest'.*

during one of their visits, which would have spread to the cottages had the crew not dug a trench to act as a fire break. In September 1884 a group of 70 YNU members arrived by steamer from Grimsby, having reached Spurn in about three hours. They found the plants 'much trodden down by the weekly tide of excursionists from Grimsby'. The excursion traffic was not all one way: excursions left from near the end of Humber Side Lane to Grimsby, both before and after the First World War.

Some people liked Spurn so much that they constructed little holiday homes on the peninsula. Early photographs show several examples of such huts. The earliest-recorded inhabitant of the 12th-century peninsula made a home in an upturned boat. He was not the last to do so! A pre-First World War photograph shows a boat called the *Dove* requisitioned as a shelter, whilst one entitled 'Happy Days at Camp Spurn' shows another. Other huts were constructed of bits of driftwood,

58 *The caravan near Warren Cottage. A caravan augmented the accommodation available for the White family at the turn of the century. The wooden bungalow, 'The Rest', being built in photograph 57 can be seen behind the bushes.*

59 *The White boys, John Dalton White and Thomas Lambert White, with Letty Stone and another servant at Spurn.*

or better-quality timber, washed up by the sea – whatever came to hand! Before he even came to Spurn to serve on the lifeboat, Robert Cross and his wife made a little shack for summer holidays on the Point. No planning laws operated in those days. Spurn was still owned by the Constable family of Burton Constable but, in the late 19th century, the family went through a period of financial difficulty. They were unable to live on their estate, and seem to have left Spurn to its own devices. Certainly no-one objected to the little shacks and huts, which proliferated all over the peninsula by the early part of the 20th century.

At the Warren a new lessee of the cottage appeared to take it over from the White family. Dr William Henry Coates had come to live at Bleak House in Patrington in 1891. He was to become a very important person in the town, as a magistrate, general practitioner, county councillor and local benefactor. He soon discovered the pleasures of Spurn and Kilnsea, and had a sort of beach hut (which he called 'Our Flat') built in the dunes, where he entertained visitors, many of them 'theatricals' from Hull and further afield. When Warren Cottage became vacant about 1908, Dr Coates rented it to use as a *pied-à-terre*. In the early years he visited by horse and trap, and when he bought a car he was probably the first person to motor to Kilnsea. His visitors made regular treks down to the little community on the Point, and entertained the locals and visitors. Lily Hopper, the daughter of James Hopper, licensee of the *Lifeboat Inn*, recollected that whenever the family visited Hull, they had the very best seats at the Hull theatres.

Erosion, the Beach and the Floods

By the end of the 19th century the erosion of the peninsula was more or less stabilised. A series of groynes ran down the seaward side, protecting the sand dunes from the sea, and building up the beach. The success of groynes in protecting beaches has never been disputed, but they are very expensive to erect and maintain. The peninsula itself is attached to the rest of Holderness, which is subject to similar forces to Spurn itself. All along the clay coast, land was being lost to the sea at an average rate of approximately two yards (just under two metres) annually. Only at Withernsea, a growing seaside resort, was any attempt made to counter the forces of erosion. Other villages were left to fend for themselves. The farmers of Kilnsea and Easington had always done their best to keep out the sea, but inevitably they were fighting a losing battle. Their only option in the 19th century and earlier was to build earth banks, which temporarily inhibited the overflow of the tides, though only until a surge in the North Sea coincided with high spring tides when the bank would be washed away. Another bank would then be built farther back, which would eventually suffer the same fate as its predecessor.

When Easington was enclosed in 1771 the bank (now called Long Bank), which separated Easington from Kilnsea, was then known as the New Bank, suggesting that it was of fairly recent origin. Its principal role was to protect Easington rather than Kilnsea from flooding. The bank's sinuous course suggests that it followed an old watercourse and, from what is known of the topography of that area before historical times, that seems likely. Much of the land between Easington and Kilnsea is below sea level and in prehistoric times formed part of a broad, well-wooded, east-west oriented valley, full of streams and pools. Several thousand years ago

60 *The White family on the beach. Colonel William Lambert White is third from the right. Colonel White's military titles came from his membership of the East Riding Royal Artillery Volunteers. He was mayor of Hedon several times in the 1890s, and was also a magistrate. He lived at Lambert House, Hedon, surrounded by ruinous pieces of Holderness churches, which he collected and displayed.*

61 *Warren Cottage, 1906, The Caravan, and the 'Rest', are still in situ.*

the coastline would have been about five miles to the east.

Concern about flooding and the loss of good agricultural land was never far from the minds of the inhabitants of South Holderness. By the 1890s the children of Kilnsea were being taken to Easington school daily in a farmer's wagon. The road between the two villages was very low-lying and the logbooks for Easington school in the late 19th and early 20th centuries often record the absence of Kilnsea children in the winter months owing to the road being flooded. An Erosion Committee was formed in Hull in 1900 because the condition of the coast was causing such concern. In March of that year representatives of the district councils of Bridlington, Hornsea and Withernsea, ecclesiastical commissioners, and principal landowners, had a meeting at which they discussed protecting the whole coast with groynes. But how to raise funds? The method favoured was an Act of Parliament with powers to levy a rate on all property owners with land within five miles of the coast. This idea was received with great acclamation by the first "half milers" ... but with a perfect wail of protest from the remaining "4½ milers", who argued that it might be 40 or 50 years before the sea swamped the first half-milers, by which time they would be dead and gone. It was soon realised that it was impracticable to levy a rate just on the first half-milers who, in any case, could not afford the

cost. In the end the members of the committee stopped meeting because they could not agree on a way forward.

Thomas Sheppard wrote in the *Naturalist* (1901):

In view of the recent articles which have appeared in the Hull papers in reference to the alarming state of affairs in south Holderness during the present month (March) the writer has visited the district (25 March 1901) and carefully examined the cliffs, especially in the vicinity of Kilnsea Land End where it is stated that the great danger lies. There was abundant evidence of the great destruction being carried on by the sea. Large strips of land, in some instances several yards across, had become detached and partly slipped down the cliffs. Several falls of clay, obviously recent, were noticed ... But I could find no signs whatever of any immediate danger of the sea breaking through and altering the channel of the Humber! In one or two places where the cliffs are unusually low – generally on the sites of ancient meres – the higher ground on each side has been connected by an embankment. Towards Spurn Point ample protection is afforded by very good groynes which stay the progress of southwardly travelling shingle, or thus protect the land from the force of the waves.

Spurn was indeed relatively safe at that time, but Kilnsea and Easington continued to be attacked by the sea. In response to the floods of the turn of the century Long Bank was raised higher in 1902. Mr William Evans, the surveyor of the local Court of Sewers, (a body responsible for overseeing the banks and ditches of a district) in his evidence to the Royal Commission of Coastal Erosion of 1909 said that 300 acres of Kilnsea was below sea level and that until the recent floods the farmers had 87 chains (one chain = 22 yards) of embankment to maintain against the sea and 126 chains against the Humber. As a result of their land diminishing and losing value many of them could no longer afford to erect and maintain new embankments. He said that there had been:

> an urgent necessity for a new sea embankment across a portion of Kilnsea Level about 5 years ago [c.1904] but the Court of Sewers knew it was impossible for the land to bear the cost. They approached the Board of Trade which offered £400 – a paltry sum. In September 1905 a storm had damaged the bank and the Court of Sewers decided to abandon it.

The events of 12 and 13 March 1906 were unprecedented in living memory. The bank by then was already half destroyed, and when there was an 'extraordinary tide and storm – 14 ft 9 inch at Grimsby' – on 12 March the sea broke through from just south of Ten Chains Road, Easington, (the sea road) and southwards to Kilnsea Beacon and Kilnsea itself. It was described as 'like a tremendous weir, … sweeping all before it on the low-lying land'. From here the rising waters rushed over Long Bank. The sea, having filled up the low lands, travelled onwards until it reached Welwick parish at the Humber side. Kilnsea with Spurn was virtually converted into an island. The sea was only prevented from joining the Humber by a few feet of clay embankment, which formed the river Humber bank. Three hundred acres below sea level from the sea to the Humber in Kilnsea were under as much as nine feet of water, as were 650 acres of Easington.

The following day the tides swept in again. A thousand acres were under water, and all the farms in the low areas between the two villages were affected. Mrs Clubley of Firtholme Farm (halfway between Easington and Kilnsea) had only 20 acres

62   Dr Coates and 'theatricals' at his holiday home at Kilnsea, c.1905. Dr Coates later rented Warren Cottage, after the White family left.

left clear of the salt water out of 140 acres of land on her farm. Mr John Newsam, who had a 400-acre farm in the same neighbourhood, had 153 acres of land inundated, and Mr George Clubley had half his 60 acres under water. The worst affected area was in Kilnsea. At Grange Farm the sea swept into the stack yard, drowning most of the fowls and doing great damage. Practically the whole of the farm's 160 acres were flooded. Further south the sea swept into Southfield Farm and put the kitchen fire out. Thirty-six acres of William Sharp's land was ruined. Fortunately, the other residents of Kilnsea lived on slightly higher ground and the sea failed to reach them.

Colonel White's gamekeeper, Mr Robinson, tried to return home at night, having waited until low water. But about midnight the gigantic waves got hold of his horse and trap, nearly sweeping them seawards, and he gave up. He tried again at six the next morning, again without being able to get through.

The postman, Barney Coy, having attempted to get through on the seaward side, almost got washed away. Apparently a most determined man, he next tried by the Humber Bank and 'after some escapes he was successful. He was, however, unable to deliver the letters at many of the isolated farms.'

The floods left many dramatic memories, but they left much more in concrete form. As the waters retreated, the inhabitants found everything scattered about, including implements such as ploughs, 'and it is by no means an uncommon thing to see drift wood, fish boxes, and even a crab pot stranded on the hedge tops'. At that time many fields had already been sown and the newspaper reported that 'The countryside presents a desolate appearance. Fields sown with wheat and beans are all wasted and rendered useless, while the grass land is badly damaged, and all the wells filled with salt water and rendered unfit for use.' The contamination of the wells was very serious, and all

63   *Landing passengers at Spurn.*

64   The 'Gloriana Ark Darts Club' at Spurn, c.1905.

the fresh water required for domestic use and for the stock had to be fetched from Easington until the wells ran pure again. Without the protection of the bank the sea came across Kilnsea to the Humber bank for three or four days every spring tide, and the road to Kilnsea and the Spurn was described as 'practically impassable every alternative week and at times is covered with three feet of salt water besides the damage which is accruing to the road itself'.

As a result of the floods the banks were mended, but the effect could only be short-term. In July 1910 the 224th meeting of the Yorkshire Naturalists' Union was held at Spurn. The report described:

> the recent ravages of the sea in the low-lying flooded land ... floods so serious as to have interfered with the character of the tongue of land at two or three points. In one place near Kilnsea beacon the sand which has washed over the fields has resulted in a new colony of Lesser Tern. The distance from the *Blue Bell Inn* is now 272 yards (534 on plaque).

So what was bad for farmers was good for Little Terns!

Life in Kilnsea and Spurn in the Early 20th Century

Despite the dangers of floods, daily life at the southern tip of Holderness was usually fairly peaceful and even self-contained at the turn of the 19th century. Easington itself could provide many services, including its four pubs – the *Marquis of Granby*, the *Sun*, the *White Horse* and the *Neptune*. The village had many craftsmen, including three shoemakers, two tailors, three wheelwright-cum-joiners, two bricklayers, a bird-stuffer (Philip Loten), and one blacksmith (a woman, Mrs Martha Petch). The village had four general shopkeepers, some of them also drapers, and a marine store dealer for the fishermen and sportsmen. And Easington still had a working windmill on the road going towards Out Newton.

Despite all those services a trip to Hull market was certainly a regular treat for many Easington residents. The 1892 directory for Easington lists three carriers – William Hodgson, James Pinder and Christopher Webster. Anyone wishing to get the flavour of travelling by carrier's cart or wagon in South Holderness before the First World War

65   *The Lizzie Helen* on land.

should read Edward Booth's *The Cliff End* (1924), which opens with a description of Tankard's Bus, a horse-driven omnibus that went to Hunmouth (Hull) every Saturday to the market:

> It is timed to leave the Market Arms at three o'clock. To make sure of a corner seat you would do well to be sitting in it at four o'clock at the latest.' Having eventually got on its way the bus moved into the countryside east of Hull and 'began to strew a trail of passengers and baskets behind it along the road-side ... With each departure there is an unmistakeable tightening of the bonds of friendship, belting the survivors in closer and more visible embrace ...

Easington's proximity to the sea and the Humber made it a popular place for both day and weekly visitors in the summer months. The traveller could take a train from Hull to Patrington or Withernsea. From there one could get a lift with the carrier to Easington, or hire a horse and carriage to proceed further. Many pubs also ran

livery stables at that time, and Patrington was a busy centre of a thriving agricultural district. When visitors got to Easington and wished to venture a little further south they could take refreshments at the *Marquis of Granby* and hire a horse from there, and set out for Kilnsea, another two miles further south. Kilnsea had less to offer visitors (certainly no shops) though some farmers' wives provided refreshments. The two pubs, the *Crown & Anchor* and the *Blue Bell*, were also well-placed to provide the traveller with both food and drink. The travel opportunities could have improved markedly at the end of the 19th century had the idea of building a light railway from Hull to Easington come to fruition.

Kilnsea was a very scattered village at that time. Approaching from the north it still appeared to be set upon a hill, though the old village, which had been on the highest ground, had completely disappeared into the sea by then. The first farmhouse was Grange Farm, on the left, and the next was Westmere, on the same side of the road. A terrace of three cottages, Rosabel Terrace, came next, with Blackmoor House (sometimes called Click'em) on the Humber side and the Primitive Methodist chapel next to Blackwell Pond. After some distance came the last building on the left before the *Crown & Anchor* – a house called Humber View. Between Cliff Farm and the sea, the church lay on the left and two small Coastguard cottages (later to be Rose Cottage) were on the right, after which no more buildings were to be seen until one reached the crossroads, where the *Blue Bell* pub was located. Taking the road north (North Marsh Lane) one passed a couple of cottages on the right and a little further up the lane was Northfield Farm. At the very top of North Marsh Lane was Beacon Cottage (also known as Headow, or Eddowes). This part-cobble and part-brick house had been built in the mid-19th century but, by the beginning of the 20th century, its situation was a precarious one. It survived the floods of 1906, and Redvers Clubley, who was apparently born in the house, told the story of how a bank was built around it to try to keep the sea out, but instead the waters came over and formed a moat, which drowned the family dog! About 1916 the Clubleys retreated to Cliff Farm as the house was washed away despite the family's efforts to protect it.

A comparison between the 1891 and the 1901 censuses for Kilnsea shows that it had suffered a marked decrease in population between those two dates. In 1891 there were 93 people in 25 households but in 1901 seven houses were uninhabited on the night of the census and the population had dropped to 79. Rural depopulation was a common feature of the second half of the 19th century, and such a drop is not unusual. Improved mechanisation of farming was partly responsible, and many young people were migrating to the towns at that time.

Living in Kilnsea at number two Rosabel Terrace in 1901 were the members of the Norwood family, headed by Everitt Norwood, a Lincolnshire man. He had come to Kilnsea to work on the gravelling and had married Mary Jane Hodgson, the daughter of William Hodgson, the licensee of the *Crown & Anchor*, in 1894. Through Mary Jane the Norwoods were connected to most of the Kilnsea families, including the Tennisons and the Medforths, as well

as the Hodgsons. Everitt and Mary Jane had eight children, including Ernest Medforth Norwood, who was born in 1904, and who wrote a memoir of his life in Kilnsea. Everitt worked as a general labourer, mainly on the farms, dyking and draining, and at hay time and harvest time he was employed full-time. He also earned money delivering oil to Spurn lighthouse. The oil was delivered to the *Crown & Anchor* by barge, 200 barrels at a time; the large barrels were then taken to Spurn by horse and cart, each cart having room for only one barrel. As there was no road down to Spurn, part of the trek was along the beach. The jetty at Kilnsea must have been more suitable for large bulky deliveries than the beach near the lighthouse, given the problems that Ernie describes in getting the large barrels down a road-less peninsula.

Most Kilnsea men were volunteer members of the team that operated the rocket apparatus, for which they were paid a few shillings for each turnout. Everitt Norwood was head man of the rocket crew. According to Ernie the men often had

66 *Kilnsea after the floods, March 1906, looking east towards the beacon.*

to walk to Spurn carrying the apparatus when a ship came ashore, and he had even seen 'elderly women' helping out. Such emergencies could occur quite frequently – 'nearly every month' said Ernie, 'a trawler would come ashore between Spurn and Easington. In those days there were no operators to guide the ship in and out of the river.' As well as taking lives the sea could sometimes be a good provider to those living on the coasts, especially after a storm. All sorts of things were found on the beach or the Humber foreshore:

> It was quite a usual thing to find a barrel of herring or a box of fish and to see a line of herring or fish hanging on the outside walls. Also a lot of timber or pit props floated in. One Saturday I went down on the Humber side and gathered over one hundred wooden blocks that were used for street laying in Hull. A lot of wood was thrown into the docks at Hull and when the lock gates were opened it floated out and washed up on the beach. Also if you reported a dog or a pig or a sheep washed up to the authorities by burying it with a little quicklime you got five shillings. Coal also washed up now and again. This was known as sea coal and made a good fire. I have known times when we had half a ton in the garden. Once a ship struck a mine and bags of flour, boxes of butter, lard and margarine, were washed up, At one time we were feeding the chickens on flour and butter mixed together. Those eggs we got in those days were really lovely!

Like the rest of the children in Kilnsea Ernie had to go to school in Easington. When he was a lad about 25 children left Kilnsea daily for Easington at 8.20 a.m. in an old mail coach, ('15 children inside and 9 outside'), which 'in its working days had plied the route from Bath to London'. The coach was pulled by Mettle, 'an old cavalry horse from the South African war'. Normally her speed was very slow and plodding, but one day her blinder (harness) fell off. 'Mettle must have thought she was back on the battle field, galloping off at a great rate, the driver (Mr George Clubley) fell off, and she delivered us safely at school somewhat earlier than usual!'

The school logbooks at the beginning of the 20th century show that Kilnsea children's attendance was sometimes erratic. Winters in the early years of the century did have more snow than was the case later in the century, and that meant no school

for the Kilnsea children. But floods were a greater hazard and Ernie remembered many occasions when the road to Easington was flooded up to three feet deep between Long Bank and Grange Farm.

For other reasons, too, many children's attendance at school was often poor. From the age of eight or so, when the threshing machine came to Kilnsea, Ernie Medforth did not attend school, but earned money for the family carrying chaff and water for the engine. For that he was paid six shillings a week, a sum that a poor family could not afford to turn down. There were other ways of making money. Ernie remembered that he used to fish in the Humber:

> with what was known as long line fishing and in those days you could bait 100 hooks and sometimes get as many fish. I used to sell them round the village or send them to Hull market with the carrier. I found a box of fish one morning and was dragging it home when he stopped me. He jumped off his lorry and said 'Here lad, let's put it on the lorry and I'll take it to fish market for you.' I used to collect rock semper and mushrooms and these also went to Hull to the market. And many a shilling have I got for getting a sheep off its back or taking a cow or heifer to the bull or taking a boar to a farm for its use.

In the early years of the 20th century many travelling salesmen were on the road. Ernie mentioned a draper coming from Hull every month, and staying the night at the *Crown & Anchor*. The grocer passed through Kilnsea on his way to Spurn every week, taking orders for next week's shopping whilst delivering the orders, or, for those who needed last-minute orders, the daily visit of the postman provided a chance to convey requests. The late Mr Peter Webster of Easington remembered the weekly deliveries to Kilnsea and Spurn carried out by his father, grandfather and uncle. The general store had been opened by Robert Henry Webster, Mr Peter Webster's grandfather, in 1877. Their regular Thursday deliveries to Spurn began in 1905 when John William Webster (Peter's uncle) used to go on horseback to deliver groceries to the families on the Point. Unfortunately John William Webster was caught in a severe snowstorm. A search party went out to look for him; he was found, and brought back, but sadly died as a result of his exposure. Robert

67 *A Primitive Methodist outing from Kilnsea to Withernsea, 14 July 1909.*

Henry Webster, John's father, decided that in future two men should go to Spurn, and he designed a cart specially for the job. They used the horse of a neighbouring farmer, Albert Clubley, and so two men went thereafter – Albert, and Peter's father, Robinson Webster.

Peter Webster's account demonstrates how potentially hazardous the journey could be to the tip of Spurn in the winter months. Every Wednesday night the two men would consider carefully what the weather was like, and what was the state of the tide and the wind. A 'blown tide' could cause difficulty. That was the result of a strong westerly wind, which would keep the water up to the chalk boulders, thus making a high tide last a lot longer. On Thursday morning the cart was loaded up before the horse arrived. The Kilnsea groceries were put on top. Typical groceries would be flour, lard, sugar, margarine, vinegar, eggs, tea, baking powder, dried fruit, prunes, rice, evaporated and condensed milk, tinned fruit and bacon. Paraffin in two-gallon tins was loaded on the front – on the shafts to keep

it clear of contaminating the groceries. Tarpaulins covered the groceries to protect from the weather, and the two men wore yellow Swedish overcoats with fur collars to keep them warm.

They stopped at each cottage and farm to deliver the order, (and pass on all the local news). When they reached Southfield Farm they could assess the state of the tide and decide if it were safe to carry on. If the Humber beach seemed suitable they went down Warren Lane to the beginning of Spurn. At that time there was no gate. Warren Lane was a rough gravel track, and from where the gate to the nature reserve is now was a mud track. At that time Warren Cottage was seldom occupied. From there they drove the cart onto the sand dunes, which lay in front of the cottage at that time, and went down onto 'the growp'. The local term for that route was 'travelling the growp' (or groop), that is, going along the Humber beach keeping one set of wheels on the gravel and the other on the firm clay/sand. In the late 19th century chalk had been laid along the Humber foreshore to protect the peninsula, but a break had been left specially for travellers by horse and cart. A line of stakes held back the chalk at that point, and can still be seen to this day. This they called Cart Gap.

Mr Webster and Mr Clubley then travelled along a rutted track, which they and other people had made, eventually reaching the little community at the Point. Having delivered their groceries, the Websters' cart did not go back empty. The lifeboatmen often gathered more sea coal than they could use, and sold the surplus in bags to the Websters, who sold it in their shop. The men collected firewood for the same purpose, and chopped it and tied it in bundles for kindling. The journey back could be just as hazardous. If the tide was fully out and conditions were right it was sometimes possible to cut across Worm Sands (Spurn Bight) rather than go along the shoreline. This would save about an hour, but was not done very often. On the return journey the Websters used to stop at Southfield Farm and at Firtholme to collect butter and eggs to sell in their shop at Easington. That was all done on a barter system. The Websters exchanged groceries for butter and eggs. Very rarely did money change hands.

The Build-up to War

Spurn's position at the end of the Humber estuary meant that inevitably it had strategic importance from a military point of view. That had been recognised during the Napoleonic Wars when two batteries of 24-pounder guns had been built on Spurn, with barracks that were later used for accommodation for the lifeboat coxswain. After the French wars Britain experienced decades of freedom from the fear of invasion, and it was not until the 1850s that the defence of the Humber was again considered. The French were again being considered as a threat and Spurn peninsula was surveyed in 1859 with a view to establishing a site there for a 12-gun battery and two 13-inch mortars, to become a part of a proposed Humber defence system consisting of a block ship near Bull Sand, and batteries at Spurn, Grimsby, Killingholme and Paull. Spurn had only just been saved from becoming an island as a result of the breaches of 1849 and thereafter. Its future was uncertain and it was therefore ruled

out. Batteries were, however, built at Paull on the north bank of the Humber, and at Stallingborough on the south bank.

The batteries were generally manned by volunteers. In 1860 a volunteer force, known as the 4th Yorkshire East Riding Artillery Volunteers, was established. It later changed its name to the East Riding Royal Garrisons Artillery, when the Territorial Army was established in 1908. In 1886 the Humber Volunteer Division of the Submarine Miners, Royal Engineers, was established. This recruited local men whose knowledge of the tides and currents of the Humber was essential for this new form of defence, which involved laying mines. Many members of these volunteer brigades found that their main activity was pleasurable comradeship in rifle practices, camps and social events. Colonel White of Hedon was the Commanding Officer of the East Riding Artillery Volunteers (Hull Artillery) in the late 19th century. Since he rented Warren Cottage as a shooting box in the 1890s and early 20th century and had extensive acquaintance with the area, it was no doubt he who suggested that Kilnsea would be ideal for a summer camp for the artillery volunteers. They came in 1904, 1905 and 1906, and their presence was most welcome to the people of Kilnsea and neighbourhood, who presented a challenge cup for the Heavy Battery to compete for. The volunteers expressed their sympathy for the plight of Kilnsea during the floods by subscribing £5 to the Kilnsea Inundation Relief Fund. In 1907 the camp moved a little further north to Easington.

The early years of the 20th century brought in a period of international unrest. Germany began building up its fleet with massive battleships, which caused its immediate neighbours, including France and Great Britain, to respond in kind. Another threat, potentially far more frightening, was that posed by the newly developed airships. Whilst the United Kingdom could only be attacked by sea, she was pretty much inviolate. Once the attack was airborne her traditional reliance on sea power was no longer enough. In July 1909 Louis Bleriot became the first pilot to cross the Channel to great acclaim and a £1,000 prize from the *Daily Mail*. But a few months before that flight the country was gripped

68 *The Lifeboat Inn and old cottages before the First World War. Note the area of cultivated ground to the right of the cart track. When the military came in the First World War and built the Port War Signal Station near this area, new allotments were created by the lifeboat families a little further north. This area, which was revealed when the ground was cleared by the Spurn Heritage Coast Project, was named 'the potato fields'. Turf banks which separated the allotments are still visible (2006) to the north of tank ditch.*

by a fever of anxiety caused by apparent sightings of a new airborne machine – the German Zeppelin. In 1909 those airship were incapable of flying at night over England. Nevertheless, several hundred people, over a four-month period, were convinced that they had seen these sinister machines, heard their whirring engines and seen their bright searchlights. One of them was a Mr Walker who, on 13 May whilst walking home in Hull at 11 p.m., observed:

> a luminous body seen through a cloud, and appeared arc-shaped, and I also heard a peculiar whirring noise. The light was high up, about a mile up, I should think. It was dark and cloudy at the time and I had the light under observation for about two minutes. I immediately called my father and mother who were in the house, and they also both saw the light as it travelled westwards.

The following night several other Hull residents claimed to have seen an airship. The hysteria that was whipped up at the time was clearly related to a period of international tension.

As a result of the increasingly tense international situation, the British government began to look again at the defences of the Humber and, in 1911, it was agreed that Sunk Island should be developed as a fortification and that Stallingborough should be strengthened. Spurn was considered, but rejected because at that time it was deemed unsuitable for heavy gun emplacements owing to its sandy nature. After war was declared on Germany in 1914, however, Spurn and Kilnsea became military forts, and this little part of South Holderness was never the same again. On the eve of the war perhaps it would be appropriate to quote John Cordeaux's view of life at the end of the peninsula as he saw it in the 1880s:

> To some the daily life of the small colony may appear uneventful and monotonous, in its practical separation from their fellows on the mainland. The naturalist … will not share this view, for there are probably few situations on our northern shores which offer greater attractions; we have seldom visited the place without finding something to interest … If all these [natural history] fail there are the infinite changes of sea and cloudland – wonderful effects of parting day, as the sun dips beyond the western wold and when for a short space the grey river is transformed as burnished copper and the oozy mudflats are purple with reflected light. Then there is the solitariness and all-aloneness of the place – never more felt perhaps than at night, when from the clearness of the air itself the soft light of star and planet glows as silver lamps let down in space, when the far off cry of shore birds comes low and subdued, and the whispering breezes through the wiry seagrass is as the tinkling of fairy harp-strings, and beyond, and above all minor notes the intermittent boom of the great sea, like a child sobbing itself to sleep in the darkness.

The peace and quiet of the place was certainly but a distant memory when the military moved in!

Four

Spurn and Kilnsea during the First World War, 1914-18

The First World War had profound effects upon everyone in Western Europe. Spurn and Kilnsea were completely transformed by war, situated as they were on the east coast at the mouth of the Humber, which was of strategic importance in the defence of Britain. Ernie Norwood, eight years old, was at school in Easington on 4 August 1914, when the headmaster announced that war had been declared on Germany. All the children were sent home and things seem to have happened very quickly. According to Ernie's account, at noon on the day that war broke out 'a contingent of the East Yorkshire Regiment marched in to Kilnsea, at three o'clock three batteries of the [Royal] Field Artillery galloped in to Kilnsea, [and] as if that were not enough excitement at midnight a company of Northumberlands marched in. Kilnsea was a 'garrison town' in less than twelve hours!'

The Building of the Batteries

The First World War was to be mainly conducted on the European mainland and in the Near East, but in August 1914 one of the priorities for the military strategists was the defence of the United Kingdom from attack by sea and (a new danger) by air. The build-up of naval power on both the German and the British side, which had begun at the end of the 19th century, focused the minds of the planners on the North Sea. The Humber estuary was almost midway between the Firth of Forth and the Thames estuary. As a place of refuge it had great advantages in a time of war. Moreover, it was the entry to the important ports of Hull, Grimsby and Immingham, and to a network of rivers leading inland. As such

it needed to be defended from attack. But the Humber has a very wide mouth (seven and a half miles between Kilnsea and Cleethorpes), making it difficult to defend. In the 19th century Paull Point Battery had been regarded as the key to defending Hull but, by the beginning of the 20th century, Grimsby and Immingham further east needed a strong defence. As mentioned earlier, in 1911 it had been decided to construct two new forts at Stallingborough and Sunk Island. At that time the work was not regarded as a high priority and in June 1914, when a meeting took place in Hull of naval and army officers belonging to the Home Ports Defence Committee, the forts were far from ready. At that meeting two admirals represented Naval Intelligence and Naval Ordnance, and three generals represented the General Staff, Royal Artillery and Royal Engineers. The party first visited Sunk Island and Stallingborough, and some alterations were suggested to the plans of the new batteries there in order to expedite their construction. They then went down the Humber to Spurn, which had been regarded in 1911 as an unsuitable site for a fort, owing to its sandy make-up. Now, however, the international situation called for a re-evaluation of that attitude. The party arrived off the Point at high tide, and prepared to disembark. Unfortunately the water was too shallow for their dinghy to reach the shore. Major-General George Scott Moncrieff, who was one of the party, wrote: 'both admirals at once removed boots and stockings, rolled up their trousers, and carried the generals on their backs, with many jests about the privilege of the Navy to carry the Army overseas'. Thus arrived the military on Spurn!

Having arrived, they proceeded to examine the site. Such a high-powered group was in a position to make decisions on the spot, and it appears that this visit to Spurn was crucial with regard to its future important role in military coastal defence. The Point itself, likened to a serpent's head by Moncrieff, was deemed ideal for the site of a battery – 'Round the seaward edge, both to east and west, was a bank of high ground, covered with rough grass, dwarf shrubs, and many wild flowers, and enclosing a flat grassy vale eminently suited for the dwelling places and recreation ground of the garrison.' The visitors could see that artillery would have an extensive line of fire, and the lighthouse would provide a ready-made vantage point for observation in all directions. The lifeboat cottages would be well away from the fort itself, and the new Port War Signal Station would occupy an independent site a little further north. The problem of the wide estuary still remained. The coast of Lincolnshire was several miles away and the mouth of the Humber would need more defence than could be provided by Spurn alone. The admirals put forward the idea of having two forts, one on either side of the river, constructed on the lines of those built in 1860 at Spithead near Portsmouth. It was hoped that the Humber sandbanks would provide a sufficiently firm foundation for these forts

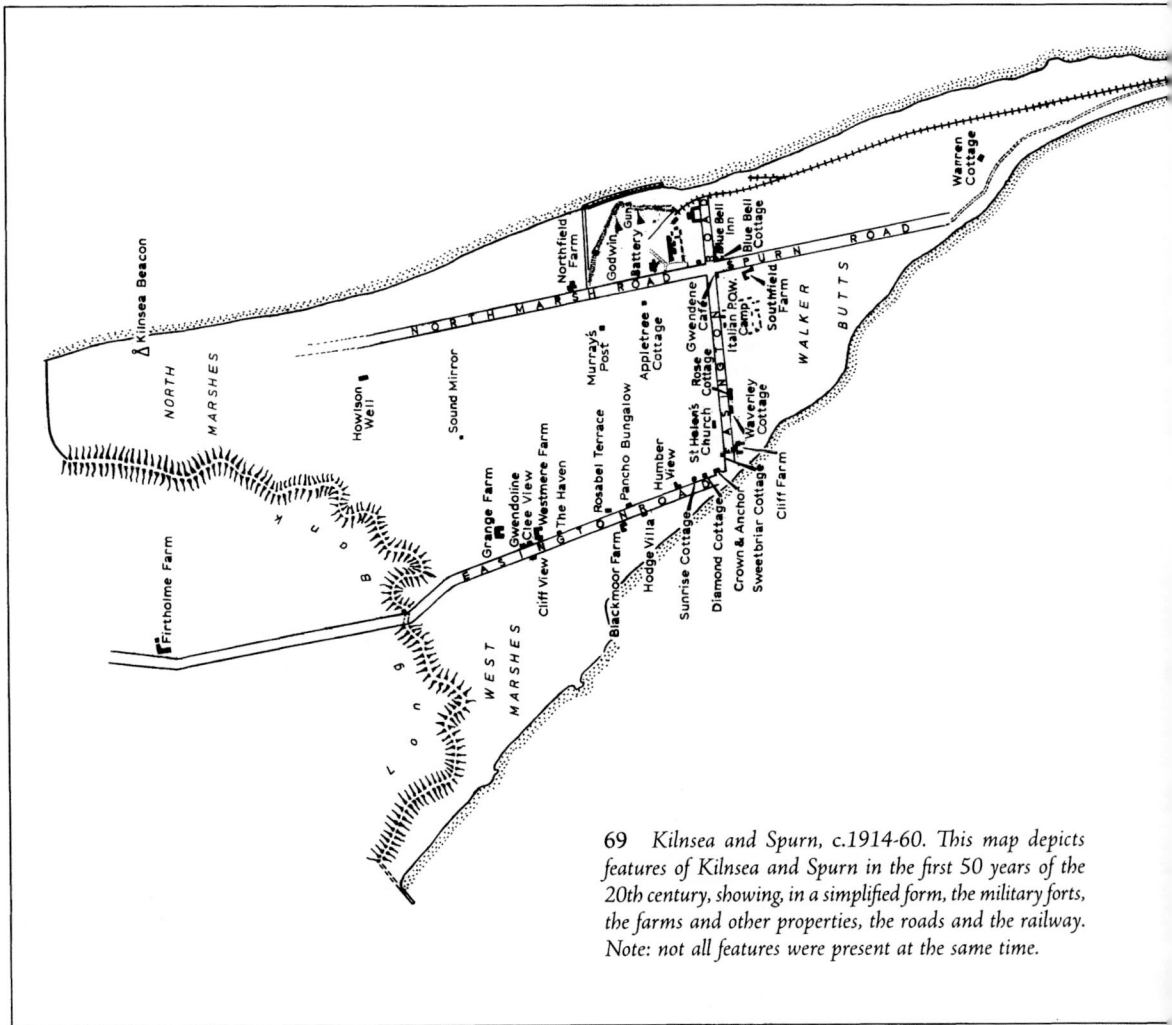

69 *Kilnsea and Spurn, c.1914-60. This map depicts features of Kilnsea and Spurn in the first 50 years of the 20th century, showing, in a simplified form, the military forts, the farms and other properties, the roads and the railway. Note: not all features were present at the same time.*

to be sited provisionally on Bull Sand, about a mile from the head of the peninsula, and Haile Sand, east of Cleethorpes on the other side of the estuary. It was agreed that the scheme should be presented to the Government, and the group left Spurn and returned to London, where they made their report.

The Occupation

Two months later war broke out, and the peace and quiet of South Holderness was soon to become a distant memory. As well as the projected military fort at Spurn, there was to be another fort at Kilnsea,

which was required to protect the estuary from the north. Accordingly, a field just north of the *Blue Bell* pub was requisitioned for what was to become Godwin Battery. At the same time, the members of the Constable family, the owners of Spurn itself, were informed that they would be required to lease the peninsula to the War Department for the duration of the war. The construction of the forts was put in the hands of Messrs C. J. Wills & Sons, a London and Manchester firm of high repute. But such large projects would obviously take some time and, in the meantime, the country was at war and the area had to be defended. Troops were sent into South Holderness immediately. Spurn and Kilnsea (as well

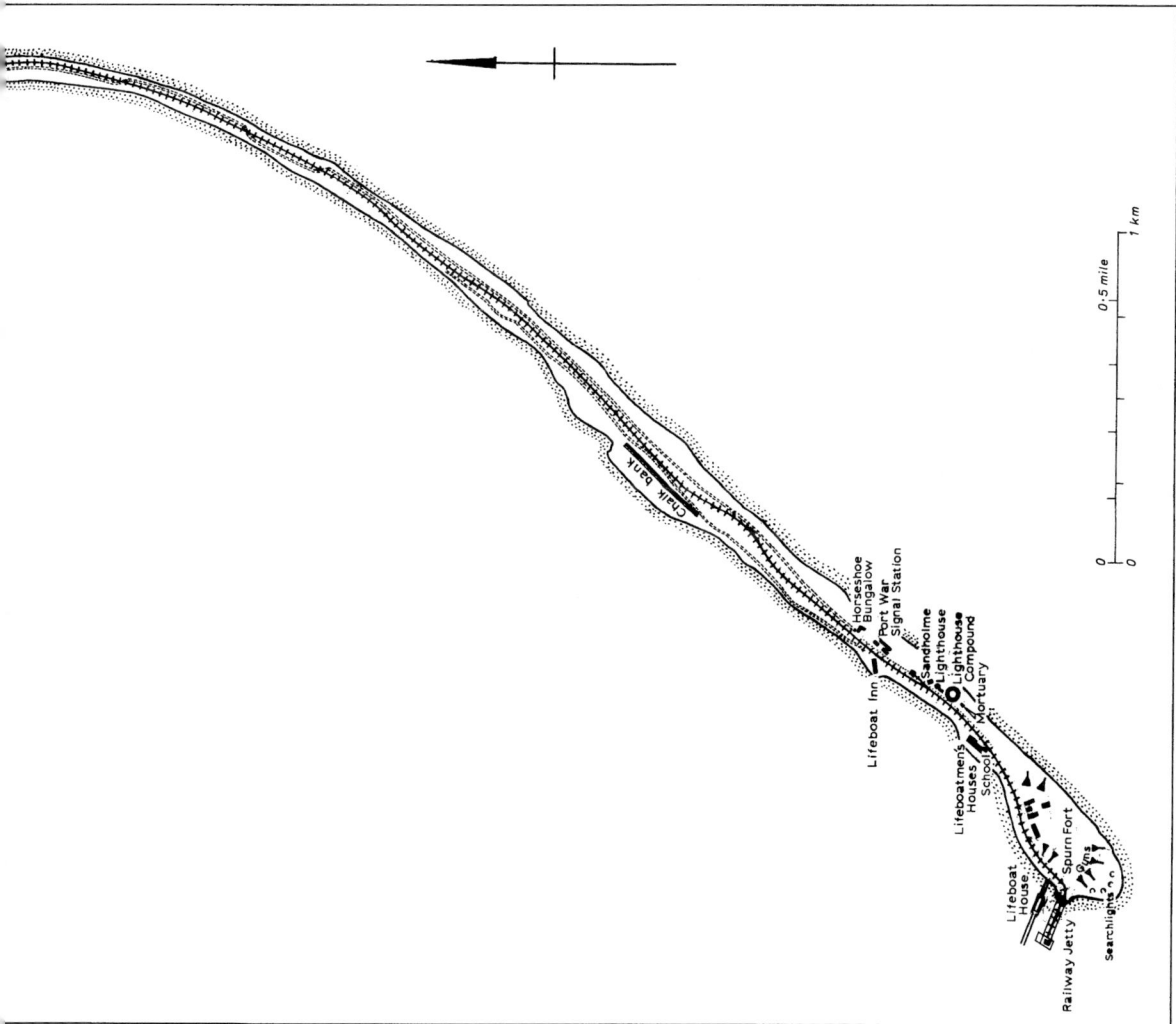

70   *Spurn Fort, 16 August 1917.*
These photographs (70-4), which
may have been taken from a balloon,
show the military installations still
in the process of construction. The
Point area was almost covered with
buildings, railway lines and concrete,
and transformed from a quiet, peaceful
wilderness to a bustling military fort.
Near the end of the Point the four
4.7-inch guns can be seen. At the end
of the railway pier a ship is unloading,
and wagons are ready on the pier.
To the left of the railway pier are the
4-inch guns, and a little further left a
workshop, hospital and the cruciform
barracks (now used by the Humber
Pilots as their base).

as Easington to the north) soon became used to the sight of military uniforms. Until the men could be provided with purpose-built accommodation the local populace had to supply it. Ernie Norwood watched his village change almost overnight. The soldiers were marched round Kilnsea to find billets, and any place that was available was requisitioned. Cliff Farm, luckily for the military, was vacant in 1914, and its house and barns provided substantial barracks (according to Ernie, for 500 men!), for the first four months of the war, Blue Bell Cottage was taken over, as was a tiny shack on the corner by the *Crown & Anchor*.

The Primitive Methodist chapel (later Hodge Villa, now Chapel Cottage) provided accommodation, and part of the terrace of three cottages, Rosabel Terrace, where the Norwoods lived, was

requisitioned. Ernie acquired 52 new neighbours! Westmere Farm was taken over for the officers' mess and all the householders of Kilnsea were expected to find room for as many men as they could accommodate. Some soldiers were taken down to Spurn Point, where they took over the school for a few months. Others marched north to Easington and found accommodation in private houses. Tower House, Easington, with its high lookout point, was particularly desirable to the military. Robert Walker, the owner, kept a diary and recorded in November 1914 that the 17th Battalion Northumberland Fusiliers had arrived from King George Dock, Hull and Lieutenant Reeves and two privates were billeted in his house and 10 privates in his adjoining cottage.

Two more officers arrived a week later, and another 10 privates were billeted in his stables and shed. Easington school was also commandeered. The children of the district, said Ernie Norwood, found the whole experience great fun, especially when it meant that they could not go to school. Barriers were erected across the roads, one between Grange Farm and Westmere, and one between the *Crown & Anchor* and the church. All residents were issued with permits to allow them to pass through the barriers. The Easington school logbook also recorded the difficulties experienced by Kilnsea children in getting to school past the barbed-wire entanglements placed upon the road between the two communities.

The concern with security at that stage of the war was not surprising. When the war broke out the Germans had an impressive fleet of ships and airships, which they had been building up since before the beginning of the century. Control of the North Sea was obviously crucial and the Germans made the first move. On 22 November 1914 three battle-cruisers, three heavy cruisers, three light cruisers and a flotilla of destroyers sailed across the North Sea from Heligoland Bight to the coast of East Anglia. In a thick mist they opened fire upon Yarmouth and Gorleston but fortunately the shells fell onto the beach or into the sea. Clearly good defences on the coast were of the utmost importance, and the government poured money and men into the establishment of the forts at the mouth of the Humber.

Trenches were dug along the coast and, for the first few months of the war, they were manned around the clock. Ernie Norwood says that 600 men camped in 'Blue Bell Field', which was the area

71   *Spurn Fort, 16 August 1917. In this photograph the two 9.2-inch guns are easily visible on the new emplacements. The concrete road between them still exists (2006), as do the concrete emplacements themselves, which give excellent views over the Point, the sea and the mouth of the estuary.*

where Godwin Battery was being built. In 1915 well over 1,000 men were stationed in Kilnsea and Spurn. Life for the residents was dominated by the military and, during the construction phase, also by the workmen, who were accommodated in temporary huts in Kilnsea and on the peninsula. Ernie Norwood found another source of income in cycling to Easington for daily newspapers and selling them to the men in the village and on Spurn.

Concern for the defence of the coast meant that troops poured into East Yorkshire from far afield. In Easington the Huntingdonshire Cyclists' Battalion occupied the school, and when the pupils were allowed to return in October the headmaster recorded that 'Many books and other things show signs of the occupation of the soldiers. Some things missing from the same cause.' The Cyclists' Battalion were responsible, with others, for coastal patrols. They sent reports back to Huntingdonshire of the difficulties encountered in riding their cycles in the high winds common in the autumn and winter. To keep up their spirits, songs and poems were written, such as the one below:

> The Huntingdon boys you've heard of,
> Who are guarding England's shore
> From Spurn Point up to Scarboro
> As it ne'er was done before.
> So here's luck to their boys in Khaki,
> We wish them a safe return ;
> And they'll always be remembered
> From Scarboro' down to Spurn.

72   Godwin Battery, 15 August 1917. This is a more distant view of Godwin Battery than the others. At the top of the photo, Rose Cottage (formerly the coastguard cottages) may be seen. The ridge and furrow of the open fields shows quite clearly. The road from the crossroads to the old village of Kilnsea passes to the south of the three-sided officers' quarters. The entrance to Godwin Battery was located where Warrenby Cottage is now (2006), and where the guard-room may still be seen. The buildings now used by Sandy Beaches Caravan Site for the camp office, club-room and stores are visible, though some of the other buildings shown on this photograph have since been demolished. The hospital can also be seen, near North Marsh Lane.

73   Godwin Battery, 16 August 1917. The 9.2-inch guns on their concrete emplacements are easily visible, pointing east. The military buildings are all in place, but the numerous railway lines all over the site suggest that the construction of the camp is still in progress. The gun emplacements now (2006) lie, broken up, on the beach under Kilnsea cliff, and the building between them, which housed the magazines, workshops and shelters, is about to follow them. The concrete sea wall, some of which is still visible at low tide, appears to be complete in this photograph, as does the blockhouse at the apex of the sea wall.

The residents of Kilnsea apparently welcomed the visitors, who provided a considerable boost to the local economy. The women of the village found new opportunities for making money: Mrs Norwood and no doubt many of the other housewives made sweet buns, jam tarts and small cakes, which found a ready market amongst the men stationed in the area.

In addition, the women of the village were asked to do the officers' washing, especially before they had acquired proper accommodation in the battery. Ernie's mother worked at the *Crown & Anchor*, which benefited from the military influx. One day an officer came into the pub and asked Mrs Norwood if she could cook some meat for his men. When the meat was delivered she found to her dismay that it was half a bullock. Recovering from her shock she asked if the Army had a butcher. One was duly found and she was able to produce a substantial meal, cooked in the *Crown's* huge oven, which was capable of cooking 18 two-pound loaves at the same time. Everitt Norwood, Ernie's father, found employment with the army, as did many more men in the village.

Construction

The construction of an enormous complex of military buildings in such a geographically unusual area was not without problems. Having decided that they could overcome the engineering problems of establishing a fortress on a sandy peninsula, the planners were faced with the difficulties of access.

74 *Godwin Battery, looking north,
16 August 1917. A closer view.
A branch of the railway line can be seen
just north of the barracks (now part of
Sandy Beaches' buildings). Part of the
hospital is visible on the west. To the
north of the officers' quarters one of the
battery observation posts may be seen,
with the railway platform nearby. That
has just (2006) been eroded by the sea
and the remains are on the beach.*

The two batteries, Godwin and Spurn, were to be
built as a unit. The peninsula was a narrow three and
a half mile strip of sand with no road to link Kilnsea
and the Point. The decision was made, therefore,
to build a single-track, standard gauge railway line.
When built it was to run from a railway jetty at
the tip of the Point, which would give access to
the deepest water and allow materials and stores
to be brought in at most stages of the tide. At the
other end the railway would terminate at the new
battery at Kilnsea.

Work on the forts and the railway started at the
beginning of 1915. Despite its short length there
were a number of problems in building the line. At
the narrowest point, the Narrows, there was already
a timber revetment, the Wyke Revetment, which had
been built by the Board of Trade in the 1880s, but
a railway line required it to be built up higher.

Most of the line (which was second-hand) was
to be single-track, but there were loop lines (or
passing places) just south of Godwin Battery, at
Chalk Bank and at the Point. In addition, both at
Kilnsea and at the Point, especially in the construction phase, many sidings and loading platforms were
needed. Near the *Lifeboat Inn*, just north of the
lighthouse, was a platform that was much used by
those manning the Port War Signal Station.

Five steam engines worked on the line in the
war years – *Lord Mayor, Frances, Somerton, Bombay*
and *Kenyon*. The massive construction work involved
with the two land forts, not to mention the river
forts, meant that the railway was a very busy one.

The battery built at Kilnsea was named Godwin
Battery after Major-General John Godwin, an
18th-century soldier, who served for 45 years in the
Royal Artillery and died in 1786. The battery was

situated on a field adjacent to the sea just north of the *Blue Bell Inn*. Considerable defensive works were needed to make the site safe from erosion, and a new earth bank was built along the coast between the two villages. It was named by the locals the 'conchie bank' because conscientious objectors built it. To protect the actual site of the fort from erosion a sea wall about 300 yards long was constructed. It may still be seen lying on the beach though it is now many yards beyond the high-water mark. A blockhouse with a connecting tunnel was built into the sea wall. It was intended as a look-out for the garrison, but was almost undermined after a particularly violent storm, when the shore was scoured out in front of the wall. To protect the foreshore wooden groynes were built at right-angles, but they were so effective at retaining the gravel that the blockhouse was almost buried by the next storm!

75 *Officers near the lighthouse looking at an airship or a balloon. It is just to the left of the lighthouse. The buildings to the left are the first lifeboatmen's cottages, and the Lifeboat Inn. Note the barbed wire in the foreground.*

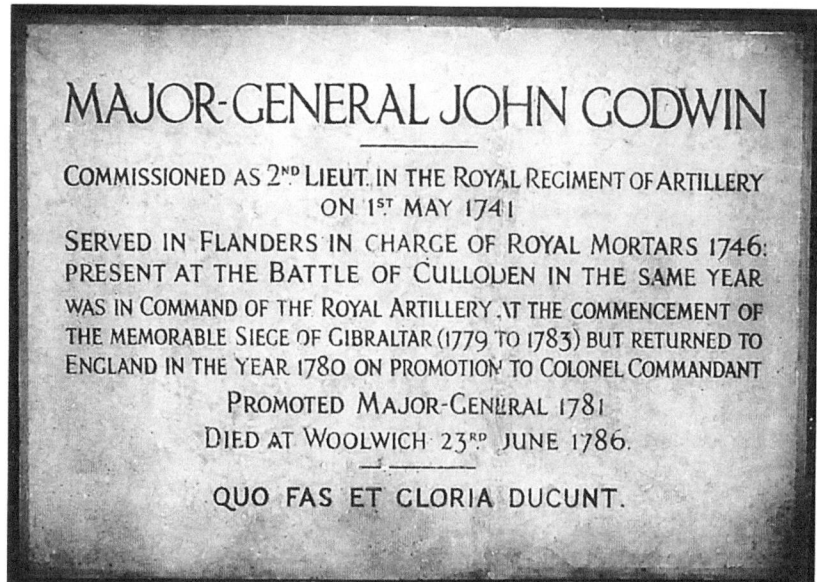

76 *Plaque to commemorate Major-General John Godwin. This plaque is in the care of the owners of Sandy Beaches Caravan Site.*

MAJOR-GENERAL JOHN GODWIN

COMMISSIONED AS 2ND LIEUT. IN THE ROYAL REGIMENT OF ARTILLERY ON 1ST MAY 1741
SERVED IN FLANDERS IN CHARGE OF ROYAL MORTARS 1746:
PRESENT AT THE BATTLE OF CULLODEN IN THE SAME YEAR
WAS IN COMMAND OF THE ROYAL ARTILLERY AT THE COMMENCEMENT OF
THE MEMORABLE SIEGE OF GIBRALTAR (1779 TO 1783) BUT RETURNED TO
ENGLAND IN THE YEAR 1780 ON PROMOTION TO COLONEL COMMANDANT

PROMOTED MAJOR-GENERAL 1781
DIED AT WOOLWICH 23RD JUNE 1786.

QUO FAS ET GLORIA DUCUNT.

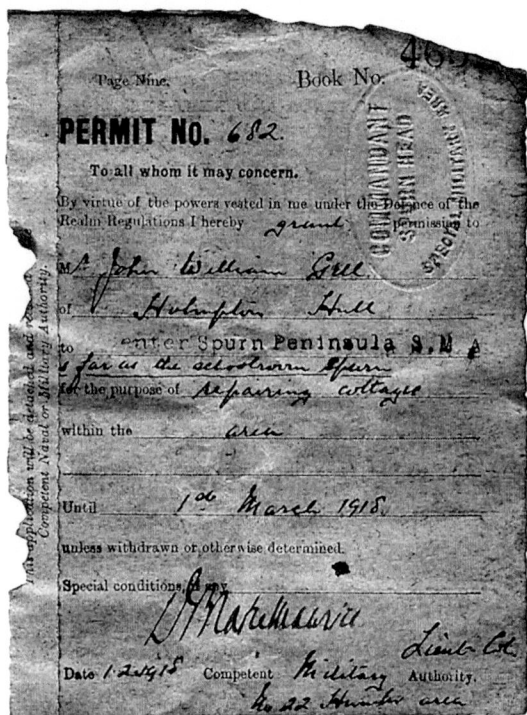

77 John William Gell's permit to go on Spurn, 1918.
Gell, a builder, worked for Trinity House and the RNLI
when their property needed repairing. He lived at Holmpton
and when working on the Point stayed with the Cross family
or other lifeboat families on the peninsula.

To protect the battery from hostile invasion a ditch filled with barbed wire and a system of fire trenches were dug. Caponiers were built at each end of the fort, to provide enfilade fire along the ditch. On the landward side of the fort a six-feet high concrete wall was built. The battery itself was to consist of two 9.2-inch guns mounted 100 yards apart. At that point the land was over 40 feet above sea level so the guns were well sited, and could turn 360° to fire over the land as well as the sea. Between the two gun emplacements were workshops, crew's shelters and underground magazines, while to the north and south were two battery observation posts with defensive blockhouses built into their base. A high wall separated the battery from the camp, which included substantial barracks built of brick and concrete as well as a hospital on the western perimeter, a separate house for the warrant officer, officers' quarters near the south-eastern corner and a guard house. Outside the camp on higher ground to the north-west an infantry redoubt known as Murray's Post was built, linked to the camp by a tunnel under the lane that ran between them. An aerial photograph of Godwin Battery and Fort in 1917 shows it to be a substantial fortress that, when fully manned, completely dominated the little village of Kilnsea.

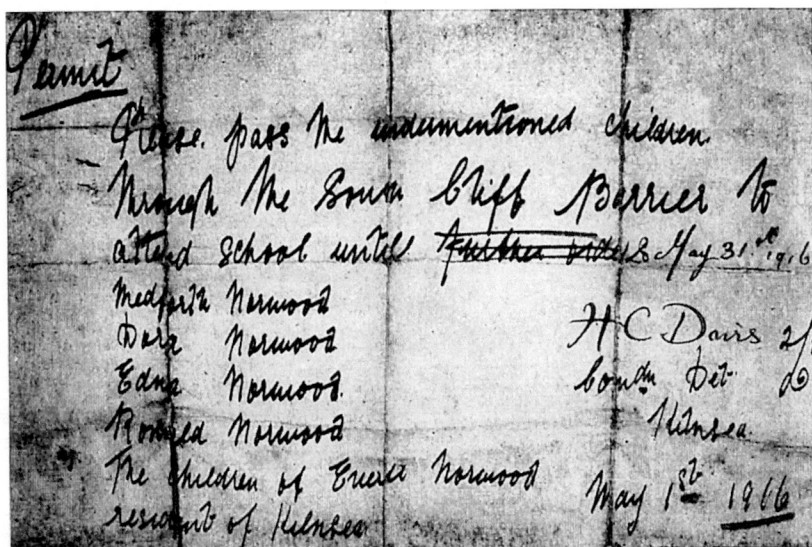

78 Kilnsea children's permit, 1916. There were several army barriers in Kilnsea.

A contemporary account gives an excellent picture of the battery when it was operational:

> During 1916 and 1917 Kilnsea gradually developed into a trim little military post. There was the diamond-shaped form, with its huge guns in their concrete emplacements, with magazine, shell-stores, and the usual accompaniments. There was the guarding parapet and ditch, the flanking posts, and the high observation towers (which nothing could disguise). There was the small parade ground, and the infantry barracks with officers' quarters and mess, neat little cottages round three sides of a trim grass plot, looking out on the waters of the sheltered bay. And there was the hospital, with fairly up-to-date equipment, ready for emergencies, though never in use except for minor ailments.

Three and a half miles south along the railway line was Spurn Fort, an even larger military establishment.

Spurn Fort

Spurn Fort covered the whole of the Point from a guard post at the entrance just near the lifeboat cottages and school, and it comprised three batteries in total. On the riverside it was surrounded by a concrete block wall, which was flanked by blockhouses. The concrete wall was constructed over sand dunes, which had to be flattened so as to be suitable for the railway line to extend to the new jetty. As one entered the fort, passing through the checkpoint, a large battery observation post lay on the left, with the first of the two 9.2-inch guns known as Green Battery about a hundred yards further. The second gun was another hundred yards south-east. These two guns were identical to the two guns mounted at Godwin Battery, and like them were situated in circular concrete emplacements. Their role was to deal with heavily armed warships, and they could cover the peninsula to the north as well as out to sea. To deal with motor torpedo boats and lightly armed vessels two 4-inch quick-firing guns of the Light Permanent Battery were placed overlooking the Humber, in concrete barbettes with magazines below. A large engine room, today almost covered by sand, supplied most of the power needed at that time, though there were other smaller engine rooms too. Overlooking the end of the peninsula four 4.7-inch guns known as the Light Temporary Battery were placed. Each pair of guns had a battery observation post situated between the guns, and shared a magazine room and an engine room. A hospital was built to the north of the Light Permanent Battery. Several single-storey barracks in a cruciform construction were built looking over the river, now (2006) partly used by the pilots stationed on Spurn. Those proved to be insufficient, and so temporary hutments made of wood and corrugated iron were erected near what is now called the 'parade ground'. The seaward side of the peninsula was honeycombed with trenches, and blockhouses on the beach were connected with tunnels.

Again, a contemporary account gives a vivid picture:

> Spurn Head had changed [in a similar way to Kilnsea]. The mounds which fringed the sea on the eastern side had given shelter to a battery of large guns, and cunningly concealed along the shore were lines of infantry trenches, covered with reinforced concrete, and bristling with wire entanglements. The southern edge had its quota of smaller quick-firing guns and searchlights. The western mound had been changed into groups of flat-roofed quarters, built of concrete blocks from the shingle and sand which is there, very substantial and comfortable; and in the hollow flats between them and the batteries was a grass plot big enough for football, where the soldiers constantly played that cheerful game ... At intervals along the peninsula were anti-aircraft batteries and searchlights, some conspicuous and dummy, some concealed and real.

About half a mile to the north, near the *Lifeboat Inn*, was the Port War Signal Station (PWSS). A Port War Signal Station was a naval establishment associated with a port or coastal base. Its function was to identify ships approaching the port, and to pass the information to naval headquarters and to the coastal artillery. Friendly ships signalled to the PWSS using flags and lights, and the signal could change daily or even hourly. Spurn's Port War Signal Station was also a fortified site, with a concrete-block wall pierced with embrasures and two blockhouses. The station had its own officers' quarters and barracks. Its tower also housed the Fire

79 'HMS Spurn', by Hugh de Poix.

Command Post, so was an important and integral part of the whole complex.

The River Forts

The river forts were planned as part of the whole Spurn development, but offered greater challenges to the engineers. In the event it was as well that the defences of the Humber were never needed, because Bull Sand Fort and Haile Sand Fort were not completed until 1919, when hostilities were over, though the work had begun in 1915. The spring and early summer months of that year were stormy, so no work could be done on the site. The first task on the Bull Sand was to minimize the tidal scour by depositing chalk all around the proposed site, as a temporary measure, until it could be replaced by concrete. Borings had shown that the sandbank consisted of fine sand down to 120 feet and that the solid chalk was well below the surface. The

next step was to sink wooden piles, on which was placed a temporary wooden platform for cranes, concrete mixers and huts for the workmen. When this had just been built, and a small sleeping hut placed upon it the chief engineer, Mr Arthur Wills, and his chief foreman went across to inspect the work. Unfortunately they were cut off by a sudden gale, and forced to stay all night, watching their boat being bashed against the piles and wondering if they would be swept away themselves. They did get off safely and work continued, though slowly.

The Sound Mirror

As work was proceeding on the Humber forts another unusual construction appeared in a field between Grange Farm and the sea. That was the Kilnsea sound mirror, intended to give early warning of aerial bombardment by airships. The name Zeppelin is often used interchangeably with 'airship' and it is certainly true that in the First World War the Germans were in the forefront of the design and production of those aircraft, built by the firm created by Count Zeppelin and by another designer, Schutte-Lanz. The airships' initial role had been surveillance, but the Germans soon began to see their potential as bombers. In the early years of the war aeroplanes were not used for combat, and the airships became the forerunners of aerial bombardment. The first airship to be seen over the Spurn area was on 12 May 1915, recorded by Robert Walker of Tower House, Easington, as having been seen over Spurn at 7 p.m. The next airship came over the coast on the night of 4 June near Flamborough and dropped three bombs near Driffield, though with little harm. The next raid was more serious. The L-9 attacked Hull on the night of 6 June and killed 25 people and wounded forty-five. It also attacked Grimsby. That was the forerunner of a series of airship attacks on Yorkshire. Hull was an easy target as the airships had only to follow the river. People were naturally terrified of this new enemy from the air, and began leaving their homes at night and going into parks or into the surrounding countryside. The airships were to them a terrifying sight, and at that stage of the war there were no anti-aircraft guns to fire on them.

At Spurn the school logbook records that in 1915 the officer in command of Spurn Fort had a bomb-proof shelter constructed for the use of the women and children, and strict instructions were given to the teacher and the families on what to do when a raid took place. Vera Cross, daughter of Robert Cross the coxswain, remembered being told that when only two weeks old she was taken into a dugout, one of which was just through the fort gate and one near the low lighthouse, to be safe from Zeppelins.

The first line of defence against aerial attack was the interception of wireless transmissions. The British were quite efficient at this and usually knew when an airship had set out from its base. When it had crossed the coast and been detected, land-based ground observers, the precursors of the Royal Observer Corps of the Second World War, could follow the airship's progress towards its target. But what was needed were watchers on the coast who could report where the airship came in. That was the acoustical sound mirrors' role. The Kilnsea sound mirror was one of three known to be constructed in Yorkshire and it probably dates from 1916. It was placed near the cliff edge just north of Godwin Battery. It still survives and is in the form of a half hexagon with a concave circle inside, and is made of concrete.

80 *Cottage on the* Crown & Anchor *corner. This little shack was one of many buildings used by the military before Godwin Battery was built.*

81 *Military hutments and battery observation post near the entrance to Spurn Fort.*

In front of the mirror and about ten feet distant from it is a concrete plinth that still carries a pipe upon which would have been mounted the trumpet-shaped 'collector head', which could pick up the engine sound of an airship coming in over the sea. Wires passed down the pipe to the 'listener', who was seated in a trench below with a stethoscope-like headset. Having picked up early warning of an airship he could note its bearing and phone the information through to the head of his sector. Like some modern radar-warning systems, the sound mirror provided only four minutes' warning! Indeed, one can think of other similar early warning systems that had been located on the cliff top at Kilnsea, notably the beacons that were ready to give warning of the Spanish Armada, and 300 years later the beacons that were ready to be fired to warn of Napoleon's invasion!

It is not known how effective the sound mirrors were in saving lives, but raids continued throughout 1916. The airships attacked Bridlington and Whitby, and then on the night of 5 March 1916 another devastating attack on Hull killed 18 people and injured 50. Robert Walker's diary recorded Zeppelin raids on the Humber district every night between 31 March and 5 April that year, with gunfire on the airships clearly audible from Easington. By then heavy anti-aircraft guns and searchlights were in place, but during the summer of 1916 more raids followed, the worst night being 8 August, when nine Zeppelins dropped 44 bombs on Hull, killing 10 and injuring 11. By 1917 the raids were diminishing

in number. The last raid of the war was on the night of 5 August 1918, when the airship's bombs fell in the sea to the east of Spurn. Hull ended the First World War as the second-most heavily bombed city in the country after London.

This assault from the air was a totally new phenomenon, and caused great alarm, though compared to what took place in the Second World War it was insignificant. An assault from the sea was the most serious concern, and indeed the *raison d'être* of the Humber fortifications. The Battle of Dogger Bank, which took place in January 1915, was to be crucial to the course of the war at sea. Admiral Hipper set out with a fleet of cruisers and destroyers to reconnoitre off the Dogger Bank and engage with the British. Admiral Sir David Beatty received advance information of the movement and put to sea. The ensuing battle, though not a complete victory for the British, caused the High Command in Germany to decide that the priority was to protect the fleet. They abandoned all thought of invasion, which in any case would have been out of the question after the Battle of Jutland in 1916, when the Royal Navy held command of the North Sea.

Civilian Population

Spurn and Kilnsea may not have played any crucial role in the course of the First World War, but since the forts continued to be manned throughout the hostilities, the neighbourhood was inevitably much changed between 1914 and 1918. The civilians who

82 Kenyon *with truck and coach. This coach is now a dwelling at 1 and 2 Cliff View, Kilnsea.*

83 *Port War Signal Station, built c.1915. This photograph shows the original First World War building, which was very similar in design to the one on Sunk Island. During the Second World War it was much extended.*

lived at Spurn Point were all specialists in their different ways. The lighthouse-keepers remained during the war, but lighting up was under the control of the military and dependent upon wartime contingencies.

The lifeboatmen of course continued their life-saving activities throughout the war. In 1913 the RNLI had decided to station a motor lifeboat at Spurn and a new boathouse and slipway was built. However, the war meant that the new lifeboat had to be deferred, and so all rescues were still carried out by the oared boat. The presence of the army and navy changed the nature of the job to some extent, as did the presence of the Port War Signal Station, with its constant vigilance of all shipping movements.

One of the most impressive rescues that occurred in the war years took place on 9 December 1915. On that night the SS *Florence*, laden with a cargo of oil, became stranded in a storm on the Middle Binks. The lifeboat was unable to get alongside and, with the seas sweeping over the ship, the coxswain, Robert Cross, asked for volunteers from his crew to jump into the water and make their way to the ship in order to get a line to it. Nobody volunteered, and so Cross himself tried to get to the ship but was unable to do so. He was pulled back by the crew and again asked for a man to accompany him. George Martin offered to help and the two men, despite being nearly engulfed by the waves, managed

to get a rope up to the ship and help eight men into the lifeboat. For that brave service Robert Cross was awarded the RNLI Silver Medal, and George Martin also received an award.

The School

A good insight into life on Spurn Point during the First World War is provided by the school logbooks. Shortly after the outbreak of war a new schoolmaster took over the little school on the Point. This was Vincent Skelton, whose elder brother, Cyril, a schoolmaster at Withernsea, was later to take over Easington school. Vincent joined the school at a strange time for everyone on the Point. For a start the term had to begin late, as the school had been occupied by the military for six weeks. Skelton began in mid-September, and found his pupils 'very deficient in general knowledge ... due to their environment, and the difficulties of communication. Many of the children have never seen such common objects as a cow, a tree, a meadow, or a cornfield.' The position of the school suggested that special lessons on the war should take the place of history and geography. The presence of the military naturally interested the children greatly. That their situation could have been a dangerous one is attested to by a bomb-proof shelter being constructed for them in January 1915. In May the children were given five minutes during an arithmetic lesson to see HMS

Illustrious using her heavy guns for target practice. Some of the raiding airships went over Spurn on their way inland. In October 1916 Skelton recorded that he was holding no school in the morning as 'the Zeppelin scare kept us awake all last night'. Skelton himself, though already over 30, wanted to take a more active role in the war, and applied to join the army in November 1915. To his chagrin, although he was accepted, he was sent back to Spurn to carry on teaching, albeit part-time, spending the rest of his time on military duties.

Skelton had joined the Royal Garrison Artillery. He was stationed with the 4.7-inch battery and also did three hours' teaching per day – two hours in the morning from 10 a.m. to 12 p.m. and one hour in the afternoon from 2 p.m. to 3 p.m. When he was on leave the children had no school. In April 1916 he asked permission to take his leave at the weekends so that the school sessions should not be interfered with. That was refused but he did manage to exchange with other colleagues several times. Nevertheless emergency guard duties often impinged upon school duties. Moreover the school was frequently requisitioned by the army. During Easter 1915 the holidays were extended for a week when the military had occupied the school, leaving it in a 'deplorable condition … two windows were broken, also a chair, a desk and a form. The floor was indescribably dirty. Several cupboards had been broken open and the harmonium damaged'. So much for military discipline! In April 1916, when a naval raid was expected, the school was to have been used as a dressing station for the wounded.

In late May no school was held on the Thursday and Friday because the army medical authorities were to occupy the building when the guns were being used during a target practice. And on many occasions the firing of the guns made lessons impossible. The problems of fulfilling two roles are made plain when Skelton wrote on 15 December 1916 that he had been on guard duty all night so no school could take place on Monday, whilst on Wednesday he had to parade at 10.30 a.m. and then carry his effects from one barracks to another, so the children again missed school. Probably they had no objection whatsoever! Certainly, they must have been highly entertained in April 1917, when

their schoolmaster was put under arrest for leaving the battery during the morning. Skelton argued that he was holding school as usual, but he was brought before the second lieutenant in charge of battery, who decided that there was no case to answer. Skelton wrote: 'This action is significant of the attitude of Sergeant Major Littlejohn – who seems to place every difficulty he can in the way of my paying legitimate attention to school duties.'

Skelton's school life was much complicated by the wartime emergency, but the children saw it quite differently. In February 1915 their PT was taken by Lieutenant R. Murray, who was the officer in command of the fort, and he also gave them instruction in flag signalling, which their parents thought would be useful to them in the future. There was also an extra bonus every Christmas during the war, when the children were given a treat by the officers. The excitement of living near a military fort was enhanced by the advent of the railway line. In May 1915 Skelton wrote that it was the first time that many of the children had seen a locomotive, and he took the chance to use it for an 'object lesson'.

It had been difficult for teachers at Spurn school to achieve full attendance even before the war, since the children were often needed to help their parents to collect sea coal or wood for fuel, or to pick up goods from wrecked vessels, whilst the girls were often required for domestic duties. During the war such absences were legitimised, because the usual deliveries of coal and other goods were made very difficult by the military barriers between Spurn and Easington.

Everyone on the Point was affected by the military presence. Day-trippers no longer arrived in steam boats from Cleethorpes and Hull, but the women of Spurn were busy with other extra domestic duties. They had military boarders if they had room, and they took in the washing for the officers. The *Lifeboat Inn* remained open throughout the war and did a good trade with the large number of men on the Point. James Hopper, who had run the pub since the late 1870s, retired to Grimsby just before the war. The next licensee was William Forster, a South African. Soon after the army came he was apparently arrested as a spy, together with his wife, a German from Dresden, who spoke very little English. Her presence, so close to a military fort, might naturally cause unease, but both were apparently released and William enlisted. He seems to have continued to run the pub in uniform, and was still there in 1921 according to a directory of that date.

Once the fear of invasion receded, Spurn Fort's role in the war diminished and some men were withdrawn. Nevertheless throughout the hostilities it was run as an operational station, and the Port War Signal Station also played an important role in surveillance. The presence of the army and the navy on the Point meant the provision of recreational facilities, and these were also available to the lifeboat families and the lighthouse families.

In 1918 Skelton tried once more to get an overseas posting, and that time he was successful. By then he was almost thirty-six. The dangers must have been well known to him by then, and he could easily have avoided the conflict. Soon after leaving Spurn he was posted to Flanders, but was only at the front for six weeks before he was almost fatally wounded, with shrapnel wounds to the neck, back and left arm. He was eventually evacuated to a military hospital, before returning to Spurn in 1919.

James Hopper left the Point, but other members of the Hopper family stayed on. His sister Eliza continued to run the post office and his brother Consitt was still the Lloyd's agent. James's daughters' autograph albums provide graphic evidence that they also spent a lot of time at Spurn during the war. As well as the autographs of friends they contain many messages and drawings by military men stationed at Spurn Fort.

Friendships

The autograph albums mainly relate to the period 1916 to 1918, when Spurn's role in the war was as a staging post rather than involving any active participation. For the soldiers, the presence of the Hopper girls, Ada, Agatha and Lily, then in their twenties and teens, must have been very welcome! An early entry in Lily Hopper's book reveals a typical military routine illustrated by hymns:

A Soldiers Table of Hymns

6.30	Reveille – Christians Awake
6.45	Rouse Parade – Art Thou Weary.
7.0	Breakfast – Meekly Wait & Murmur Not
8.15	Coy; Officers Parade – When He Cometh
8.45	Manoeuvres – Fight the Good Fight
11.15	Swedish Drill – Here we Suffer Grief & Pain.
1.0	Dinner –Come ye thankful People Come
2.15	Rifle Drill – Go Labour On
3.15	Lecture by Officers – Tell me the Old Old Story
4.30	Dismiss – Praise God from Whom all Blessings Flow
5.0	Tea – What means this eager anxious Throng
6.0	Free for the night – Oh Lord how happy we should be.
10.0	Last Post – All are safely gathered in.
10.15	Lights Out – Peace perfect Peace
10.30	Inspection of Guard – Sleep on Beloved

Charles Nichilson [sic] 19 July 1916

A rhyme was customised by another soldier to make it relevant to Spurn:

There ain't no sense in dodging bombs
    afore they start to drop,
There ain't no sense in flopping when the
    shells ain't goin' pop,
But when you're calmly smoking & they
    get you on the top,
There ain't no sense in staying if you've
    not been told to stop.

There ain't no sense in hiding 'cos fatigues
    is out on view,
There ain't no sense in slacking round
    instead of buckling to,
But if the sun is shining & the sky's
    uncommon blue,
There ain't no sense in doing work that
    someone else can do.

There ain't no sense in scoffing 'biere' until
   you're fit to burst,
There ain't no sense in swiggin' 'vin' until
   you're fair immersed,
But if you finds a bottle, an' you're feeling
   at your worst,
There ain't no sense in leavin' it for
   someone else's thirst.

There ain't no sense in fighting, with a
   bay'nit and a gun,
There ain't no sense in killing, or bein'
   killed for fun,
But if you're mixed up in a war the other
   chap's begun,
There ain't no sense in chucking it until
   the job is done

There ain't no sense in grumbling if they
   station you at Spurn,
There ain't no sense in cussin' till your
   tongue begins to burn,
You're bound to get away after a short or
   long sojourn,
So when you get your ticket, see it isn't
   marked 'RETURN'

W.B. R.A.F. SPURN 7/10/1918

The drawings and paintings in the books are lively and give an immediate flavour of some aspects of life in what amounted to a garrison town on Spurn Point. One telling painting shows a woman's shoe filled with flowers. It is dated 11 November 1918, which was of course Armistice Day.

The Kilnsea parish registers show only one illegitimate birth that might be related to the war, and one marriage of a Kilnsea girl to a soldier, though there were to be many more marriages, both between the wars and during the Second World War. Kilnsea was such an isolated community before the military arrived that it must have felt like quite a jolt when so many strangers arrived in its midst. The hospital at Godwin Battery was used for convalescent soldiers during the war. Ernie Hodgson said that he did not like the fact that when he'd got friendly with the soldiers they would go off to France, never to be heard of again.

Life in Kilnsea during the war did not involve great deprivation. As Ernie wrote:

> Although there was rationing it did not seem to affect us a great deal, as we were able to get eggs from the farms, and an occasional joint of meat. Most people kept chickens and pigs, and we got our flour from the local mills; and there was plenty of fish to be caught in the Humber. Life went on very well – the only thing that worried us was the

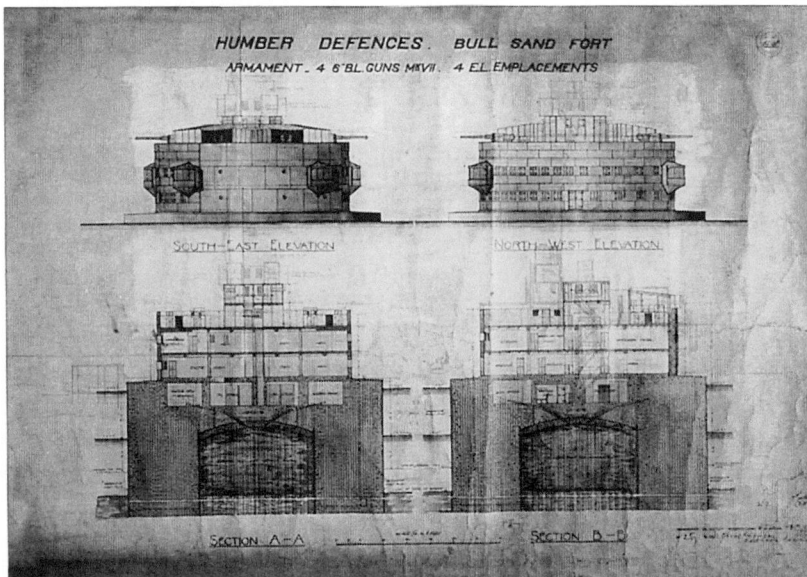

84   *Bull Sand Fort plans.*

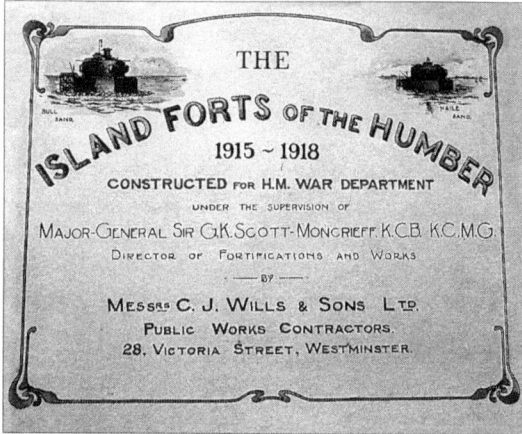

85   Title page of Humber forts book.

86   Kilnsea sound mirror, 2000. Now a listed structure.

Zeppelins going over on their way to bomb Hull. Sometimes they were only about 50 feet high when they passed over Kilnsea.

Ernie Norwood left school at 13 and went to work at Southfield Farm. As part of his job there he visited Godwin Battery regularly to collect the swill, and found a lucrative hobby in searching through it before it went to the pigs. He found that the soldiers were very careless with their cutlery. Each soldier was issued with a knife, fork and spoon when they joined up. If they lost them they had to pay a day's pay – a shilling – to replace them. Ernie charged them sixpence for a set! He also collected bones from the swill, 'for which I got five shillings a hundred weight, also I got the same price for scrap metal, so I earned myself quite a nice bit of cash. On several occasions I found rings and even a gold watch, which I gave back to the RSM.'

Work had continued steadily on Bull Sand Fort and Haile Sand Fort throughout the war. Once the platform on top of the piles had been finished, a small portable railway and a crane were put in position for all the material had to be unloaded from barges. Offices for the staff and sleeping huts for the workmen ensured that no time was wasted. To get onto the platform personnel had to climb a vertical ladder, or, if they were special visitors, they could climb into the lowered bucket of the crane and be swung over 'like a bag of cement or a box of rivets'.

Armistice

Ernie Norwood, being too young, was not conscripted, though he did join the Royal Navy as a regular soon after the war. Like every village in Britain Kilnsea sent many of its young men to war. Two of them never came back: John Richard Ombler was killed at Flanders in April 1916 at the age of

87   'The glad eye'. A sketch from the Hopper girls' autograph albums.

88 *Robert Cross, coxswain of Spurn lifeboat. Cross was described as 'a fine man to look at, the embodiment of strength and vigour ... at the same time, the most modest and unassuming of men. It is with reluctance and hesitancy that he will speak of his achievements.'*

26, and George William Tennison of Grange Farm was killed in action in France in April 1917 aged twenty-two. Gravestones in Kilnsea churchyard now commemorate two other deaths that were associated with the First World War. They each read:

'A sailor
of the Great War
21st February 1916'

Every city, town and village had lost some of its rising generation and the war memorials that sprang up in the years after the war are a poignant remembrance of them. But there had to be celebrations, and in Easington the parish council decided that there should be a parish meeting on 7 April 1919 'for the purpose of taking into consideration the festivities on Peace Day'. At that meeting it was

resolved that the parishioners of Skeffling, Out Newton and Kilnsea should be invited to join with Easington in the peace festivities, and that there should be tea and sports for all. Everyone was to be personally solicited for voluntary subscriptions by Messrs A. Grantham and J. Clubley, and the management of the sports was to be in the hands of Messrs Henry Clubley and A. Grantham. A field to hold the sports was to be provided by Mr C.F. Biglin. At the next meeting three men from Kilnsea, Mr William Tennison, Mr Edward Sharp and Mr M. Hodgson represented their village, but Skeffling let it be known that it was going to have its own celebrations. Mr Robinson Webster 'magnanimously offered' to supply all the tea and sugar required from his grocery business, and it was decided to buy six home-fed hams from Welwick.

The Peace Day festivities must have been tempered by the losses that the villages had sustained, but no doubt a good time was had by all on Saturday 19 July, which the government had designated the day for the national celebrations. (It had been on 19 July 1588 that the chain of beacons blazed out to warn of the coming of the Spanish Armada.) Certainly the children of Easington and Kilnsea walked in procession, waving flags, from their school to the YMCA hut where the tea was served. Medals to commemorate the occasion, which were provided by the Easington coastguards, were distributed to the children.

The so-called Great War was known at the time as the 'War to end all Wars' and probably the inhabitants of this little corner of Holderness hoped that that was the case. But the war had left behind many reminders in the form of a vast array of military buildings, barbed wire entanglements and, in the middle of the river Humber and on the southern side, the two forts. Within two decades they were to be needed again.

Five

Spurn and Kilnsea between the Wars, 1919-39

The First World War had a long-lasting impact on the Spurn area. The end of hostilities did not mean the total withdrawal of the military, who stayed for almost another 50 years. Spurn Fort and Godwin Battery were to play a part in another European war in 20 years' time but that could not be foreseen when the War Department decided to formalise its control of the peninsula in 1919. According to the terms of the 1914 lease, Spurn had to be returned to 'its original state' before being returned to the Chichester-Constable family. Demolishing the fort and all its appurtenances would have cost far more than the land was worth, so the War Department decided to compulsorily purchase it for £7,800, despite Brigadier Raleigh Charles Joseph Chichester-Constable's objections. As he later said 'they took the easiest way out. Not that its original state was anything to write home about.' The War Department accordingly bought 335 acres, which included the whole of Spurn Head apart from a small area around the lighthouse.

The Post-war Batteries

In the period between the wars the role of the military at Spurn and Kilnsea underwent many changes. Godwin Battery at Kilnsea was chosen after the First World War as the principal site of the army's activities, and most military personnel were withdrawn from Spurn Fort which, owing to its relative isolation, was an unpopular posting. Gradually, too, most of the armaments at the Point were withdrawn. Two of the four seaward-facing 4.7-inch guns were withdrawn in the early 1920s,

followed by the two 4-inch guns facing the Humber in 1928. The two 9.2-inch guns that comprised Green Battery were disarmed in 1933. Sadly, that last action caused a fatality. When the barrels were being loaded onto a barge a gunner was killed when one rolled onto him. Only 30 Royal Engineers were based at Spurn to maintain the buildings and equipment and look after the remaining guns and sea defences, and even they were diminished after 1932 when civilians, often formerly Royal Engineers, replaced many of the military personnel, both at Spurn Fort and at Godwin Battery. At Godwin Battery the guns were fully maintained, so that the local Territorial Army could train there. However Spurn Fort was still used for short-term postings for training, and June Collins (née Hopper) who spent her early childhood on the Point, remembers soldiers staying for a week or so at a time in the 1930s. Bull Sand Fort also continued to be manned by a small detachment. Soldiers were given a very short posting there, it being even more unpopular than Spurn!

Those soldiers remaining on the Point had the advantages of services such as electricity, running water and sewage that were not available to the lifeboat families, but a posting on Spurn in the inter-war period cannot have been very popular. The soldiers made the best of it, however, and there was plenty of fraternisation between the servicemen, the lifeboat crew, the lighthouse-keepers and their respective families. Christmas was a special time for everyone on the Point. The school logbook on 18 December 1931 records that the previous day 'all the children were invited to a party at the battery. The affair was a wonderful success: everything that

89 *The removal of the 9.2-inch guns from Spurn Fort, 1933. The guns were loaded onto barges in 1933, when unfortunately a fatality occurred, when the two gun barrels collided whilst being loaded.*

could delight the heart of a child was thought of. Santa Claus arrived on the roof in the moonlight and descended by means of a ladder.' Every year a similar party took place.

Protecting the Peninsula

The military's decision to stay had long-term consequences for the peninsula. The need to maintain Spurn Fort and Godwin Battery ensured the preservation of good sea defences, so the groynes and revetments were well looked after between the wars, and indeed new groynes were erected, notably near the old lifeboat cottages. The work begun in the 1850s by the Board of Trade, in protecting the eastern side of the peninsula from the sea, was continued by the Royal Engineers remaining on Spurn and by the workmen whom they employed on the groynes. Without that intervention Spurn would surely have been breached.

The most time-consuming task for the army was the maintenance of the sea defences. Redvers Clubley, born at Kilnsea in 1900, was closely involved with looking after the groynes almost all his adult life. In 1980 he commented unfavourably upon the use of a new material for the breakwaters – concrete. He had always favoured pitch pine, and had made the piledriver himself. It was a simple hoist-gear

that lifted a one-ton hammer that could batter a pile into the ground a quarter of a foot when dropped from six feet. The piles themselves were either 24 feet or 16 feet long. The hammer was raised by a winch manned by eight men – four to a handle on each side of the structure. There were no other mechanical aids, but four piles a day was not an unusual achievement. On the remote beaches of Spurn, manpower proved to be more efficient than all the encumbrances of modern machinery.

Another method favoured by Redvers was even more 'low-tech' and involved driving stakes into the beach, leaving them four to six feet above the level of the sand, and then throwing thorny branches over them and compressing them to form a thicket wall. Deposits of sand were left in the hedging and a natural barrier was created. Redvers' relative, John Craggs Clubley, who lived at the converted coastguard cottages now known as Rose Cottage, also worked on the groynes, and had been trained originally by John Ombler, the superintendent of the Spurn and Kilnsea sea defences, in the late 19th century. Craggs was celebrated locally for his skills: 'He would go along inspecting the groynes and take a plank off here or put one back there as sand built up or was eroded. Craggs Clubley gathered the seeds of grasses, and planted them to help the natural defences of Spurn.'

Godwin Battery

Throughout the inter-war period Godwin Battery continued as an active base, both for the local military establishments and as a venue for Territorial Army camps. At those camps the 9.2-inch guns were always fired. Everyone in the village was warned when the guns were about to fire so that the windows in their houses could be opened just a little in order to allow for the blast.

Les Park, a sergeant in the Territorial Army, spent much time at Godwin Battery in the inter-war period. He first went there in 1927-8 and attended weekend camps and annual summer training camps thereafter. He recalled that there was neither piped water nor electricity at the fort; indeed the soldiers regarded both the Kilnsea and Spurn fortifications as having been left unfinished at the end of the First World War:

> As regards water the Humber Defences relied on Bull Sands Fort. The RASC brought it by the tank load. The defences were lit by oil and even the magazines used candles which were enclosed in an elaborate manner to avoid explosions … We were taught that no candles must be of the same length to avoid a blackout, say three burning out together.

Apparently there had been plans to bring piped water from Hull to Easington, Kilnsea and Spurn, as early as 1916. On 3 July 1916 the minutes of the Public Health Committee of the East Riding of Yorkshire Council record that the labour would be provided by soldiers billeted in the locality and on 9 October 1916 it was recorded that the War Office had agreed to pay the district council for laying the water mains. Shortly thereafter the War Office decided to lay wells instead. The matter was raised again in 1917 when it was found that the plans for wells were impracticable. Again no action was taken.

Bull Sand Fort, along with Haile Sand Fort, had its own water supply from underground springs pumped by the engines. But at various times an epidemic of something resembling dysentery would break out. That occurred because clear water could only be obtained when the pumps operated at a certain rate. If their speed increased they brought up deposits of sludge and slurry. Park remembered a camp on Bull Sand Fort one Whitsun when 'every man jack was queuing up. A shocking time, the MO was at his wit's end.'

Park's comment about the forts never having been finished may be explained by the fact that, after

90   RAF aerial photograph of Godwin Battery, 22 June 1937. The southernmost gun emplacement appears to lack the concrete apron. Earlier and later photographs show the two emplacements as identical. It may be that part of the southern one had been temporarily camouflaged. 'Murray's Post', the First World War infantry strong point, is visible, situated to the west of the battery perimeter, and linked to the northern boundary of the battery by a fire trench. This outpost is still in situ, though much overgrown, and on private land. Also visible is Appletree Cottage, thought to have been erected in the 1930s on land belonging to Southfield Farm.

91   *Bull Sand Fort.*

the initial worries about invasion during the early years of the First World War, the focus of the war moved away from Great Britain to the continent and the Mediterranean. After the war the Territorial Army used Godwin Battery only in the summer when nights were short, so that some of the fort's inadequacies did not pose a serious problem. The camp was certainly extensive and well built: 'There were barrack blocks, cookhouses, latrines, dining rooms, wash-houses and a large well-equipped hospital ... and a fine officers' mess.' Despite those advantages, the Territorial Army sergeants found that no provision had been made for a sergeants' mess, so they commandeered the hospital for their own quarters. Les Park said of the guns of Godwin Battery as he found them in the inter-war period, 'they were very conspicuous, big concrete circles, could be seen for miles, by any plane, but they belonged to the Zeppelin era, we even had some actual shrapnel shells in the magazines to fire at the Zepps.'

As well as providing a venue for Territorial camps, Godwin Battery had other uses in the later

1930s. In 1935 the Lord Mayor of Hull, Archibald Stark, set up a fund to provide holiday camps for the poor children of the city in commemoration of the Jubilee of King George V. These camps used the facilities at Godwin Battery, which was ideal for the purpose, providing suitable accommodation, sea air and a fully equipped hospital for medical needs. If the children were especially lucky, they also had a trip on an unusual railway line down the peninsula. The holidays went from Friday to Friday, with 120 children coming at a time. Teachers, who also rotated their duties and organised games, swimming and other activities, accompanied them. Carrie Leonard and her mother had a café and shop opposite the camp and they were well placed to cater to the children's needs. They made many friendships with both children and teachers. The benefits derived from an unaccustomed holiday are attested to by one story Carrie told of a little boy who hid in a ditch when it was time to leave, having enjoyed his stay so much he wanted to extend it. June Collins (née Hopper) recalled that in the summer in the 1930s some huts near the lighthouse were also used for camps, first for children with TB and then for holidays for deprived children.

The Lifeboat

After the war, which had brought special crises for the Spurn lifeboat, life went back to normal on the station. Robert Cross had served as coxswain throughout the war, and continued to serve at the helm during the inter-war years and well into the next war. His total years of service, when he retired in 1943 aged 67, were 38, and during those years he experienced many changes, including the transfer of management from Trinity House to the Royal Lifeboat Institution, two world wars, and the changeover from an oared lifeboat to a motorised craft. In 1914 a new boathouse and slipway had been constructed for the new motorised lifeboat that the RNLI had decided should be stationed at Spurn. However, owing to the outbreak of war and lack of materials, the new boat could not be built. Spurn's last oared boat, a 38-foot Liverpool class boat, the *Charles Deere James*, had to serve the station from 1913 until 1919 when the new boat arrived on station. This was the *Samuel Oakes*, a 40 foot by 11 foot Watson class non-self-righter, costing £7,156, a sum of money

92 *Building the new lifeboat house, 1923.*

93 *The* City of Bradford I *being pulled up the slipway, late 1920s.*

provided by a legacy left by a Mrs Laing of Barnes. A motor mechanic was now needed, the first such crew member being Mr Denby Dunley. The *Samuel Oakes* remained at Spurn until 1923 when, thanks to the generosity of the people of Bradford, who raised the necessary £12,758, a new lifeboat, the *City of Bradford*, joined the Spurn station. The old lifeboat house was too small for this boat, and so a new boathouse and slipway were constructed. That boathouse remained at Spurn, much photographed, until 1995. Vera Cross, the coxswain's daughter, remembered that, from being quite a small girl, her

94 *Christening the* City of Bradford II *at Bridlington, 1929. The girl in the cloche hat with flowers, to the right of the steps, is Vera Cross aged eleven.*

95 *The lifeboat crew in front of the coxswain's house, 1930s. Left to right: William (Bill) Jenkinson (second coxswain), John Major (mechanic), Walter Hood, Robert Cross (coxswain), Samuel (Sam) Cross, William Robinson, Stephen Kendall. Robert Cross's fishing boat, Holly, is the boat in the photograph. The Spurn crew, like other lifeboat crews, wore jerseys in a distinctive pattern.*

96 *Civic dignitaries' visit to the Spurn station, 1931. A new, longer, slipway had been built for the City of Bradford II, with a legacy from Mr S. Crabtree Helm of Bradford. To mark this gift a memorial tablet was unveiled on the boathouse and a certificate on vellum was presented to Robert Cross by Sir William Priestley, chairman of the Bradford branch of the RNLI. This picture shows the presentation ceremony, which was attended by many people from Bradford. The Reverend Holt of Easington is in the centre of the group.*

job, once the crew had a call-out, was to run to the lighthouse, whether it were night or day, knock on the big door, and ask the keepers to rush down to the lifeboat house to help with the launch.

In 1924 the RNLI decided to rename the Spurn lifeboat as the Humber lifeboat, the name it has since kept. The *City of Bradford I* was replaced in 1927 by a slightly longer boat with twin propellers, the *City of Bradford II*. A longer slipway was built to accommodate the new boat. Though the older boat left in 1927 she returned and served as the emergency vessel from 1930 until 1932. It was at that time that the crew was reduced from ten to eight, as from thenceforth oars did not power the lifeboat. Now different skills were needed, but the bravery and expertise shown by the lifeboat men remained undiminished. Robert Cross was a much-decorated coxswain. His first medal, a Silver, was awarded for the rescue carried out during the First World War, when the SS *Florence* was stranded on the Middle Binks. In October 1922 two vessels went aground on sand banks at the mouth of the Humber. One, a fishing smack, was almost submerged and the crew had climbed into the rigging. The conditions were appalling, and the lifeboat was washed right over the wreck and filled with water. Having got her righted the lifeboat men

returned to the wreck, but she had sunk, and sadly there was no sign of survivors. Cross and his crew then went out to the steam trawler *Mafeking*, which had sunk, but fortunately the crew had got off in boats and been picked up. Cross received a Bronze Medal for that rescue, and then in November 1925 he was awarded a bar to his Silver Medal for a rescue which took place in what he said was the worst weather in all his 23 years of service to date. The SS *Whinstone* ran aground on a sandbank with seas breaking over her. Using a breeches buoy, Cross and his crew managed to get six men safely off the ship.

The rescues for which medals were awarded were those which brought the most attention, but the lifeboat crew never went off duty and never knew what the next day would bring. Their daily lives remained much the same as during the war; quiet routine punctuated by sudden emergencies. They took it in turns to man the watch house, which was still on the dunes just above their houses, in a prime position to see all sides of the peninsula. Day and night in four-hour watches a man was stationed there, ready if he saw a ship in distress to run down the dunes and ring the bell that hung just in front of the coxswain's house. The crew earned extra money by gravelling and fishing, and they saw probably rather more of their families than did most working-class men of that time.

Life on the Point

Vincent Skelton was discharged from the army in 1919, and returned to Spurn, where he remained in charge of the school until 1921. In 1919 the authorities decided that soldiers stationed on the Point could bring their families, an innovation welcomed by Skelton, who only had 11 children on the register at that time. Once he had left the army, Skelton had problems with finding accommodation at Spurn, so he usually lodged at Kilnsea and travelled to Spurn on the train, which seems to have had a rather erratic timetable after the war. On 19 September 1919 he wrote in the school logbook, 'Heavy storm of sand wind and rain raging have intention of leaving by train at 2.30 as that is only way of reaching lodgings at Kilnsea tonight', Skelton, who was still suffering from his traumatic

injuries sustained in Flanders, obviously found the arduous journey difficult. In December 1919 he went to look at a hut that was for sale and was thought to be suitable for living accommodation. Skelton was not successful on that occasion, but in March 1921 he was handed the key of the schoolmaster's house, which was situated on the eastern side of the railway line about a quarter of a mile north of the lighthouse.

The new ruling that military men would be allowed to bring their families did not result in a large increase in the pupils at the school. In the 1890s the average number of children attending Spurn school had been twenty-two. By the First World War the numbers had halved, and by the early 1920s only six or seven children occupied the school. The school was described by Skelton in 1921 as 'no more than an infants' school'. His nephew, Robin Skelton, the poet, described Vincent Skelton as talkative, enthusiastic and sociable, and Spurn's return to a quiet backwater may not have

97　*Leaving the Point in the train, 1931. This is the occasion of the civic dignitaries' visit to Spurn (see fig. 96). Because of the lack of a platform the visitors had some difficulty in boarding the carriage. Robert Cross is closing the carriage door. Irene Major and her brother are on the left. Reginald Rashley, a lighthouse keeper, looks on. Sarah Cross, Robert Cross's wife, is the lady with folded arms.*

98 *Spurn school, c.1928. Back row, left to right: Violet Bowgen (lighthouse), Miss Annie Ingleby (teacher), Peggy Washington (lifeboat), Reggie Rashley (lighthouse), Nancy Hodgson (Medforth Hodgson's daughter), Stephen Kendall (lifeboat), Vera Cross (lifeboat). Front row: Joyce Reed (Army), Ronald Kendall (lifeboat), girl unknown, Ruby Warr (Army), Leslie Kendall (lifeboat), Alma Washington (lifeboat), George Washington (lifeboat), Irene Major (lifeboat).*

been to his taste. He left soon afterwards to take a more demanding job as the village schoolmaster at Long Riston.

Skelton's successor was Annie Ingleby, whose comments in the logbook give many insights into life in that unusual situation. In February 1923 two boys from the lighthouse, Harold Rashley, aged 12, and Reggie Rashley aged seven, arrived at school late. The door was always shut when scripture lessons began, so the boys were refused entrance until the lesson was over. They left and did not return that day. The next day they arrived with an apology from their mother, giving as the reason for their lateness 'the difference in lighthouse time'. Miss Ingleby's lessons included dancing, using a musical box that played 15 different tunes. This was preferred over the American organ, which was 'somewhat stiff and does not lend itself well to lively music'. One of the lifeboatmen, Mr Hood, brought a gramophone into the school to play a message from the King and Queen on Empire Day. French lessons were given to the older children after the infants had gone home.

By the late 1920s the numbers of pupils had risen to 16, much helped by the large Kendall family. In February 1920 Frederick Kendall joined the crew

as second coxswain, and remained until 1933. When he and Hannah, his wife, arrived they already had two sons; a third, Ronald, was born that May, and Hannah had another four boys and two girls whilst at Spurn. Ronald wrote his reminiscences of life for a young boy on the Point. His account shows that, despite the proximity of a military fort, daily life in the Victorian cottages on the Point after the war was little changed from what it had been in the 19th century.

Meals were cooked on the kitchen range, but to augment that most families had Primus stoves, which were kept in the washhouse. Each house had a closet in the yards next to the washhouse. These were emptied frequently, and the men dug deep holes in the sand, at low tide, to bury the contents. On Saturdays in the Kendall house everything including the stove was cleaned, and while that was being done a stew was cooked on the Primus stove in the washhouse. Then the kitchen stove was lit and bread made, and after dinner everyone was bathed in the galvanised baths in front of the fire. That was a familiar ritual in households all over Britain, but by the 1920s piped water would have been available to most of them. At Spurn, however, the families still depended upon the water that was collected from their gutters. It ran into a central tank behind the cottages, and each household had to take it in buckets to their own personal tanks in their yards. To make this water drinkable it had to be boiled of course, but in the early 1930s the water had become contaminated, so a new system was devised to supply the cottages. Spurn Fort's water had originally been brought by rail, but after the war it was conveyed weekly from Grimsby by the MOD supply ship *Sir Herbert Miles* and pumped into storage tanks on the railway pier. Some time thereafter a huge water tank was placed on top of the low lighthouse. That supplied the garrison by gravity feed, and in 1932-3 the lifeboat families were allowed to use it too.

Spurn Fort had its own generator to supply electricity, but the lifeboatmen still depended upon paraffin lamps. Great entertainment was provided for the Kendall family by their wireless set, which was powered by a small accumulator, recharged by the soldiers at the barracks. At first it had two pairs of earphones that they had to take turns at using, but later they acquired a loudspeaker and everyone could listen at the same time.

Despite their isolation the residents of the Point were well provided with food. As they had done in the 19th century, the families kept chickens and ducks, so eggs were plentiful. The Kendall family's chicken run was on the seaward side of the railway line not far from the lighthouse. The run was left open in the daytime and the hens roamed freely. Fish and shellfish formed a regular part of their diet. Most of the lifeboatmen had boats, which they kept in front of the cottages: half of the day when the tide receded they were left high and dry. They set stakes on the seaward side of the Point, with lines stretched between carrying baited hooks to catch codling. They also caught plaice and haddock with nets from their boats and went crabbing. The largest boat was used as a market boat, which took the catch to Grimsby to be sold, a much-appreciated addition to the lifeboatmen's incomes.

The gravelling, which had been such a source of contention in the 19th century, still carried on into the 20th. The barges would come down the Humber at high tide and anchor on the Binks where, as the tide receded, they were left high and dry. The

lifeboatmen, and men from Kilnsea and Easington, wearing leather harnesses, would shovel up the gravel and carry it in buckets onto the barges, using one ladder to carry them up and another to walk down. Ronald and the other children earned a few pennies from looking after the locals' horses, on which the Tennisons, Clubleys, Sharps and other men used to ride bareback along the sands.

Vegetables were grown in the allotments, which were still scattered around, some just south of Chalk Bank, and some near the lighthouse. The sandy soil was improved with quantities of seaweed, poultry droppings and whatever else was available. Granger, writing in the *Naturalist* in 1926 mentioned 'attempts at cultivation in small plots … potatoes, French beans and peas being grown in the early spring. About a month before new potatoes were on the market in surrounding districts, there was a limited supply in Spurn village.' Mr Webster and Mr Clubley brought down other provisions to Spurn from Easington. As before the war the orders were given to the postman and dropped off at the shop run by Mr Webster, who delivered them once a week. Every Saturday Eric Keyworth, the butcher, came down too. Ronald described his unusual cart as:

> more like a stage coach; the driver's seat was high up in front and the back all enclosed to protect the meat. When a flap door was opened all the meat, scales, block for chopping, knives, etc. were revealed. Mr Keyworth liked a drink and often partook of a few drams on his journey to and from Spurn. I know he had a few mishaps. The track along the beach was quite hazardous especially when negotiating some of the sand dunes. Steve (brother) once told me that the horse and cart had rolled over onto its side and remained there until someone walking on the railway sleepers came across it. The horse still laid in the hafts with the butcher laid asleep alongside him.

The people on the Point also had regular deliveries of dairy produce. In the 1920s:

> Fresh milk was delivered by a Mr Sharp in his pony and trap. It was supplied by John Clubley who had a farm near Easington. He supplied fresh butter when ordered. In those days milk was carried to your door in a big milk can holding a few gallons and ladled out in gill or pint ladles.

The postman in the Kendalls' time was a Mr Moore, who had a special hut allocated for his sole use just outside the fort. Here he would sit to have his lunch, accept letters for posting and grocery lists for Mr Webster. In the inter-war period much toing and froing went on between the people of Kilnsea and the people on the Point. One regular was Redvers Clubley who came to Spurn with a horse and cart 'collecting odds and ends', mainly found by the lifeboatmen and children, who would chalk their initials on the goods so that Redvers knew whom to pay. He was to keep that collecting habit up almost to his death some 50 years later!

The residents of the Point were not lonely, especially in the summer months, as parties often visited them from Cleethorpes. Before the war the day-trippers had arrived in paddle steamers. After the war smaller boats 'dressed over all' were commoner:

They came four or five at a time to look out for each other and returned the same way because of the dangerous tides running at the mouth of the Humber. They would embark between the [Railway] Pier and the Lifeboat House. They [the passengers] were assisted ashore on running planks by one or two of the lifeboatmen. The boats would then stand just off the beach, moored to each other until the passengers were all ready to go back again. As they embarked the hat was passed round each boat in turn. When all were safely aboard they would head back to Cleethorpes.

On the day the boats were expected the children would walk towards Kilnsea with fish baskets to gather sea holly to sell to the visitors at two pennies per bunch.

The pub had closed just after the war, so the women of Spurn filled the gap with tea and cakes. Relations also came to Spurn to stay with the lifeboat families. Despite their house already being

99 *The lifeboatmen working on crab pots, early 1930s. Near the cottages was a row of sheds where the men stored their nets, buoys and oars, and where Ronald Kendall recalled them working and chatting, mending their nets and crab pots, sawing and chopping wood. Two of the Kendall children are in the picture.*

full the Kendalls had many visitors in summer. Ronald wrote that feeding them was no problem, with plenty of fish, crabs, eggs and chickens. Sleeping accommodation was a different matter:

> … every inch of the house was used, every blanket, every pillow, anything that looked like a pillow, every coat, every mat, in fact anything that could be slept on or in was used. Once down and in place no one dare move until the morning, otherwise you might get a big toe up your nose or things of that nature.

Many lively social events took place on the Point in the inter-war years. Just inside the fort gates was an old Army mission hut where whist drives and concert parties were held, often involving fancy dress. Ronald's father and the other lifeboatmen dressed as minstrels, but more usually they dressed in 'drag'. There was no lack of music as Fred played the melodeon and mandolin and others played accordion and mouth organs. The people of Kilnsea often attended

100   Wally and Redvers Clubley returning from fishing. Wally and Redvers could turn their hand to anything – fishing, farming, collecting any useful materials washed up by the sea, working on the sea defences, and in later years doing odd jobs on the nature reserve.

too. Carrie Leonard remembered dances being held within the lighthouse compound, with accordion music. Edie Clubley (now Wheeler-Osman) remembered attending the whist drives, and being taken down the Point and back on the sail bogie. In winter things were quieter, but a huge Christmas party was held at the barracks that everyone attended and all contributed to the preparations. There was a massive tree with a present for everyone, prizes for games and plenty to eat and drink. Christmas shopping tended to be done in Grimsby, when the mothers and children were taken over in boats to buy extra treats. Ronald wrote of the oranges, apples and nuts ordered collectively by the families and delivered in bulk at Christmas.

After the First World War most of the soldiers had left, but many of the buildings, the guns, look-outs, tunnels and fortifications remained. The children were not supposed to enter the fort, but of course they did! The fort gates were only just past the school, and the sentry box stood at the gate, though it was only rarely used:

> Inside the gates to the left a deep trench was dug into the hillside. At a guess I would say about 250 yards long, then lined with concrete with a concrete reinforced roof. [N.B. this was the dugout that acted as an air raid shelter during the First World War] It was parallel with the peninsula. Entrance was gained by climbing concrete steps up to its limit and entering short trenches built the same way which joined the main trench. At various places concrete gun emplacements would be found that overlooked North Beach. They were never used after the First War and deteriorated, the roof caving in and filling up with sand. Of course these were very dangerous and strictly out of bounds which made it more thrilling and daring for us to venture into. Many's the time we have dared each other to go through the trenches often crawling on hands and knees through dark narrow places. With being small we could climb in from the gun emplacements and come across those who had entered from the steps area. Many places in the Fort were out of bounds to children but we were allowed to walk on the path through the fort which ran right through to the Pier, but sometimes we would look in their mess just off the road and the soldiers would pass sandwiches etc. through a small window to us. There was also another building nearby which housed the large accumulators used to supply electricity to all the barracks and the searchlights.

101   *Sail bogie at Spurn, early 1930s. This shows, below the lifeboatmen's look-out hut, the underground shelters provided in the First World War for protection from airships. One of the women may be Florence Regan, and the uniformed lifeboatman is probably Walter Harding, a member of the crew from 1926 to 1932.*

Life at Spurn was dominated by the weather. Summer days, as now, can be idyllic, but wintertime was often bleak. Cold winds, high tides and snow never deterred the children from playing outside. Sledges were made, or curved pieces of wood from barrels were used, to slide down the dunes during the infrequent snow. And of course the children did not need snow: the dunes were wonderful for sliding down at any time. At Easter the mothers would hard-boil and colour eggs for rolling down the dunes. And just like school children elsewhere they had their seasonal activities: whips and tops being appropriate for Easter.

The Railway Line

The railway line built during the war provided the inhabitants of Spurn with a new way of getting off the Point. Before the war their main route away from Spurn tended to be via the Humber, and across to Grimsby and Cleethorpes, for shopping

and leisure. After the war the families often took the train to Kilnsea in order to go shopping in Easington, though they had to walk between the two villages. Afternoon school on Fridays finished early, enabling the children to accompany their parents and help carry the groceries.

Of the five steam engines that had worked on the line when the forts were being built only *Kenyon* remained after the war. She pulled a goods wagon, a water tank and a single passenger coach, which had come from the North London Railway Company. It had five compartments, two of superior class and quite well-upholstered, if a little shabby, and three of lower class with dividing partitions only reaching seat level. In that coach it was rumoured that a murder had taken place, and that an 'X' still marked the spot! *Kenyon* lasted until 1929, when she cracked a cylinder cover and became unserviceable. She was not replaced, and the coach, which remained for a few years, was pulled by what were to become the most common vehicles on the line

– the petrol-driven railcars. By the mid-1930s the coach had been moved to Kilnsea to become part of the dwellings at Cliff View.

All the railcars were known by the people of Spurn and Kilnsea as the Drewry cars, though only the earlier railcars were made by that firm. Two railcars operated on the line by 1920. One was open-topped with two sets of back-to-back seats. The first actual Drewry car was ordered by the War Department in 1919 and arrived in 1920. It could seat 12 people, and had open sides that could be covered with a pull-down screen. That vehicle did not stay long and was replaced by a smaller type that carried only six people on two seats, could be driven at either end and had a full-length canopy and side curtains. It was destroyed by fire about 1930. Later railcars were made by Hardy Motors of Slough and by Hudswell Clarke Co. of Leeds.

In the early years of Spurn railway another vehicle ran on the line. Lieutenant E.A. Lees of the Royal Engineers was the Officer in Charge of a detachment of the 16th Fortress Company at the end of the war. He adapted a pre-1914 two-seater Itala sports car by giving it a pair of railway wheels at the front and having metal-flanged rims fitted to the back wheels. It was apparently first used by a group of officers who formed a concert party and needed to travel between Godwin Battery and Spurn Fort. Lieutenant Lees left about 1920 but the Itala remained, to be used by the lifeboat men. It eventually lost its bonnet, mudguards and lamp and came to be referred to as 'The Bitsa'. It was still being used in the 1930s and Ronald related a story that the flanges on the wheels were so thin that one day when it passed over the points that led to the engine shed near the lighthouse the front wheels went one way and the back wheels another! He also had plenty of tales about what he called 'The Bogie'. That was one of the famous sail bogies that became the most celebrated form of transport of Spurn railway. Several different bogies were in use between the wars. Most of them seem to have been converted plate-layers' trucks, about five feet by six feet. They were equipped with a plank that protruded fore and aft and had a hole at each end into which a mast to carry a sail could be fitted. At least three different sail bogies have been identified on the line, including

one that belonged to the War Department and one that belonged to the lifeboatmen. The army's bogie was motorised for a time, until it came to a bad end when it smashed into a wagon. Ronald remembered the lifeboatmen's bogie, which was used to carry fuel for the lifeboat as well as giving the families a bit of independence on the line when the railcars were not available, and described it thus:

> Two axles with flanged wheels were placed on the line, then a wooden platform with shaped pieces of wood at each corner for handles. A long plank about nine inches wide going down the centre and protruding to about four feet at either end, and four U-shaped irons underneath were lifted up and placed with the irons fitting over the axles. There were two holes in the platform, one either end, for a mast (properly reinforced of course), which carried a lug sail. It was always a thrill to ride the bogie. When there wasn't any wind we had to push it, get into a run and jump on, but when the wind was OK it could travel very quickly. Sometimes it would travel so fast the sail could be lowered quite a distance from our destination. The brake was a shaped piece of wood that one held between the wheel and a reinforced piece of timber bolted into place on the underside of the platform. It needed a bit of strength to operate. Whenever the bogies were in use permission was needed from the WD. Therefore they were lifted off the line immediately after use.

Ronald also described a small trolley, with just room enough for two people to stand on, which was propelled by pumping two handles up and down. Steve and Leslie Kendall had been playing with it one day and got it going too fast as they raced onto the Pier. 'Before the end of the Pier they jumped off, the trolley hitting a sleeper that was bolted onto the line. At the very end of the line it reared up and toppled over into the river – I'll say no more.'

There were many dangers for children on the Point, and the Kendall children seem to have found most of them! Doctor Cripps of Patrington was the nearest doctor, so medical help was not close at hand. Arthur, aged about one, was playing on the sand in front of the cottages when a railcar went by, frightening him and causing him to fall onto the line when the car ran over his hands. His father plunged them into cold water, and then jumped into the railcar to be taken to Kilnsea and thence to

Hull Infirmary, where the baby spent many months having grafts and operations on his hands. In order to prevent the children getting too close to the line near the cottages, sleepers were laid alongside soon after Arthur's accident. Ronald and his friends went down into any dugout and tunnel that they could find. Dares were often involved and once Ronald was dared to be thrown off a groyne near the cottages. He was swung to and fro by his arms and legs and then thrown, landing awkwardly about nine feet below and damaging his shoulder permanently. Little Bernard was once lost for hours and eventually found asleep in a boat well out in the bay.

New Neighbours

In 1931 a new schoolteacher, Mrs Campbell, arrived at Spurn. She was to remain at Spurn for 10 years, an extremely popular person both with the pupils and with the other residents. A widow twice over, she had two daughters, Gwen and Jackie, by her first marriage, and a son, Malcolm, by her second. She moved into the little wooden bungalow not far from the lighthouse, but about 18 months after her arrival she was badly burned when a fire occurred in the bungalow. Spurn Point was not well equipped to deal with fire. The schoolteacher's bungalow was quite a distance from the other cottages and any source of water, and the only fire-fighting equipment at the time was an old-fashioned fire engine, described by Ronald Kendall as 'a round tank on wheels with a pair of shaft-like handles for pulling it along. A bar at either end worked on a rocking system, one or two men lifting it up and down and working the pump.' Mrs Campbell was off work for nine months with her injuries, and her bungalow was badly damaged.

By the 1930s the lifeboat families, the lighthouse-keepers' families and the schoolteacher were not the only residents of the peninsula. An army officer called Francis Fewster, who had been stationed at Spurn with the Royal Engineers during

102 *The Fewsters' bungalow between the wars. The Fewster family kept to themselves on Spurn, feeling themselves somewhat superior to the other inhabitants, though Fewster was happy to entertain army officers above the rank of lieutenant in the bungalow! The railway ran very close to the bungalow, which had an attractive garden, with a bird bath and statue made by Enid Fewster. In 1941, part of the bungalow had to be taken down to make room for the new concrete road.*

103 *The other Fewster bungalow. This bungalow began as a small shack, and was apparently rented for holidays. Trevlynn Hildred and her family stayed here in the summers of 1932 and 1933. This picture shows Trevlynn and her father. The shack was later taken over by Dan and Florrie Fewster and extended. Their grandson Denis Hopkin was a regular visitor in the later 1930s.*

the war, managed to acquire a wooden L-shaped bungalow, which had been used for officers' quarters, and was situated near the Port War Signal Station. He initially used it as a holiday home. However, in the late 1920s Fewster suffered a serious accident whilst on active duty in Bermuda and, as a result was paralysed from the chest down. He was pensioned off from the army but, having a daughter by his first marriage and two young sons by his second, and wishing to educate them privately, he decided that moving into the bungalow (later named Horseshoe Bungalow), would enable the family to live very cheaply. So about 1928 Francis (Frank) and Hettie Fewster moved in, joined by Enid, Eric and Alan when they were not at school in York. A well equipped workshop was built at the back of the bungalow, furnished with a large paraffin engine for driving a metal-turning lathe and other equipment. Water came from a large tank upon the roof, a septic tank was built and the Fewsters lived in surprising comfort and gentility, with central heating installed and a generator providing electricity. (Only the army camp had this at that time!) The Fewsters continued to live in a colonial style, furnishing the bungalow with antique furniture and silver and dining with silverware, table napkins and good china. An extension was built on the seaward side in which was a bedroom for Frank Fewster, with a window through which at that time he was able to look out to sea, and furnished with hooks on the

ceiling so that he could be lifted easily out of bed and widened doorways for his wheelchair. Hettie and Enid Fewster created an attractive garden in the angle around the bungalow, with a piece of statuary made by Enid.

The Fewsters were given permits to travel on the railway, and they used the sail bogies when the railcars were not running. Otherwise they walked on the sleepers, which were set evenly for ten paces followed by a short pace. Hettie thought nothing of saying whilst they were having tea – 'I need some eggs,' and the boys would walk to Kilnsea and back to get them. The Fewsters were to remain on Spurn for nearly 10 years and, in the early 1930s, were joined by Frank's brother Dan and his wife Florrie in a much more modest bungalow, formerly a little fisherman's shack, a little to the north. This shack appears to have been available for 'holiday lets' in the early 1930s, for Trevlynn Hildred, now of Coventry, remembers having holidays on Spurn in 1931-2, having come over from Grimsby where her family lived. Dan and Florrie Fewster lived in a far plainer style than did Frank and Hettie. Like them they got most of their water from rain, but they had no bath, and their lighting was 'by a glass-chimneyed type wick lamp. They were visited in the summer by their grandson, Denis, who found plenty to do on Spurn. The lighthouse was a source of great interest, and the keepers welcomed children as a distraction from routine. Denis and his friends used to get out the chassis of one of the old sail bogies and run it on the lines: 'We would all push it as hard and fast as we could and then jump on and coast as far as we could. I have wondered since whether anyone checked whether the "Drewry" was due along the line at the same time!' A quieter activity for rainy days was reading. A small library of books was kept in the schoolroom, looked after by Vera Cross, the daughter of the Spurn coxswain.

Another dwelling on Spurn, called Sandholme, was located just to the north of the lighthouse. This was a wooden bungalow that had presumably been built for the military during the First World War. In the late 1920s and early 1930s the Regans lived there. James Regan was a Sergeant in the Royal Garrison Artillery and, when he was stationed at Spurn in 1920, he met and married Florence Hailes, the daughter of Charles Hailes, a lighthouse-keeper. Mrs Regan, who had twin daughters, ran a sweet shop at Sandholme in the 1930s.

The Wildlife and the Naturalists

During the First World War the vast array of military buildings and increase in personnel might have been expected to have a deleterious impact on the wild life of the peninsula. The YNU Protection of Birds Committee of 1914 had reported a successful nesting season for the Little Terns, with 'The watcher G. Hall, the best man we have had on the ground,' and despite the disruption from the military activities there was similar success in 1915. In 1916 the committee regretted that they had no watchers on Spurn despite having applied to the Humber Garrison for permission – 'The General Commanding Officer there gave a most decided answer that no watcher could be allowed.' He did allow notices to be posted for protection of both eggs and birds, but that did not prevent some destruction. Moreover the presence of the new railway had deterred the birds from nesting nearby. In 1917 the lighthouse keeper and his assistant proffered their assistance, subject to the agreement of Trinity House. A stringent prohibition against disturbing the birds was issued, and the Officers of the Royal Garrison Artillery at Spurn made it their business to enforce it. On 30 June 1917 a Major

Pauley stationed at Spurn undertook to see that all the eggs were marked with indelible pencil (thus making them valueless to collectors). In 1918 the Committee reported:

> We have not been able to do any protecting during the year. Trinity House would not allow any keeper or man from the lighthouse to assist so the birds had to take their chance … The Commanding Officer would give a permit to a watcher, but Trinity House stands in the way.

After the war, despite the continued presence of the military, naturalists were allowed to return to Spurn. On the August Bank Holiday weekend of 1919 a Yorkshire Naturalists' Union meeting was organised in South Holderness. The choice of such a busy weekend made arranging accommodation difficult, but the members managed to secure the *Hildyard Arms* at Patrington for their headquarters. They travelled by wagonette to Kilnsea, then went along the peninsula and back, thence to Dimlington, before being taken back to Patrington in wagonettes. The party noted the two huge towers of Godwin Battery supporting enormous range finders, which dominated the skyline, and the 9.2-inch guns, surrounded by 'quite a village of new houses and huts'. Across the Humber they noted 'enormous piles forming a barrier stretching almost all the way across the estuary' to prevent submarines entering the river, and the new Bull Sand Fort that dominated the entrance to the estuary. Some of them used the railway to get down to the Point, 'though station buildings, ticket collectors, and even tickets and fares, were dispensed with'. What a bonus – a free railway journey down the peninsula!

The naturalists feared the worst from the invasion of the peninsula by so many army personnel, but found that despite the traffic and the soldiers, the flora and fauna had not been too much disturbed. The sea holly still flourished, and the Little Terns and Ringed Plover had bred successfully. The only problem seemed to be the burning of some areas by cinders from the steam engine. The botanists also remarked that having travelled by road halfway across the country to get to Spurn, and noted few wayside flowers on the way, they were delighted by the:

104 *Master Gunner Johnson at Kilnsea, 1930s. He is standing alongside Carrie Leonard's bungalow.*

wealth of bloom that delighted the eye on the few miles of sand dune at Spurn; big clumps of Musk Thistle occupied disturbed ground; Ragwort, Wild Celery, Carrot, Sea Rocket and Sea Holly gave masses of colour, the beauty of which was enhanced by contrast with the yellow sands and the foliage of Sea Wormwood, Sea Buckthorn and the dune grasses.

The geologists noted that because the increase in groynes had protected the fragile coastline, the peninsula appeared to be stronger and more stable than before the war, with higher beaches of sand and shingle. The sand dunes were higher on both the sea and the riversides, and firm sand from the Warren as far as the lighthouse meant that carts now had relatively easy access to the Point. Several bores had been put down in the Kilnsea area for water, because a good spring had been found under the Bull Sand and it had been hoped that water could

have been found on the peninsula and further north, though a later report in the *Naturalist* reported no success in that respect.

Sadly the *Naturalist* in the 1920s continued to record the large numbers of eggs taken, despite posters being put up at Kilnsea, Easington and near both batteries. One unfortunate effect of the peace was to allow the egg collectors to return to Spurn, though on the positive side the Little Tern protection scheme had resumed. The watcher was paid £20 per season in the early 1920s, and in the later 1920s two watchers were employed. One of them, Medforth Hodgson, was the former landlord of the *Crown & Anchor*, now working as a maintenance engineer for the army on Spurn. The practice of marking the eggs was continued, and the children of the Point were employed upon that task too: Vera Cross remembers that even her mother got involved. Crows and Magpies raiding the nests were also a regular problem. The War Office was very co-operative with the bird-watchers, and in 1930 the *Naturalist* recorded that:

> three enamelled notices very plainly and eloquently lettered have been erected on double poles at the approach to all the sides by arrangement with the War Office. The CO has sponsored our attempts to preserve as a sanctuary the nesting headland and has issued instructions to all N.C.O.s that every care must be taken to preserve these birds.

Another innovation at Spurn was the placing of bird perches on the lighthouse. The powerful light had the effect of attracting migrating birds, some of which dashed themselves against the light and were killed. The bird perches were placed around the light in March, taken down in early November and stored in the 'mortuary'. During very busy migration periods the perches seem to have been fairly effective.

Travel was still difficult before the Second World War, and most of the naturalists who did get as far as Kilnsea did not go down to Spurn often. Henry Bunce started to visit Kilnsea in the autumn of 1929, and he and his friend, Len Smith, became regular visitors from about 1935. They did most of their bird-watching in the Beacon area, which was studded with pools and dunes and provided excellent habitat:

There was a lovely pond, which dried up in June or July. The Little Terns used to nest in the pond's edge in horses' footprints. There was a weird assortment of a donkey or two, and a dozen cattle, which they [the farmers] used to drive down every morning having milked them, and then fetch at four in the afternoon. Glorious rough pasture was kept short-cropped by the cattle – lovely. Every spring a high tide would flood the Beacon field, and when the Little Terns arrived they could fish in the field, and in the fresh water dykes. Lots of debris was brought in by the sea – fish baskets, fish floats, ropes, bits of cork, and the Ringed Plovers used to nest in them.

Henry and Len spent most of their time there in preference to Spurn, and also walked from Westmere Farm over to the Humber, to the shingle point where Oystercatcher and Ringed Plover bred. This they christened Sammy's Point (after another feature of the same name at the mouth of the river Hull on its east bank). Henry remembered the roads of Kilnsea as being so quiet in those days that cows could graze on the grass verges with no fear of traffic.

Travel

Until the late 1920s visitors to the tip of South Holderness were few. Those that did come disembarked at Patrington station and still had 10 miles of winding roads to go before they reached Easington, Kilnsea and Spurn. If they had timed it right they might be able to get a lift from one of the carriers' carts that made regular trips between

105 *Connor & Graham bus in the 1920s. The first Connor & Graham bus was a Model T Ford.*

the villages, or they could hire the services of a driver with a wagonette at a local inn. There was no public transport in the area until the arrival of two young Geordies in 1921. James H. Graham and Campbell Connor were shipwrights who were out of work because of the depression. Relatives had told them that there were no buses in South Holderness, so they decided to come to Easington and try their hands at starting a service. They arrived with a brand new 14-seater Model T Ford called 'Dixie', which made its maiden trip into Hull on 21 October 1921. The bus was very popular and James and Campbell bought another, which they called 'Britannia' after James Graham's little daughter. Connor & Graham's buses were soon tremendously popular. The early services went to Patrington to connect with the trains, and went to the eastern border of Hull (they were not allowed to go further than Marfleet, where the trams started). Connor & Graham's buses continued the tradition of carrier's carts in doing errands for people, delivering parcels, waiting patiently for stragglers and altogether providing an important social as well as transport service. Though the name of Connor & Graham was retained, Campbell Connor soon moved into farming but remained as a sleeping partner until his death. The firm was eventually taken over by James Graham's son, Thomas.

Buses were obviously a great boon at a time when very few people had cars, so a comment made in 1928 when another YNU meeting took place in South Holderness that Kilnsea Warren and the middle bents were 'denuded' of birds because of the increasing numbers of people arriving in cars is somewhat surprising. No road existed down Spurn for motorised traffic of course, so the cars could go no further than the Warren. However a trip to Spurn would have made a good 'spin' from Hull, and in October 1925 Easington Parish Council was so concerned about speeding through the village that it arranged for notice boards to be erected at the northern end of Easington warning motorists of a five miles per hour speed limit through the village!

Some 'unofficial' trips took place on the railway in the inter-war period. In the mid-1920s a Hull char-à-banc proprietor, presumably with some con-nivance with contacts at Spurn, was advertising a trip to Kilnsea with a ride on the train to Spurn. Once this was brought to the attention of the military authorities it was soon stopped!

Kilnsea between the Wars

After the First World War, Kilnsea settled back into relative tranquillity. Farming continued to be the main way of earning a living, and most of the farms remained with the same families. Indeed the continuity was remarkable, and provides a great contrast with more modern times. Grange Farm, the largest farm in the village, was still in the hands of the Tennison family: William (Bill) Tennison farmed it from about 1908 until he retired in 1930, when his son Ernest took over. Just along the road at Westmere Farm, George Edwin Clubley, formerly of Cliff Farm, who had taken over about 1902, carried on farming there until his death in 1938. Blackmoor Farm (at that time usually called Clickham Farm), on the Humber side of the road, was a smallholding, where lived William Sellars, formerly of Grimsby, and his wife Annie. They remained in Kilnsea from c.1904 until the late 1940s.

George Edwin Clubley's father, John, who had been the tenant of Cliff Farm since the 1870s, had died in 1891, but his wife Elizabeth continued farming the land with the help of her children until 1918, when her nephew John Robert Hunton Clubley took over the tenancy. He had fathered no less than 19 children by two wives, and he worked the farm with the help of his sons, Redvers and Walter (Wally), and other members of the family. Life was hard for the Clubleys with so many dependents: Carrie Leonard recalled a particular mealtime when she saw Edith Clubley throw flat fish caught from the Humber, but neither gutted nor cleaned, into a pan, and once cooked, tossed onto newspaper for the numerous offspring to eat as best they could.

The same continuity in farming tenancy and/or ownership could be observed at Southfield Farm. Here the Sharp family still remained. Until 1880 they were tenants, but in that year William Sharp bought the farmhouse and land from the Thompson family. His brother Walter was running the farm at that time, and when he died in 1889 William's

106 *The Tennison family outside Grange Farm, c.1920. Left to right, back row: Gertrude, Ada, Ernest, Milly, Jack, Mary, Mabel, Dorothy, Anna. Front row: Phyllis, William, Mary, Grace.*

son farmed the land until he too died in 1913. It was then that Edward, his son took over. Edward Ainsley Sharp (Ted) had married a Clubley (Eliza) as had his grandfather before him, and they were to stay at Southfield Farm from the First World War until 1953. The only other farm of any size in Kilnsea was along North Marsh Lane. That was North or Northfield Farm, and it too demonstrated the continuity of tenancy that characterized Kilnsea in the late 19th and early 20th centuries. North Farm had been built by and for the Tennisons just after the enclosure of the open fields. Bill Tennison (1867-1946), who had been born on Spurn, where his father Robert was a lifeboatman, was farming it in 1901, but after he moved to take over Grange Farm his son John (1886-1965) took over. Father and son probably managed the land together, since

the fields abutted each other, and both farms stayed with the Tennisons until well after the Second World War.

The Pubs

The *Crown & Anchor*, which had been built in the 1850s by the Tennison family, remained within that family for over 70 years: Medforth Tennison's daughter Kezia married William Hodgson, and their son Medforth Hodgson ran the *Crown* until about 1925, when he was forced to give it up. His successor, William (Bill) Whiskers, also formed a long-lasting association with the pub, remaining as its landlord until the late 1930s. The *Blue Bell*, unlike the *Crown*, was a tied pub, owned by Hull Brewery, and it had many tenants in the inter-war period. It flourished during the First World War and thereafter, because of its proximity to Godwin Battery, and because it was at the terminus of the railway line between Spurn Fort and Kilnsea. It was also said that many of the military officers had shares in Hull Brewery and encouraged the men to give their custom to the *Blue Bell* rather than the *Crown & Anchor*!

New Bungalows

Kilnsea village increased somewhat in size in the inter-war period, not with brick-built houses, but with bungalows of wood or corrugated iron, some built by a Hull firm, R.G. Tarran. June Collins (née Hopper) remembers that there were several on land between Rose Cottage and Blue Bell corner, but no trace of them now remains; it is probable that they were used as holiday homes. Most of the other bungalows were erected in the late 1920s and early 1930s, on land alongside farms, and were built for farmers' relatives, rather than as holiday cottages. That was certainly the case with the two little bungalows just to the south of Grange Farm. The first, called Gwendoline (now Yew Cottage) was built *c*.1930 as a retirement home for the owner of Grange Farm, William Tennison, and his wife. The bungalow next door, Clee View, was built for William's daughter, Phyllis, and her husband Jack (Ernest) Codd, who was a train driver on the Kilnsea to Spurn railway. Both those bungalows were constructed of corrugated iron. Across the road was a small wooden bungalow, where Phyllis's sister Grace lived with her husband Albert Warner. They remained there until about 1933 when the Clubley family became the new occupants. Redvers Clubley extended the accommodation by the purchase of a large wooden bungalow (formerly officers' quarters) from one of the forts. The complex of buildings was even further extended when the former North East London Railway coach became redundant soon after the *Kenyon* steam engine that had pulled it was scrapped in 1929. After Redvers and Wally Clubley had finished with their various purchases and conversions there were several dwellings at what became known as 1 and 2 Cliff View. The front bungalow was converted into two independent residences, the railway coach was provided with a corrugated iron corridor so that the resident could move across from one compartment to another, and a fireplace with a proper chimney was installed in the large living compartment. Counting the original wooden bungalow, four separate dwellings were necessary to accommodate the many members of the Clubley family who lived there.

Just along the road, in Westmere Farm's fold yard, another bungalow was built, and it too was an example of bungalows built for the relatives of farmers. George Edwin Clubley and his wife Eden (née Blenkin) lived at Westmere, and the bungalow was built for her brother, John Blenkin. After George Edwin Clubley died in 1938, Westmere Farm was sold to the Mitchells, a Hull firm of hauliers, who insisted that the bungalow should be moved. The Clarksons, who were living there at the time, bought a small plot of land near the *Crown*, from William Sellars of Blackmoor Farm, and the bungalow (which was said to be built on orange boxes!) was taken down and re-erected there.

Another new residence had an even more interesting background. The 'iron chapel' built for the Primitive Methodists in 1885 was apparently little used by 1919 so it was closed and converted to a cottage. Ernest Tennison, the son of William of Grange Farm, married Daisy Clubley in 1919, and they moved into what became Hodge Villa (named after Henry Hodge, the benefactor who built it as a chapel) that same year. The *Crown & Anchor* also had a little satellite bungalow. That was Sweetbriar Cottage (later called Kew Villa), which was built between the *Crown* and the church in the 1920s by Medforth Hodgson, after he left the *Crown*, though he did not live there until some years later. Along the road to the sea, a bungalow, later called Sunny Cliff, appeared next to a field that was to become a prisoner of war camp in the Second World War. The Sharps of Southfield Farm built their own satellite bungalow up North Marsh Lane. This bungalow, later called Appletree Cottage, was erected on land belonging to Ted Sharp, and his son William (Billy) lived there with his wife for a short time.

At the crossroads near the sea another new bungalow, which was to become an important centre of village life, appeared in the mid-1920s. Mrs Lucy

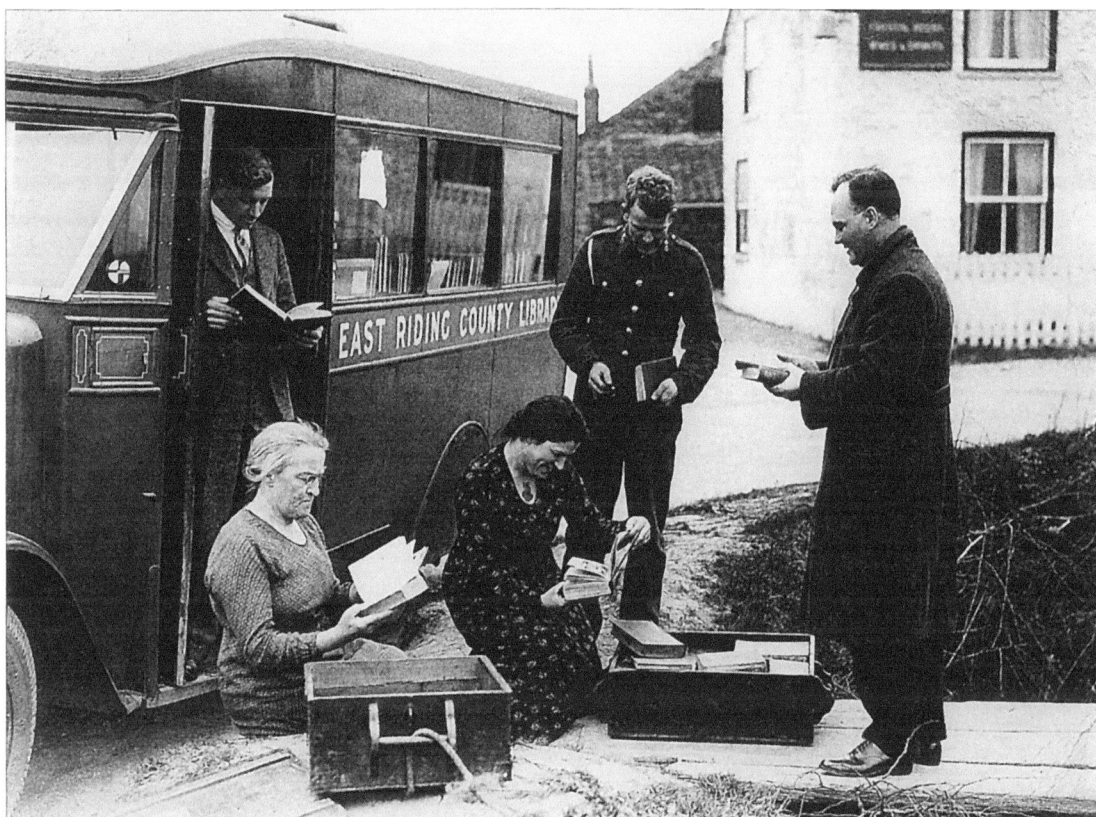

107 *Visit of the mobile library to Kilnsea, 13 March 1935. The photo shows Carrie and Lucy Leonard outside their bungalow, near the* Blue Bell Inn. *The East Riding of Yorkshire mobile library still visits Kilnsea.*

Leonard, of Cliff Farm, Out Newton, who had become widowed in 1924, had the bungalow built at the crossroads on a corner opposite the *Blue Bell* public house. The bungalow was later named Gwendene (now Fourways). The Leonards (Lucy and her daughter Carrie) ran a successful shop and café from that site so conveniently close to Godwin Battery. Thanks to the lively personalities of Carrie and her mother, the café became in effect the social centre of the village, and was to flourish for some 30 years.

At the end of the First World War, Warren Cottage, at the north end of the peninsula, was apparently deserted; indeed two references in the *Naturalist* describe it as 'a ruin'. When the War Department bought the peninsula in 1919 the sale included Warren Cottage. By that date OS maps show several buildings around the Warren.

The caravan and hut which had been erected just south of Warren Cottage by the White family were at some time moved to Easington, for they appear in a postcard of a view in Vicar Lane. The cottage itself got new tenants in 1929, when a lifeboatman, George Washington, left the Point and moved in with his family. Edith Wheeler-Osman (née Clubley) remembers staying there with her friend Peggy, one of the Washington children. After the Washingtons left, the cottage was used on occasion for permanent staff regulars (instructors) attached to the Territorial Army, and their wives. When naturalists began making regular visits to Spurn and Kilnsea in the 1930s they began to cast envious eyes on Warren Cottage, which they realised would make an ideal *pied-a-terre*. At that time the Warren area was still quite wide, surrounded by a rich habitat, with marsh, rough grassland and sand dunes. In 1938 enough naturalists (mainly from the West Riding) were visiting Spurn to make it worthwhile to keep a communal log. A report in the *Naturalist* for 1939 stated that 'in 1938, between July 25th and November 2nd there have been competent field ornithologists on Spurn Point on 26 days. Notes have been made on species seen and subsequently tabulated in the "Spurn notebook" and "roll call" thoughtfully provided by Mr R.M. Garnett using his abbreviations.' It was Ralph Garnett too, who suggested that the garden of Warren Cottage would make an ideal site for a ringing trap. However, before the plans could come to fruition the war came and the Warren area became part of the military defences.

If one were to try to sum up what Spurn and Kilnsea were like in the inter-war period, with the benefit of hindsight, it was a time of quietude between two wars. Certainly Kilnsea expanded during those inter-war years, and new blood came in. The old saying that Kilnsea people found it difficult if not impossible to get over Long Bank and leave, and that were it not for sailors being washed up (alive!) on the shore all the inhabitants would be dangerously inter-bred, now needed adjusting. The parish registers record numerous marriages taking place in the interwar years between Kilnsea girls and the military personnel working at Godwin Battery and Spurn Fort. The social life seems to have been quite lively, especially when it was augmented by the presence of the army.

From the mid-1930s onwards the clouds of impending war began to loom ahead. This time, however, defence preparations would not have to be put in place from scratch as various armaments and military installations had been retained at Kilnsea for the Territorial Army. Moreover, in the 1930s Bull Sand Fort and Haile Sand Fort had been kept on care and maintenance with 13 men on Bull Sand Fort and rather fewer on Haile Sand Fort. Nonetheless the military situation at Spurn and Kilnsea could scarcely be said to be on a war footing! At the coronation of George VI and Queen Elizabeth, a celebration was held at Spurn with a sports meeting followed by high tea in the barracks and a bonfire and fireworks afterwards, with dancing and whist to finish. Jollifications were to be short-lived, however: in September 1938 Europe appeared to be on the verge of war. It was obvious that Hitler intended to annex Czechoslovakia, and conflict seemed inevitable. The Government ordered the manning of coast and anti-aircraft defences and the Humber defences were reactivated. The Heavy Regiment Royal Artillery/Territorial Army was mobilised and reached Kilnsea by 11.30 p.m. on 26 September, whilst the stores came next day. George Edwards, who was visiting on a bird-watching trip at that time, remembered that Spurn was manned by extra troops and the railcar was towing an open wagon to and from the Point with ammunition and stores. Haile Fort's inadequacies were revealed at that time, when its guns were found to be obsolete. Nothing useful remained there but searchlights and engines.

Spurn and the Humber defences were not ready for war, so perhaps it was fortunate that Chamberlain came back from Munich with his piece of paper 'Peace in our time', and on 5 October the troops stood down. But it had been a useful exercise for the real thing, which was to come a year later.

Six

Spurn and Kilnsea during the Second World War 1939-45

By early 1939 war with Hitler's Germany was inevitable. The Treaty of Munich had only deferred matters. In March Hitler invaded Czechoslovakia, and the British government began making preparations for the conflict to come. In April the Ministry of Supply was set up to co-ordinate munitions (a step suggested by Churchill as early as 1936) and compulsory conscription for men aged 20 and 21 was brought in. Spurn received an early visitor presaging war, when the *Graf Zeppelin II* made reconnaissance flights over the East Coast of Britain. The airship had been sent to spy on the tall towers that had been erected along the coast and that were to be part of the Chain Home network, the early radar system that was to be crucial in the defence of Britain. On two occasions the airship flew over Yorkshire – on 31 May and 3-4 August. On one of those occasions, probably the latter, Carrie Leonard photographed the airship over Spurn Point.

1939

In August the Emergency Powers Defence Act passed, and the Admiralty began to requisition Hull's trawler fleet. The last bird-watchers' visit to Spurn took place in late August, the visitors being George Ainsworth, Ralph Chislett, George Edwards, Ronald Garnett and eight others. The atmosphere at Kilnsea and Spurn still seemed peaceful; but as they passed homeward through Hull, shopkeepers were sandbagging their windows. Subsequent visitors who carried binoculars were liable to be arrested and detained for interrogation. Chislett's report in the *Naturalist* mentioned Swallows and House

Martins nesting in the empty gun emplacements at the Point. They were not to be empty much longer. On 22 August the so-called 'Precautionary period' began, and the Territorial Army were called up to man the coast defences. Les Park's unit was mobilised on 24 August.

108 Graf Zeppelin II *over Spurn Point, 1939. This airship, on a spying mission, was seen over the Yorkshire coast on 31 May and 3-4 August 1939. It was probably on the latter occasion that it was photographed by Carrie Leonard.*

On 1 September Germany invaded Poland, and Britain declared war on Germany on 3 September. Carrie Leonard, running her café at Kilnsea, opposite the military camp, remembered it well:

I stood and looked with pleasure at my peaceful little kingdom – the silence was unbroken except by the murmur of the calm sea. But, 'Hell, what was that?' A sudden and prolonged clattering, thumping and banging, shouting and roaring had broken out. The Army had moved in.... 'Well, Carrie,' I said to myself, 'what happens next?' To which I replied, rather weakly, 'I suppose something will have to be done, but I'm bothered if I can think of anything.' The next thought struck me like lightning. 'I suppose I'll have to introduce myself to the men.' ... I seemed to feel eyes on my neck and turning round with an effort, I tried vainly to meet the eyes of the hundred or so grimy soldiers who were examining me from all angles. [but] I was the independent Carrie Leonard, owner of 'Gwendene', saviour of the trippers, a godsend to perspiring fathers of fractious families, a boon to mothers of mewling masses. This was just one more holiday crowd to be dealt with, and, in the true fighting spirit of the Leonards, I coped. ... 'Say, Miss, can you tell us where we can get some tea and cake, please?' This was my big moment, and I lead the way to 'Gwendene'. Here I proceeded to make tea for my first war-time customers. Little did I think then of the thousands of cups of tea I should make for the troops before the war was over.

Carrie's café became a home from home for these men who, at the beginning of the war, had been 'torn away from loved ones and herded together like cattle'. Like Carrie herself, no-one knew what was happening – some thought that bombs would fall that very day. Most thought that the war would be over in six months.

In Easington Cyril Skelton recorded in the school logbook on 11 September that a class of infant evacuees was being taught in the Church Institute by a Hull teacher who had come with them. At the little school on the Point, Mrs Campbell recorded in the logbook:

We started war with Germany at 11.15 a.m. on September 3rd. I opened school on September 4th although a message was broadcast that schools would be closed. As Spurn Point is military ground and the troops are in occupation, the children are safer and out of mischief while in school. Mr. Cross has unfastened the gate on his side of the school yard and in case of an air-raid warning the children can be under parental care within two minutes.

The defences at the beginning of the war comprised two 9.2-inch guns at Kilnsea, and four 6-inch and two 4.7-inch guns at Spurn. The latter were facing the river and an early task of the gunners was to move them to face the sea. Given the state of unreadiness of the Humber defences it was fortunate that the first six months of the war (commonly known as the Phoney War) were relatively quiet. Unlike in the First World War, Germany did not have a fleet powerful enough to

109 *Sketch from Vera Cross's autograph album. This is probably a coastal defence light in one of the emplacements on the Point.*

110   *Haile Sand Fort. Haile Sand Fort is smaller than Bull Sand Fort.*

challenge Britain's naval supremacy, so an attack on the area by sea was unlikely. Attack by air was a different matter, and the priority was to improve the anti-aircraft weapons, because light machine guns were the only defence available in the early months of the war. Moreover, the guns that were available were very visible from the air. 'The 30 foot Barr and Stroud took some hiding. The gun platforms were easily seen from the air,' said Les Park. As no trees grew in the vicinity the gunners had to scrounge whatever bits and pieces they could find as camouflage. Camouflage paint would have been an answer, but they had neither paint nor the men to do the job. Sid Scott, stationed at Spurn early in the war, remembered a severe shortage of ammunition, and telegraph poles being used to mimic anti-aircraft guns, whilst canvas pill-boxes were made to fool the German reconnaissance aircraft.

An early task for the military was to get the river forts ready for action. In the interwar period

Les Park had made several trips over to Bull Fort, but he had never been to Haile Sand, or even heard from anyone who had seen guns fired from it. Its guns were quick-firing, and they had been declared obsolete at the time of the Munich crisis in 1938. The pieces had gone and the pedestals upon which they stood were in the process of being broken up. When war broke out one had already been smashed up, but the other was saved. In effect Haile had no armaments, only the searchlights and engines, manned by the Royal Engineers. The week before the war began, on 25 August, James Alexander Omer, who like Les Park had been called up and sent to Spurn the previous day, was sent with a small party of men by tug to Haile Sand Fort. They found that the roof of the only available barrack room was open to the skies and water was flooding the whole place. They spent about 11 weeks on the fort, getting wet through almost every day. At that time they had to carry their rations from Grimsby across the sands.

Les Park was given the job, with 20 reservists, of taking 12-pounder guns and ammunition over to Haile from Spurn. They set out on 10 October, and were to stay on Haile until the guns were mounted. Unlike Bull, Haile Sand is connected to the land, though not easily accessible. When the party had landed they put all the gear on the apron and went inside to close up for the night. However, the sentry came a little later to report to Park that the tide had come in, and the water was washing over 'that stuff' outside. The boxes weighed about 12 hundredweight, but the waves had moved them about like pieces of wood. The men dashed out to get as much off inside as they could, getting soaking wet in the process.

Bull Sand Fort was better equipped than Haile Sand Fort at the beginning of the war, probably because it had been regularly visited in the inter-war period. It had had four 6-inch Mk VII guns, two being in turrets, and two outside, but those two outer guns were replaced by twin six-pounders soon after the war began. That also happened at Haile Sand Fort in 1941. A story from Les Park emphasises how *ad hoc* the arrangements at the beginning of the war were, when the Humber defences were being reactivated. It was very foggy and the foghorn on Bull 'konked out'. One of the gunners was provided with a large hammer and a stopwatch, and every so many seconds he had to hit the bell!

On 12 October, when Les Park and his party were getting ready to go over to Haile Sands Fort they saw a Grimsby trawler that had gone ashore on the sands near the tip of the Point. Her crew were passing the time by playing football with some soldiers from the fort. The ship, the *Saltaire*, had first run aground in a gale before dawn that morning. Coxswain Cross took the lifeboat out to her and, after great difficulty, managed to get the nine-man crew off. Later in the day the wind dropped and the crew returned to the ship over the sands as the tide went out. Unfortunately, as the tide came in again the wind freshened, and the trawler listed badly, the crew taking refuge in the wheelhouse. The lifeboat went out again and fired a line over to the ship. A breeches buoy was fixed up and three men were hauled over before the trawler's nets, which had been washed overboard, fouled the lines of the breeches buoy. Eventually a second breeches buoy was fixed and three more men got aboard the lifeboat. The remaining three men were hauled ashore by soldiers, though two of them were badly hurt in the operation. Thanks to the skill of Robert Cross and his crew no lives were lost and Cross received the RNLI's Silver Medal, whilst Motor

111 *The Point from the Port War Signal Station, 1940. The* Saltaire *is visible, beached on the eastern side of the peninsula.*

Mechanic John Major received the Bronze Medal and the crew were awarded the RNLI's Thanks on Vellum. That was one of the first war services for the Humber Lifeboat. There were to be many more.

Another memorable mission took place on 3 November 1939, when the SS *Canada* of Copenhagen was holed by enemy action some miles north-east of Spurn. As her holds filled with water 40 members of the crew launched the ship's boats and were eventually picked up. The remaining 13 men and the captain remained on board. The Spurn lifeboat launched and sailed up towards the *Canada* in a strong south-easterly. She found the ship anchored off Holmpton, stood by through the night and then transferred the captain to a tug so that he could report to the ship's agent. However, the ship developed a serious list and the mate asked the lifeboat to take off the rest of the crew. By that time the ship was surrounded by floating timber from the deck cargo and the lifeboat was damaged whilst getting the men off. By 10.30 a.m. all men were safe and only five minutes later the ship sank. The lifeboat took the men to Grimsby, having been out in appalling weather for over 18 hours. The *Canada* wreck was to remain *in situ* throughout the war years, and indeed still lies where she sank to this day.

When the war broke out the evenings were light until late, so the lack of electricity at Spurn Fort and at Godwin Battery was not a problem. As the nights drew in it was clear that the facilities had to be updated quickly. Park described the situation in the sergeants' mess at Kilnsea where they used two petrol Pifco lamps, which created a similar effect to exhaust fumes, and induced sleepiness. Accordingly, between October and November, conduits were laid down to Kilnsea and right down the peninsula to carry the electricity. A little earlier a three-inch water main had been laid down to supply Spurn Fort, which until then had been supplied with water from Grimsby and from Bull Sand Fort. Spurn had modern services at last. However the accommodation for the first Territorials left something to be desired. In the inter-war period the sergeants had used the hospital as their mess. On the declaration of war Park found the hospital was reactivated:

then it was out with the sergeants – where were we to go? We found a little wooden rope store, cleaned it out and used that. We suffered, but murmured not, but the officers' mess was a real posh place, and all the troops had brick-built barracks, water for washing and baths. The watch shelters were all up to scratch, even had metal beds but if you had three little seagulls on your arm you'd had it!

In early November 1939 there was a 'pea-souper' of a fog, which lasted all day long. It began clearing about 5 p.m. and observers at Spurn heard a seaplane start up and move off the sea near the battery. They had no idea at that stage what it could be, but they did occasionally get planes limping in from the RAF station at Donna Nook on the opposite side of the river, so could not assume that it was hostile. The plane circled Spurn very low and, as it went over the anti-aircraft searchlight unit, water dropped off the floats, and Major Reader, the Battery Commander, said, 'I think it is an enemy plane.' The searchlight started up and exposed the plane, which put all its lights on, 'riding lights, cabin lights, the lot'. The searchlight doused its lights, thinking it was 'some poor straggler trying to get home' and the plane flew off towards the Point and began machine-gunning Bull Fort. The Lewis gunner on the fort, Lance Bombardier Charlie Dunham, dashed out to his gun and was hit on the thigh by a piece of metal when the round hit the plating on the fort and splattered. This became famous as the first casualty of the war in Britain. Dunham was taken to York for treatment and the piece of metal was taken for inspection. 'Charlie came in for some leg-pulling and … developed a limp worthy of an Oscar.' In fact the plane turned out to have been mine-laying all day. Shortly afterwards a cargo ship, the *Manatee*, blew up and sank off Trinity Sands. Initially it was thought to have been hit by a torpedo, but it turned out to be one of the first magnetic mines. Some were dropped around Shoeburyness, and some in the Humber. Park said:

we had seven ships piled up in the Humber mouth – a terrible tangle … We had over 200 mines washed up on the Yorkshire coast at that time. We saw them on the beach and the orderly sergeant used to take a picket out, knock it in the sand and secure the mine and inform the Navy who took them it away. We tied up dozens, never gave them a second thought until one Saturday such a crash, and one had washed up and gone off; a great big hole a bus could be put in, great jagged lumps of metal hanging round. We treated mines with more respect after that!

Respect was certainly necessary: on 17 October 1939 six German destroyers left Wilhelmshaven and reached the Humber mouth in the early hours of the 18th. Five of them carried 60 mines each and laid them between the Humber estuary and Withernsea. That minefield eventually claimed seven ships. The Humber region was not only the first area in the country to be the unfortunate victim of magnetic mines but also of the dropping of mines by aircraft as opposed to ships. On the night of 21/22 November Heinkel He 115s were observed laying mines in the Humber, and in the estuaries of the Stour and the Thames. Those aerial mines were described as looking like sailors' kitbags suspended by a parachute. That new threat – magnetic mines delivered from the air, which were set off by a passing ship's magnetic field – was terrifying. In the weeks before Christmas several ships were blown up by mines near Spurn, including the SS *Mangalore*, which was struck by a drifting mine and broke in two as she lay at anchor in the Hawke Roads on 24 November, and two days later the SS *Pilsudski*, a Polish liner under charter to the Royal Navy, which was struck by a mine and sank off the Humber. The lifeboat crew was kept very busy attempting to rescue the crews from such disasters.

Carrie Leonard remembered the scenes at the camp during the first weeks of the war as a state of 'unorganised chaos'. The camp was not ready for so many troops, who had to be fed and, if possible, made comfortable. However at Godwin Battery, Kilnsea, as at Spurn Fort, things were getting organised by the first Christmas of the war. A canteen was opened, and Carrie herself considered closing the café and working there as manageress. Perhaps wisely, since she liked to be in charge of things, she decided to carry on with the café. She became very closely involved with the camp anyway, because concerts and dances were soon planned, and Carrie and the other ladies of Kilnsea threw themselves enthusiastically into these activities. The first concert was held just before Christmas:

All the folks from far and near were invited and gathered round in their best bibs and tuckers. Some concert it was too!!! There was a bevy of Bright Young Things who showed far more leg than was necessary and made Bold Bad eyes at the Officers, who sat in the front row looking very impressed and trying to look important.

1940

The winter of 1940 was one of the most severe for many years. Even on the coast the temperature dropped well below freezing point for many weeks and ice floes were seen on the Humber. The buffer oil in the guns, a liquid that it was almost impossible to freeze, did so. Park remembers that the soldiers were ordered not to march in line up to the guns, as that would leave a pattern in the snow like pointers alerting the enemy to their position! Instead they walked on different tracks hither and thither, to baffle the enemy planes! Because of the prolonged cold weather the new underground water pipe down the peninsula froze up. The soldiers had to wash and shave in melted snow, and fresh water was brought down to Spurn on the railcar and was strictly rationed. Carrie Leonard remembered the snow being four feet deep with frequent blizzards. Getting supplies from Kilnsea to Spurn was a great problem. That was before the road was made and the railcar had to be dug out of snowdrifts all the way down to the Point.

1940 was probably the most crucial year as far as Spurn and Kilnsea's role in the war was concerned, when the threat of invasion became very real, as the German army began to advance on the continent. The importance of the Humber region in the defence of Britain was recognised, and apparently Winston Churchill, then First Sea Lord, made a visit to Spurn at that time. Another dignitary, the Princess Royal, visited the Point on 16 April, in her travels round the country looking at YMCA facilities for the troops. She arrived on the railway, as there was not as yet a road down the Point. She met Robert Cross and his family, and the other members of the lifeboat crew, as well as military personnel stationed on the peninsula. Her journey was made on the Hardy railcar, and was memorable for ending rather abruptly, when the

112 *Wedding group at Easington, on the occasion of Gwen Jackson and William Broom's marriage in 1940 at St Helen's, Kilnsea. Gwen Jackson was one of Mrs Campbell's daughters by her first marriage. Left to right: Lucy Leonard, unknown soldier, Mrs Campbell, Jackie Jackson, unknown soldier, Vera Cross. Jackie was Gwen's sister.*

113 *Ken Webster and REME men near Spurn lighthouse, 1939-40. They seem to be leaning on a gun emplacement for a Lewis machine gun.*

driver overshot the platform and she had to walk along a hastily placed plank onto a sand dune. The railcar was actually pulled by a steam locomotive, because by that time the railcars had been augmented by a LNER steam engine, which had been sent from Hull. No engine driver came with it, however, and Horace Burton, who was a civilian working for the Royal Engineers, and not a trained engine driver, was expected to drive it. Fortunately a corporal with railway experience arrived and after some problems Burton learned to handle the engine, which was nicknamed *The Black Sapper*.

114   *Visit of the Princess Royal to Spurn, 16 April 1940. Front row: Robert Cross, coxswain and HRH The Princess Royal. Back row: William Jenkinson, Walter Hood, Samuel Cross, George Stephenson, Samuel Hoopell, Walter Biglin, John Major.*

115   The Black Sapper, *1940.*

Many of the men who manned the various forts must have considered that they had reached a rather remote area of Yorkshire, but Godwin Battery and Spurn Fort were positively luxurious compared to the Humber forts. Bull Fort, out in the middle of the Humber, had to be manned continuously, and 'the old iron bucket', as Sid Scott called it, must have seemed somewhat like a prison. When Scott was told that he had to 'go to Bull' he thought at first that at least it would make a change from Spurn. With his fellow soldiers he marched down the railway jetty, which consisted of 'a few iron pylons and wood planks'. Waiting alongside was a large Royal Navy launch with a 'chirpy sub' in the wheelhouse. The men that could squash in got into the wheelhouse and the rest were in the after-end in full marching order, stuffed in like sardines. They passed many wrecks on their way to Bull, 'ships going nowhere, a bit of bow, stern, upper-structure, masts, funnels … a small ship [which] must have been rather smart in her time, mahogany wheelhouse, square brass ports'. When they reached the fort they had to

perform acrobatics to climb aboard wearing and carrying all their kit, and watch their steps on the mossy planking.

There was very little to do on Bull Fort. The men played cards, and there was a small store where they could buy sweets and cigarettes. Scott described how, in order to pass the time, they were reduced to schoolboy games: at high tide they would stand on the lower deck as long as possible before a heavy wave came too close and they had to rush for the stairway. Another trick was to run across the apron before the wave came over. That could have resulted in tragedy, but no-one came to grief whilst Scott was on Bull. He was one of the men running the power plants, both inside and outside the fort. These were semi-diesel petrol and paraffin, which were started on petrol and when they reached a certain temperature were changed over to paraffin. That was probably the warmest place on Bull Fort, and the operators could make toast on the red-hot manifolds! However, being on duty at night-time on the upper deck in a gale was not a pleasant experience.

116   *A view of Spurn in 1941 from Vera Cross's autograph album. A compressed view of the Port War Signal Station, the lighthouse, various military buildings and the YMCA.*

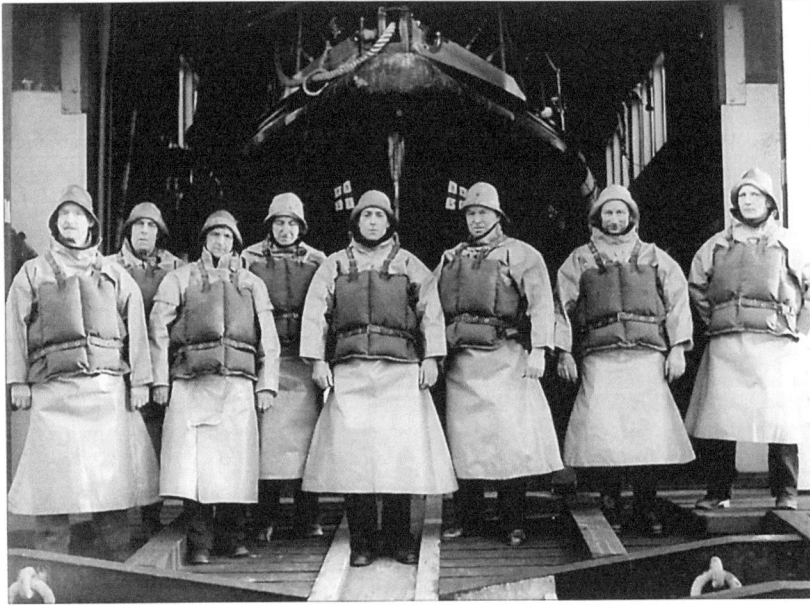

117 *Spurn lifeboat crew. Left to right: George (Dod) Hopper, Samuel Hoopell, John Major, Walter Hood, Samuel Cross, Robert Cross, Walter Biglin, William Jenkinson.*

The accommodation in Bull Fort was cold and damp. The rooms were made of steel and there was serious condensation, as all the doors and shutters had to be closed at night. The men turned in wearing all their clothes, and some even wore their greatcoats. The men slept in tiered bunks, and the on-going watch had to remove their bedding so that the off-coming watch could bed down. Hammocks could also be slung across the rooms. The food was basic: porridge for breakfast with jam; stew and vegetables for dinner followed by rice or custard; 'that cake the cooks made damp, thick and yellow'; cocoa at night that was only just warm by the time it got round to all the men.

At Spurn Fort by early 1940 facilities were improving. In addition to a NAAFI canteen there was a YMCA – two interconnected huts where tea, sandwiches and cakes were sold. It had facilities for table tennis and darts, and a piano for home-made entertainment. The YMCA was run by two ladies from the West Riding, Miss Nancy Ambler and Miss Kathleen Sutcliffe. They were volunteers, and they had their own accommodation inside the YMCA. As more servicemen moved into the area a NAAFI was opened, operating first in a canvas marquee on the Point, but soon replaced by a permanent building

The lifeboat crew and their families now found themselves virtually living in the middle of an army camp and potentially on the front line! Enemy mine-laying off the Humber meant that shipping in the area faced a new threat to add to the usual hazards of difficult navigation and poor weather. A rescue that has been described as 'one of the most outstanding of the Second World War' took place on 12 February 1940. Two lifeboatmen were off sick that evening, when the coastguards reported that red flares had been seen east-south-east of Donna Nook, so Robert Cross launched the lifeboat with a reduced crew. In tremendous seas and driving snow the *City of Bradford II* reached the stricken ship, the steam trawler the *Gurth*, which by then had struck the shore and had heavy seas pouring over her. The rescue involved no less than 20 attempts to save the crew of nine, and was carried out in complete darkness. Robert Cross had to use all his many years' experience to plan his tactics and carry them out. Motor Mechanic John Major, at the engine controls, was often almost submerged, and the rest of the crew of the lifeboat were repeatedly knocked down by huge waves, and were only saved from being washed overboard by clinging to the handrails. After six of the men had been brought onto the lifeboat its port engine stopped, having been fouled by a rope. Several more attempts were made to rescue the remaining three men, on only one engine. They were eventually got off and the lifeboat made its way into deeper water, where Robert Cross, using a knife of his own design, cleared the propeller. The lifeboat reached Grimsby at 10.35 p.m. and landed the rescued crew. For that mission Coxswain Robert Cross was awarded the RNLI's Gold Medal and the five lifeboat crew were each awarded a Silver Medal for one of the most outstanding rescues of the war. Later in the year Cross was awarded the George Medal, a gallantry medal only second highest to the George Cross. The George Medal was only instituted in 1940 and Coxswain Cross was the first civilian to receive it.

By the spring of 1940 the so-called 'Phoney War' was over. The Germans were approaching France and plans were being made for the defence of Britain. In late spring/early summer the German offensive on the Continent accelerated. In May 1940 Germany invaded Holland, Belgium and Luxembourg, and between 27 May and 5 June the British Expeditionary Force was evacuated from the beaches of Dunkirk. Such huge numbers of soldiers had to be accommodated somehow, and some of them came to Spurn and Kilnsea. Carrie wrote:

> I always feel a lump in my throat whenever I think of those lads. One youngster suffered very badly from shell-shock and he would come into the café and sit for hours by the fire. In spite of my efforts, I always used to feel tense when he came in, for he would carry on a normal conversation for quite a long time then without warning he would break out in tears, sobs, and mournful howls. Things like that used to increase my hatred of war and made me work even harder for the boys who came round this way.

The Humber defences were now on the front line. Once Paris had fallen on 14 June and the enemy

118 *Kilnsea and Godwin Battery, 24 March 1941. The infantry camp established alongside the bungalow now called Sunny Cliff can be seen south of the road. The military hutments north of Warren Cottage are visible, as is the railway line. The three rows of anti-tank blocks erected from the Humber towards the sea are perhaps still in the course of construction. The ridge and furrow of the open fields is very clear.*

119 *The Royal Observer Corps at their post near the lighthouse, c.1943. The Port War Signal Station is in the background. Inside the post are Dick Atkinson and Alf Shearsmith. In the foreground are Albert Linley and ? Ellerby.*

occupied the western coast of Europe Great Britain was directly threatened. The Germans moved their airfields close up to the Channel, where shipping was dangerously vulnerable. Hitler's plan to invade, code-named Operation Sealion, targeted the South Coast, but the entire coast of England was vulnerable, and it was decided to construct a ring of coast defence batteries to cover every probable or indeed possible landing place. Coastal Artillery was, as a result, greatly expanded in the second half of 1940, and the Humber defences were completely reorganised. The railway, which had served well enough during the First World War, was not able to cope with modern transport requirements, and it was decided to have a road down the peninsula. It was built in concrete sections, with points where the railway crossed it in either direction. The shape of the peninsula had changed subtly in the 20 years since the railway had been built and, indeed, during a strong storm surge in 1942, a section of the railway

at the narrows collapsed, and gangs of men were delegated to make concrete sandbags to build up the banks. The concrete road was finished by early 1941, and the road and railway worked together to link the camps at either end of the peninsula. On the Point itself was a road that linked the batteries, in a sort of 'horseshoe sweep' as it was described by Les Park.

Behind the *Blue Bell* pub, a Naval installation had been built just after the war started. Les Park remembered a 4-inch gun there from his first period at Kilnsea and Spurn, 1939/40:

It was put in by the Navy and was put up for the D.E.M.S training defensively equipped merchant service [ships], I believe. Anyway it was purely a naval site and nobody seemed bothered with it. We at Kilnsea certainly had nothing to do with it in those early days. One day we had a party of seamen come along in a coach. The only one in uniform was Chief Petty Officer, gunnery. We watched and wondered as the 'squad' disembarked and made for the *Blue Bell*. Having refreshed and satisfied all other needs they proceeded to said 4-inch equipment. The bucket, rammer and ammunition were brought down. There was no drill as such. The gun crew had cloth caps, mufflers, jackets etc. The C.P.O. got them around and the gun was loaded. They banged off about twenty rounds at various elevations, just pumping rounds out to sea, no question of a target. It was primarily to let them know and see the gun firing. They also had two Lewis guns for anti-aircraft work, which they mounted on the rails; there were 100 rounds per magazine (we only had 47 (50) on our Lewis guns). Anyhow they all had a bang and a good time was had by all, pack up, call at the *Blue Bell* and away.

Park's contempt for that amateur attitude on the part of the 'Senior Service' comes over strongly, but it appears that this site was soon expanded, and it became an important part of the beach defences, with '13-pounders, spigot mortars, Oerlikons and such'. As to the D.E.M.S. site, that was to remain for several years, being crucial to the war effort. Before the war started the possibility of arming British merchant ships had been considered and, when war was declared, Germany announced that every vessel of the British mercantile marine was to be regarded as a warship. Due to shortages of equipment, merchant ships were often forced to go to sea without any armaments. Gradually, ocean-going ships were provided with defensive weapons, but small coasters and fishing vessels remained mostly without them during the early part of the war. The usual armaments were anti-aircraft Lewis and Bren guns. The scheme to arm ships and to train men in gunnery was known as D.E.M.S. – Defensively Equipped Merchant Ships. Bases where men, both from the Merchant Service and the Royal Navy, could be trained, were all over the coast, including the one at Kilnsea, at the back of the *Blue Bell* pub.

As well as the threat from the sea, a new threat had now come into being – attack from the air and, near Warren Cottage at the north end of the peninsula, an anti-aircraft installation was built, initially with a battery of two 4.5-inch guns. Rows of about 30 huts and a NAAFI, for a mixed corps of *c.*40 men and *c.*50 women were built between the present gate to the reserve and

Warren Cottage. Other buildings (some still there) were erected nearer the cottage. Lewis guns, which were all that were available at the outset of the war for air defence, were later replaced by Bren guns, 3.7-inch anti-aircraft, and Bofors guns, both around the Warren area and up and down the peninsula. The Spurn area was soon bristling with defences. Carrie Leonard described the Point as 'looking like a giant's neck covered with a rash of spiky guns and large blister-like Nissen huts'.

On the Humber side of the peninsula, almost opposite the lighthouse, an Observer Corps post was set up. The Royal Observer Corps was ancillary to Fighter Command. They took men who might be elderly, or not fit for the forces, or too young to join up. They also took some women. The corps became 'Royal' in 1941. It acted as a second arm of surveillance to radar, which aircraft could fly underneath. The observer posts were dotted around the countryside in places where the corps

120   *The Point during the Second World War. This photograph shows the Royal Observer Corps's mess, which is the building with the sloping roof on the left of the road. The observer post is on the right.*

could have all-round vision. Spurn was the only permanent post in the country at that time, being isolated from any town. The post was placed near the lighthouse on a high sand dune with good vision on most sides (apart from the view blocked by the looming lighthouse!). The Spurn post was brick-built, and constructed to provide shelter and warmth for the two men on duty. The building was divided into two sections, one being roofed and the other open to the sky. In the covered area was a table, covered by a large-scale map of the area and heated by a coke stove. One of the men on duty was always looking at the skies with binoculars, searching for aircraft, and ready to spot, identify and track both friend and foe. The other man was ready at the plotting chart, and able to report the observation to group headquarters. They had to establish the height of the aircraft and put it on a calibrated height bar. There were four stations in South Holderness – Spurn, Withernsea, Easington, and Sunk Island. They all worked together and were in constant communication. The headquarters were at Knavesmire, York. At night-time the observers were able to plot by sound – in a five-mile sound circle. The unit at Spurn consisted of eight men with two on duty at any time. The spells were eight hours and they worked 48 hours a week. Alf Shearsmith, who was stationed at Spurn as a member of the corps from 1943 to 1945, has written a vivid account his life there. The men of the corps had a pretty good billet by the standards of the area. It was apparently the envy of many other people stationed on the peninsula, having 'combined bathroom and toilet facilities, a comfortable lounge with open fireplace, which provided the hot water, and sleeping quarters for eight with another open fire, which of course was essential to survive the severe winter storms. The edifice was entirely brick-built, with a lean-to sloping roof and blast wall.'

A new infantry camp made up of 20 wooden huts was set up on the southern side of the road from the *Blue Bell* to the church (where Sunny Cliff is now). From Kilnsea in the north, the peninsula and estuary now bristled with defences – the Warren anti-aircraft establishment, various mobile anti-aircraft posts on the Narrows, the Port War

Signal Station, which monitored the movements of shipping near the lighthouse, Spurn Fort covering the Point itself, and the two river forts, Bull Sand and Haile Sand, now fully functional. Spurn was getting ready to take its place on the front line.

The soft contours of Spurn Point and the coast running north became punctuated by concrete and iron defences – tank blocks, tank traps, pill-boxes, barbed wire, iron fencing, stakes, anti-invasion scaffolding and so on. Most of the pill-boxes still visible on Spurn and at Kilnsea were erected at that time, though there were some that dated from the previous war. Enormous resources were put into defending the coastline in a very short time. Well over 20,000 pill-boxes were built in Britain between January 1940 and June 1941. The measures that were taken in the area were aimed firstly at making movement of invading troops difficult on the ground. Tubular fencing was erected from an area just north of Kilnsea village as far as Warren Cottage, and lines of anti-tank blocks (large concrete cubes) were put in place right across the peninsula just north of the entrance to Spurn and along the beach north of Kilnsea village. Some of them still remain, though the most striking ones, which were laid out in three rows of blocks, were broken up in the 1970s, when some were moved and used as sea defences. Further down the peninsula in the Chalk Bank area, two anti-tank ditches were dug. That furthest south still remains, being best viewed on the eastern side of the peninsula, with some of the tank blocks still *in situ* on the beach. The railway line, which passed through that area on the western side, made its way between two blocks that also still remain to this day. The part of the peninsula known as 'wire dump' is still punctuated by the spiral upright iron spikes that held the barbed wire in place.

For the personnel stationed at the forts, things began to change in the spring of 1940. As a result of bombing raids on Hull and mine-laying on the coast Spurn and Kilnsea experienced much more enemy air activity. Sidney Scott recalled that, after a particularly heavy night of anti-aircraft fire, the staff running the NAAFI left the Point, and the two elderly ladies who ran a YMCA hut providing tea, cakes, table tennis and darts also left shortly after,

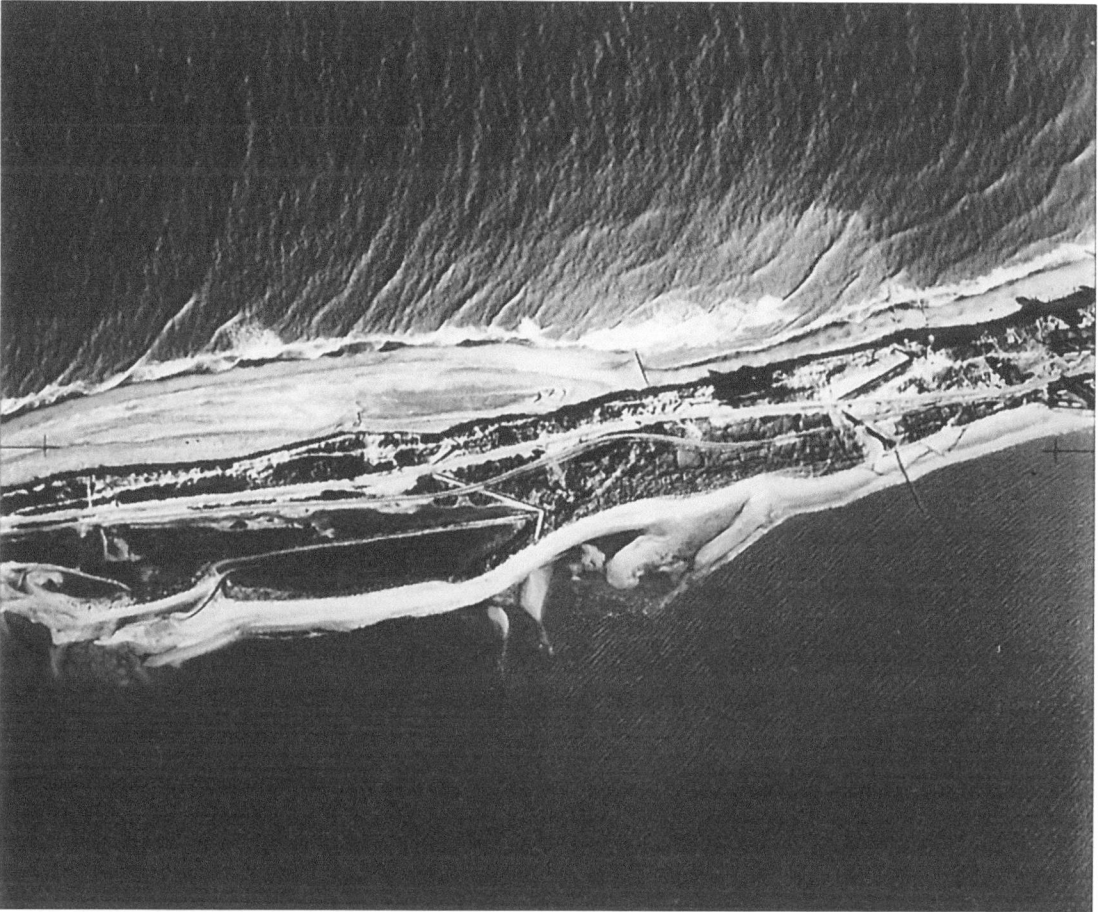

121   *Chalk Bank area in 1941. It is possible to see two anti-tank ditches, though only one, now a listed structure, is visible today. Between the two ditches are former allotments, subdivided by earth banks and now known as 'the potato fields'.*

to be replaced by two men. Incidentally these two men were suddenly taken away from their post by the Military Police in late 1940. The rumour was that they had been accused of flashing lights at enemy aircraft and asking pertinent questions of military personnel.

During the invasion scare period all leave was cancelled, and all members of units, whether on watch or not, were on 'stand-to' at dawn, whilst increased patrolling took place at night in the dunes forward of the guns' positions. Until that time gunners had not been issued with bayonets, but these were now issued, together with instructions on how to use them, and the soldiers were also trained in unarmed combat. The men were also apparently

encouraged to use their rifles to fire at low-flying aircraft, though only when they were in groups.

At Tower House in Easington Robert Walker and his daughter Violet found that, as in the First World War, they were living in a house that the military required for billeting and surveillance (the tower itself giving some of the best views of the surrounding countryside). Robert, an old man by the outbreak of war, dreaded the disruption that would be caused by soldiers using his house and land. In 1939 the vicar's wife, Mrs Robins, called on Violet to help with the war effort. Mr Skelton, the schoolmaster, organised the distribution of gas masks and registration cards were issued to all. Air-raid alarms began in October 1939, and Robert Walker recorded them all in his diary, as well as the constant disturbance that he was suffering as a result of living in a house being used by the military. In May 1940 'Flying Officer Mummery here at 8 p.m. about billeting two men,' and in June 'Major Robinson, Captain Robertson and Lt Moore from Kilnsea here and went on roof of tower.' Later in the month Walker was asked for permission to take the tower over for use as a day-and-night observation post. Trenches were dug in his field, and more men were billeted in the house. Access to the tower room was only possible through the house, and daily life became increasingly difficult for the Walkers. Now in his eighties, Robert decided that he could no longer bear the disturbance, and in October 1940 the Walkers bought a cottage near Ilkley and prepared to leave. Finding even a few more days at Tower House insupportable (the diary records damage having been done to the house and furniture already) they moved temporarily into 1 Cliff View at Kilnsea, to board with the Clubleys. After visiting his wife's grave on 15 October, Robert and his daughter left for Ilkley. He died soon afterwards. Throughout the war Tower House continued to be used by the military, though now in the ownership of Redvers Clubley and his wife, Doris (who had been a maid there for the Walkers). The Clubleys only used a few rooms in the house and many decades later Redvers' nephew, Roland Wheeler-Osman, remembered that army beds were still in the tower rooms.

Robin Skelton, the poet, in his biography of his father Cyril, the village schoolmaster, recalled the many changes brought to Easington during the war. Near the schoolhouse a searchlight battery was installed, with anti-aircraft guns as well as searchlights. Mr Skelton became an air-raid warden and chairman of the Invasion Committee, which involved collecting together emergency rations and hiding them away. Mrs Skelton ran the Women's Royal Voluntary Service, organised the knitting of socks etc, ran a canteen in the church hall, and brought cinema to the village. Everyone was supplied with gas masks, of course. A little later in the war a radar station manned by the R.A.F. was built on the site of the old mill (now covered by the gas site). 'We gazed awestruck at the strange construction of slowly spinning metal, and the notices forbidding entry.'

The increased military activity in the area led to the removal in March 1940 of a much-loved Kilnsea landmark. The Kilnsea Beacon, which had given guidance to mariners since 1895 and provided a favourite playground for Kilnsea and Easington children, was taken down and never replaced. It was considered too useful a landmark for enemy aircraft. For the same reason the lighthouse, having been converted to electricity, was not usually lit at night, apart from a simple navigation beacon on a lower level. The lighthouse-keepers were of course retained, maintaining the equipment and ready for duty when required. Their 'light duties' must have seemed quite desirable to some, though admittedly they were stuck in a rather isolated spot! At the same time as electricity came to the lighthouse it was also brought to the lifeboat houses, which no longer had to rely on oil lamps for light.

On 19 May 1940 the minelayer *Princess Victoria* struck a mine and sank off the Humber with the loss of 37 of her crew. In June 1940 all leave for the lifeboat crew was cancelled. Mrs Campbell the schoolteacher recorded in the logbook on 7 June that SS *Orangemoor* had been torpedoed and her son was missing. She carried on working and recorded several air-raids in June, which meant that the children had very broken nights, being moved to the shelters most of the night. On 4 July Mrs Campbell recorded, 'We have been told to prepare for immediate and instant evacuation. The Education Authority has granted permission to close school at once until August 19th. So I close today.'

At the beginning of August the Battle of Britain began. If Hitler were to invade successfully he had to destroy Britain's air power. Accordingly Germany began to systematically bomb radar sites and airfields. Much of the action took place well south of Spurn, but around the Humber area were many airfields, which sent aircraft both on bombing missions and on defensive attacks on German aircraft over England. The Battle of Britain, which lasted from July until September 1940, resulted in victory for Britain, because Hitler failed to destroy the R.A.F. and, in September, he called off Operation Sealion, having realised that Britain's superior air power meant that a seaborne invasion would not succeed. The Humber defences, like the defences around the South Coast, were not to be needed after all, but they remained in place just in case. Spurn and Kilnsea forts, of course, were still important to the war effort in many other ways.

The enemy was very active at that time in laying mines in the Humber and Tyne. Many cities and towns on the East Coast were the targets of bombers in August and September. Spurn school reopened in late August, but Mrs Campbell, having had her son's death confirmed, now had another, though lesser, blow. On her arrival back at Spurn just before the start of term, she was informed that her little bungalow was to be taken down – 'razed to the ground by 8.30 p.m.'. The bungalow lay in the way of the new concrete road that was being built down to the Point, and Mrs Campbell had to find accommodation in the lifeboat cottages. Undeterred she carried on and, on 11 October she recorded that eight children – five boys and three girls – attended and that she usually had 100 per cent attendance. In spite of air raids she opened each day at nine o'clock:

> The children have made, in school, a pillow for each child, and mattresses, that each child may lie on their bunks immediately on being taken into the shelter. We had a great amount of 'tubing' packed with kapok washed up near school. The children opened the tubes, extracted and dried the kapok, and it has been most useful. They have in addition made blankets by knitting and by cloth, so that everything for comfort has been done that can be done.

Mines continued to take their toll of ships off Spurn: on 12 September 1940 SS *Gothic*, a tanker carrying a cargo of creosote and sailing from the Humber to Billingham, was sunk by a mine off Spurn Point. Twelve crew were lost from that ship. On 14 October 1940 the Trinity House tender *Reculver* was sunk by a mine off Spurn Point, and on 28 October 1940 a cargo ship, the SS *Sheaf Field*, was sunk by a mine near the Sunk Light vessel, and another, the SS *Sagacity*, was sunk by a mine off Spurn Point. Mine-laying continued throughout November despite the efforts of minesweepers, two of which, both minesweeping trawlers, the *Manx Prince* and the *Cortina*, were sunk off the Humber in November and December.

1941

The second winter of the war was, like the first, a cold and stormy one. The steam engine, the *Black Sapper*, which had been brought to the peninsula in 1940, left in 1941, and the Hudswell Clarke railcar (always called the Drewry by everyone) was the only vehicle on the line thereafter.

In 1941 bombing raids on Hull and other Northern cities became commonplace. The Humber provided an excellent flight path for guidance inland, so the people on the Point were also vulnerable to attack. At Kilnsea, Carrie soon became accustomed to air raids but wrote that she would never forget her first one. Many of the 'Ack Ack' boys used her café and they told her that after their training they could not wait for 'Jerry' to put in an appearance. Carrie described the first serious air raid, when:

> The night was bright with flares and gunfire, and all Hell seemed to be set free in that small corner of England. Bangs ... bursts ... bombs on the beaches ... a real blitz. Then came the moment we had been waiting for! – up went the shell, like a bolt of vengeance from the gun; there was a blaze of vivid flame in the sky, a muffled roar then a scarlet streak in the sky streaked towards the earth, swooped across the Point and landed on the sea ... Then came the dawn. No medals, no parade in glory, no barrels of beer ... nothing but a smoke-streaked sky, a smell of cordite and a wreck in the river. But the boys were not disappointed; the thrill of having made their first 'kill' was all they wanted, and that thrill would be lived again in that distant future when the world would be at peace once more ...

The first major raid of the war on Hull took place on the night of 13/14 March 1941, when 78 enemy aircraft dropped 39 tonnes of high explosives and 4,500 incendiary bombs. Their target was the docks but they also went for residential areas. They were taking advantage of the full moon, which gave excellent visibility to the bomb crews, and the toll was high: 40 people were killed and 79 seriously injured. Another big raid took place on 18 March 1941, when north and central Hull were hit. A paint factory and a gasworks were damaged, roads were blocked, 700 fires were started, 94 people were killed, and 70 were seriously injured. The Humber anti-aircraft

122   *Port War Signal Station wartime Christmas party.*

guns fired 2,500 of the 8,500 rounds used by AA Command during that night.

At the little school on the Point Mrs Campbell recorded in the logbook the disruption caused by the raids: on 11 February she recorded that they had raids on three nights in succession. 'Last night and the night before were very hectic. The children were in the shelter again until after midnight – I did not open until ten o'clock this morning.' On 21 February she recorded that 'We have had many disturbed nights and I fear the children take cold when carried from bed to the shelter.' Possibly the children welcomed those breaks in routine. They certainly relished being in the middle of a military camp! Bombs fell on Easington on the night of 25 February and over 50 windows were broken, including one at the school. On 27 February Cyril Skelton, the schoolmaster, recorded that a Heinkel bomber had passed over the school flying low, and men of the searchlight party in the field next to the school were in action with machine guns. Routine went on regardless, even at the school. At Spurn a very sad event happened in April: Mrs Campbell went to Birmingham for her Easter holiday, became ill whilst there, and died. Vera Cross, who sometimes helped out at the school, recorded in

the logbook, 'The children of Spurn have lost a very kind friend.'

Mines continued to be a constant hazard to shipping in the Humber area. Many ships were struck by mines and lives were lost. Throughout 1941 the lifeboat was busy, and the crew often put their lives in danger. One rescue on 27 February 1941 occurred when the *City of Bradford II* was launched at 3 a.m. in snow and a full gale, because the Port War Signal Station had reported the explosion of a mine in the convoy anchorage. Later a message was received that a vessel had sunk. The lifeboat first found the SS *Venus* in trouble at the mouth of the Humber because she had fouled the boom defences there. After requesting tugs to tow her off, the lifeboat began to search for the vessel that had been reported sunk. Seeing distress rockets to the north-east, Robert Cross and his crew headed in that direction, straight into an area where many mines had been dropped only a few days before. Instead of the sunken ship, they found the air-raid balloon ship *Thora* aground on Trinity Sands with heavy seas sweeping right over her. Coxswain Cross took the lifeboat round the *Thora* into shallow water on the sand bank and then, using the engines, he held the lifeboat in position in heavy seas whilst the eight men from the balloon ship jumped aboard. The men were taken to Grimsby and the lifeboat was back at her station by 9.30 a.m. Robert Cross received the RNLI Bronze Medal for his actions in that rescue.

On 30 June a new teacher, Mrs Beal, came to the little school on Spurn. On 2 July she was shown round by Vera Cross, and she started her duties the following day, recording that she was 'Practically without stock of any description.' She soon found that she was in a war zone when bombs were dropped on the Warren area on 10 July and the children spent most of that night in the air-raid shelter. It was during 1941 that a landmine landed on the wall of the lighthouse compound, demolishing part of the wall, a naval hut and Sandholme, an ex-army hut converted to a house. The Regan family, who had lived there for many years, were made homeless and had to move into one of the vacant lifeboat cottages. Happily no lives were lost.

Enemy activity in the Humber and North Sea continued to take a heavy toll of ships despite the vigilance of the Army and Navy and mine-sweeping activities. On 12 May the steamship *Fowberry Tower*, which had left Hull en route for the USA, was sunk by a German aircraft off the Humber with the loss of six of her crew.

Either the same aircraft or another was shot at by anti-aircraft fire the next day. It crashed into the water and two survivors were picked up by a balloon barrage drifter. On 10 June the patrol sloop *Pintail* and steamship *Royal Scott* were both sunk by mines. In early September the minesweeping trawler *Strathborne* and the mine destructor vessel *Corfield* were sunk by mines off the Humber – most of those minesweeping vessels were based in Grimsby docks, which was the largest base for minesweepers in the British Isles. Later in that month the steamship *British Prince* was sunk by enemy aircraft. The losses in the Humber carried on into the winter, with the bombing and sinking of the steamship *Marie Dawn* on 3 November and the steamship *Corhampton* on 16 November. A sister ship of the *British Prince*, the *Welsh Prince*, only launched the previous year, was sunk off the Humber en route from London to New York on 7 December, and a week later the steamship *Dromore Castle* was sunk by a mine south-east of the Humber and a motor anti-submarine boat fouled the boom in the Humber and sank. Two more ships were lost before the year end: the steamship *Benmacdhui* and the Free French minesweeping trawler *Henriette*, both sunk by mines off the Humber.

123 *The Port War Signal Station during the Second World War.*

124 *D.E.M.S. Wrens at Kilnsea, 1944. Left to right: Louise Clarke, Rose Thorpe, Evelyn Williams, May Beck.*

1942

By 1942 the threat of invasion had receded and many of the men who had been stationed at Kilnsea and Spurn were moved to more useful tasks elsewhere. Nevertheless, the forts still remained of crucial importance to the war effort in a variety of ways. The Port War Signal Station just north of the lighthouse, operated by the Navy, continued to monitor all traffic at sea and into the Humber, as it had done during the First World War. The buildings on that site had been much expanded during the early years of the war. On the ground floor were the Coastguards, and now they were joined by the Royal Navy and later by the Royal Marines. Being a very busy estuary there was great need for a signal station on Spurn. At the beginning of the war Vera Cross, the coxswain's daughter, was 19, and had just left boarding school where she had acquired secretarial skills. Petty Officer Jago, the head chief coastguard in the area, asked her if she would be prepared to work for the Navy at the Port War Signal Station, to which she readily agreed, remaining there until 1947.

The road down to the Point was now fully operational. Lorries could now use it and local tradesmen were able to deliver milk and other fresh supplies. Nevertheless the railcar remained essential, especially for the transport of personnel at both ends of the line.

By 1942 men in coastal batteries were being replaced where possible by Home Guard, whilst fully trained women, both Auxiliary Service (A.T.S.) and Naval (Wrens) were beginning to play a more active role in military establishments. Louise Clarke, a Wren who had trained at Rochester and then worked for six months at Yarmouth, came to Spurn in 1942. She was one of the D.E.M.S. Wrens, and she remained at Spurn and Kilnsea until 1944. Her task was to work on the Naval D.E.M.S. site situated at the back of the *Blue Bell* pub. She described the naval tracer range, which was located in a large building about 30 feet high in the front and 50 feet in the rear. Here gunners were trained to use the armaments that they would use on board ships. In the tracer range everything was made to scale, with the trainees firing at model aircraft, and machines that could register their success of failure. The Wrens' job was to maintain the equipment and to work on other armament in large Nissen or Nissen-type huts (some of the huts put on Spurn and Kilnsea during the war were made by the Hull firm of Tarran, and were of a slightly different design), which were alongside the tracer range. To get to their work they had to manoeuvre between barbed wire barriers and, (far worse!) negotiate a passage past two geese called Harcroft and Lysander who lived at the back of the pub, where:

> you went into this big tracer range with Nissen huts where the Wrens worked. There was a very large table where they put the guns for maintenance. In front of the *Blue Bell* was a 12-pounder gun. Also apart from having the tracer range they had a plane coming over with a sleeve at the back and the men training on the range tried to hit the sleeve. They had a contraption like little cups with explosive inside and these with red silk parachutes were sent up and they used to fire on these for training too. Where they had mountings further out they took other guns – Oerlikon guns and ammunition. The Wrens had the job of painting them grey. They were the sort of guns you had on ships. The Naval officers who ran the range did not live at Spurn, but came out from Hull every day. Lt Commander Kurtain and staff were in charge. They came out with a different class or team – a coachful of men, every day – Ruskies, Americans came to Kilnsea and Spurn from Hull for the day. Americans came down for training and to see how things were done.

The D.E.M.S. Wrens lived in a brick-built hut alongside the lighthouse. As it had originally been meant for officers, by the standards of the day it was quite luxurious, 'nicely painted with lino floors', two toilets and two bathrooms. It was lit by electricity and was 'really cozy with a boiler house to heat the water and a stove with a tall chimney to heat the room'. The windows were quite large and the Wrens had to put up big wooden boards with vents to hide the lights inside until they went to bed. There were 10 Wrens in the hut. For their meals they went to a canteen near the Port War Signal Station, next to the Drewry shed, where at first they had a remarkably good cook, called Mrs Dale, who was soon poached by the officers! There was also a 'YM' (social facilities run by the YMCA) and a NAAFI nearby. At the NAAFI they would have a band sometimes. The YM tended to be 'just for eats and things'. In the lighthouse compound were quarters for Naval officers and Naval personnel, as well as the lighthouse-keepers' accommodation. Two of the stewards who worked in the compound were Wrens from Louise's hut. However each area was totally separate, and Louise and her fellow D.E.M.S. Wrens apparently kept very much to their own part of the peninsula and tended to fraternize only with

Navy personnel and keep themselves separate from the Army. She remembers:

> four or five different establishments – Able, Baker, Charlie, Dog, Easy. Able was the far end of the Point [Spurn Fort presumably], Baker was south of the lighthouse, Charlie was north of the lighthouse, Dog was… [perhaps the Warren] – didn't refer to it much, Easy was Kilnsea [Godwin Battery].

The Wrens sometimes walked to the lifeboat cottages. Louise Clarke remembered two elderly ladies there selling greeting cards, writing paper and sewing materials in a room in one of the cottages. Those would be the Hoopell sisters, whom Vera Cross lodged with after her father retired. Vera remembered them doing all the washing and ironing for the officers on the Point, though she has no recollection of their having a little shop. On one occasion some ATS (Auxiliary Territorial Service) girls came down as part of a mixed battery of Army and ATS. Two of the girls were drivers and they were placed in the little room at the end of Louise's hut where they usually kept their bikes. Others were placed in the Nissen huts. Several times the Wrens went up the lighthouse to have a look round:

125 *The lighthouse compound during the Second World War. The circle of paving stones in the centre of the compound shows where Smeaton's lighthouse stood. The D.E.M.S. Wrens' quarters were in the brick building at the bottom of the picture. Inside the compound extra buildings were erected, and some structures became two storeys. Officers were quartered there during the war.*

It was spotlessly clean. There was a fire there. You could see your face in the gleaming brass. One of the men (or both) was making something [a carpet?] with hessian, with a very large needle and wool, stitching over and over again in numerous colours. One of them already had done a roll of it.

To get to work the Wrens had to go down to Kilnsea every day. At first they got a lift but then got bikes, though if weather was particularly bad they would 'pinch a lift in an army truck and put their bikes inside it'. The road of course was brand new then. They also went on the old Drewry but never saw a steam engine or the sail bogie.

When they could get time off, they went mainly to the *Blue Bell* pub, unless transport was going to the *Marquis of Granby* in Easington. John Clubley was the landlord of the *Blue Bell*. He was in the army so worked as a soldier in the day and ran the pub at night. The Wrens also helped Carrie at the café – Louise said that there was nowhere else to go and they got to know people that way. The menu was 'Egg and chips, sausage and chips, beans and chips.' When they first arrived (all in their early twenties) they were carefully chaperoned:

> Petty Officer Smith was in charge when we first came to Spurn. She was not young. Because there were so many men the Wrens had to troupe [sic] out in a crocodile! She took her duties very seriously. When she left a younger Petty Officer came. She was more liberal.

In November 1942 Les Park was posted back to Spurn, but now as master-gunner. He found many changes; most notably the road had been built. The armaments had been augmented – 'The twins had arrived along with the 6 and all the bits and pieces.' Like Louise, Park remembered that behind the *Blue Bell* pub were beach defence guns, a 12-pounder according to Louise and, according to Park, in 1940 the armaments also included two Lewis guns for AA work, 'which they mounted on rails. There were 100 rounds per magazine. We only had 47 (50) on our Lewis guns.' When he returned in 1942 'a whole lot of beach defence had been formed – 13-pounders, spigot mortars, Oerlikons and such'. When Park was master gunner he had:

apart from 6, 4.7, 4 in Naval, six-pounders, two 13-pounders, no. 7 dial sight and such. (These were for beach defence, we hadn't any horses, just manhandle them or towed by truck.) Add to this we had six spigot mortars, 72mm I seem to remember, and we practised with these firing at oil drums of the beach – beach defence again. In for good measure four Oerlikons, add small arms, bombs, grenades all needing drill and training etc. etc. A day was pretty full.

1943

In January 1943 the big guns at Spurn and Kilnsea, like others in coastal defence, were put on a care and maintenance status. The war in Italy was going well for the Allies, and the artillery camp on the site of what is now Sunny Cliff became a camp for Italian prisoners of war, who were mainly put to work on maintaining the sea defences. The prisoners were dressed in brown uniforms 'emblazoned with huge circular and square coloured patches, just in case they managed to get themselves lost'! Louise remembered them marching past the *Blue Bell* – 'The Wrens were not pleased to see them as they used to pinch the red parachutes and use them as neckerchiefs.' Carrie remembered looking into their Nissen huts and seeing home-made spaghetti draped over the rafters to dry! Towards the end of the war they were given considerable freedom, and some of them ended up staying after hostilities had ended. Arthur Piggott, who was staying with his grandparents in Kilnsea whilst his father was in the army, remembered the Italian POWs well too:

> They were keen to obtain bits of alloy and Perspex that we had scavenged from crashed aircraft, and they would fashion them into rings, bracelets and cigarette lighters. They would also ask for small portrait photographs which they would somehow fit into the top of the rings – a marvelous piece of design and ingenuity.

Tony Regan, who was a young boy during the war, also remembered the Italian POWs fishing on a homemade raft off Kilnsea, tethered by a long line from the shore. When the line broke and the raft went adrift, there was panic on because the people on shore thought they were trying to escape, 'but the two men were only too pleased to be rescued'.

126 *The lighthouse area during the Second World War. A First World War mine can be seen to the right of the Wrens' hut.*

Many other people in the area during wartime were skilled craftsmen. The lifeboatmen made models of boats and other home-made objects. Carrie Leonard's and Vera Cross's autograph albums are full of delightful drawings by military personnel. And at Christmas 1941 the men at Godwin Battery decided to spend some of their spare time in making presents for orphaned children. Carrie wrote:

> They contacted the matron of the local orphanage, and as there were a couple of hundred of the men, they asked for a corresponding number of the children's names and promised to make toys for them. The names went into a hat back at the camp, and each man drew a name … each toy showed just how much care, thought and time had been spent on it. One in particular impressed me, both by reason of the time and care that had been taken with it and the beauty of the craftsmanship. It was a model of a pleasure yacht, and the decks were all inlaid with small plates of glass so that it was possible to see below the upper deck into the cocktail bar below. Here, everything was complete to the tiniest detail. There were tiny bar counters, a minute cabinet, and even the tiny scarlet painted stools had not been forgotten.

In the winter of 1943 Alf Shearsmith, aged 24, came to the Royal Observer Post at Spurn, to join 'Easy One, Group Ten, Midland Area'. He was to remain until 1945. Alf had been born with both feet turned inwards and had to undergo many

operations. When the war broke out he was very keen to join the R.A.F. but he was graded three, which meant that he was unfit for that service, so he joined the Home Guard. Later his interest in aircraft led him to apply to join the Royal Observer Corps. He did not know the Spurn area before he was posted there, but, like other service personnel travelling to Spurn, his journey began at the Baker Street terminal of Connor & Graham's route out to South Holderness:

> on a small wooden-seated saloon bus at the Baker Street terminus in Hull, a city in total darkness because of blackout regulations. The passengers are a mixed bunch of villagers and military personnel returning from leave to the many service camps covering the four-mile length of land from Kilnsea to Spurn Point … As well as collecting fares the conductress has several other duties: delivering parcels, calling for doctors' prescriptions and medicines, and looking after passengers' welfare. This makes for an entertaining but slow journey; also an extremely uncomfortable one – the hard wooden slatted seats definitely leave an impression on one's rear! Rattling along at a slow pace of knots through the winding country lanes, we pass several army camps and, near the village of Ottringham, numerous high radio masts … The only passengers to dismount at Kilnsea are the military, many of whom belong to the massive anti-aircraft establishment nearby. Those left usually have a long wait for the driver of a rail passenger contraption, who needs

Bull Sand Fort.
proceeding 4th Aug 1941.
Gunner Lutherd
R.A.
3rd August 1941.

" We're off on another
job o' work."

HSpifford. (L/Sgt.)
17/2/41.

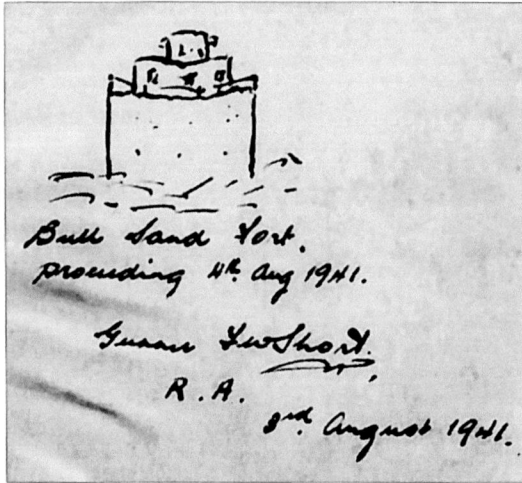

127 *From Vera Cross's autograph album.*

pints of Dutch courage to give him the strength and daring necessary for their remaining journey down the Spurn peninsula. ... The truck taking us on the four-mile trip is nicknamed 'The Drury' ... It is powered by two diesel engines and built like a tram, with engines and controls at both ends to save turning round; more wooden slatted seats ensure that one receives two deep impressions of one's journey! When the driver, a man of few words, finally appears, we are ready for four miles of shake, rattle and roll, dropping people at small gun emplacements on the way, where we criss-cross the narrow concrete vehicular road. This part is the worst – 15 mph top speed and so noisy that conversation is impossible. I have never experienced such shaking except, perhaps, at a fair.

Hull was still being bombed in 1943, and in July three Dorniers that had been involved in a raid on Hull were brought down, one 15 miles east of Spurn, another over Long Riston and the third was shot down into the sea just off Spurn Head. All the crew were killed. On the night of 2 October a Junkers 188 was seen half a mile from the lighthouse. Having been lit up by the searchlights it banked too steeply and then crashed on a mud bank just offshore, and exploded. That was apparently the first aircraft of its type to come down in Great Britain. Again, all the crew were killed.

It was in July 1943 that another contingent of Wrens came to Spurn. These were destined for the

Port War Signal Station, to release the men who worked there for a more offensive role. One of them was Sybil Blewett, who wrote:

Sixteen V/S (Visual Signallers) Wrens, having finished training in Morse/Semaphore/Flag hoisting at HMS *Cabbala* in July 1943 were drafted to Spurn Point to take over the PWSS from Naval personnel. (They were none too keen to go, I recall!) ... We worked the Navy watch-keeping system. That was the core, a Petty Officer (P/O) arrived to be Executive Officer, a V.A.D. to care for our health, a cook and several stewards to feed us ... Already at the PWSS were Lloyd's Shipping Service men, Chiefs and P.O.s who were recalled for war service, led by Lt. Jago. All of these lived in houses in Easington. In addition the XDO [Extended Defence Officer] and four officers lived in the Officers' Quarters with some Marines nearby.

Most of that first group remained there until VE Day (May 1945). Sybil and her fellow Wrens took to life on the Point pretty well:

At first we were wishing we were in Portsmouth as Spurn seemed so isolated, but surprisingly it was a busy station, signal-wise. Fishing trawlers, naval craft, the lifeboat and American liberty boats (one went aground at the end of the Point of course!) went in and out through the boom vessels. Bombers from Lincolnshire flew out overhead, keeping us all on our toes ... We shared the Point with a whole garrison of gunners, Royal Observer Corps, lifeboat personnel and their families. There was plenty of amusement and a very lively YMCA. When we had shore leave we went to Hull (for the day) or to Beverley, Leeds, or York for longer stays. The whole Point buzzed with activity – we could boat or swim on the Humber side. Some of us had bicycles so we went exploring; I remember going to church in Patrington … I am sure that many of us who were there at the time came to recognise our stay as something precious. There was much beauty to be seen from the bridge as the sun went down over the sea and sand. The wind sometimes howled overhead and the sea and the Humber met in great showers as we dashed over to the YM. But, we were young and everything was fresh and exciting, and we were proud to belong to the Navy.

Like the D.E.M.S. Wrens the PWSS Wrens used bicycles to get about, or went on the railcar to Kilnsea. The tennis court near the PWSS was little used because 'tennis balls were few and far between and racquets irreplaceable', but table tennis was available in the YMCA, and there was plenty of entertainment and dances.

Indeed Spurn and Kilnsea must have been a very lively place when they were packed with military personnel, most of them young and prepared to have a good time when they could, and mindful of the dangers they were soon to find themselves in. Carrie Leonard threw herself into the social life of the camps, and was the life and soul of any event. Her reminiscences are full of anecdotes about the wartime jollifications. Her two autograph albums demonstrate the artistic and literary skills of some of the people she met. Many too were musical, and numerous concerts and other musical events took place at Kilnsea and Spurn during the war years. The first one Carrie mentions took place in 1940, a low point in the war, when men who had been brought to Spurn after Dunkirk needed moral support:

To raise the drooping spirits of the men, the boys of a Coastal Defence Unit decided to give a concert, and very soon all the usual preparations were in full swing. To take the minds of the returned men from all they had gone through, the gunners concentrated upon making fun of their own efforts. One of the sergeants walked on to the stage and gave a very amusing demonstration of a gun team in action. He impersonated a stuttering sergeant and when one

of the stage hands gave the warning of approaching aircraft. he bawled 'f-f-f-f-f- … well, its too late to f-f-fire now, but f-f-f-f-fall out and we'll f-f-f-fire when they come back.' Small thoughtful entertainments like these soon helped the Dunkirk boys to get a normal grip on life again, and they left us in a happier state than that in which they arrived.

128 *From Carrie Leonard's autograph album.*

When things were fairly quiet at the camps it was sometimes possible for wives to visit their husbands. Carrie remembered one such occasion when the men had worked hard to brighten up the camp, and had constructed as a 'crowning glory, and the pride and joy of every man's heart a huge clean bed of sand, carefully edged with white stones which they had carried from the beach with much toil and labour. Laid out on the sand, in small white round pebbles, was the regimental badge of the unit'. They had spent days searching for pebbles of the same shape and size, the pattern had been carefully measured and marked out. 'When they had all been collected at the guard room, the whole group was led round to inspect 'the badge' … there was Mick, rooting happily in the middle of it, and stones were flying wildly in all directions; not one was left in its original position'.

1944

In March 1944 there was much excitement when the A.T.S. were to be stationed at Kilnsea. Like the Wrens, the A.T.S. had come to the camp to relieve men for duties overseas. Carrie watched as the first truckload of girls arrived, and inspected 'the wilderness which was to be their new home'. It did not take them long to find her little café, and they found Carrie to be a sympathetic listener. She soon became privy to their secrets, and several romances started over the café tables. The behaviour of the A.T.S. girls was rather different to the men they replaced. On one occasion, after a reorganisation of the huts, one girl, having been told that she would have to go into another room and leave her friends, burst into tears. Another 'bolshie' one organised a 'lock-out strike'. No-one was to be allowed to enter the hut until the officers agreed that the girls should remain with their friends. A password and signal was agreed upon in case anyone had to leave the hut for any reason. Carrie recorded that 'All turned out well, fortunately, since the punishment in the army for mutiny is rather severe. The girls had their own way and everyone was happy.' When the A.T.S. arrived, air raids had become less common, but one night the alarm sounded and the guns went into action. Carrie wondered how the girls were standing

up to it, for the sky was a sheer mass of flame, and bombs were bursting all round the site. The next day, some of the girls came in, and:

> far from being shaken they told me some of the amusing things that had happened during the raid. One of the girls was on the Height and Range Finder, and looking into it she saw an 'object' which she reported, 'Parachute with black object attached'. Immediately the officer in charge grabbed a Sten gun, and followed by the sergeant major, who also had a Sten, he made his way to the beach. The girls could hear them shouting 'Hands up!', in a voice full of excitement, and they roared with laughter, for just after they had rushed away the object was recognised as a canister of incendiaries. The idea of the dignified officer shouting at a canister appealed to their sense of humour and he was never allowed to forget his lapse from dignity.

In February 1944 Robert Cross and his wife left the peninsula, after an association of 43 years. Cross had first served on the crew from 1901 until 1908, then returned as coxswain in 1912. His retirement was truly the end of an era. At 67 Robert Cross the lifeboat coxswain was well over retirement age, but he had been asked to stay on until a suitable replacement was ready. In 1940, when Cross received the Victoria Medal and the RNLI Gold Medal for the rescue of men from the steam-ship *Gurth*, a testimonial stated that 'from 1906 till the time of the present war he has taken part in a hundred and eighty-six launches of the boat with the saving of 150 lives. Since September of last year the boat has been the means of saving 11 crews totalling 207 men.' Other rescues were to follow, too numerous to mention, but one was outstanding and took place when he was aged sixty-six. On the evening of 6 January 1943 the extended defence officer at the Port War Signal Station asked the lifeboat to go to the aid of 'Phillips Defence Unit no. 1', which was a large anchored craft with anti-aircraft guns mounted upon it. This had broken from its moorings and gone ashore inside the boom defence. The weather was cold with heavy snow showers, and the crew must have been delighted when they were told that a tug had gone to the aid of the vessel and they could return home. However, just as they had hauled the lifeboat back inside the lifeboat house Coxswain

129 *The Port War Signal Station Wrens at Spurn, November 1944. Left to right: Joyce Green, Gladys Wesley, Nan Ireland, P/O Armitage, Florence Roxborough, Margaret McAloon, Jean St Pierre, P/O Law, Sybil Cheverton, Betty Probert, Agnes Hindley, Audrey Cooper, Joan Scotchmer, Connie Thompson, Nurse Wilkinson.*

Cross received a telephone call reporting a vessel aground on the Binks. The crew stood by, intending to go out when the tide turned, but then were told that another defence unit, no. 3, had also broken adrift and become entangled in the boom defence. The men were firing distress rockets and were in great danger. The lifeboat was relaunched and by the light of searchlights from the shore that both helped and hindered the rescue efforts, Cross and his crew eventually rescued the men. This took five attempts, and the lifeboat sustained considerable damage from the long steel spikes that surrounded the defence unit and were intended to deter boarders. The lifeboat landed the rescued men but the vessel on the Binks remained in trouble, so the crew, despite their tiredness, had to go out again. At 3 a.m. the lifeboat found the trawler *Almondine* lying on her side with water pouring over her. Despite almost insurmountable difficulties, and after no fewer than 12 attempts, Cross and his crew managed to get 19 men off the trawler. The skipper and officers

remained aboard and were just debating whether they should also abandon ship, when their ship's lights went out and radio contact was lost. The lifeboat searched for them for an hour and a half, but eventually had to give up and take the survivors back to Spurn. Cross later learnt that the *Almondine* had been found by a tug drifting at the mouth of the Humber and been taken in tow. For that rescue Robert Cross received the RNLI's Gold Medal, his reserve mechanic, George Richards, was awarded the Silver Medal and crew George Stephenson, Samuel Cross, William Major, Sidney Harman and George Shakesby received the Bronze Medal each. When Coxswain Cross retired the RNLI drew up a list of his achievements, including the fact that he had taken part in the rescue of no fewer than 471 lives!

The Cross's daughter, Vera, who was secretary to the Extended Defence Officer at the Port War Signal Station, remained until after the war. Both Robert and his wife Sarah loved Spurn and were

130 *'The BOP [Battery Observation Post] boys' at Kilnsea.*

involved with every aspect of its life. Cross's replacement was John Mason, whose wartime job was on a minesweeper. Having been offered the job of coxswain of Spurn lifeboat he gave his wife Lily a glowing account of the place they were to move to. Lily found that the reality was very different. After travelling from Hull on a Connor & Graham bus for two and a half hours, then half an hour on a rattling railcar, she arrived in the pitch black of a Spurn night:

> The next morning all I could see was sand and water, the North Sea and the river Humber, and Spurn Point sandwiched in between ... The sand seemed to get into everything. Everything in the pantry had to be covered up. We couldn't set the table without having to wash the crockery. Sand got into the washing ... There were heaps of sand when we shook the rug.

Lily hated every solitary minute of it, but she had to stick it out until 1949.

People were always coming and going at Spurn, and it was in 1944 that Hilda Sparrow, in her late teens, came to the peninsula as a cook to the Wrens. Hilda stayed on the Point for just over a year, but when the officers' cook went off sick they asked her to take over. They lived separate to the Wrens. Better food than Wrens – had more choice. Some wanted kippers, some kedgeree, some sausage and bacon.

Messy going on!' She remembered particularly the winter she was there, yet another really hard one, when they had to be dug out of their huts as the snow was so deep.

Probably weather was one of the things that many of the military personnel will have remembered from their time at Spurn. Living on a flat narrow peninsula surrounded by water the elements seem very close at hand. Hilda remembered the glorious summer when they could lie on the beach and sunbathe. She remembered the dark summer nights when some of the girls working on the peninsula would have assignations on the beach (and had to beware the big searchlights that might suddenly illuminate them)! Sybil remembered the wonderful Spurn sunsets she saw from the top of the Port War Signal Station. Alf Shearsmith of the Royal Observer Corps remembered many hours during the warm summer days lazing on the beach, 'surrounded by barbed wire and concrete defences'.

By 1944 the Spurn and Kilnsea forts' principal role was for training rather than their previous defensive tasks. As Carrie wrote of that period, 'Troops came and went, and there was constant activity on the Point, but even so, the whole world seemed to be holding its breath waiting for that supremely important event, the opening of the Second Front!! 1943 came and went, and everyone said "it will happen in Spring", but Spring came and went and still the world waited.' During the long run-up to D-Day all leave was cancelled as any information had to be kept top secret. However the fateful day, 6 June, came at last:

> One morning I walked past the Ack Ack site and noticed that everyone seemed to be walking about in a daze. I had no radio and the newspapers arrived about 11 o'clock, so I had no idea that anything unusual had happened. Then one of the girls saw me and said, 'It's happened, Carrie', and that was the way in which I learned of the event for which the world had been waiting. The invasion of the Continent had started!! The whole world's attention was focused on that little strip of the Normandy beach, and the question in everyone's mind was 'Will they be able to hold on?' Here, on the Point, we felt really helpless for we could do nothing, and we could only think of Milton's words 'They also serve who only stand and wait.'

At the end of 1944 the 9.2-inch guns at Kilnsea were removed from their mountings. However, vigilance over the skies was still very necessary. On 23/24 December a unit of Heinkel 111s carrying V1s (known as buzz bombs) came over the East Coast to bomb Manchester. They missed their intended target, with some landing in Yorkshire. At Kilnsea Carrie and her friends were all looking forward to what they were certain would be their last wartime Christmas:

Because of this we were all taken by surprise when, on Christmas morning, we were awakened by the first 'Buzz Bombs' we had ever seen. This activity of the enemy after such a long period of quiet made a terrific difference to all our plans, for most of the boys and girls who had expected to be off duty were kept at 'Action Stations', and instead of the bright, cheery time we had expected, we played bridge for the whole of the evening with two of the boys who were fortunate enough to be off duty.

Whilst all the military activity was going on throughout the long years of the war, daily life still carried on in Kilnsea. Most of the young men of the village had left, but the older men that remained played their part in the war effort, if only by keeping the farms going. At Westmere Farm a branch of the Clubley family had been farming since the beginning of the century. George Edwin Clubley, born 1868 at Cliff Farm, had died in 1938. His wife and son John kept the dairy farm going, but John by then had another job, as licensee of the *Blue Bell* pub. At some stage during the war his mother Eden moved into the pub, leaving the farmhouse to the military for accommodation. The *Blue Bell* tended to be the pub favoured by the military personnel stationed at Kilnsea and Spurn, but nevertheless the *Crown* too flourished throughout the war years – there could never be too many licensed premises near an army camp!

131 *Mock holiday brochure produced at Spurn during the Second World War. 'Meadowsweet' is Spurn Point and 'Avverbottle' is Kilnsea.*

132   *Olive and Craggs Clubley with their daughter Ivy Piggott and grandson Arthur returning from fishing, early 1930s.*

The largest farm in Kilnsea was still Grange Farm. Ernest Tennison and his wife Daisy (née Clubley) were running that farm during the war, with the help of one farm labourer, Harry Docherty. Over the road at 1 and 2 Cliff View lived Mrs Edith Clubley, her son Wally, her other son Redvers and his wife Doris and other members of that large family. Another branch of the Clubleys, headed by John Craggs Clubley, lived at Rose Cottage, two former coastguard cottages now converted into one. Craggs and his wife Olive had raised a very large family in that little cottage. Craggs himself was now an old man but there was still quite a large group of people living at his cottage. His two sons Ken and Lambert and he and his wife were joined by his daughter Ivy, whose husband Thomas Piggott was serving in the Army in Malta. Arthur Piggott was nine when war broke out and his brother was just over a year older. The two boys enjoyed living in the middle of a military zone. They travelled to school at Easington in a horse-drawn wagon covered with a green canopy 'similar to those seen in old cowboy films', with long forms down each side and had blankets to keep their knees warm. In exceptionally bad weather the Kilnsea children were ferried to school in Mr Jack Tennison's Fiat saloon.

Arthur remembered the headmaster, Mr Skelton, as a tall and distinguished-looking man, who with his wife, in charge of the infants, ran the school with great discipline and efficiency. Like most teachers of that period he did not hesitate to use corporal punishment. Cyril Skelton's son, Robin, was to become very famous indeed, as a poet of international fame. Arthur remembered:

We were at war with Germany and the school windows were crisscrossed with sticky tape to reduce flying glass should the school suffer an air attack. One near miss I do remember was when a German bomber returning after a daylight raid flew low over the school with guns blazing. We needed no persuading to dive for cover under the desks. The enemy plane was fired on by the guns stationed beyond the school, about where Turmarr Villas now stand. Unfortunately this was one that got away. One of our stranger lessons was being taught to knit squares for blankets for the troops and what with gathering nettles and rosehips, presumably for medicinal purposes, we all felt that we were helping the war effort. All this new-found patriotism along with normal school lessons kept us busy. Nobody really needed confirmation of a war going on as there were constant reminders such as the firing of the guns in the evening and the sky ablaze with many fires from the nightly bombing of Hull and the other docks along both banks of the Humber. No-one slept much during the evening and many school days were cancelled because of it.

Arthur's uncle was in the Home Guard and with his friend shared a Browning automatic rifle and one bullet! One of the warden's tasks was checking on the blackout, and Kilnsea must have seemed to be right in the thick of it at times as the air raids became more frequent:

> with sirens screaming their warning nearly every night. We could not resist going out to watch, even though we were not really allowed to. It gave us a great thrill to see enemy bombers caught in the beam of the searchlights and how we would cheer if one was hit and had to turn back with engines billowing smoke and flames.

Wartime rations were very restricted, but near the sea the meagre fare could be augmented with fish, eels and crabs, and most people managed to obtain a few rabbits. Arthur's grandfather Craggs certainly had many skills in snaring rabbits, which he passed on to the two boys. Sea coal could be obtained from the beach and they were often sent with sacks to gather as much as they could when the tides had washed up a good haul. One day they got more than they expected:

> The snow blew into our faces as we struggled with the wet bags of coal, making our task even more unpleasant than it already was. Suddenly we spotted a large wooden packing case washing up on the tide. We pulled it onto the beach and quickly smashed it open. We found it contained dozens and dozens of tins. Printed on the tins were the words 'Pagoda cakes' ... and inside we found individually wrapped soft sweets, about fifty to a tin. They were about an inch long, conical shaped and spiralled as if made with an icing bag. They were also of many colours and very decorative. Throwing caution to the winds we decided to sample a few and found them to be extremely sweet and delicious.

They gave up coal-gathering and filled the sacks with Pagoda cakes instead. When eventually they told the family of their discovery more people enjoyed the cakes. It was only some time later that they found that the cakes had been destined for troops serving abroad, and were actually 'worm cakes'!

Those episodes where cargoes came ashore were quite frequent in Kilnsea and Easington. Robin Skelton remembered one occasion when a whole cargo of lard in hermetically sealed containers landed on the beach. Everyone came out, with perambulators, pushcarts or wheelbarrows. All was safely stowed away by noon but the Customs men heard of the windfall:

> They met with blank stares, evasions, and very little hospitality. Searches produced nothing, until it was decided that they had better be mollified. One of two of the most richly endowed beachcombers surrendered a small portion of their loot. The Revenue men departed ... and village ovens were soon filled with home-baked pies and bread as never before. The supply lasted until the end of the war.

The people of Kilnsea and Spurn were much changed by the coming of the military to their small corner of Yorkshire. Carrie said that she felt that she had 'met a world' and made many friends that she would never forget. In their turn many of the military personnel never forgot the time they spent in that unusual posting. As Carrie wrote, 'Most of the men on their arrival complained bitterly about the place, but most were loath to leave. Many have written from far-off fields wishing they were back.'

1945

The New Year of 1945 brought a stream of good news. To the people at Kilnsea and Spurn it was almost like a peacetime spring:

> By now, we were certain of victory and all we had to do was wait for it as best we could. At last came that never-to-be-forgotten day in May, VE Day. Naturally some of the gunners made their way to the pub to celebrate, and after a while out they rolled, and they crowded around the old iron cannon which stands outside the pub as an ornament. They had a sergeant with them who entered into the spirit of the game and he drilled them in earnest. They yelled for ammunition, and as none was forthcoming, they tore up lumps of grass and hurled them into the air, all the while carrying out their gun drill perfectly. At last, one of them yelling that the plane was at crossing point, hurled his 'shell'

into the air, and down it came on his unsuspecting head, knocking him unconscious. That seemed to sober them up slightly, but when the lad recovered they formed up in three ranks and marched away noisily in search of fresh sport. The war in Europe was over, and these men had played their part in winning this victory.

On the Point the celebrations were just as joyful. Miriam Shead, whose husband Douglas, was the lifeboat engineer remembered:

> What a night! Everyone on Spurn was invited to the Army Recreation Hall, high ranking to the unknown, of course the officers had the pick of their choice, quite a few of our friends just stood around. I could see some were not too happy, so when I got the chance, I spoke to the bandmaster & asked him to play some music that would get everyone on the floor. We sure did, changing partners, knees-up, Can-Can ... the lot, even getting hold of the officers and making them dance to 'Maybe it's because I'm a Londoner'. We all danced, laughed and sang our heads off. Some people finished at the Point collapsing on the sandy beach. Some even finished

up in the water – that was Spurn's way of declaring PEACE to all our boys and girls.

Carrie observed the changes as the place took on a peacetime air:

> The beaches were cleared and paths made through the maze of barbed wire. A few visitors began to arrive. Certainly it was not by any means a peacetime summer, as there were still plenty of troops around, and some units still had several shooting practices. There was also plenty of barbed wire draping itself about the place. Still one must not complain, as at least one could wander along the shore, swim, or sunbathe.

They were now waiting for VJ Day. One of Carrie's bridge-playing friends returned to his barracks one day, where a huge piece of paper on his bunk read 'The War's over, Mr Attlee says so' written on it. Carrie's first thought was for all the boys she knew, 'who were prisoners of war in Japanese hands, and the ones who were in Burma fighting. To think at last that they were free!'

Seven

The Post-war Period, 1945-59

Although the war had officially finished on 15 August 1945, Spurn and Kilnsea were to be affected by it for many years to come. The military did not in fact leave until 1959, and there were to be periods in the 1950s when the Humber defences were reactivated. Nevertheless, the people of the district could breathe more easily, and many celebrations followed the ending of hostilities – victory teas, sports events and family parties when loved ones returned home from distant parts.

For the little school on Spurn Point the end of the war marked the end of its life. The educational authority decided that it was no longer viable, and the improved transport facilities offered by the road down the peninsula meant that, like the Kilnsea children, the children on Spurn could be bussed to Easington by Connor & Graham. On 21 November 1945 Mrs Beal, the teacher, recorded in the logbook that two men had been to itemise the furniture and the coal. A list was sent to county hall. On 23 November the vicar of Easington fetched the prayer and hymn books and 13 December was the last day of Spurn school. The Easington logbook on 11 January 1946 records that 11 Spurn children had been transferred to its school.

Throughout the war the Point, indeed the entire peninsula, had remained inaccessible to all but the lifeboat crew, the lighthouse-keepers and the military. The wildlife of the area was apparently little disturbed. School logbooks indicate that the children were encouraged to study the bird life and some soldiers with time on their hands took an interest too. From about 1943, when the focus of the war shifted from the home front, many troops left the peninsula and only small numbers remained to

man the batteries and take care of the sea defences. To some extent the peninsula reverted to its pre-war isolation. However the road was a new factor and, as more people came to have cars, Spurn's isolation was soon to be breached.

Spurn Bird Observatory

1945 was a significant year for the naturalists, for it marked the establishment of the Spurn Bird Observatory. Warren Cottage, well-recognised by the ornithologists as the natural headquarters for

133   *Ralph Chislett, chairman of Spurn Bird Observatory, is standing outside Warren Cottage.*

an observatory, was now vacant. Ralph Chislett, an accountant by profession, had delayed his retirement until the end of the war. He and his wife Lilian then moved from the West Riding to Masham, in the North Riding, but Spurn was always a site of particular interest. The Army Lands Department was requested to allow Chislett and his colleagues to lease Warren Cottage. That was agreed (the lieutenant-general in charge at York, Lieutenant-General Sir Phillip Christleton, was an experienced ornithologist), and Spurn Bird Observatory was set up, under the auspices of the Yorkshire Naturalists' Union.

Chislett wrote of the Warren area before the Second World War thus:

> Often had we looked at Warren Cottage with its garden and trees and bushes surrounded by a hedge, and by rabbit-eaten turf and Marram Grass. Pied Flycatchers and Redstarts were often present, and occasionally Barred Warblers. The entrance to the Warren was then closed to motorists. The road did not exist. A single rail-track ran from Kilnsea to the Point, traversed by a lorry [sic], sometimes propelled by wind and sail, to serve the needs of the lighthouse keepers, the lifeboat crew, and the military camp at the Point. Guns and their servers, and barbed wire were absent from the Warren.

They found the area somewhat changed after the war. Warren Cottage itself had been used throughout the war by the military. It was sur-rounded by army buildings and Nissen-type huts stretching as far as the present gate. Barbed wire was there in profusion, and gun emplacements, in a semi-circle of four, were located just south of the buildings. The peninsula was still mined, and visitors to Warren Cottage had to be very careful in certain areas. The railway track remained, behind the cottage, but now the Point was accessible by a concrete road, which ran between the cottage and the Humber foreshore.

Members of the YNU set about furnishing and equipping Warren Cottage. The principal people involved at that time were George Ainsworth, John Lord and R.M. Garnett. Women were few: Eva Crackles was the exception. She was then more of an ornithologist than the botanist that she later became. She made her first visit to Warren Cottage on 24 March 1945, and came again on 2 June, when 'we followed the new military road from the *Blue Bell* inn.' In October 1946 she recorded in her diary 'I was driven down to Chalk Bank by Mr Chislett, who has a big car and is very generous in giving lifts. Barbed wire in marsh.'

The cottage has two small bedrooms, a kitchen, and what became the common room, a room that had once been two. There was no bathroom and no toilet. Carrie Leonard, who lost a lot of customers for her café after the military left, now found herself catering for the bird-watchers.

134 *Spring-cleaning Warren Cottage, 1954.*

135 *Eva Crackles and a friend walking towards Warren Cottage, 1950s. The building on the left remains, and its western section is now the Yorkshire Wildlife Trust's Information Centre.*

136 *Chalk Bank 1951. Many military buildings still remained in this area. Note the barbed wire, after which 'Wire Dump' was named by the naturalists.*

Every effort was made to provide coverage for the migration periods – March to June, and July to December. Several retired people like Chislett himself were able to cover weekdays. At that time only a minority of people had cars, and access to Spurn by public transport involved quite lengthy journeys, especially for those who came from the West and the North Ridings. The nearest railway station was Patrington, from where a bus provided the link to Kilnsea. As described by Chislett, several of the members of the observatory were teachers, who brought pupils to Spurn to help with recording. Anyone who thought they were coming for a holiday was given short shrift. In the *Naturalist* of 1946 Chislett wrote:

The most interesting development of 1945 has been the establishment of a ringing station at Spurn, which had been under consideration before 1939.

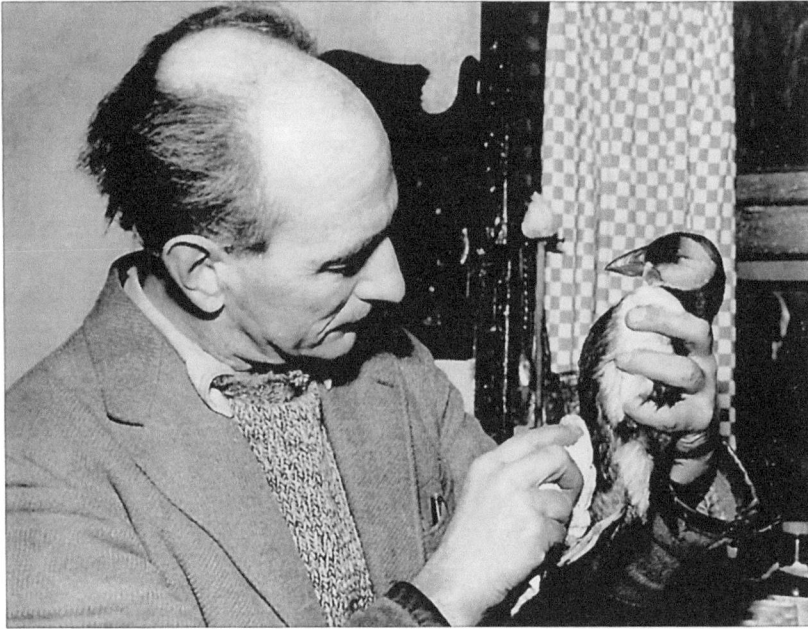

137 *George Ainsworth with a puffin.*

Garnett, Ainsworth and C.E.A. Burnham who, with J. Lord and myself form the Ringing Sub-Committee [of the YNU], met there in September for the selection of a suitable site. With the war over the War Department readily gave consent and has indeed been most helpful in many ways, amongst other things loaning the use of a hut pending release of Warren Cottage.

An early requirement was to build a Heligoland trap at the Warren and, on 17 November 1945, the observatory ringed its first bird, a blackbird, which was recovered near Grimsby on 19 February 1947. In the early years of Spurn Bird Observatory bird-ringing was the absolute priority for most of the naturalists staying at Warren Cottage. Ringing had begun in the early years of the 20th century, the first person in England to practise it being Henry (Harry) Witherby (1873-1943), a noted British ornithologist and founding editor of *British Birds* magazine. The study of migration was no new thing at Spurn and Spurn Bird Observatory was standing on the shoulders of people like John Cordeaux and H. Eagle Clarke, who had been such stalwarts of bird recording in the Humber area at the end of the 19th century. In 1937 the British Trust for Ornithology began co-ordinating the ring-

ing of birds, having taken over the scheme begun by Harry Witherby. The first bird observatory in Britain, Skokholm, had been established in 1933. Spurn Bird Observatory was the first mainland observatory, and it was to be followed by many more. Heligoland traps, large constructions made of wood and wire, are usually funnel-shaped. Birds can be driven into them and moved down to a narrowing section where a catching box allows the ringers to remove them and ring them. Until 1956 that was the usual way of catching birds. Thereafter mist-nets, a Japanese invention, allowed birders to become more mobile, and to catch birds in more localities. The nets were made of very fine black thread and, when hung vertically from bamboo poles in front of bushes or shrubs, were almost invisible to birds. Another Heligoland trap was erected in 1949 in the Point dunes, but it had to be taken down in 1950 and moved to Wire Dump, because during the reactivation of the Humber defences during the Cold War the army bulldozed the dunes in front of the gun emplacements to improve sight lines. In 1951 a double-ended trap (later made into a normal Heligoland trap) was built in the Chalk Bank area, but it was abandoned in 1972. In 1956 Chalk Bank East trap was erected in the dunes on the seaward side, but it was almost washed away in 1963, when the sea came over at that point. The trap had to be taken down. In 1960 a trap was built at the rear of what was to become the Pilots' Tower on the Point, and was removed in 1978. In 1966 the Hollow Trap on the Point was built.

From the beginning of Spurn Bird Observatory the daily census was an essential part of the routine. Every evening those people staying in Warren Cottage congregated in the common room for the recording of the 'log'. That routine has gone on every day since. As well as keeping a log, the accreditation of any bird observatory is based on its having a defined recording area that has been covered for at least two years, with coverage being maintained for at least the main migration periods. The observatory must be able to offer training/ringing facilities to visiting ringers and be able to arrange accommodation for visitors. Spurn's recording area encompassed the peninsula, and went as far north as the road from the *Blue Bell* to the *Crown*. It has been slightly extended in more recent years. Over the years Spurn Bird Observatory became increasingly attractive to bird-watchers and, during the migration season, some people found themselves having to bring tents and sleep outside.

Soon after hostilities had ceased people began to make use of the new road to go onto the peninsula, though they were still barred from the Point itself. At that time a Little Tern colony was located near the lighthouse, watched over by Spurn Bird Observatory. The SBO reports regularly expressed concern about the day-trippers who began to visit on a regular basis in the summer. The report for 1946 complained of 'much disturbance to birds by picnickers ... It is hoped to be able to afford more effective protection in 1947 but the use of the road by cars makes the problem rather difficult.' Entrance to the camp on the Point was still barred in 1949, both for the general public and the naturalists, who could not visit the Heligoland trap in the dunes except via the beach. The observatory organised regular weekend patrolling of the ternery but the 1949 report recorded '30 pairs attempting to breed at the main colony [i.e. on the east side of the Point] but no young were found, the site being over-run with trippers'. In *Gleanings from the Log 1948* – 'To

keep picnickers and sunbathers away who had come by car was all but impossible. Notice-boards were ignored; likewise the terns screaming overhead. After a fine Sunday the embryos in very few eggs remained alive.'

Military Activity

The end of hostilities did not mean the withdrawal of the military presence. Although the military retained a presence on the Spurn Peninsula, the superior barracks and other buildings at Godwin Battery at Kilnsea made it more convenient to use that as a centre rather than Spurn Fort on the peninsula. At the end of 1945 some huts at Godwin Battery were used for German prisoners of war, who remained until 1947. In 1948 the 9.2-inch guns at Godwin Battery were finally scrapped but the battery remained in army occupation until the dissolution of coast artillery in 1956.

During the immediate post-war period the only military activity on Spurn itself was the regular maintenance of the sea defences carried out by the Royal Engineers. The Territorial Army was reconstituted in 1947 and became responsible for coastal defence. In 1948 most of the temporary buildings around the Warren (what Chislett called 'the hutments'), were taken down, and the naturalists announced plans to put up a fence and plant bushes to attract birds. The observatory's landlord, the Lands Branch of the Army at York, was very happy with their tenants and the clerk of works, Mr Iveson, and the garrison engineer Mr Batchelor were always thanked warmly in the annual reports. It must have seemed in the late 1940s that the Army would gradually withdraw entirely from the Humber area. However during the early 1950s the Cold War ensured that Spurn again became the centre of military activity, when the guns on the Point and at Godwin Battery were taken out of care and preservation and placed on six hours' notice. Indeed, at Godwin Battery a new gun emplacement was installed overlooking the sea.

In 1950 the Point dunes were bulldozed to allow better sighting for coastal batteries. The sea buckthorn and elders were to take many years to regenerate. Aerial photographs show a strange

138 *The new military sea wall and gun emplacement at Kilnsea, c.1952. Both these features were short-lived. The southernmost battery observation post may be seen beyond the gun emplacement.*

landscape at the end of the Point with half of the area flattened. Just to the west of the *Lifeboat Inn* an anti-submarine defence was constructed. This was a line of metal posts ending in a platform. On the opposite bank of the Humber was a similar line of posts, and the two were linked by an underwater boom. In the Warren area two new bungalows were built for the caretakers of new anti-aircraft guns, which were placed there as the Cold War intensified. These buildings were later to become respectively the residence of the warden when the Trust took over, and the 'annexe' to the observatory. Down on the Point an eccentric character called Jack Johnson was in charge of the diesel generator that provided the houses with electricity. The Regan family were still at Spurn in the post-war period. Tony and his twin brother Peter remembered Johnson, who lived at Horseshoe Bungalow, going round in summer and winter 'in a shirt and trousers, sometimes in boots and sometimes in a boot and a shoe or a sandal and a boot. About once a month you would see him dressed in a smart suit and trilby going off to no-one knew where, looking smart as a button stick.'

At the end of 1950 a new use was found for the Nissen huts on the Point itself. At R.A.F. Patrington was a Sector Operations Centre to which national servicemen were being drafted. Because the accommodation at that time was insufficient for the number of men it was decided to reopen

Spurn Camp to accommodate the overflow of R.A.F. personnel caused by the call up of reservists during the Korean War. At that time national service was increased from 18 months to two years. Richard Loughlin was one of those young men posted to Patrington, and was one of the first to find himself living at Spurn Point:

We understood that the camp had not been occupied since the end of the Second World War. I recall talking to one of the advance party who had been involved in cleaning the place up and preparing it for our arrival, and he said 'It really was a dreary, desolate place – like an old Western movie ghost town, with sand everywhere blown in by the winds of many years and some of the old wooden doors on the huts were hanging off or missing'

Howard Frost, who was later to write a history of the Spurn military railway, paid his first visit to Spurn in 1955, and he recalls accidentally stepping into one of the fenced areas:

I was concentrating on watching a bird in front of me and stepped over a low wire into a shrubby area. Then suddenly, a sixth sense reminded me of the warning all bird observatory visitors were given at the time: 'Avoid the fenced areas!' I stepped back, walked round the perimeter and, on the opposite side, hidden behind a bush, discovered a freshly painted notice in red letters on a white background: KEEP OUT OR BE KILLED. I still shudder at the thought of how close I came to being a unique Spurn statistic!

139   Aerial view of the
Point after bulldozing by
the army, c.1951. As this
photograph shows, the end
of the Point was cleared of
vegetation very effectively. It
took several years for it to
grow again.

140   Constructing the anti-
submarine boom, c.1952.

Alan McKinstrie was commissioned in the RAF in early summer 1951, and instead of being sent to Korea as he had expected, found himself at Spurn:

> The officer I replaced told me that when the first batch arrived to reopen the East Coast radar chain, they got to Spurn to find no huts whatsoever. On the point of retreat the officer in charge sent his car and driver to the mainland to find a chimney sweep who duly arrived complete with his extendible bamboo-pole chimney brushes and these were used as prods (as in the Swiss Alps after a snowfall) and the huts were duly found buried in the drifting sand. They were dug out and thereafter every airman had to spend time ever day with a shovel beating back the advancing sand ... I was to come to have a high regard for the airmen when I learnt that our water supply was a one-inch pipe running the length of the causeway, which could change course overnight fracturing the pipe. When the break was found and fixed the pipe was blown free of contaminants and supply resumed, firstly to the hospital storage tank, then to the cookhouse tank and thence to the airmen's ablutions.

Spurn in the 1950s was not so well equipped as it had been during the war, and only the NAAFI canteen, selling soft drinks, 'inedible cakes and cigarettes etc', with a 'beat-up piano and a table tennis table and games of Housey Housey!!' was available for recreation. However a bus ran from the camp to Withernsea most nights, and 'we enjoyed our social life in what we found to be a pleasant little seaside resort with its cinema and dance pavilion.' Loughlin said 'Spurn Point holds special memories of primitive living conditions in inclement weather and long evenings crowded around the stove and young men trying to come to terms with the probability of having to take up arms yet again in an insane world about to explode.'

Arrol MacInnes was another young RAF man stationed at Spurn. The first time that he saw Spurn – a place about which he knew nothing – was when he was sent on fatigues from Patrington to take a load of coke, which was the only fuel at Spurn. He said that as he came round the *Crown* corner and saw the peninsula lying across the bay, he felt all the hairs rise on the back of his neck! He remembered that the only time that the parade ground was used whilst he was there was when the airmen paraded on it for the accession of Elizabeth II.

The observatory reports record the difficulties that the naturalists experienced when the military presence was expanded. In the report for 1950:

> the peninsula has been well watched. The fact that we have not surpassed the 1948/9 total [presumably of birds ringed] is due entirely to military activities. During much of the year sand was shifted all around the Point trap, which became buried in the autumn so that only by the greatest effort (and military help) was part of the material salvaged and moved to the wire dump area where it was re-erected.

Another problem for the observatory was the holidaymakers. Notwithstanding the military activity, people began to flock to Spurn at weekends. Of course, the naturalists preferred to have the peninsula to themselves, so their comments in the logs may exaggerate the problem. Warning notices erected by the War Office were everywhere, and they were joined by notices appealing for people to keep away from the nesting birds. At that time the Little Terns were nesting near the lighthouse and Chislett recorded that 'June was a melancholy month in those early years' when day visitors made their successful breeding almost impossible. The bait-diggers and fishermen were 'too preoccupied to be any threat to the nesting birds, but the number of footprints, particularly among the Little Terns' nests, illustrates the dangers.'

In 1949 the passage of the Coast Protection Act placed responsibility for coastal protection upon the maritime district councils. As a result of the Act in 1949 John Dossor & Associates were commissioned by Holderness Rural District Council to report on the protection of the Holderness coast. They recommended that the groynes be maintained on the eastward side of the spit to defend new land. In fact, throughout the later 1940s and into the 1950s, the sea defences at Spurn continued to be kept up, with the result that erosion was held in check, whilst around Godwin Battery the concrete defences were proving to be effective. A weak point was perceived to be the stretch of coast from opposite the *Blue Bell* southwards towards the Warren. In 1950-2 a new concrete sea wall was built here by the MoD. Its life

141 *The new sea wall being constructed, c.1952.*

142 *An earlier view of the Narrows.*

was to be fairly short. Its first test was the storm surge of 1953 when a 400-foot gap appeared in the wall. Although it was repaired shortly afterwards, by 1958 it was outflanked, and it was accelerating the erosion further south. Though still standing in the early 1960s, and dubbed 'The Promenade' by holiday-makers, it was rapidly being washed away.

On 17 February 1956 the Minister of Defence announced that the coast artillery was to be abolished since modern weaponry developments had made it redundant. All existing coast artillery units were to be converted to new roles or completely closed down. During 1957, the Army set about the task of dismantling the defences and disposing of the armaments, many of the guns being cut up for scrap on site. After 400 years, the Humber defences ceased to exist.

Whilst the war was going on the railway along the peninsula had remained of use despite the new road. Once hostilities were over it was still found to be useful, and the Hudswell Clarke railcar ran five trips daily for both people and goods, with an addition of two evening trips a week paid for by the RNLI. The work on the sea defences was ongoing, and was carried out by prisoners of war as well as regular troops so the railway still had a role.

However the decision was taken in 1951 to close the Spurn railway, and over the winter of 1951-2 the rails were taken up along the peninsula. The Hardy railcar had been scrapped on site in 1947. The Hudswell Clarke railcar was taken down to Bicester Military Railway in Oxfordshire. More or less the only reminder of 35 years of the Spurn railway line was the track left embedded in the road at those points where the railway had crossed it.

The Lifeboat

After the war, life on the Point for the residents was much changed. A constant bustle of activity had been provided by the Army at Spurn Fort, the comings and goings from Bull Sand Fort and Haile Sand Fort, the Navy working from the Port War Signal Station and living in the lighthouse compound, the Wrens in their respective barracks, the Royal Observer Corps in their quarters and the coastguards working from the tower. Now the only residents of the peninsula were the lighthouse-keepers and their families (who now had the compound to themselves), and the lifeboat families. John Mason, who had taken over as coxswain of the

Humber lifeboat in 1944, left (much to his wife Lily's delight) in 1949. He was succeeded by a Tynesider, Captain William Anderson, a master mariner who was called out on his very first day at Spurn to a Spanish ship in trouble. Captain Anderson and his wife Ethel settled down very well at Spurn, and in 1952 they were joined by their daughter, Doris, and her husband, Robertson Buchan, who became second coxswain. Buchan, a native of Peterhead, whose father had been a lifeboat man, had plenty of experience. Born in 1913, he first went to sea at 15 on a drifter, later skippered trawlers from this port and, during the war years, was in command of minesweepers based at Grimsby, where he also worked on naval escort vessels. He met his wife, Doris, at Fowey, a Cornish port to which she had travelled to meet her father, who was master of a vessel carrying ammunition for the 8th Army. Robertson was on one of the escort vessels and the two met and married soon afterwards. After the war the couple moved to Peterhead where Robertson took a shore job, but in 1952 the second coxswain's job fell vacant and they moved to Spurn. Seven years later, in 1959, he took over from his father-in-law as coxswain. Captain Anderson said 'The retiring

143 *Humber lifeboat crew, c.1956. Left to right: R. Stork, R. Appleby, B. Major, R. Buchan, S. Cross, W.S. Anderson (coxswain), D. Fox, L. Wells.*

144   *The families of the lifeboatmen in 1962. The photo includes Mrs Buchan, Mrs Staves, Mrs Appleby, and children.*

age is 60 and I have gone beyond it ... It is time for a younger man to take over.' He did not move far – one of the 10 cottages was vacant and so the couple stayed for a time until Captain Anderson's health meant that they had to move away. When he died Ethel moved back to the Point, and stayed for several years more.

The *City of Bradford II*, which had given sterling service since 1929, was by the 1950s getting to be an old boat. In 1954 a new lifeboat was built at Cowes. She was a 46 foot 9 inches Watson-class boat, powered by two 40 HP diesel engines. She arrived after a 'storm-torn voyage round the coast of Britain'. The cost of £29,593 was again provided by the City of Bradford Lifeboat Fund. Christened *City of Bradford III*, she lasted almost 20 years.

Despite being isolated, the people of Spurn still had access to religious services. Whilst the army was on the Point during the two wars religious services were held weekly, and the lifeboat and lighthouse families could take part. Robert Cross and his wife were Methodists and whilst they were at Spurn regular services and Sunday Schools were held in the schoolroom. However by the 1950s the vicar of Easington, the Reverend Leslie Erving, came to the conclusion that Spurn needed a proper place of worship. Many huts on the Point were not in use,

and in 1954 he asked the military authorities if the church could take over one near the guardhouse, hut number 44, as a place of worship. His request being duly granted, people rallied round to furnish the church and the *Hull Daily Mail* reported on the visit of the Bishop of Hull, the Right Reverend H.T. Vodden, to the 'outlandish peninsula' to dedicate the new church, which being no larger than six yards by ten yards 'must be one of the smallest in Yorkshire'. The Reverend Erving's son David recalled:

> My dad had a large number of churches to care for – Easington, Kilnsea, Holmpton, Skeffling, Welwick and Spurn. He created Spurn Church in 1954 out of an old army hut. When one of the lifeboat families (Robertson Buchan was the lifeboat second coxswain at the time) had a baby to baptize he improvised a font by using an upturned lifeboat bell.

Playtime on the Point

For the younger children living on the Point, life was idyllic, as it had been for those before them. The freedom to roam, the proximity of water, the excitement provided by the army buildings everywhere, tunnels, little sheds and Nissen huts and the wildlife all contributed to a wonderland for a child. Tony Regan said:

Looking back at the Spurn of my childhood, it was
a wonderful place for a child to be brought up ...
Some of the older children rigged a rope high up
on the 'magazine' as the old disused lighthouse was
called ... and when the tide was in it was great fun
to swing out from the magazine and let go, finishing
up in the water. Many underground tunnels lay all
over Spurn, and all the kids knew every one of them.
Of course, fishing and messing about in boats was
always a great source of fun for us.

Rosie Robertson, whose father was the Spurn
mechanic in the late 1940s and early 1950s, also
remembered her happy childhood:

We'd leave after breakfast and often not return until
teatime. The men taught us to whittle daggers, rifles
and six-shooters from driftwood for our cowboys
and Indians games. We could all make a bow and
arrow. But ... the best and most exciting game we
had was one I can't think of now without shuddering
and marvelling that we weren't all killed! When the
Army left Spurn, as well as the fort and all of those
buildings, they left behind a whole warren of tunnels
under the sand, shored up with what I remember
as planks, but which were probably pit props. We
would crawl on our hands and knees through these
tunnels, which were very prone to collapse in parts
and we'd often have to dig past roof-falls! We could
have been buried alive. Our parents didn't know we
did this – they knew we wandered through all the
old army buildings and the pill-boxes, but I don't
even know whether the adults were aware of the
existence of tunnels like those!

So life for a young child was wonderful, but
less so when they became teenagers. The eldest of
the three Buchan boys, Robertson, born in 1944,
came to Spurn with his family in 1949. His younger
brothers were Stewart and Jo. The boys had a great
childhood but, as they grew into teenagers, they
found the life at Spurn increasingly restricted. Once
the school bus had deposited them back home the
only companions were the other children. After-
school activities were closed to them. No friends
could come round to see them. As their family did
not have a car they were more or less imprisoned on
the Point. In fact the problems for growing children
were the most usual reason that lifeboatmen left the
Point after a time. And before their wives had access
to cars themselves, and could get employment away

from Spurn, the women too sometimes found that
life was restricted. It was not until the 1960s that
these things were to change.

The Lighthouse

Although the lighthouse was lit by electricity after
the war (and from 1957 was fitted with automatic
acetylene gas light), it still needed constant maintenance, and continued to be manned by a principal
lighthouse-keeper and two assistants to provide
a constant watch. Richard Loughlin, in the early
1950s, remembered meeting the head keeper and
engaging him in conversation:

He was an oldish, bearded, sailor-type, wearing what
looked like a sailor's coat or uniform and a shiny
peaked cap. I remember him remarking what a
lonely life it was and how it was proving difficult to
get young men to train for lighthouse work as there
was 'nothing in a place like this for a young man
with a family'

The low lighthouse, which for many decades
had been used by Trinity House to store explosives,
finally lost that role in 1956. It retained the water
tank on the top, though now that Spurn had a water
main it was no longer required. The suggestion
has been made on a number of occasions that the
tank should be removed, as it gives the lighthouse
a rather odd appearance, but that seems unlikely
to happen.

Every year during the migration seasons, as
had happened before the war, perches were placed
on the lighthouse to help birds who were attracted
to the light, and to attempt to avoid the large-scale
slaughter that had become common. The ornithologists staying at Warren Cottage sometimes spent a
few hours overnight at the lighthouse to see what
birds were being attracted, and 'perhaps to pick a few
birds from the rails'. That was especially worthwhile
on misty nights.

More Naturalists

Spurn Bird Observatory did not just attract ornithologists. Warren Cottage offered accommodation
for naturalists of all kinds and in the summers of
1947 to 1950 parties of entomologists came to stay,
with their nets, pooters (insect-collecting tubes) and

sugaring equipment. An article by W.D. Hincks in the *Naturalist* of 1951 gives a good account of their findings and the look of the peninsula not long after the war. Spurn at that time offered quite a range of differing habitats to insect collectors. The Walker Butts area included the so-called 'Marsh Meadow', a pond, the Walker Butts Bank Dyke (a smaller feature than the present Canal), whilst to the east of Warren Cottage lay a considerable area of Phragmites, also with a pond. To these were added the marram dunes, the Warren area, the saltmarsh, Chalk Bank and the Point area, with its covering of sea buckthorn, elder and wild flowers. The entomologists armed themselves daily with packed lunches, or lunch was taken at the cottage if they were working near to it, and:

> after the evening meal, taken at the Kilnsea café [Carrie Leonard's café, Gwendene], on our return to the cottage, diaries were written up, specimens were mounted and often identified, textbooks and microscopes having been brought by most members of the party. Discussions of the day's collecting accompanied the mounting which often went on, of necessity, until the early hours of the morning. On suitable evenings moths were collected, often in numbers, from the lighted windows of the cottage, with paraffin lamps, car lights, or 'at sugar'. Occasional evening or 'after dark' excursions were made, usually, but not entirely, by the lepidopterists.

Hincks described the area investigated by the entomologists and he gives a good picture of how it had been left after the war. Many of the hutments erected for the military had been taken down, but 'are still lying about, making the place unsightly'. The garden of Warren Cottage, though it has been 'badly cut down and damaged during the past few years', still contained a Corsican pine, whitebeam, bullace and sycamores. Privet was dominant with some bushes over 10 feet high, and in the summer scented the air around the cottage. Apparently the soldiers staying at the Warren had made some attempt at cultivation by planting brassicas, which by the late 1950s had run to seed. In the marshy area to the east of the buildings, rabbit warrens covered the ground, and shelducks used the burrows as nesting holes. Further down the peninsula, at Chalk Bank, a salt marsh lay to the north-west of the chalk bank

that ran the length of the broader part. At that time a channel about two feet deep and a yard wide ran along it and the plants there were characteristic of salt marsh. Hincks's description of what he calls 'the main ridge and seashore' differs very little from what we see today, though he describes 'newer dunes on the seaward side' that have grown as a result of the groynes and other barriers put up by the military during the war. The party visited before the 'Canal' (see below) was created, and Hincks's description of the dyke that preceded it is interesting. As now, the dyke was divided into two parts that on the western side were described as 'foul'. The section on the eastern side, was of considerable interest to the entomologists. In winter and early spring it was full of water, but dried out gradually so that in high summer it consisted of shallow isolated ponds and stretches of mud, attracting dragonflies and other interesting insects.

The 1953 Floods

For the people of the East Coast of England, 1953 was a year that would be remembered for a very long time. Easington, Kilnsea and Spurn lie sandwiched between the Humber and the sea, and the inhabitants know well the power of the tides. In the early 1950s many of those still living remembered the great flood of 1906, when so much land in South Holderness lay underwater. But for many years no really big tides had threatened the triangle of land at the tip of Holderness, and only the regular nibbling away of the sea took the land. However, the last day of January 1953 was to become one of those days that they could never forget.

It began with a depression described as 'unremarkable', located in the early hours of 30 January just to the south of Iceland. As the day went on and the depression moved eastward it began to deepen and, by midday on 31 January, it was centred over the North Sea between Scotland and southern Norway. Meanwhile an area of high pressure had built up to the west of the UK, and the conjunction of high and low pressure areas so close to each other resulted in very high winds. All day on 31 January winds of Force 10 and Force 11 drove water down the North Sea as though into a funnel. The waves they generated were more than eight metres (24 feet) high. As the 'surge' travelled southwards it gained in speed and intensity. That night it brought devastation to the East Coast of England, hitting Holderness in the early evening and then affecting Lincolnshire, East Anglia, Kent and finally, and most devastatingly, the Netherlands. Almost 2,000 people were killed in that surge, 200 of them in England. South Holderness, where the surge struck first, came off fairly lightly, though it did not seem like that to those who were affected.

On that day, 31 January, weather forecasts had warned that strong winds were approaching North Sea coasts. That was before the days of television, and only those at sea were likely to have been really concerned. Mr Peter Webster, who with his wife was running Easington Post Office and shop, has left an account of that night and subsequent nights. The Websters had closed the shop early as few people were venturing out, and they settled down for a cosy night by the fireside. At that time Withernsea had no less than three cinemas, and a bus had left Easington earlier to take some villagers to the pictures. The Websters heard on the radio that a car ferry was in trouble in high winds in the North Sea, and that a mountainous gale was blowing, up to 80 m.p.h. Then a policeman knocked on their door and told them that he had experienced great difficulty in getting along the road from Kilnsea because the water lay across it in several places. The Websters went out into Easington Square to find that:

> water surrounded the *White Horse* and the drain which took rain water was gushing out water like a fountain at least 2 feet high. It was obvious from the briny smell it was sea water and not rain, so we realised then that Easington was in peril. Several people came out of the *White Horse* and we agreed to stop all traffic trying to get to Kilnsea.

Mr Webster, a magistrate and a former fighter pilot in the war, was a good man in a crisis. His first task was to alert the authorities and, since it was a Saturday and council offices were closed, he began with the local police. Unfortunately that was the night of the police annual dance, and all Holderness officers were enjoying themselves at Beverley, whilst their duties had been taken over by Hull Station.

Mr Webster had some difficulty in explaining where Easington was located! Eventually he managed to contact the Beverley dance hall and the local officers were pulled away prematurely from their dance.

It was soon apparent that the sea defences and the Humber defences had been breached by the surge. The land was being attacked by the waters on both east and west. Between Easington and Kilnsea at that time there were few hard defences, but only what Mr Webster described as 'a grass and sand bank just south of the cliffs'. That bank, known as 'The Bents' (a favourite courting spot apparently) had completely disappeared and seawater covered all the farmland towards Kilnsea and in the direction of Skeffling. Between Easington and Kilnsea lay Long Bank, which served to defend the low-lying land on its north and south sides from higher-than-average tides. On the Humber foreshore were sand dunes and a bank, which, in normal circumstances, would have been enough to keep the river back. But these were not normal times and it was soon apparent that the sea and the Humber had met across the narrow stretch of low-lying land between Easington and Kilnsea. This area was not densely populated, but there were several scattered farms and cottages, and all were affected. The Kilnsea people who arrived at 10.30 p.m. on the bus from Withernsea were told that they would not be able to get back to their homes that night, and were soon offered accommodation with friends and relatives. Others who lived on the outskirts of Easington tried to reach their flooded homes. Mr Webster recounts the adventures of one passenger on the bus, a farm manager, Mr Harold Bosman, who farmed on Peter Lane and realised that his livestock were in peril as they could not get away from the floods. Rather than seek shelter with the rest of his family he set out for his farm to drive the animals onto higher ground. He had to work in freezing water, waist deep, and finally had to find refuge on top of some of the hay and straw in one of the buildings. In the morning he was rescued from a chaff stack by a boat manned by farmers.

The Websters tried to phone all the farms and houses likely to be affected by the floods, but most overhead telephone lines were down. However, they

145 *Inspecting the damage at Kilnsea caused by the 1953 floods. Looking north towards Easington.*

146 *Damage to the sea wall at Kilnsea, 1953. The view is north towards Godwin Battery, where one of the battery observation posts can be seen.*

did get through to Mr George Colley of Firtholme Farm, which lies on the main road between Easington and Kilnsea. The family, which included a young baby, had retreated upstairs, because there was three feet of water in all downstairs rooms and it was still rising. By that time the police had arrived and because Firtholme was so close to the sea, and was in the place where the worst breach had occurred, it was decided that a rescue attempt should be tried before dawn. A fire brigade van had arrived with a rowing boat and a party set out down the road

towards the farm. They could only get a short way along the road and, once they reached the water, the boat was launched with two firemen rowing. However, it was dark and once they got out of the reach of the lights of the van the boat ran aground on top of a submerged hedge. And when the men got out of the boat to try and refloat it, they plunged into a deep ditch, well over waist deep. They had no choice but to abandon the boat, find the road surface, and wait until first light when they could see what they were doing.

No-one in Easington knew what was happening in Kilnsea that night, but they found out later that many were very badly hit by the floods. On the corner in Kilnsea, opposite the *Blue Bell* pub, was the cottage and café run by Carrie Leonard. She had lived in the village since just after the First World War, but had never experienced anything like the events on the night of 31 January. Carrie said that at about 4 p.m. there were tremendous winds, and then the water began to come into the bungalow from both the river and the sea. The Humber water was full of sewage – 18 inches of foul water. Carrie had several workmen due for an evening meal that night, but quickly realised she would have to leave. She'd already laid the table and when she came back the next day it was virtually untouched, but with cat's paw marks all over the tablecloth.

People like Carrie, living in that part of Kilnsea where the river and sea were only a quarter of a mile apart, were particularly badly affected. Present-day Kilnsea has several hundred caravans. In 1953 there were only a few, but two, which were in a field just south of Southfield Farm, were obviously very vulnerable to the flowing waters. One was owned by Henry Bunce, a naturalist who had been visiting Spurn since the 1930s. Fortunately he was safely at home in Hull on the night of 31 January. His caravan was lifted by the waters, and ended up

spiked on top of the tank traps near the gateway to Spurn. His neighbour, a lady named in the *Hull Daily Mail* as 'Mrs J. Williams, young mother of two children, Carol, aged nine and Bruce, aged eight', had made Kilnsea her home after spending a holiday there the previous year. She had bought a caravan with 'oak-fitted furniture', which Ted Sharp allowed her to put in his field. Mrs Williams recalled the horrors of that Saturday night in an interview with the *Hull Daily Mail*:

The children had been ill with flu and they were frightened as they listened to the howling gale. Mrs Williams, herself alarmed, drew the curtains, turned up the radio to the loudest pitch and got nearer the fire. A few minutes later, however, she saw a tell-tale stain. The sea was creeping through the floor. It came through the door and in minutes they were ankle deep in water. Then came the knock on the door. Mr William Sharp, who was on hand only because his car had broken down, had come to the rescue. She remembered how Mr Sharp had taken young Carol on his shoulders, and told her to wait until he returned. She remembered with horror, how, with a clothesline tied around her waist and the other end tied to Mr Sharp, she waded through armpit-deep sea to safety. 'I have never been so frightened in my life,' she said. 'Funny the things you rescue in an emergency. I grabbed a bag and

147 *Coxswain William Anderson and second coxswain, his son-in-law, Robertson Buchan, inspecting the damage after the 1953 floods.*

put in anything I saw – a clock, a pair of scissors, two toothbrushes, a cigarette lighter (I don't smoke either) and a pound of butter which I saw floating across the room.'

The Williams family were given shelter at Cliff Farm. A week later, when she went to look at the wreck of her home, Mrs Williams found that the side had been ripped off and all the fitted cupboards and furniture had been swept out to sea. On the muddy floor of what remained of the caravan she found her wristwatch, and the remains of the dress she had been making for a wedding, whilst two fields away she found what remained of her store cupboard – raisins, apples, onions, rice, sugar, all mixed together and caked with mud.

Pat Stevenson and her parents, Mr and Mrs Robinson, were running the *Crown & Anchor* public house in 1953. The *Crown* overlooks the Humber and the water soon washed over the road and began lapping against the pub walls. They had managed to keep most of it out but when a neighbour came round they opened the back door and it all came in. The *Crown* provided its traditional hospitality nevertheless.

Further down the peninsula the lifeboatmen had expected trouble when they heard the weather warnings, but probably not in their own homes! Hardly surprisingly, they were called out on the night of the 31 January. They had to leave their families to cope with the storm without them, and it was 24 hours before they could get back. Because phone lines were down, at midnight the BBC had appealed for anyone to contact the Humber lifeboat with a message that barges were in trouble 15 miles off Withernsea. Off-duty coastguards tried to signal through by lamp from Easington, but the lifeboat had already gone out and eventually picked up the men from the barges, which had lost their tow. They were at sea altogether for 29 and a half hours. 'We were first called out at 5.30 p.m. to a ship and just before we got to her we received a message saying they would be all right. Before we could get back we were called to the Spurn lightship, which was adrift, and after that to a barge under tow. After five hours punching the weather we were informed that there was nobody aboard the barge and we were not required. We finally returned home at 11

148 *Flood damage to the old inn, 1953. The wall was rebuilt, only to be pulled down with the rest of the building in the 1970s.*

o'clock the following night.' Meanwhile the Humber had washed right through the lifeboatmen's homes, and such was the force of the wind and waves that spray had been thrown right over their houses. The wives had to fend for themselves; the lifeboat was called out five times between the Saturday night and Monday. When the men had chance to view the damage they found rubble, driftwood and smashed boats piled up against their houses, and mud covering the ground floor. For several nights the families retreated to the accommodation within the walled enclosure where the old lighthouse had been, as it was more sheltered from the force of the waves.

Ironically, however, what the lifeboat families needed most urgently was water. The water main, which brought the only water supply down the peninsula, had been fractured and without a supply of running water they could not have fires because they were linked to the heating system. Water had to be brought down in lorries and, when the Women's

Royal Voluntary Service workers took clothing to Spurn, they found that the housewives were also in need of soap and scrubbing brushes to clean out their homes.

Meanwhile, back in Easington, people spent a sleepless night wondering what the next high tide would do. The Websters gave shelter to several policemen who catnapped on chairs. In the morning everyone was relieved to find that the gale had died down. However, seawater covered all the farmland between Kilnsea and Easington and in the direction of Skeffling. The high tide fortunately stopped about six inches short of flowing over the land, and a party set out to rescue the Colleys from Firtholme. Someone had had the idea of sending to Hull for a high-wheeled tractor that was used for taking loads of timber from the docks to the timber yard. The regular driver had taken the keys home with him, but the police tracked him down and the tractor was given police escort to Easington. The rescue attempt was successful, and the Colley family clambered aboard and were taken to relations in the village. By that time the authorities had got organised and, when Mr Webster and his party returned to Easington, they found the square full of vehicles. Most belonged to council officials, who had taken over the *White Horse* as their headquarters and were making arrangements to have extra telephones installed. They were to remain there for some days.

Once there was no fear of loss of human life people turned their attention to their stock. Because the surge had happened at night without warning no precautions had been taken and though many people helped to save as many head of cattle, pigs, and poultry as possible, it was estimated a few days later that 100 cattle, 300 sheep, 200 pigs, and 3,000 to 4,000 head of poultry had perished in the area. Those that were rescued were soon housed by neighbours. It was not only stock that concerned the farmers. The damage to the land was considerable, and large areas of land were likely to remain flooded for some time. The East Riding County Council fire brigade was soon standing by with all the pumps at their disposal to move into the area, where millions of gallons of water must be thrown back into the sea if the farmland was not to be completely poisoned with salt.

Two days after the flood Peter Webster decided to try to get through to Kilnsea to replenish people's grocery stores. 'I made arrangements with my good friend and rival grocer, Mr Louis Curtis, that if I made it through to Kilnsea I would visit his customers as well as mine and take orders for foodstuffs and other requirements. Food rationing was still in force and people might have had vital supplies wasted by the flood water.' He went with Clarence Stothard on his tractor to Kilnsea. They found that most of the houses had been flooded, and people needed groceries urgently. It was necessary to contact the Ministry of Food (Rationing), Leeds, and get permission to replace all rationed foodstuffs without marking the customers' ration books or counting out their coupons. The army barracks at Beverley sent a high-wheeled lorry and two soldiers to deliver orders.

The priority now was to get the water off the land. Hull Fire Brigade had two large pumps taking water from the drains and over the Humber Bank onto the mud flats by Monday. More trouble was expected because the tides were predicted to continue to rise higher each day for over a week. However by the Monday the water level had gradually lowered and lorries and DUKWs (amphibious vehicles, commonly called Ducks, which were American trucks converted to go into water for the D-Day landings) were able to make frequent trips to the Point through the water, which still covered the road between Easington and Kilnsea. On Thursday 5 February everyone still feared a return of the floods, as further high tides had been predicted. The *Hull Daily Mail* on 5 February reported that:

Farmers and farm workers working on the rebuilding of the sea and river defences are ready to abandon the task to rescue livestock remaining in the area if the sea breaks through again. While they waited they continue working with the only excavators available on the rebuilding of the Easington seabank. They are waiting for 15-20 more excavators which are being drafted into the area to continue the work which was started with limited equipment early on Tuesday morning. The whole of the Army's equipment has been diverted to the most vulnerable areas in Lincolnshire, and Holderness was having to take second place. By the weekend 30 more excavators may be at work on the Easington and

149   *Flood damage in front of the cottages after the floods of 31 January 1953.*

150   *'The Canal', c.1956. The lines of anti-tank blocks can be seen on the far side of 'the canal'.*

Humberside banks rebuilding the sea walls ... It is a race against time. In eight days the highest tides, up to 30 or more feet, are expected. Throughout the night farmers and their employees worked incessantly checking and rechecking the state of the winds and tide and their effects on the temporary rebuilt coastal defences which have been erected so far. Until early today farmers and their workers kept watch along the vulnerable Easington seabank and the broken-down defence wall of the Humberside area, but the threatened storm which Easington and Kilnsea were warned about stopped eight miles from the flood area.

For a while heavy snowstorms and high winds added to the problems but then thankfully the weather calmed. Families that had been evacuated again from the low-lying zones of Kilnsea returned, as all fear of further flooding of the area had passed for the time being. The *Mail* reported that their men folk had actually refused to leave the village, being determined to attend a darts match in the *Blue Bell* public house that had been planned in advance of the floods!

A week after the floods the *Mail* reported that about 14 or 15 excavators, tractors, bulldozers and dumpers were working on the breached Easington sea bank. A drainage board official said they had a full week to rebuild the sea wall. Sand was being excavated from the rear of what was left of the old wall and the resulting trench was being filled with clay. The fear was that the tides expected the following weekend might be accompanied by wind, and that the sea would come in again. With that in mind work went on at top speed. Six large trailer pumps, pumping about 3,000 gallons a minute, were at work clearing the floodwaters in the Kilnsea and Weeton areas. The pumps were moved from place to place, and the water was pumped back into the river or into drains where the water level was lower. Nevertheless, thousands of acres were still underwater and it was estimated that it would be weeks before the land was cleared. All-out efforts were going on to ensure that banks were as high as possible before the next high tides on 14 and 17 February.

As people returned to their flooded homes, the full impact of the floods became apparent to them. Mr and Mrs G.W. Horn and their young family lived at Southend, Easington. Mrs Horn described her feelings when she made the journey home. 'There was thick mud everywhere. We have put the hosepipe over the rooms and the furniture. The drawers won't open because they are too swollen. The clothes that were hanging in the hall are saturated and sea-stained.'

Once the emergency was over the farmers were able to assess the long-term damage. Much of their

151   *Working on the sea defences near the High Bents, late 1950s. Left to right: Roland Cooper; Eric Parish; Charlie Scott.*

152 *The Crown & Anchor in the late 1950s. The photograph shows the Crown & Anchor before it was extended. The outbuilding to the left was later taken down to improve access to the rear. Land alongside the pub was used for caravans until new regulations forced their removal.*

153 *Connor & Graham bus at Spurn Point, 1954. Bob Ellerby is the driver.*

land was rendered useless for at least one cropping season. What was to happen to their farmhands? If they left to work in the town, there would be little likelihood of their returning. The *Hull Daily Mail* reported that 'One farmer is faced with a wage bill of £42 per week for seven employees, who can do little or nothing because of the effects of the flooding.' One positive side-effect was that 'the work

will also absorb Easington's unemployed – two. Men from Hull's unemployment register are unlikely to be called as the work is regarded as specialised. In nearly every case drivers and maintenance men will come with the machinery.'

As soon as the threat of more flooding had gone it was necessary to consider new and improved flood defences to ensure that such a catastrophe did not recur. The temporary banks built immediately after the disaster were not enough, and so new hard defences were built in the next few years along the Humber foreshore and the sea. Mr H.B. Hewetson, of Preston, came up with a novel idea – to use the anti-tank concrete blocks that still lay in three lines running from the sea to the Humber. He suggested that they be lifted and made into a sea wall, which would be concreted in. Other concrete tank blocks lying around the East Riding could also be utilised for such a task. His suggestion was not taken up until the 1970s, when the three rows of blocks were indeed lifted and placed at the Narrows to protect the peninsula! Mr Hewetson remembered the floods of 1906, 'when a quarter of a mile of land went in a night', and he was perturbed that so little had been done since then to protect the land. He said he was afraid that if the coast was not protected it may not be long before people will walk on the beach to sit on the foundation stone of the present Kilnsea church!

The landscape of the area changed somewhat after the events of 1953. In 1954 a flood bank was constructed between the *Crown* and the gate to Spurn and, as a result, what is now known as the 'Canal', quite a large watercourse in two sections, was created. The Humber bank northwards, from 'Chalky Point' towards Easington, was also raised and from Easington southwards towards Kilnsea a new flood bank (New Bank) was built inland of Long Bank, with the material to make it being taken from an area to its east, creating what is now called Easington Lagoon.

Kilnsea in the Late 1940s to 1950s

There was still a strong military feeling to Kilnsea long after the war had finished. From Godwin Battery, southwards through the Warren and down to Spurn, the military remained, albeit in relatively small numbers, until 1959. The church registers show many baptisms and marriages relating to the forces for decades after the war. Many Kilnsea girls had married military personnel, and some settled down in the village and found work with the military even after they had left the services. For example Thomas Piggott, Arthur's father, who had married Ivy Clubley, became a plumber on Kilnsea camp

154   *Connor & Graham bus stuck in a snow drift at Kilnsea, 1947.*

after the war, and Thomas Jardine, who had married Dorothy Tennison, went to work at the Warren as 'equipment attendant' and lived at one of the bungalows. Many older men, like Medforth Hodgson, Jack Codd and Edwin Hodgson, who had all worked for the army, lived out the rest of their lives in Kilnsea, whilst some military men such as Major Hambrook, and Group Captain Smyth-Piggott bought or rented property and stayed a while. Lieutenant-Colonel Henry Guy Brownlow was a regular visitor in the late 1940s and 1950s. 'He went down the Point to do some birdwatching and was stopped by the guard. He said I was the commander in chief at Spurn in the war [a somewhat exaggerated claim] – and so was let through!'

Farming in Kilnsea carried on in much the same way after the Second World War as it had done before, though it became increasingly mechanised. Ernest and Daisy Tennison remained at Grange Farm until the late 1950s when they sold the farm, now reduced from 218 acres to 145 acres, to Leslie and Alma Marshall. The Clubleys had left Westmere during the war and, after a few changes of tenancy, Albert and Miriam Gautier came to run the dairy farm from about 1951. Alongside the farm they built a bungalow, Carlyon, which still remains. William Sellars of Blackmoor Farm died in 1947, but his widow Annie remained for a few years. Thereafter, that smallholding changed hands many times. After the Second World War Evelyn and William Tennison were living at Cliff Farm, and the land associated with it was farmed alongside other Tennison land along North Marsh Lane. When they left, Albert and Beatrice Hall were there until the early 1960s. After the war Ted Sharp of Southfield Farm used some of his land for caravans, but the land and farmhouse had been badly affected by the 1953 floods and, in August 1953, Ted and his new wife Doris retired to Blue Bell Cottage, selling Southfield Farm to Arthur and Nellie Clubley, who were to remain there for over 40 years. The only other farm in the village was Northfield Farm, a Tennison holding since the enclosure in 1840. Since that time its land has been gradually eaten away by the sea, and indeed the farmhouse itself had got much closer to the cliff.

155   Carrie Leonard at home, early 1950s.

Kilnsea had supported two pubs with no difficulty up to and including the war, but in the post-war period the run-down of military personnel meant that two licensed premises were struggling to stay in business. Nevertheless John B. Clubley, his wife (and mother) carried on running the Blue Bell until the mid-1950s, when they retired to the West Country. Ernest (Jack) Codd and his wife tried to make a go of the pub for a year or so, but then in 1957 Hull Brewery decided to sell the Blue Bell, and it became a café. A shop was later combined with the café business. The demise of the Blue Bell must have been welcome to the licensees of the Crown & Anchor. After the war these were Archibald and Dorothy Butler, followed by the Smiths. Then in 1951 Harry and Anne Robinson arrived in Kilnsea. When a reporter from the Yorkshire Times visited the area in June 1957 he found Kilnsea 'more restful than rewarding ... There is not much doing there nowadays, for even the soldiers have gone and the sprawling WD site is deserted'. At the Crown & Anchor 'Mr and Mrs Harry Robinson are host and hostess to many visitors to the area in the season and to many ornithologists who are concerned with the bird-ringing station and observatory at Spurn all the year round'. Harry Robinson died in 1959,

156 *View from the lighthouse, 1957. Most of the military buildings still remained at that date, and were in good condition. They included numerous Tarran and Nissen huts, many brick buildings, and the row of wooden huts near the entrance to the fort.*

but Anne (always called Ma) remained in charge of the *Crown* for over 30 years, helped by her daughter and son-in-law.

Unlike today, in the post-war period Kilnsea had good transport links. Connor & Graham, the local bus firm, provided a regular bus service, and were also prepared to go up and down the Point on request. But sometimes inclement weather meant that Kilnsea and Spurn were cut off and Connor & Graham could not get down. The winter of 1947 was a particularly memorable one when, from late January until late March, almost the whole of the country was gripped in freezing temperatures, with snow accumulating everywhere. Kilnsea and Spurn were cut off for some time. Eva Crackles recorded in her diary on 1 March 1947:

> Spurn has been cut off. I travelled on the first bus to get through. Called at Carrie Leonard's cafe. She said 'Good God, what have you come for? You'll never get away again.' Walked between walls of snow along the road to Spurn from the *Blue Bell*. I walked down the shore on the river side at the beginning of Spurn. When I came up the shore the water became deeper; the tide was coming in under the ice. I panicked and got icy water in my boots. I did get back to Hull!

Kilnsea was beginning to attract retired people from outside the area by the 1950s. For example, at Gwendolyn (now Yew Cottage) William Lyndoe, a retired grocer from Hull, and his wife Rachel lived from 1949 to 1963. A retired army officer lived at The Haven for several years. In 1949 Blue Bell Cottage was bought by Group Captain Smyth-Piggott. He was a keen member of Spurn Bird Observatory and 'lived there for much of his time for a few years, dispensing hospitality', wrote Ralph Chislett. The Clarksons, Madge and Samuel, who retired from the jewellery trade in Hull, had lived at Sunrise Cottage since 1935 and, after Samuel died, Madge remained there with her niece Margaret Walling until the late 1950s. After her mother died in 1954 and she was no longer tied, Carrie Leonard left Kilnsea and achieved her long-term ambition of going to sea as a stewardess. She worked for North Sea Ferries, but never broke her links with the village, visiting it frequently until her death in 2004.

The coming decades were to bring many more strangers to Kilnsea. The army was preparing to move out by the late 1950s, and the sale of Spurn Fort and Godwin Battery was to bring many changes to the area.

Eight

The Early Years of the Nature Reserve, the Late 1950s to the Late 1960s

The Nature Reserve

By the 1950s it was becoming clear that a confrontation was brewing between the naturalists who wished to preserve Spurn's special qualities as a sanctuary for wildlife, and those who wanted to exploit it commercially. As described in the last chapter people had begun flocking to Spurn, drawn by its unique qualities of landscape, natural history interest and, perhaps most important, the wonderful unspoilt sandy beaches. Unfortunately though, the visitors were in danger of destroying what they came to enjoy. It was becoming clear to those interested in conservation that Spurn needed special protection. The focus was on the Little Tern colony.

Interest in nature conservancy in Great Britain was growing in the 20th century. The creation of nature reserves was seen as one important way that special areas could be protected. In 1912 the Society for the Promotion of Nature Reserves (SPNR) was created by Charles Rothschild, with the aim of creating an integrated string of reserves across the country. Well ahead of its time, the SPNR aimed to collect and collate information on land that retained 'primitive conditions' and to preserve them for posterity. With that aim, in 1915 a provisional list of potential reserves was presented to the Board of Agriculture. These consisted of some 284 sites covering Britain and Ireland, graded into three categories. Many of those sites remain prime places for wildlife to this day. Unfortunately the First World War, and the death of Rothschild, meant that the movement came to a halt, and it never recovered momentum between the wars. Interest was revived after the Second World War when the government set up the Wildlife Conservation Special Committee (the Huxley Committee) to examine the needs of nature conservancy in England and Wales. In 1949 the Nature Conservancy was established. It was authorised to own or lease National Nature Reserves (NNRs) or enter into a Nature Reserve Agreement whereby the owner, lessee or occupier allowed the Nature Conservancy to implement a management programme for conservation on their property. Under the National Parks and Access to the Countryside Act 1949 it was given powers of compulsory land acquisition and the authority to formulate by-laws for the protection of each reserve. The Huxley Committee also recommended the creation of Sites of Special Scientific Interest (SSSIs) to provide some protection for areas outside the statutory reserves. All those measures were applicable to Spurn.

Visitors to the Observatory had long realised Spurn's value for wildlife, and they were supported in 1952 by the *Yorkshire Evening Post*, which carried correspondence suggesting that Spurn be declared a nature reserve under the provisions of recent Planning Acts. The Little Terns were still being disturbed by visitors – '18 eggs were found in a heap on one day' by people checking the ternery. In 1953 George Ainsworth wrote:

> holiday-makers and fishermen appear to ignore the birds – but the presence of these people keeps the birds off the eggs. Several visitors have dogs with them which roam the ternery and naturally are attracted to the eggs and young. This state of affairs has been going on now for some years. Many eggs are laid but very few young have been reared. This cannot go on much longer and unless vigorous measures are taken to make Spurn a Nature Reserve we shall have no Little Terns nesting there before so very long.

157 Cars and cyclists at Spurn, late 1950s. At that time there were no car parks, and on a hot weekend in summer people parking in the lay-bys caused problems on the peninsula.

158 Richard Wood, M.P., electioneering at Spurn Point, September 1964. Coxswain Robertson Buchan and his wife are in the foreground.

A document of 1953, sent to Richard Wood MP, gives an interesting insight. It states that between the wars no attempts had been made to exclude the public but, because there was no made-up road, the area was little frequented, because it is relatively remote from any large centre of population. Now that there was a good concrete road 'the motoring public' had begun to discover the attractions of the peninsula. It was becoming increasingly popular and

coach trips had been organised from Withernsea and Hull, though that seems to have been stopped by the military authorities, who were becoming increasingly concerned, firstly because of the threat to military security (bearing in mind that it was 1953 when the installations were being expanded) and secondly because people having picnics in the dunes and on the beaches were leaving their cars on the single-track road, and blocking it for military traffic. The War Department considered taking action to abolish the public right of way down the peninsula and the county council and the Holderness Rural District Council had agreed that if it were essential on security grounds, they could well raise objection 'during the period that the present emergency continues'. However the rural district council wanted the public to enjoy the amenities of Spurn so far as that could reasonably be secured, and the county council also felt that if the road were closed they would ask that it should be reopened when the emergency has passed. Apparently the War Office had encountered legal difficulties in the way of closing the road to the public and discussions were still proceeding as to alternative means of protecting their interests.

The document acknowledged that the influx of holidaymakers was perturbing the naturalists. The Nature Conservancy, whilst not prepared to establish a National Nature Reserve at Spurn, had informed the county council that they were about to notify the area as one of Special Scientific Interest and would favourably consider any proposal of the county council to establish a local nature reserve in the area. Caravan sites were already encroaching on Spurn: 'in contravention of planning control, a site for trailer caravans was recently established close to the northern end of the Spurn peninsula'. That site was the land on either side of the road from the *Blue Bell* to the gate. At the time of writing planning permission had been refused and an appeal against the refusal was before the Minister of Housing and

159 *Looking north from the lighthouse, 1951. This photograph shows the Port War Signal Station during a period of renewed military activity.*

Local Government. One matter that was raised at the public local inquiry into the appeal was the possible increase in the threat to wildlife that might result from the establishment of a holiday camp so close to a site of special scientific interest. There was a rumour that Butlins were interested.

Another threat to wildlife was raised in the letter. Apparently there had been a proposal to establish an air-to-sea rocket firing range at Holmpton. A public inquiry was held and strong local protest was expressed. So, at the beginning of 1952, the Air Ministry put forward amended

160 Blue Bell Inn corner, 1964. At the rear of the Blue Bell Inn the foundations of the D.E.M.S. building can still be seen. The irregular field beyond straddles the line of an ancient lane leading from the old village of Kilnsea to the Humber foreshore.

161 Sunny Cliff, 1964. The bases and some blast walls of the military hutments associated with the artillery camp/prisoner of war camp are still visible.

162   *From the 'parade ground' looking towards the military buildings, November 1964. The anti-submarine boom may be seen stretching out into the Humber. Most of the First World War military buildings shown in the photograph still remain to this day, and some are now used for the Humber Pilots' base.*

proposals to establish the rocket range across Spurn Peninsula itself. Although the conservancy council and the Yorkshire Naturalists Union had raised strong objections it appeared that the matter was still under consideration 'by the Inter-departmental Committee dealing with land requirements'. In the event the proposal was dropped.

Ralph Chislett, at about the same time, came up with reasons why Spurn should be made into a nature reserve. He cited Spurn's unique ecological and biological interest for scientists. Students of marine natural science – marine biology, marine botany, ecology, ornithology, geology and entomology all visited the place and took advantage of the facilities offered by the bird observatory. With the sea to one side, and a great estuary to the other, the peninsula was unique in Yorkshire; and without complete parallel anywhere else, possessing a very unusual flora and fauna of its own, due to its position, and the twice-washed daily estuarial mudflats and salt marsh. Because of its geographical position, it was

one of the best places for the study of migration of birds in Europe.

It would seem that Richard Wood MP found the naturalists' case compelling for, in April 1953, he wrote to George Ainsworth that there were many other places that people could visit for a day trip and he therefore felt that 'the wildlife and the military authorities were of the first importance ... and I think that if the road were closed by the War Department that would be a happy answer to the problem'. He offered to write to the War Office himself.

In 1955 Dr Elizabeth Evans of the Nature Conservancy decided to visit the peninsula to see for herself, a visit that probably took place in the summer. In August she wrote to the command land agent, at Shenfield, York, to say that the Nature Conservancy was interested in the Spurn Peninsula and would give full support to any proposal to declare it a nature reserve 'under Section 21 of the National Parks and Access to the Countryside Act. 1949'.

The idea of closing the peninsula at certain times of the year was mooted – 'for the sake of the breeding birds alone, from April to early August', and it was also suggested that drivers and passengers in vehicles needing to make the journey down to the lighthouse and lifeboat cottages should not leave the road 'except for legitimate business'. George Ainsworth decided that a publicity campaign to save Spurn might help, though Chislett feared that it would only serve to draw attention to what Spurn had to offer. Several local newspapers gave support to the campaign, notably the *Hull Daily Mail* and the *Yorkshire Post*. Chislett did not think that the media attention had much effect:

> except to send more people down to Spurn at weekends; and to rouse the Rural District Council to the possibility that a nature reserve, with controlled access by the public, might not benefit some farmers who wanted to let caravan sites and otherwise improve land values, on which their own ideas of 'amenity values' depend'

An exchange of letter in July 1956 between Major L.E. Andrews, Royal Engineers, at the War Office and Lt-Col W.B.L. Manley, is of interest:

> Dear Bill, ... Regarding your request that we should close the road between mid-day Saturday and Sunday night each week, I find that the Holderness Rural District Council objects to the road being closed until such time as the draft map prepared under the National Parks and Countryside Act, 1949...has been finally determined. In the face of this opposition I regret that we cannot accede to your request. ... I can confirm that it is possible that we may dispose of the majority of the land, although other departments, e.g. the Admiralty, have certain interests which they may wish to take over. I suggest therefore that you communicate with our Land Agent at York and indicate the area you would wish to take over.

In September 1956 Ralph Chislett produced a document summarising what areas any Spurn nature reserve should cover:

163   *The 'parade ground', May 1964. The military buildings on the right have since been demolished, and the new lifeboat cottages have been erected on the site.*

We consider that the whole peninsula south of Kilnsea should be included. The small area now cultivated north of Warren Cottage should continue so. Subject to being free of liability in respect of erosion, drainage, etc. on both sea and Humber side, we could probably raise a fund to buy the land above Warren Cottage back towards Kilnsea now cultivated by R. Clubley and to hold it for him to continue as at present. If the area from the south-east side of the guns enclosure to the place where gate-posts exist near to the rise to the narrow ridge were excluded, we should be handicapped, but could still carry out our work. A Nature Reserve need not mean exclusion of the public, but only exclusion from certain areas in the breeding season, and from other areas where research work is carried on, and the regulation of behaviour (shooting, egg collection etc.).

The growing hostility between locals and the naturalists is demonstrated in Chislett's next statement:

> One of the members of the Holderness Council is Mr Sharp, who we believe farms near Easington and is the brother of the Mr Sharp who owns a little land near Kilnsea. The mentality of both appears to be that of small landowners who want to draw as much rent as possible from as many caravans as they can crowd onto their land.

The naturalists had help in high places: Ainsworth mentions support from the Honourable Richard Wood, the local MP, who 'is, as you know, the son of Lord Halifax. I have had letters from Lord Hotham and Lord Middleton who are apparently interested in the preservation of Spurn.' Rumours were rife now that the army was preparing to move out. Chislett in September wrote to Evans 'At a time when the guns have been removed and those who keep them have lost their jobs, there are sure to be rumours.'

By October 1956 several protagonists were interested in what happened to Spurn. They were broadly split into two camps: those who wished to protect the peninsula from damage by the general public, and those who wished the public to have unfettered access. In the first camp were the War Department, which still owned the peninsula, the Yorkshire Naturalists' Union, which ran Spurn Bird Observatory, and Nature Conservancy, which though not prepared to put Spurn forward as a National Nature Reserve was determined to protect it if it could. In the second camp was Holderness District Council, which was determined to keep the road open, the *Holderness Gazette*, which supported local people's access to a local beauty spot and Easington Parish Council, which had associations with some people with a vested interest in buying the peninsula should it come on the market. East Riding County Council generally seemed to be siding with the lobby concerned to protect Spurn from too much public access. The county council in 1956 was still dominated by the local gentry, and might be accused of representing an elitist view, in comparison with the rural district council, on which served local farmers and businessmen (though Chichester-Constable of Burton Constable was a rural district councillor).

In a document drawn up by Dr Evans of Nature Conservancy the current state of the peninsula was described in some detail: all along the peninsula were many signs of army activity, such as barbed wire and 'various forms of concrete'. Part of the peninsula was thought still to contain mines, which were being cleared by local army personnel. Notices were placed at the entrance to warn visitors that they entered at their own risk. Particular interest focused upon the way people have travelled down the Point because of the disputed right of way. Before the road, apart from the railway line, a horse and cart could make its way along the peninsula using the footpath and the sands. Since the war the new concrete road has been used by an increasing number of people to get to the easily accessible beaches, and at peak weekends in summer 'the hordes of cars parked along the track are a real hindrance to authorised traffic'. However, much as they might wish to do so, the War Department could not close the road to the public because of a disputed right of way. Following instructions given in the National Parks and Access to the Countryside Act, 1949, Easington Parish Council had prepared a map of footpaths and rights of way, including a path down the peninsula, following the concrete road. That map was accepted by the Holderness Rural District Council, but experts for the War Department had drawn up a different map, showing that the footpath, which did indeed run a short way along the road, soon left it to go

164   *View from the Port War Signal Station/coastguard tower of the old inn and the anti-submarine boom, August 1966.*

along the peninsula near the western shore, actually traversing the beach for part of the way. That map, which was supported by the county council (and is more accurate historically), was to be brought up at an inquiry as an objection to the parish council's map. It was acknowledged that the right of way down Spurn Peninsula was one of the most difficult cases to be dealt with under the 1949 Act and that it might not be settled for several years. In the meantime the War Department was continuing its interest in the right of way problem, despite the fact that it was planning to give up Spurn as a military base. When this was to happen (probably in a year or so) it was thought that the Admiralty might take over, so the closing of the road would still be a matter of importance to the government.

The Nature Conservancy document stated that the Holderness Rural District Council was firmly against the closing of the road to public traffic, even if the footpath were kept open. A possible

hidden agenda, which might have been affecting the district council's attitude, was mentioned here – 'Rumour has it that this view is put forward by a vocal minority who have financial considerations at the back of their minds.' It was well known that some local businessmen were interested in buying Spurn for leisure activities, such as a holiday camp. The document stated that the county council was anxious to reach some settlement satisfactory to all concerned. They had expected the War Department to win their case against Holderness RDC, and to settle the whole problem by closing the road. If the area was now put on the market who would want to buy it? The county council considered that Spurn was of no economic value and, from the coast protection point of view, a liability. They would firmly oppose further caravan development in the district, and were 'not unsympathetic' to the local naturalists. If the Nature Conservancy were to take the lead in establishing a National Nature

Reserve, the council would give them every support, but in the present complex situation they would do nothing.

The YNU report of 1956 stated that there had been strenuous efforts to have the peninsula declared a nature reserve. Dr E. Evans of Nature Conservancy had consulted with the landowners and planning authority but 'strong Yorkshire support especially from the East Riding is needed'. In 1956 the terns had a better year because day-trippers did not come in large numbers owing to a very wet summer. However, there was clearly tension between the naturalists and those people who wished to visit Spurn to enjoy its scenery and extensive beaches. The peninsula had been closed to the public for so many years during the two world wars that it was understandable that, as more people acquired cars and motor-bikes, Spurn was regarded as an ideal day trip from Hull and further west.

In March 1957 members of Spurn Bird Observatory informed Dr Evans that there was a movement of troops out of the peninsula. She wrote to Colonel Manley asking for information 'as we need to be in a position to move quickly if there is a likelihood of a change in Spurn's status'. A flurry of letters passed between the interested parties, and it is at that point that the Yorkshire Naturalists' Trust (now the Yorkshire Wildlife Trust) is mentioned in the correspondence, though they were involved well before that time, many of the same individuals being represented on both the YNU and the YNT. Dr Evans wrote that 'we offered to keep [the Chairman of the YNT] in touch with future developments and so to avoid competition between two organisations as happened over Colt Park Wood'.

The correspondence, which has survived in the archives, from 1957 between Dr Evans of Nature Conservancy and various military persons demonstrates the close links between them. Those negotiations proceeded outside the public domain and, when local people in Easington and district complained after Spurn was bought by the YNT that they were never given the opportunity to purchase it themselves, they clearly had a point:

26th March 1957 Major L.E. Andrews, War Office to Manley. Dear Bill I am afraid that formal alienation proposals for this area have not yet reached the War Office, but as you have advised the Command Land Agent of your interest you may rest assured that you will not be forgotten.

28th March 1957 Manley to Evans. ... it would be quicker and best if you made direct contact with the Command Land Agent at Command HQ. ... If you care to mention my name you may find that you get on a more personal footing as he and I were well known to each other during the war.

Once it became likely that Spurn was to be sold, the name of Brigadier R.C.J. Chichester-Constable was mentioned, since the peninsula had been compulsorily purchased from him in 1925 and had to be offered back. If he wished to take up the offer it was thought that he might be prepared to lease it as a nature reserve. If he did not, then the Nature Conservancy hoped to persuade the Yorkshire Naturalists' Trust to take over the area itself, with support from the Nature Conservancy. The matter was first discussed at a meeting of the YNT council on 23 March 1957.

A new protagonist had also come on the scene. The Humber Conservancy Board was apparently interested in Spurn Head. R.M. Sandford for Command Land Agent at York wrote to Dr Evans on 2 April 1957:

You are quite correct in your understanding that the military authorities are vacating Spurn, and a very comprehensive report is now in process of preparation by various branches of Northern Command and which will be sent to the WO during the course of the next three weeks. Thereafter instruction will be awaited from the WO as to the steps which are proposed with a view to disposing of the WO's interest in Spurn, either by sale or by transfer to another Department. I made a point of ensuring that a note was included in the report referred to, covering both the interest of the YNU in their bird-watching, ringing and recording activities and the preservation, as far as possible, of Spurn as a bird sanctuary, and the interest of the NC on similar lines. I will have an opportunity of seeing the report in its final form before it is sent to the WO, and I will ensure that these two points are adequately covered.

A document from Nature Conservancy set out the arguments for and against Spurn being designated a National Nature Reserve:

FOR:

1. The peninsula is in an ideal position for protection since there is only one access route by land.
2. The area would provide valuable teaching and study facilities for Hull University and schools.
3. The fact that the area was a nature reserve would provide a tremendous stimulus for local ornithologists.
4. The Conservancy, being a national body, is in the strongest position to act quickly as the present situation crystallises.

AGAINST:

1. If the Conservancy were to acquire the area, they would have to take over the right of way case from the WD.
2. Coast protection obligations might prove a liability.

Recommendation

Spurn peninsula is of sufficient scientific importance to warrant its acquisition as a national nature reserve by whichever means seems most appropriate.

Despite that recommendation, Spurn was not considered suitable as a NNR when the matter came before the Committee for England in mid-April. However the YNT was beginning to take a very active interest in the future of Spurn and, on 21 April 1957, Clifford Smith of the YNT wrote to Dr Evans asking for information, including the likely responsibility of the new owner with regard to maintaining the shoreline against the action of the sea. He also asked whether the present roadway constituted a right of way, and what would be the status of the buildings vacated by the War Office. He also wanted to know how negotiations might be conducted for acquiring ownership of part or all of the area, and what were the pros and cons of acquiring part only of the property. Nature Conservancy replied that Spurn was very suitable for a local nature reserve and that all reasonable help and support would be given with that object.

In July discussions in the Nature Conservancy concerned a proposal from Frank Mason, Honorary Secretary of Hull and East Riding Wildfowlers' Association, that a bird sanctuary should be established at Spurn, governed by a committee of wildfowlers and naturalists in equal numbers, on the lines of the Humber Wildfowl Refuge. Dr Evans was quite supportive of that suggestion – 'I am sure it would be worthwhile meeting them to find the extent of common ground.'

Matters were not moving very fast in the negotiations but the YNT's interest in the purchase is clear from an undated letter from Wilfred Taylor of the YNT to Nicholson for the Nature Conservancy:

> Some of the legal aspects, particularly in relation to the maintenance of the sea defences against erosion by the sea and the right-of-way are still somewhat obscure. It is however an area of great interest to Yorkshire naturalists; not only have they watched over the colony of Little Terns for more than fifty years, but they have also established the main Yorkshire ringing station at Warren Cottage. If the YNT can find a way through these two difficulties it will be prepared to make an offer when the property is put up for auction. Such an offer would be unlikely to exceed £2,000 or the value of the land and there might be a bidder who could make some use of existing buildings and offer more. We do not think, however that the ERCC will permit holiday camps or caravan sites on the promontory so there may be little competition.

Local people were largely ignorant of those negotiations and discussions. No love was lost between the different interest groups. The attitude of some naturalists (and indeed a certain class prejudice) comes over from the secretary of an ornithological society that had visited Spurn in August 1958, and wrote to thank Spurn Observatory, saying 'the biggest bugbear was the host of beach-lollers with portable radios, deckchairs, tents, and rubber ducks etc'. The antagonism between the natural history lobby and the 'beach lollers' came to a head in 1958 when the YNU applied to the Secretary of State for War to close the peninsula entirely from 15 April to 15 August. The ban was to include walkers as well as those in cars or on motor-bikes. Many local people were incensed by that proposal and a petition was organised, volunteers made house-to-house visits and within a week they had 1,500 signatures. The lifeboat crew supported the petition, because visitors served to break down the families' isolation, whilst lifeboat wives provided refreshments for the day visitors.

The matter of closing the peninsula went to the county council for consideration at the end of February. The debate, according to the *Holderness Gazette*, 'provided the most exciting scenes in the Chamber for a long time'. All the Holderness councillors spoke against the motion. Alderman Connor spoke for local people when he said the proposal:

> had aroused a good deal of disquiet not only in the area immediate to Spurn Point but throughout the district ... Spurn Point had an amenity to offer, for when the wind was to the east people could go to the west side and enjoy the amenities and vice versa ... It was not a place that catered for the ordinary seaside tripper or visitor, and the people who went there were not vandals ... The Naturalists were applying to do something which many other people had tried to do, such as the War Department, without success.

Those councillors who supported the closure of the peninsula said that it was unique so far as birds were concerned, and that unless there was some restriction of access, Spurn would lose that unique characteristic. They pointed out that the public had never had a right of way along the road, since it was a private road built by the owners of private property, and the footpath to the end of Spurn did not follow the military concrete road. Lord Hotham referred to YNU evidence that there had indeed been great disturbance of rare birds. It was for the Secretary of State to decide what he should do about the long-term future of Spurn, but the General Purposes Committee had agreed to support the restriction on travel down Spurn by 13 votes to five. Lord Hotham felt that it would be a great pity if it was said in the future that they had not been able to maintain it as a sanctuary and support the preservation of very rare bird life. As a compromise the peninsula was closed from April until July rather than August, the busiest month for day visitors.

The petition was expected to reach 3,000 signatures before it was sent to the Secretary of State. Those opposing the naturalists hoped that the government would decide against the closing of the peninsula, or alternatively might announce the holding of a public inquiry, when strong representations would be made from the local authority, organisations and individuals.

The army's evacuation of Spurn was imminent. The War Department passed the matter to the Ministry of Housing and Local Government, and a meeting was held in London on 6 August 1958 at which all interests were represented. In the *YNT Newsletter* for September 1976 Dr Wilfred Taylor, who was president of the Trust during those negotiations gave his account of the lead-up. He said that he was very friendly with one of the Northern Command Estate Agents and learned from him that the War Department was considering putting the promontory up for sale. The Trust told him that they would hope for an opportunity to bid as the area was ideal for the creation of a nature reserve:

> The Trust was finally notified that the sale of the Spurn Promontory was to take place at the Ministry of Housing & Local Govt on 6th August 1958 and that the chair would be taken by Sir Edward Playfair. Some 18 national and local bodies sent delegates. Four members of the Trust were present at this meeting and the President – as chief delegate – was supported by the Hon Secretary and the Trust's legal advisor, Bryan Burstall.

Richard Wood, the MP for Holderness, reported later on that crucial meeting:

> It became clear that none of the authorities present were prepared to take over the financial burden of maintaining the present sea defences. The YNT who were one of the authorities present at the meeting were however willing to acquire the Head. As it is an area of special scientific interest the Nature Conservancy also favoured the proposal. The War Department land lying to the north of the area acquired by the Trust is to be sold by public auction subject to the interest of the former owners of the agricultural and or their successors. The price for which the Head was sold to the YNT was agreed between the Trust and the War Department as fair and reasonable to both parties. The War Department will be selling off the hutting and reserving certain other valuable assets.

165   *View from the Port War Signal Station/coastguard tower of the old inn when the anti-submarine boom was being removed and other buildings demolished, July 1967.*

At that stage prospective purchasers were given to understand that the coast protection works necessary to preserve the peninsula had cost £17,000 per annum. It was stated at the time that between 1945 and 1960 12 men were engaged in the full-time maintenance of the defences at Spurn. Obviously local authorities would not or could not take on such a burden on behalf of their ratepayers. Later the *Gazette* asserted that prospective buyers were not informed that this responsibility was to be waived.

As stated above, Godwin Battery at Kilnsea was also redundant and, in 1959, it was put up for sale, being advertised in the sale catalogue as 'Fort Godwin the Valuable Gun and Camp site'. No particular wildlife interest existed in this site and the sale went ahead without opposition from the natural

history lobby. That sale took place openly with a sale catalogue produced, itemising the site and its buildings (see below). Matters were managed differently with Spurn Fort, and the *Holderness Gazette* continued to suggest that the sale was conducted in a clandestine manner. In April 1959 the newspaper reported that the future of Spurn had been raised at meeting of Holderness Rural District Council by Councillor Robinson, who said there seemed to be 'a veil of secrecy' over it. He said that if there were no commitment to continue the defences then Spurn had been 'given away'. Some might say that this was confirmed in early April 1959 when it was reported that the War Office was to sell Spurn to the YNT for £1,500. Mr Clifford J. Smith, the secretary of the Trust, assured the *Gazette*:

> We have no intention of closing the peninsula to the general public. Our intention is to run it as a nature reserve. There will be one or two minor regulations to keep people off areas where birds are breeding, but if the public co-operate with us there will be no restriction other than that.

Incidentally the Port War Signal Station, which was still being used by the coastguards, was excluded from the sale (though in the early 1960s the coastguards moved to a purpose-built tower on Sandy Beaches Caravan Site at Kilnsea). The two lighthouses were also excluded from the sale. At that time the War Department was still paying one shilling per annum to Trinity House to use the low light as a water tank. The land sold to the Trust totalled 470 acres including the foreshore between the high-water mark of ordinary tides and the low-water mark, with a right of access reserved along Spurn road and across the sand dunes 'for the purpose of inspecting and maintaining the piling and boom defence barrier'. In 1961 'the low light stump' was given up by the War Department, and Trinity House wrote to YNT to ask whether they would accept it. They refused, not wishing to take on the responsibility. There was to be a reprise of that situation after 1985, when the high lighthouse went dark and Trinity House wanted the Trust to take it on.

The *Gazette* continued to complain of the secrecy of the sale:

As far as can be ascertained no advertisements appeared regarding [the sale] and it would have passed unnoticed had it not been for a Holderness resident who saw an article in a Midland newspaper. ... That the low figure of £1,500 has been accepted as payment for such an important and valuable strip of land has astounded Holderness people, but what they want to know now is who is to be responsible for the annual maintenance charge of £17,000 for sea defences. It is obvious that the Naturalists will not be able to meet such a charge. The question is, if they are not to be held responsible for this why weren't the Holderness RDC offered it under similar circumstances? It appears that no one cares what happens to the sea defences now, and these may be left to fall into disrepair. Men who know the coast in these parts warn us that if this is so the sea will breach the peninsula at the narrowest part and in a very short time the Point will become an island.

The *Gazette's* alternative future for the peninsula demonstrated that it supported those businessmen who wished to establish a holiday camp on Spurn:

> What has escaped most people's attention who have been deliberating on this subject is the enormous potentialities in developing this site as an 'Island in the Sun'. It is a natural beauty spot that could be one of the most attractive holiday centres in the country, bounded by the blue sea on one side with calm waters on the other, it lends itself ideally for all kinds of aquatic sports and pastime. It has all the romance and colour of a south sea island with its white soft sandy beaches and tranquillity. With ocean going liners and river traffic passing within a stone's throw it has a charm of its own and the numerous buildings still in repair and water laid on, provided the basis of a ready-made holiday camp. We venture to suggest that with a nominal charge to cars visiting the peninsula the whole of the £1,500 could be cleared this year. As a pull-on trailer caravan site (not static or permanent) a section of the peninsula could become a veritable gold mine without any expenditure for development whatsoever. Holderness is crying out for outside revenue and the development of this site could alter the whole outlook of this part of the Riding.

In April 1959 the national newspaper the *Daily Mail* carried the story of the sale of Spurn. It suggested that the Trust got the peninsula for £1,500 when it was worth £50,000, and that they got a secret tip-off from the War Office that they could buy nine lifeboatmen's cottages, two bungalows, roads, electricity and water services and barracks holding 2,000 men for a bargain basement price. 'Have the birdmen the right to make a private club of the dunes and bathing beaches that gave pleasure to thousands?'

The lifeboatmen too were concerned. Crewman Elvin Stott said – 'Other people are annoyed because they are to be locked out but we will be locked in. They say they will give us keys but what about our friends who want to come and see us? It will be like living on Alcatraz.' His wife, who catered for visitors, said 'This was my little sideline but without visitors I shall have no custom.' 'Weather-beaten' Robertson Buchan, the coxswain, said that his main worry was keeping the road open – 'Who is going to be responsible? Not the birdwatchers. I think they would like to see the Point become an island.' Mr Wilfred Lunn, a Withernsea printer (and proprietor of the *Holderness Gazette*, which had led the campaign against the Yorkshire Naturalists' Trust), waved an arm over the vast site and its buildings – 'I feel we have been cheated. Look at this – it is a ready-made holiday camp with all the chalets and a choice of river or sea-bathing.'

The Observatory secretary, George Ainsworth, said 'We are not keeping the Point for the few – we get hundreds of people from all over the world. If we do let the public in we may have a man with a white armband taking admission and car-parking fees.' Wilfred Taylor described the negotiations with the War Department once the decision had been made to sell. The Hull firm of Messrs Todd & Thorpe was chosen as valuers, and it was agreed that both parties should make an independent valuation. Messrs Todd & Thorpe based their valuation upon the fact that all work on the sea defences would shortly cease. They estimated the probable life of the promontory thereafter as five years and, as they had been informed that the rents were £180 p.a., they simply multiplied those two figures together and obtained a final figure of £900. The Trust then instructed Messrs Todd and Thorpe to negotiate with Col Gillingham, who indicated that the War Department's valuation was £2,000. A price of £1,500 was finally agreed

166 *St Helen's Church, 1964.*

and on 2 April 1959 a deposit of £150 was paid. Taylor stated that members of the council had undertaken to raise £850, the Spurn Bird Observatory £200 (later increased to £250, and apparently all Chislett's money) and the Rowntree Village Trust had promised £500. The Society for the Promotion of Nature Reserves also promised £300 (later increased to £375).

The New Regime

Once it had became clear that Spurn was to be a nature reserve the *Gazette* concentrated upon campaigning for access to be available to all. Editorials continued to talk up the fears that Spurn would only be available to the select few:

> We understand fences are to be erected at the entrance to the peninsula, and it is obvious that the Naturalists will close it to the public on the slightest provocation. We would remind members of this august body that other people who may not qualify for the title of naturalist or ornithologists still derive a great deal of pleasure from bird-watching and studying the fascinating flora and fauna in this part of the world and who studied it at Spurn long before the naturalists came on the scene. It is felt that this reserve has been handed over for the exclusive use of the few at the expense of the pleasure and enjoyment of many thousands.

In August 1959 Ralph Chislett wrote to the newspaper championing naturalists' trusts, which were:

> composed of people with ideals ... who give their time freely and pay their own expenses. They employ local people where possible ... Trade is brought to local people. They do not interfere with local agriculture. They desire local co-operation. All that is asked of local people is that the purposes for which a property was acquired shall be respected; that nothing be done to spoil the features that give a place its special interest ... Too many thoughtless visitors, even at weekends only, can harm the features that give a property its distinction and can interfere seriously with the work of those making long-term studies in Natural Science ... Where a property is acquired by a trust it does indeed mean that it has an interest for people who live far beyond the locality in which it is situated, which might rather be a matter of local pride otherwise.

Gradually the hostility began to die down. In an article in the *Holderness Gazette* on 21 August entitled 'Spurn – All Quiet' the reporter wrote:

> It would seem that as long as the YNT allow access to the Spurn peninsula there will be little objection on the part of the public to paying the 1/- car park fee now being charged. Last Sunday hundreds of motorists visited Spurn and were able to go where

they pleased; some picnicked among the grassy sand dunes, others found pleasure in a walk round the point, while many preferred to sunbathe on the beaches, especially on the river side which was sheltered from the cool breeze off the sea. There were no notices prohibiting the public from any special areas as far as could be seen and it was a very pleasant day for those who were there.

The Yorkshire Naturalists' Trust set about finding a warden and also requested volunteers to help with patrols of the ternery. The Spurn Bird Observatory accepted some responsibility for that role and a local farmer, Mr J.R.P. (Redvers) Clubley 'kept a watchful eye over the peninsula'. On 1 March 1960 Peter Mountford became the Trust's warden, living in one of the bungalows (now the 'annexe') that had been built for the caretakers of the anti-aircraft guns. For the first few years Spurn Bird Observatory paid half of the warden's salary. The Observatory apparently found his presence very helpful, and recorded that 'blank days were avoided for the log'. Moreover visitors were able to make use of his bungalow as extra accommodation and 350 visitors stayed overnight at the Observatory in 1960.

Many of the defunct buildings on the peninsula were of no use to the YNT, and preparations were made to take down and sell those which could be re-erected elsewhere. In June 1960 a big sale took place of many of them, including all the Nissen huts near the entrance to the fort on the Point. The sale was covered in the *Hull Daily Mail*:

The Spurn NAAFI ... was knocked down by a demolition company for £280 on Thursday. A nearby sectional Army building was bought by farmer Clifford Drescher for £305. It was said it would eventually become Hollym village hall. Both buildings were included in an auction of hutting and Army camp installations conducted on the site. There were 34 lots and about 50 bidders. Two large armoured steel look-out towers went for just over £127 to Mr Alfred Hutchinson, farmer, cattle dealer and licensee of the White Horse Inn, Hutton Cranswick. Farmer F. Northgroves bought the NAAFI dormitory building for £212 10s intending, he said, to use it as a workshop. Twenty Tarran and Nissen-type huts went from 50 shillings to £30 or more, according to size and condition, and storage tanks ranged between ten shillings and £25.

Hollym Village Hall is still in use. Spurn Bird Observatory also found a use for some of the huts – from 1961 an old army hut was used to provide a lookout point on the Narrows.

Near the lighthouse Horseshoe Bungalow still stood. Vacated by Jack Johnson at about the time that the army left, it had been taken over by Harry Nicholson, a Cottingham butcher and county councillor, who used it as a holiday home. When the Trust bought Spurn he managed to persuade the Trust to let him stay on. Throughout the 1960s Nicholson also allowed Cyd and Wyn Barker of Hull to use the cottage. (Cyd was very good at maintaining the fabric.) The Barkers probably spent more time at the bungalow than did Nicholson. The Barkers remembered those years with enormous fondness:

We used to go shrimping and also get cockles and mussels in the bay ... The coastguard station was at the back of Horseshoe Bungalow. There were binoculars on a swivel and you could see the donkeys on Cleethorpes sands. If anyone went on the Binks they would open a sliding door and yell 'Off sandbank. Off sandbank.' A lifeboatman kept chickens in a Nissen hut round the back of the bungalow. The postman, Peter Snaith, brought milk, papers, post, groceries etc.

Once the military authorities gave up their interest in the peninsula they no longer needed Haile Sand and Bull Sand forts. In 1956 both forts were handed over into the care of the Humber Conservancy Board by the Ministry of Defence. Finding a buyer for these two huge fortresses in the estuary might be expected to be problematical. One suggestion was that Bull Fort could be used by the Humber pilots who, at that time, were still working from the pilot cutter. However in 1964 the board became the outright owner when it purchased both forts from the ministry. The board itself was amalgamated into Associated British Ports (ABP) in 1969. Weather-monitoring devices and navigational aids were installed on the forts. Bull Fort's bell was rung automatically by a gas-pressure hammer.

In 1962 the end of an era came for the Observatory with the retirement of two of its stalwarts. Ralph Chislett, who had been chairman since 1945, stood down, and George Ainsworth retired as honorary secretary to the Observatory. Ralph Chislett's influence on Spurn Bird Observatory cannot be overstated. Indeed, his influence upon the recording and photographing of birds in Yorkshire and further afield was enormous. But Spurn had a special appeal for him and, after his retirement in 1945, he and his wife Lilian spent much time there. He was as generous with money as with his time: it was Chislett who first rented Warren Cottage from the War Department, then making it available for fellow naturalists to use: when the Yorkshire Naturalist Trust needed money to purchase the peninsula Chislett made a substantial contribution. In 1960 he was the obvious choice to be chairman of the Spurn Management Committee and he held that position until his death, aged 80, in 1964. In his tribute to Chislett, published in the *Naturalist* of that year Bob Dickens wrote:

> In his late seventies, he not only endured the minor discomforts entailed in a three weeks' visit to Spurn in October-November, but he thought nothing of travelling from Masham to Spurn and back in a day – a round journey of some 200 miles. Arriving in time for breakfast he took the opportunity of sorting out records, ringing and observing birds, as well as undertaking the various duties in which his position as Chairman involved him.

George Ainsworth was a teacher at Malet Lambert School in Hull, who for many years spent much of his leisure time at Spurn, trapping and ringing birds. The YNU report for 1962 for the Spurn Bird Observatory stated that:

> to do justice to George in full cry in the mouth of a Heligoland trap would need the descriptive verve of a sports commentator. His energy and common sense often expressed with humour have smoothed away scores of difficulties. Without his optimism and enthusiasm the Observatory might never have been …

Chislett and Ainsworth, though very different characters, worked together on the SBO Committee for 18 years. Ainsworth stayed on the committee until 1972, and in that year an article on him by John Cudworth (succeeding chairman of SBO) and Bob Dickens paid tribute to his gift for enthusing and inspiring people to take an active part in Observa-

tory work, most especially in the ringing of birds. 'Any report to him of an unusual or interesting species was inevitably greeted with the question "Did you ring it?"'

In 1963 Peter Mountford, having served as warden for the reserve's first three years, resigned and took a job with the Nature Conservancy Council (now English Nature). In his time Spurn had begun to attract visitors on a large scale. 1964 brought a period of stability of management to Spurn. In that year John Cudworth (who had been a regular at Spurn since October 1949) became the chairman of the Observatory, and the Trust appointed a new warden, Barry Spence, to replace Peter Mountford. John Cudworth was to remain chairman until 1999, a period of 37 years. Barry Spence was to remain warden until 2002, a period of 38 and a half years. Spurn itself experienced many changes in those years, but at least its management was stable.

Barry, a native of Northampton, had come from Fair Isle, where he had been assistant warden for two seasons. Having been interviewed with other candidates at York railway station by Dr Taylor, the president of the Trust, Barry was offered the job, and after being given accommodation overnight at York, was driven by Dr Taylor to Spurn on a late December day. Spurn does not look at its best on a dull day in winter, but Barry decided to accept. He started on 1 February 1964. He was given accommodation in a bungalow at the Warren. That had been the quarters of Thomas Jardine who was the caretaker of the military buildings, and his wife Dorothy (née Tennison). When the military left, a caretaker was no longer needed. Part of it was used as a rest room for trust members for a few years, and part became Barry's home. Later, having married and with a growing family, he used the whole bungalow. The 'annexe' had become part of the accommodation for the Observatory, thus increasing the capacity to 17 and improving toilet facilities.

In the 1950s bird watchers did not engage in sea-watching but in 'ocean-gazing'. As telescopes and tripods became more widely available, visitors to the Observatory spent more time scanning the sea and in 1965 the first sea-watching hut was erected in Clubley's field (named after Redvers Clubley who farmed it), for the exclusive use of people staying at the Observatory. New facilities for the ornithologists were provided in the 1960s: in 1966 the Hollow Trap on the Point was built; and in 1968 a military building on the Point was converted to a ringing laboratory.

When Spurn was bought by the Trust in 1960 its life was expected to be short. Between 1945 and 1959, 12 men had been engaged in full-time maintenance of defences at Spurn. Once the Royal Engineers left, the sea defences began to crumble. A charitable body whose purpose was the protection of wildlife could not afford to pay for the necessary repairs and maintenance to the groynes. However, even after the army left, some care was taken that the groynes should carry out their purposes of trapping sand and keeping up the beach level. The chairman of Easington Parish Council, Mr Tom Graham, recalled that 'the Humber Conservancy Board employed a man on the peninsula to keep an eye on erosion and by simple methods he was able to keep that under control'. When between 1963 and 1965 some dunes eroded due to a col-

lapsed revetment, the prophets of doom for the peninsula began to seem only too correct. Chalk Bank East Trap was washed away at that time. The Trust was fortunate to have access to the advice of Redvers Clubley, whose practical experience in beach maintenance was second to none. In 1964 the charge for cars was raised for the spring to autumn period in order to limit the traffic and number of visitors. Nevertheless, at the August bank holiday 250 cars visited the peninsula. Record numbers also stayed at Warren Cottage and organised parties came on week, weekend and day visits. The Trust's ownership of the foreshore was explained in the 1964 report:

> There has been considerable misapprehension on the part of some visitors about the rights of the public on the foreshore, or to land there from boats. When the Trust purchased the Promontory the land together with the foreshore was conveyed to the Trust so that the common rights applicable to most of the foreshore in Great Britain as Crown Land do not apply to the foreshore at Spurn which is now private land.

167 *Blackmoor Farm, 1964.* The Riverside Hotel *now stands on the site of this former smallholding.*

In the early 1960s, with the growing popularity of car ownership, a visit to Spurn was becoming more and more popular. On 28 June 1963 the *Holderness Gazette* stated that 'A well known local personality' had positioned himself at the war memorial in the centre of Patrington … and counted vehicles passing from Hull in the direction of the coast. He found at the end of the day that many more vehicles travelled in the direction of Easington and Spurn Point than Withernsea! Entrance to the peninsula at that date was two shillings per vehicle (10 pence). This popularity threatened the birds and other wildlife, and it was claimed in 1964 that the numerous visitors were flattening the marram grass, and thus killing the roots that hold the sand dunes together. In an attempt to discourage visitors the Trust raised the entrance fee to the reserve from two shillings to five shillings in the summer of 1964.

As a result of that increase many people, rather than drive down, began to leave their cars by the gate and walk. The *Gazette* reported that the Trust's warden, Mr Barry Spence, had admitted that the idea of charging was to limit the number of people going onto the peninsula, because it is a nature reserve:

> If the naturalists are not a very selfish and high-handed group of people they should realise that people still regard the peninsula as their part of Holderness and that there is still a free right of way down it on foot, and that with all the thousands of pounds that must have been taken from the motorist they should have done something about providing better facilities for them to travel on the Point. What this organisation is doing with the money goodness knows, but they are certainly letting the peninsula go to seed … Vice-chairman of Withernsea Council said that in her opinion the Trust obtained the land against the wishes of the people – 'I understand that the actual area reserved for bird-watching activities is only a very small part of the Point. I don't think they should put birds before people. The price of 5/- is absolutely exorbitant and out of all keeping. As far as I can see the Naturalists are more interested in the peninsula as a moneymaking racket than they are as a bird sanctuary.

At that time the peninsula was quite broad at the northern end, and some were quite happy to stay in that area, where there were dunes and saltmarsh. Their cars, on summer weekends, some-

times stretched from the gate as far as the *Crown & Anchor* pub. The maintenance of the road was a matter that caused difficulty at times. In 1965 the *Gazette* recorded that, for the third time in 10 months, Spurn was cut off by a large mound of sand, blown across the road by a strong easterly wind. People delivering essential supplies had to telephone the estimated time of arrival at the sand barrier so that members of the community could meet them and manhandle the goods across the sand. The problem of getting rid of sand from the road was only resolved several years later when the warden, Barry Spence, was provided with a tractor for that purpose.

In 1964 plans were put before Holderness Rural District Council to use 21 acres of land between Easington and Kilnsea (apparently in or near Easington Lagoon, part of today's Beacon Lagoons Nature Reserve) as a disposal site for chemical trade waste from a firm at Saltend. Meetings were held in Easington to voice strong opposition. The Trust and Easington Parish Council were united in their opposition to that plan. They were told that a sub-committee of the rural district council had ear-marked the site as suitable, and that representatives of the Ministry of Agriculture, Hull and East Yorkshire River Board and Medical Office of Health had all visited the site and thought it was satisfactory. Councillor Frank Hill told the *Gazette* that:

> in his opinion this land was just about the worst they could have chosen. … this waste was very poisonous when it came into contact with air and with water. What worse position could they put it in than near the seaside where in summer there were children and visitors?

A letter was sent to the council with a form signed by 450 people objecting to the scheme. Easington Parish Council was promised that an anonymous well-wisher would provide legal assistance free of charge. The *Hull Daily Mail* pointed out that the burial site involved was near the beach and 'with coast erosion at 10-12 yards per annum the refuse will soon be rolling about on the beach.' In May 1964 the plan was dropped. The owners of the land, Hull and East Yorkshire River Board, had decided not to sell it.

168 *Sweetbriar Cottage and Cliff Farm, 1964. Sweetbriar Cottage is now called Kew Villa.*

Another threat was the proposal to dredge for sand and gravel on the seabed off Spurn, an activity that did take place and that is still causing concern. Interestingly, considering that at the time of writing (2006) the peninsula is still intact, albeit much attenuated in the northern part, by the middle of the 1960s news items were already appearing regularly in the local press about the concern felt by the lifeboat personnel that the peninsula was soon to be breached. Coxswain Buchan said:

No-one knows when the sea will break through and cut us off. It could be within the next year or it could be in 10 years' time. Once we are cut off I feel that will be the end of the station. You won't get men and their families staying on what would virtually be a desert island.I would hate to leave. But should the Point be breached we will have to pull out.

In 1966 members of the East Yorkshire Joint Advisory Committee for Coast Protection Works asked for major sea defence work to be carried out on Spurn by army engineers, with the government to bear the cost of materials. The cost was estimated to be £200,000. Nothing came of that proposal however.

During March 1967, high tides caused damage on the Humber side near the entrance, and the hut there was nearly undermined. Redvers Clubley advised that thorns should be put alongside the road between Narrow Neck and Chalk Bank, a successful measure that resulted in the building up of a substantial sand bank along the road. From December 1967 until February 1968 an outbreak of Foot and Mouth disease nationally closed the peninsula to the general public – an event that was to be repeated in 2001.

1968-9 was the year that electricity came to the peninsula via overhead wires. Hitherto the lifeboat cottages and other buildings had been supplied by a generator and storage batteries. They were nearing the end of their useful life and in any case the supply they provided was no longer adequate for modern needs. The RNLI carried out a thorough review, including the feasibility of transferring the station

169 *Northfield Farm, 1964. The farm, which was owned by the Tennison family, was demolished in the late 1980s. The little corrugated iron building with a porch is the former Easington Church Institute. It was removed from Easington Square and sold to the Tennisons for £25 when a new church hall was built in 1936.*

from Spurn elsewhere, but no other place was suitable. A meeting was held with representatives of the RNLI, the YEB and the Trust to consider various methods of providing a better supply. An overhead line carried on poles was the only practicable method of installing a supply. The nature of the ground and the threat of erosion damage ruled out other methods. In view of the services rendered by the lifeboat station the Trust gave its consent, but requested that the route of the line be chosen so as to inflict the least damage possible to the bird life and appearance of Spurn. A route was inspected and agreed to. The poles, which carried the wires, were all numbered – later, when they were painted in large lettering by members of the Observatory that was a great help to those seeking to identify the location of a bird! Nevertheless not everyone approved of a line of poles going down the peninsula and marring the landscape. It was probably forgotten that it was not the first time: telephones came to Spurn in the late 19th century

and telegraph poles are shown on photographs and drawings thenceforth. At some point before the Second World War those poles came down and the phone lines went underground. 1969 was also the year that Rothampstead Experimental Station installed a moth trap at the Warren. Thus began many decades (still ongoing) of moth trapping and recording at Spurn, carried out by the YWT warden, Barry Spence.

In 1969 a major new development, which would have resulted in the total transformation of the area, was suggested for Spurn. Partly to 'protect' the peninsula, and partly to make use of colliery waste, it was decided that Spurn Bight could be filled in! That was by no means the first time that such a scheme had been suggested. In the Parliamentary Session 1865-66 a Bill was promoted to embank and reclaim an area of 3,857 acres between Spurn and Sunk Island. It did not pass the Committee Stage in House of Commons, but in a Royal Commission Report of 1906, set up as a result of the Kilnsea floods of that year, William Stickney, a land agent who acted for the Constable family, suggested that the scheme should be looked at again, and that the clay bank could be faced with 'refuse' from Frodingham Iron Works at Scunthorpe. Nothing came of that but in 1957 a reclamation scheme for 4,600 acres in Spurn Bight was considered with an estimated cost of £1.5 million, and in 1969 the Central Unit for Environmental Planning produced a study called *Humberside: a feasibility study*. That was a year or two before the creation of 'Humberside' (an unhappy creation of national government which only lasted from 1976 to 1996). At that time the population of the East Riding and North Lincolnshire was expected to expand. An extra 75,000 people were expected to inhabit the area and the document looked at ways of accommodating them, both in relation to the built-up area and to industrial development. The land on the northern shore of the Humber between Paull and Spurn seemed to the planners to be ripe for industrial development. A further 12,000 acres of mud flats in Spurn Bight could also be reclaimed – the potential was enormous. To fill the bight would require a depth of 10 to 15 feet of spoil raise it above the level of spring tides. The total filling required 'could amount to as much as 250,000,000 cubic yards'.

That was a time when wildlife conservation was not a top priority, but the prospect of losing the Humber mudflats, with their rich diversity of birds and invertebrates, appalled many people. They were to be appalled still further when it was revealed a few years later that plans were in hand for the reclamation to be carried out by bringing 'pulverised fuel ash and coal spoil' from the Selby coalfields, which were about to be opened. The spoil would be carried in capsules via a pipeline into Spurn Bight. The East Yorkshire Conservation Council, led by Dr Derrick Boatman, responded to the threat to the lower Humber by producing a report entitled *Wildlife Conservation on the Humber*, in 1974. The press were alerted, and bodies such as the Nature Conservancy Council, the Royal Society for the Protection of Birds (RSPB) and the Trusts of Yorkshire and Lincolnshire added their voices to the opposition to the plans. In 1975 the Selby Coalfield Inquiry was set up, and the East Riding Conserva-

tion Council suggested that it should investigate the possibility of back-stowing spoil and ash in the mine rather than bringing it at great expense to Spurn. Simultaneously, studies on the ecology of the Humber stressed the national importance of the habitat. In June 1976, when the first draft of the Humberside Structure Plan was produced, it was stated that 'the case for the reclamation of Spurn Bight using solid waste from Yorkshire and Humberside is not proven'. So happily the plans came to nothing.

The Lifeboat

In 1959 the timber 'saw tooth' wall built in front of the lifeboatmen's houses was reinforced with concrete to protect them further from high tides. In 1960 a big celebration took place of 150 years of life-saving at Spurn. The *City of Bradford III*, dressed overall, went out to inspect the Spurn lightship. With her was the much decorated 84-year-old Robert Cross (he died aged 88 in 1964) and many dignitaries.

In the 1960s the lifeboat crew and their families were still living in the Victorian terrace of cottages built in the 1850s. Some idea of their daily life can be gained from a contemporary newspaper article:

> The families live rent free in the 100-year-old terraced block of houses... Most of the men have cars, and there is a daily bus service available at request to the [local] bus company ... Groceries are delivered once a week and the postman is also the milkman and paper boy. Every man is allowed one day off duty a month with two weeks and two or three days' holiday a year according to years of service. There are no reserves. If a launch is called with a man off duty the boat goes out with one man short. The lifeboat can operate with six men if necessary. ... The system of call-out is both simple and speedy. A telephone rings in Coxswain Buchan's home. In rapid succession the coxswain presses eight electric bell switches, all individually linked with the homes of the other seven crew and the station electrician, the only shoreman. (If there should be an electric failure he hand rings the huge brass bell outside his home, and there is also a siren.) Dressing as they run, the crew sprint the 150 yard stretch to the boathouse. Each man knows his job. The doors are opened, oil skins are taken out of the open wardrobe at deck level and the radio operators make their preliminary calls for position of the craft

in trouble. All is ready to launch and the coxswain orders the release of the fastening rope. No more than seven minutes have elapsed as the 22-ton lifeboat glides down the 120 ft slipway and hits the water at 40 mph. The crew have a right to share in any salvage money claimed as a result of their actions but they often waive this right in the case of a privately owned yacht which is not insured. Last year the lifeboat was exceptionally busy with 24 launches. ...Winching the lifeboat back into the boathouse is a delicate operation which can only be done in calm weather.

The fact that some of the families had cars now meant that the wives who could drive could take jobs away from the peninsula. For the first time they were not 'imprisoned' on the Point as their husbands were. The school had been converted into a community hall, where bingo and whist sessions were held and Christmas and New Year parties organised. A library, restocked at three-monthly intervals was also run in the old school. Mrs Buchan, wife of the coxswain, said that the people of the Point could get hold of their Withernsea doctor faster than the townspeople can get hold of theirs, and two of the crewmen were expert first aid workers. Twice a month the Reverend Leslie Erving travelled from Easington to conduct services in the small Anglican church.

170 *Coxswain Robertson Buchan at Spurn, n.d. After the removal of the railway lines in 1951-2 the lifeboatmen extended their gardens towards the road as may be seen here.*

171 *The lifeboat cottages, February 1967.*

172   *Humber lifeboat crew, 1961. The photograph shows: R. Appleby, B. Gerrard, E. Davies, C.Alcock, R. Buchan (coxswain), E. Stott, T. Alcock, R. Stott.*

By the 1960s Spurn was regularly visited by officials and dignitaries. For example, the then Arch-bishop of York, Dr Donald Coggan, made a pastoral visit to the peninsula in May 1964. He could not go out on the lifeboat because of inclement weather, but he was taken over the lifeboat house by the coxswain, Mr Buchan, and also called in at the little church. The Lord Mayor of Hull was also Admiral of the Humber and, from 1962, the visit of Hull civic heads was an annual event, arranged by Eric Fenton, chairman of the Hull branch of the RNLI. It became the practice for the party to be given refreshments at the *Crown & Anchor* after the visit to Spurn. The crew and their families were not safe from electioneering either! In September 1964 Richard Wood MP, visited Spurn and, after picnicking on the Point, he addressed the community near the lighthouse 'on the subject of pensions and education' and then asked for questions. One problem the men of Spurn put to him concerned the question of collecting refuse from the Point. They said that rubbish was not collected and had to be thrown into the sea, with the result that empty bottles were often washed ashore and broken, becoming a danger to the children and visitors.

In January 1963 the pilot cutter, the *J.H. Fisher*, was sunk in a collision with a 10,000-ton tanker in thick fog and a snowstorm. Since 1908 the pilots had worked under the auspices of the Humber Conservancy Board. They originally used sailing cutters, which by the early 20th century had been replaced by steam cutters that were anchored in the mouth of the Humber. Boarding boats were hoisted in and out of the water as required, initially oared boats that were later replaced by motorized boats. The boat gear on the *J.H. Fisher* was arranged to ensure rapid and easy working of the boats in heavy weather. In really inclement weather the cutters had to enter the river to seek shelter. Shifts in the sand banks, very high tides – all the cutters were vulnerable when on station in such a situation. The pilots themselves were the owners of the cutters, the working expenses of which were deducted from the pilotage dues. At the time of the collision 22 crew and 18 pilots were on board the *J.H. Fisher*. While they were being resued the Humber Conservancy Board was hustling together an emergency crew of pilots recalled from leave to man the port's other pilot cutter, the *William Fenton*. At that time the move nationally was towards shore-based pilots, as pilot launches had become faster, and because it was recognised that pilot cutters on station were very vulnerable to collisions such as this. In line with that trend the pilots were to move from their station at the mouth of the Humber onto Spurn within just a few years.

The winter of 1963 was the coldest since 1947. During the last week of January the Humber mudflats were completely frozen and piled high with pack ice. The water supply to the lifeboat cottages froze up, and they were dependent for some time upon just one standpipe, inserted with some difficulty into 'sand as hard as concrete'. When the thaw came it revealed leaks everywhere, especially in the complex system that had once fed Spurn Fort. The YNT had the costly task (partly subsidised by the RNLI) of blocking off the subsidiary pipes and reconnecting the cottages to the main supply, which thankfully had not frozen.

In 1965 oil was found in the North Sea for the first time. The 5,600-ton drilling barge, the *Sea Gem*, working 42 miles off the mouth of the Humber, was the first rig to find hydrocarbons. She was a former work barge with a drill deck, later fitted with legs. On 17 September 1965 signals were sent to the Cleethorpes base in code reporting that gas had been found, and by Sunday 19 September it was clear that this was an important find. On Wednesday 9 December 1965 a 40-foot flame was ignited at the top of the rig (the first to appear in the North Sea) signalling the start of tests to measure the quality and quantity of the find. The triumph of that discovery was to turn to disaster when, on 27 December, only two days after they had been celebrating Christmas on the rig, the crew began making preparations to move the rig to a new position two miles away. Whilst the legs were being lowered two of the

173 *Lifeboatmen and their families on the Point, 1963. Back: D. Buchan, L. Staves, G. Appleby; front: R. Buchan, B. Sayers, T. Alcock, E. Stott, R. Appleby, J. Sayers, C. Staves, R. Stott. In 1963 the crew's names and their families were: Robertson Buchan (coxswain) with 12 years' service, five as coxswain and seven as second coxswain, three children; Tom Alcock (second coxswain), nine years' service; Elvin Stott (bowman), seven years' service, one child; Cliff Staves (deckhand), eight years' service, two children; Mike Davies (deckhand), three years' service, three children; Arthur White (deckhand), the newest member, having joined the station in February, three children; Bob Appleby (first mechanic and chief radio operator), 15 years' service, one child; Eric Davies (second mechanic and assistant radio operator), four years' service, two children.*

eight legs suddenly crumpled. The rig began to tilt sideways and men were thrown out of their bunks, whilst others on the upper deck were thrown straight into the icy waters of the North Sea. Fortunately for some of the crew the British cargo ship *Baltrover* was only a mile or so away when the rig collapsed.

At Spurn the lifeboat crew had been looking forward to a party, to which all the members of the lifeboat community had been invited. Their wives had decorated the former schoolroom, prepared food and a small bar had been erected and stocked. All that was immediately put on hold as the crew scrambled for the lifeboat. She was out on the *Sea Gem* mission for nearly two whole days – probably the longest call-out in the service of the Spurn lifeboat. The men lived off tins of self-heating soup, corned beef, biscuits and tea. The Spurn lifeboat took out a party of divers, but conditions were too bad for them to dive. Divers went down eventually but no-one else was found. Most of the crew were rescued by the *Baltrover* or by helicopters that had been called out in the emergency. By the time these helicopters had arrived nothing could been seen of the rig except for one of the legs sticking above the water and a mass of wreckage. Thirteen men were lost as a result of that disaster.

A reporter writing in January 1966 had a rather impressive turn of phrase when describing the Humber lifeboat as 'poised for the call of duty on the storm-racked toe of Spurn with the quivering intensity of a greyhound in its trap', and the coxswain, Mr Buchan, as 'small, compact and with the clear eyes of a sailor man ... not afraid to take the calculated risk'. Second Coxswain Thomas Beverley showed the reporter around the lifeboat – 'There's a grappling line stowed down there,' he said:

a breeches buoy line, searchlight, white flares, blankets and jerseys, and a scaling rope ladder. In the crew's cabin amidships the iron rations are stored, nine tins of self-heating milk, nine of cocoa, four of corned beef, eight bars of chocolate, 200 cigarettes and two bottles of rum. In an adjoining locker is the rocket gun, with its cartridges, and 120 fathoms of rope carefully stowed so that it runs out freely. Then there are the flares, each with a distinctively shaped knob so that it can be identified by touch in the dark.

On 2 April that year the pleasure boat *Anzio* went aground off Donna Nook. She was on her way from Tilbury to Inverness where she was to run summer pleasure cruises. She was a steamer that did not carry any lifesaving appliances. The *City of Bradford III* was launched just before midnight and spent all night in a severe north-easterly gale, searching unsuccessfully for survivors. With no chance of getting alongside the vessel Buchan decided to veer down upon her. During that operation heavy seas were breaking over the *Anzio* and the *City of Bradford III*, and three lifeboatmen, Beverley, Staves and Knaggs, were washed off their feet, and though hurt went immediately back to their stations. At that point 15-foot waves were breaking over the wreck and there was no sign of life. The lifeboat stayed on the scene and at one point there was only five feet of water beneath her keel. When there seemed to be no hope and only the masts and funnel could be seen the lifeboat headed back to the Humber, having spent more than eight hours at the scene. Buchan and his crew put themselves in great danger in trying to find the crew, and awards were made by the RNLI to Coxswain Buchan and to T.M. Beverley, J.L. Sayers, motor mechanic, C.T. Staves, bowman, C. Staves and E.L. Knaggs. Ten men lost their lives on that night, including a father, two sons and two brothers.

The Lighthouse

From the late 1950s Spurn lighthouse no longer needed full-time lighthouse-keepers. It was made fully automatic and was operated by a time switch – the end of an era indeed. In 1963 the lighthouse attendant, Mr Len Greenstead, who was an ex-Army colonel, only needed to call in twice a day to check that the lights were in working order, and to open and close the blinds that protected the lights from sunlight. Alongside the lighthouse the compound of Smeaton's lighthouse, where the keepers had lived, was to have a new role. In the later 1970s Hull Trinity House leased one of the cottages to Hull College of Further Education and another to the department of geography, Hull University, to use as field centres. From 1967 the old inn over the road on the Humber side was leased to Hull

University botany department, so students from both institutions were well placed to study the geography, ecology and wildlife of the peninsula. In the late 1960s several military buildings near the Port War Signal Station were demolished, and another Spurn object of interest, the anti-submarine boom, was taken away.

Kilnsea in the Late 1950s to Late 1960s

Whilst all those changes were going on at Spurn things were changing at Kilnsea too. Like Spurn Fort, Godwin Battery was no longer needed by the army. Its disposal was fortunately somewhat less contentious. The camp had plenty of accommodation, and was perfectly suited for conversion to a caravan park. Caravan sites were springing up all along the Holderness coast as people became more prosperous and had a little more leisure time.

On 20 October 1959 'Kilnsea, Fort Godwin, the valuable freehold gun and camp site with extensive buildings and a house, in all about 25 acres,' was auctioned by B.L. Wells & Son in Hull. The sale catalogue makes fascinating reading. At that time, because the sea defences had been well kept up, the site was intact. The gun battery was still separated from the accommodation units by a concrete wall with double iron gates. The two tall battery observation posts (complete with a pair of nesting Little Owls) towered over the site. Some buildings would provide residential accommodation without any conversion: the warrant officer's bungalow near the battery was one such. Throughout the site were numerous toilet blocks (with the emphasis on male facilities), a multitude of wooden huts, Tarran-type huts, garages, two large buildings, formerly a hospital and a sergeants' mess respectively, a former NAAFI perfectly suited to adaptation for recreation for caravanners and so on. All were available for the purchaser, who would be able to live in Warrenby Cottage (Lot 2), described as 'built of cobble stone and brick'. That last shows that the cottage actually pre-dated the First World War camp. As it has since been substantially modernised and extended several times, it is difficult to imagine that house as a 19th-century building, but undoubtedly it was originally part of the village. A small part of the

campsite, 40 feet by 25 feet, near the cliff top, was reserved from the sale, as it was expected that the coastguards would move out of the Port War Signal Station on Spurn to a purpose-built tower there. (They did do so, though only for a few years.)

Godwin Fort was bought by Mr and Mrs Burgess, who were well-prepared, having been in America 'studying modern trends in popular seaside holiday-making'. They announced their intention to introduce many new ideas to the new site. The *Holderness Gazette* in March 1961 carried a piece describing their plans for a 'super caravan and chalet site' and announcing that they had applied earlier to Holderness Borough Council for planning permission for the caravan site with 250 'first-class static caravans'. Plans were also in hand to convert some buildings into chalets, with the provision of a lookout tower, presumably utilising one of the battery observation posts. Several months had been spent in clearing the site, which they hoped to make the most up-to-date holiday camp in the country. The name chosen was 'Sandy Beaches'. By September 1963, 140 caravans had been moved onto the site. A former barracks had been transformed into a self-service shop, whilst hot and cold showers and a launderette had been opened. The former NAAFI hut had been converted into a licensed club, available for both caravanners and locals. Plans were in hand for the creation of a paddling pool 'on the site of one of the gun emplacements [with] the other made into a sand pit for the kiddies'. The East Yorkshire coast was particularly popular with people from the West Riding, and many of the new caravan owners came from there.

Most of the locals seemed to welcome the newcomers on the campsite. They did indeed bring new business to the little village. By the 1960s more and more visitors were coming to Spurn and Kilnsea. The *Blue Bell Inn* had already closed, but the café established in the former pub did a good trade. The *Crown & Anchor* flourished. Ma Robinson, with her daughter Pat, provided sandwiches and meals on demand, as well as alcoholic refreshments, to people staying at Spurn Bird Observatory and to day and weekend visitors. The people who flocked to the peninsula came for many reasons. Those who wanted amusements could go to Withernsea

174   *The visit of the Archbishop of York to Spurn (in the flat cap, extreme left), May 1964. The wooden huts inside the fort gates have been removed by this date. They were sold off site soon after the Yorkshire Wildlife Trust bought the peninsula. Most other military buildings still remained.*

175   *The 150th anniversary of the Humber lifeboat, June 1960. The City of Bradford III, dressed overall, went out to inspect the Spurn lightship. With her was the crew, with Robert Cross, former coxswain of the lifeboat (aged 84), and many dignitaries.*

176 *John Cudworth and others sea-watching from Kilnsea sea wall. The line of tank blocks may be seen behind them.*

177 *Barry Spence, Yorkshire Wildlife Trust warden, with a long-tailed duck, 1969.*

a little further up the coast. Those who came to Spurn and Kilnsea came for the wonderful, fairly empty sandy beaches, with access to both the sea and the Humber, for good beach fishing (many of the people who bought caravans on Sandy Beaches were anglers), and of course for the superb bird-watching opportunities. In the 1960s many of the birdwatchers who came used the buses and stayed at the bird Observatory. Once at Spurn they tended to stay for a few days. The 'twitchers' of the present day who drive in, tick a small bird off their list and rush off again, were many decades in the future, though in 1951 Eva Crackles had recorded in her diary that she was beginning to become more interested in botany than birds, because of 'a rebellion against trends towards mere list ticking and rarity hunting'.

In June 1964 the *Holderness Gazette* reported the breaking-up of a little museum that might have drawn in even more visitors had it been kept together and exploited better. This was the museum begun by Philip Loten in a room at the rear of the *Neptune Inn*. After Loten's death it had a chequered history, being eventually taken over by a Mrs Speight who lived at Blackwell Villa. By the 1950s there was little interest in the quirky exhibits and, after her death and that of her son, it was decided to sell the collection in small lots. People came from as far as 200 miles away for the auction, and the roadside adjacent to Blackwell Villa was 'cluttered with alabaster busts, paintings, antique furniture ... stuffed birds, tame and wild, and foreign birds of prey, egg collections, swords and clubs.' Montages of toenails, feathers, and moths' wings ended up in many private houses in the area. It was a sad end to a wonderful part of Easington's local history.

In August 1964 the *Holderness Gazette* carried predictions of what South Holderness would be like in the year 2000. It makes interesting reading, given the plans already described, to fill in Spurn Bight and use the north bank of the Humber for industrial development:

> Extensions to the Hull docks and to shipping facilities will expand down the Humber and by the year 2000 one can visualise a large quay and docks at the Patrington side of Hawkin's Point, Sunk Island, capable of receiving large ships of both passenger and cargo from Europe and the world .... Hedon, Thorngumbald, Keyingham and Patrington will be major centres. Withernsea, as a seaside resort, should benefit enormously ..., and one can even see Easington to Kilnsea, (with the Spurn peninsula as we know it today having disappeared – the lighthouse being an island) being one of East Yorkshire's popular seaside resorts. Reclamation schemes may have taken in much of the land at Welwick and Skeffling Humber regions.

Few of those predictions came to pass, but in 1967 Easington became the site of a terminal

178 *The mortuary, 1968. This attractive little building dated from the 19th century. It was presumably built to accommodate the bodies of people from wrecked vessels, though it was not used for this purpose (so far as is known) in the 20th century.*

179   *The lifeboat house and the railway pier, 1963. This photograph gives an excellent view of the railway pier, still in very good condition in 1963.*

to process North Sea gas, the first in the British Isles. Until that time gas came from coal supplied by urban gas works. The natural gas had to be distributed via pipelines to customers, who needed to have their appliances converted to burn it. The introduction of natural gas led to a rapid increase in the amount of gas sold. Oil price rises made gas much more attractive to the industrial and commercial markets and gas demand rose still further. The terminal at Easington was to become very extensive as new oil and gas fields were discovered in the North Sea. The terminal no doubt contributed to Easington's economy, though how much is in dispute. The sprawling gas site on the cliff top certainly gives the northern part of the village an industrial appearance, and it has expanded significantly over the years. At the time of writing the gas fields near the British coast are in decline and a new undersea pipeline to Norway is being laid to bring gas to fulfil about 20 per cent of this country's needs for many decades to come. Just north of the Easington terminal is a small wind farm, and plans are in hand for more wind turbines off the Humber.

Nine

Towards the Millennium, 1970-2000

Contrary to expectations when the Yorkshire Naturalists' Trust acquired Spurn in 1960, the peninsula had still not been washed away a decade later (and neither had it done so by the year 2000)! The last 30 years of the 20th century did, however, see many changes that affected both the permanent and temporary residents on the peninsula. Towards the beginning of the period, the lifeboat families were provided with new modern houses. At about the same time, the pilots transferred their base of operations from their floating vessel at the entrance to the Humber onto dry land on the Point. Another major change occurred when the lighthouse went dark and when the Spurn lightship was removed from its station at the mouth of the Humber. In the same period, too, the coastguards returned to the Point but only for a short time before moving out again. At the north end of the peninsula, Spurn Bird Observatory continued to flourish from its base at the Warren. A noticeable feature of the late 20th century was the growing attraction of Spurn to visitors, who came in increasing numbers to enjoy a family day by the sea or for a day's bird-watching or sea-fishing. As bird-watching became more widespread and popular, so the numbers of bird-watchers visiting Spurn increased, especially during the spring and autumn migration periods. Another feature of that period was the clearance by the Yorkshire Naturalists' Trust of many of the former military buildings – much to the regret of military historians!

Spurn Nature Reserve

The Yorkshire Naturalists' Trust, first established in 1946, was by the 1970s expanding its collection of nature reserves, and the income from Spurn tended to be applied to the whole Trust area rather than be ploughed back into the reserve. Barry Spence, the Trust's warden at Spurn, was left to manage Spurn with little interference, though a management committee with representation from Spurn Bird Observatory as well as from the Trust met regularly to consider matters concerning the peninsula. In 1971 a survey of visitors, based upon 1,225 interviews, reported that the majority of people valued Spurn for its peace and quiet, and hoped that it would be preserved in a wild state. They commented adversely on the derelict buildings, difficulties of parking and inadequate toilets. Some, though not all, of those criticisms were addressed over the next few years.

Ten years after the peninsula became a nature reserve Spurn still had many military buildings of no use to the Trust, which described them as 'ugly and obtrusive'. In the 1970s their historic value as relics of the military's presence on the peninsula was little appreciated. In 1976 several of these MoD buildings were demolished, though the Trust recorded that 'a lot of unsightly structures remain and it is hoped that [we] will soon get grant aid to clear them'. It is true that the buildings, or some of them, were potentially dangerous, especially for adventurous children. The money was eventually forthcoming from the Department of the Environment and by 1979 all the gun sites and concrete blockhouse at the Warren had been demolished, as had the *Lifeboat Inn*. That last was a considerable loss. The row of cottages that adjoined the former inn were the only remaining relics of the very early days of the lifeboat and the plaque, which commemorated the subscription raised when the houses were built in 1819, disappeared when the building was demolished. Perhaps it may yet resurface?

Another very sad loss was the so-called 'mortuary', a building that dated from some time in the 19th century. That lovely little building with round windows was apparently built by Trinity House to give temporary accommodation to the bodies of ship-wrecked mariners. Vera Cross, who lived at Spurn from 1919 until 1939, said that it was never used for that purpose whilst she knew it, but it was used as a store for the perches that were placed upon the lighthouse for migrating birds. Fortunately some of the buildings, including the huge gun emplacements on the Point, were made of such thick concrete that they were left for military historians of the future to appreciate. In 1981 the triple rows of concrete anti-tank blocks, which went from the Humber to the sea just north of the reserve entrance, were removed and placed on the seaward

180 *Moving the anti-tank blocks to protect the Narrows, March 1981.*

side of the Narrow Neck with the aim of combating erosion at that point.

When the nature reserve first opened to the public, Redvers Clubley, whose knowledge of Spurn was unrivalled, was employed by the Trust to clear sand from the road with his tractor and trailer, and collect the entrance money in the summer months from a hut sited near the gate. At other times the entrance money was collected by the warden somewhere along the peninsula, wherever he happened to be. In 1973 the management committee began to investigate the possibility of providing Barry Spence, who now had a wife and two children, with a new house 'in a style suitable to its setting ... [and] upgrading the whole entrance area to Spurn'. A sketch design, which included a warden's house, an entrance control point, a lecture room and a display centre, was prepared, but because of financial restraints no further progress was made. Instead, in 1974 a rather more modest establishment was opened in a former army building described as 'a dilapidated old shed' just in front of Warren Cottage. Officially opened on Sunday 25 May by Colonel B.N. Reckitt, this information and sales centre was staffed on a part-time basis by Barry's wife, Christine. At the same time that Christine Spence began to help her husband, Redvers Clubley retired at the age of 75. In 1975, when it cost 30 pence for access by car, the Trust had reported that 62,000 people had visited the Point with an especially high count of about 2,000 on one particular bank holiday day. Clearly a centre such as this would fulfil a manifest need. In June 1976 the Point had to be closed to traffic because there was no space left for parking cars. As that was just before the demolition of the lifeboat cottages the car-parking on the Point was very limited. People often parked in the passing places, causing even more problems. In 1975 the passing places on the road were properly marked and speed-limit signs erected, thanks to Maurice Nethercoat, who was Clerk of Works to the Trust at that time. In 1976 the Trust still had the intention to build a more ambitious centre, and a visit was made to Gibraltar Point to view the facilities there. The subject of toilet facilities (or rather the lack of them) came up frequently. In 1976 the Trust had asked Holderness Borough Council to put toilets on the Point, but were told that that was not the local authority's responsibility. The demolition of the Port War Signal Station (or the old coastguards' building as it was known by then) in 1979, meant that those toilets were no longer available, and the YNT report of that year stated that 'the absence of any alternative provision [of toilets] presented the warden and his family with many difficulties during the summer'.

In 1978 Harry Nicholson, believing himself to be the owner of Horseshoe Bungalow, just north of the main lighthouse, decided that he no longer wanted it, and offered it to Cyd and Wyn Barker, who had been using it as a holiday home since the early 1960s. However, when they looked further into the circumstances of ownership prior to the sale, they discovered that it was not his to sell, since it actually belonged to the YNT! The Trust, for its part, that same year decided to use the bungalow as accommodation for their summer warden but, over the following winter, when Cyd Barker found that the building was not being properly maintained, he approached Major Ian Kibble, the Trust secretary, and suggested that the building needed someone (him) to keep it in good order. He offered to supply the summer warden with a caravan in exchange for a lease on the bungalow. The Trust agreed, and Cyd negotiated a very good deal – £25 per annum for 21 years, with the opportunity for other members of his family to take it over at the end of the lease if they so wished. In 1995, having spent over 30 years in Horseshoe Bungalow, the Barkers decided that the maintenance was getting too much for them, and most reluctantly they left the Point. The bungalow was pulled down the following year.

Erosion

Against all the predictions Spurn, and most importantly its road, was still intact in the early 1970s. In the 1960s there had been some damage to the road between Narrow Neck and Chalk Bank but, on the advice of Redvers Clubley, hawthorn clippings had been used to fill the gaps, and the rubble from buildings demolished near the Port War Signal Station was also used quite effectively.

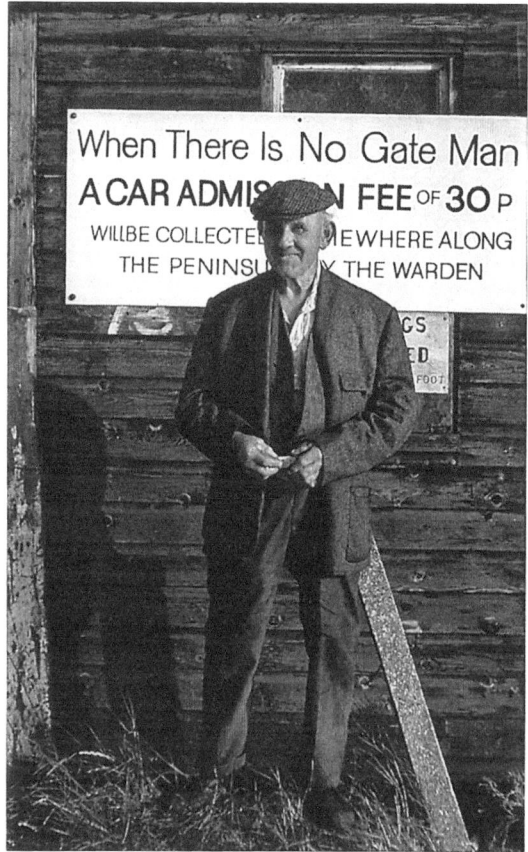

181   *Redvers Clubley at the reserve gate, 1974.*

However, the ageing sea defences were falling into disrepair by the mid-1970s: the wooden groynes were being attacked by marine borers, and even the concrete sea walls were crumbling. In 1971 Holderness Rural District Council commissioned a *Report on Sea Defence Works*, by their surveyor, H.D. Howlett. He concluded that to bring the system back into operation would cost nearly two million pounds, plus annual maintenance. Such a sum could not be justified, so nothing was done. In 1974 the groynes near the Warren collapsed, and erosion increased to their south. The 1950s sea wall (the Promenade), which went from Godwin Battery as far south as Clubley's Field, was collapsing fast, as was the sea wall that protected the battery itself (now Sandy Beaches Caravan Site). The later 1970s saw a period of high winds and surge tides. On 3 January 1976, winds of 70 to 105 m.p.h. tore through the whole country. A surge tide coincided with spring tides, resulting in tides up to 1.8 metres higher than predicted. Sand was stripped off the beach, gaps were made in concrete walls, and the flooding was the worst since 1953. The road on the high Narrows was undermined, and cost £6,000 to repair. Two years later, in January 1978, the people on the Point were cut off, when part of the military concrete road just south of the Warren was badly damaged. The floodwaters reached the threshold of the 'annexe', came within four yards of Warren Cottage and flooded the information centre and other buildings. At Chalk Bank the tide was level with the top of the bank of chalk, and those rabbits that had survived the myxomatosis outbreak were drowned. No more rabbits were seen at Chalk Bank until the late 1990s. The new section of road, which

was laid in a loop to the west of the old one later that year, was the first of many new sections in that sector over the next 30 years. Also damaged was the water main that ran down the peninsula just below ground. Some 300 metres of pipe work was washed away, and it took five weeks to repair. A similar length of telephone cable also disappeared. Thus began a period of constant reaction and reappraisal, as the northern section of the peninsula became progressively narrower, and the vital link to the Point put in jeopardy. In 1978 Trinity House, which was responsible for the lighthouse, made a contribution to the costs of renewing the road. In the future the Trust's tenants were to pay a higher and higher proportion of the cost of keeping the road and communications open when the sea took its toll.

182   *The Warren area with lorries from Easington gas site bringing clay to make a bank, 1983. Much land has been lost since this photograph was taken, and the 'annexe', which is the building furthest east, is now (2006) almost on the beach.*

North of the reserve the impact was just as bad. Gillian Granger made her first visit of the year in late March:

> I went to Spurn first, then back by the cliff to Beacon Lane beach. It's all a dreary scene of violent devastation – the sea has smashed the cliffs, ripped out bushes and bundled them into tight piles. It has undermined the road beyond the Warren, and a diversion has been made. The Beacon Lane area is as bad, debris carried right across and over the bank to the fields beyond. Lakes have been left on the fields at Spurn and Beacon Lane. The beach is now wider than ever, sand and shingle having been carried onto the fields ...

In 1981 the gas terminal at Easington was extended, and as a result a large amount of clay was excavated. It was used to make a new bank to protect Kilnsea and the northern end of the peninsula from erosion. Maurice Nethercoat, clerk of works for the Trust, estimated that more than 700,000 tons of clay were dumped, graded and consolidated at that time. The bank went from north of Big Hedge (the mound at the northern end is still *in situ*), right down past the Warren as far as the concrete sea wall at Narrow Neck.

In September of the same year, lorries were thundering up Beacon Lane taking clay to make a sea wall along the coast there in order to protect the Sandy Beaches caravan site. The clay banks did indeed hold back the sea for some years, though 1983 was another bad year for flooding when the sea washed over the clay bank, leaving liquid mud all over the road, and when 30 feet of land disappeared in one night.

Of course, Spurn and Kilnsea were not the only places being threatened by the sea. All along the Holderness coast the clay cliffs were crumbling, as they had done for thousands of years. Various schemes have been put forward to alleviate the losses. In 1986 the *Holderness Gazette* reported a scheme to use colliery waste to construct a reef all along the Holderness coast. Other suggestions included the construction of an offshore reef of old tyres.

To itemise the damage done by the sea to the northern part of the peninsula in the 1980s and 1990s would be both tedious and depressing, so a brief summary of events will have to suffice. More road collapses occurred in the 1980s. In 1988 another section of road had to be built and a water main repaired. By then the clay bank was right on the cliff top and was being eroded in its turn. After a quiet year in 1989, gales and high tides again battered Spurn and Kilnsea in 1990, in late February and again in October. By the end of the year the boulder clay bank had gone completely and there were already small 'bites' into the underlying boulder clay behind it. The following year, 1991, saw the danger months of January and February pass without incident. However, in April high tides flooded part of the Warren compound and the concrete road between the 'loop' roads was undermined, so that the whole length collapsed. The remaining dunes north of the concrete sea wall were severely damaged and the revetment and the remains of the boulder clay bank were washed away. A temporary road of metal panels was put in to bypass the break in the road. A few months later a new tarmac road was built on the west side of the peninsula near the line of electricity poles, running from the base of the old gun-site just south of the Warren to join the original concrete road several hundred yards to the south. In November the northern point of the sea wall began to collapse, and the water main and telephone cable were broken. By that time people were coming to expect trouble almost every winter. 1992 was a quiet year, but in 1993, in both February and November, more flooding and damage ensued. One feature after another was lost throughout the 1990s. The concrete sea wall, which had been looked after by the military right up until the late 1950s and had looked impregnable, cracked and collapsed. After high tides in January 1995, the old coastguard tower on Sandy Beaches Caravan site was only seven yards from the cliff edge, and the two large gun emplacements were hanging over it. In early March the gun emplacements went over the cliff and the tower was balancing on the edge. The tower was later demolished as a safety measure. With the regular flooding of Clubley's Field a band of sand, shingle and small balls of boulder clay about 10 metres wide changed the nature of its eastern border to that of a saltmarsh environment.

183 *The Warren area, 1983. The structure in the corner of the field is a Hi-Fix Radio Navigational Transmitting System, placed there in 1970. The sea-watching hut can be seen near the cliff edge. It has since been moved back many times, as the cliff has eroded.*

184 *The Blue Bell shop, 1977. Since the late 1950s when it closed as a public house, the Blue Bell had been run as a café and later as a shop.*

The year 1996 was made memorable for the damage caused to certain stretches of the peninsula by incursions of the sea. The worst period was in late February, when sections of the road were lost both at the northern end of the peninsula and, more surprisingly, just north of Chalk Bank. The only access to the Point was by four-wheel drive vehicles following a route, partly on the beach, and partly along the Spurn footpaths, to just north of Chalk Bank hide. Work was soon under way on the construction of two bypasses consisting of a part concrete, part concrete-matting road from pole 25 to pole 30 (where it rejoined the old road) and a concrete road north of Chalk Bank along part of the Spurn footpath. All that work was completed by the end of March. About 80 metres of water main from near the start of the Spurn footpath was lost and the water main from the southern end of the Narrow Neck to the north end of Chalk Bank also had to be replaced, with much of it laid on the surface. The stretch of the peninsula from the Warren as far as the Narrows was now only a few yards wide. Since 1996 further new sections of road have been built as the sea and the Humber have encroached but, remarkably, at the time of writing (May 2006) a road still goes down to the Point, the lifeboat families still live there, and the pilots and the VTS service continue to be based on Spurn.

Spurn Heritage Coast Project

After the Second World War the government began to recognise that the British countryside needed protecting. During the war itself many acres had been ploughed up for the production of food, while farming was becoming increasingly mechanised and areas of natural beauty were under threat. The National Parks Commission was created by Act in 1949, and in 1968 became the Countryside Commission. Attention became focused not only on the creation of national parks but also on the preservation of outstanding areas of unspoilt coastline. The concept of 'Heritage Coasts' was born, a scheme designed to give protection to coastlines of special scenic or environmental value against inappropriate development. In 1970 Spurn was suggested as a potential heritage coast, an initiative welcomed by the YNT, though in the event Spurn was not to be one of those so designated in the first tranche. The suggestion came up again in 1978, but it was to be another 10 years before Spurn, in October 1988, became officially designated as a heritage coast. At the same time the Spurn Heritage Coast Project, composed of the Countryside Commission, the Nature Conservancy Council, Humberside County Council, Holderness Borough Council, Easington Parish Council and the Yorkshire Wildlife Trust, was established. The partners agreed to fund a three-year project and employ an officer to devise and implement a programme of development in the heritage coast area, which was to cover the whole

Spurn and Kilnsea area, to extend north as far as Long Bank. The first project officer, appointed in the winter of 1988-9, was Tim Collins, who had since 1986 held the position of Conservation Projects Officer for the South Holderness Countryside Society. (See below.)

The project brought some much-needed money to Spurn, and was responsible for many new initiatives including fencing, tree-planting, the creation of new ponds, the construction of new birdwatching hides on the Chalk Bank and near the canal and the improvement of grassland at Chalk Bank by the use of sheep-grazing. To improve facilities for visitors a car park was constructed on a small field just north of the entrance to the reserve, and the car park at the *Crown & Anchor* was enlarged and planted with trees and bushes. In 1989 land east of Long Bank was bought by the South Holderness Countryside Society (see below), and the project worked in conjunction with that society to excavate a scrape at Beacon Ponds and build a new hide there with an adjoining bank. Unfortunately the very high tide of October 1990 flooded the hide and destroyed much good reed-bed habitat almost immediately after the work had been completed.

The early to mid-1990s were to be the most fruitful years for the Spurn Heritage Coast Project. In 1993 Jeremy Seeley was employed as a heritage coast ranger on a three-year contract, so that the project now had two full-time staff, together with others employed on short-term contracts. In 1993 the *Blue Bell*, which had closed as a shop, came on the market and was purchased by the Trust and leased for the use of the project. It was completely gutted and then refurbished. On 9 October 1995 the Blue Bell Visitor Centre officially opened. It included a tea room with an adjoining exhibition of displays on the history of the area. Also on the ground floor were the offices of the project while on the first floor the rooms had been converted to a self-contained flat to provide accommodation for the Yorkshire Wildlife Trust's warden, should his bungalow at the Warren be washed away! At the time of writing Barry Spence, now retired, still resides in the bungalow, whilst the flat has been taken up by the current YWT warden of the reserve. In 1996 Spurn became a national nature reserve. Peter Pearson, the then chairman of the Yorkshire Wildlife Trust, said 'Spurn Point is now firmly placed in the premier league of nature reserves. It is not only a national nature reserve, but a national asset.'

In 1996, when Humberside County Council was abolished and the East Riding of Yorkshire Council, covering rural East Yorkshire, replaced it, the funding for the Spurn Heritage Coast Project was much reduced. Tim Collins left in 1996 to take a job with English Nature, and his replacement was Chris Berry, who was also responsible for the Flamborough Heritage Coast. Since 1998 there have been several changes of staff, many of the initiatives begun by the project have been allowed to lapse, owing to lack of both personnel and funds and the post has been mainly desk-based. Both heritage coasts are still in place, but the heritage coast officer tends to focus on policy rather than any active management.

An initiative of the Spurn Heritage Coast Project, which had long-term implications for Spurn, was the commissioning in 1991 of a report from Dr John Pethick of the Institute of Estuarine and Coastal Studies, University of Hull, on 'the processes currently acting on Spurn, to contrast them with the processes which were responsible for the accretion of

the spit in the past, and to make recommendations for the restoration of the natural processes'. Since the 1960s the theory postulated by George de Boer, Reader in Historical Geography, University of Hull, that Spurn was subject to a 250-year cycle, had largely been accepted. Pethick, however, now challenged de Boer's theory by suggesting instead that the changes in the spit's shape in the 13th and 17th centuries could have been caused by sea level variations. He stated that the position and continuation of the spit was due to the presence of a complex glacial till foundation, which maintains Spurn in a relatively constant position despite the rapid westwards retreat of the mainland of Holderness. He stated that the present head of Spurn lies above a glacial till ridge, which runs along the line of the Binks and the outer edge of the bight. He also suggested that the 19th-century breach was probably the result of a change in sediment transport conditions in the bight following the draining of land and creation of Sunk Island, exacerbated by the large-scale removal of gravel and cobbles for commercial purposes in the first half of the 19th century. He noted that the introduction of groynes and hard defences after the breach of 1849 had resulted in the formation of a dune field along the neck, which had inhibited the wash-over

185 *The Warren area, 1985.*

processes that he suggested had maintained it in earlier times.

When the study came out it was said that 'one of the main conclusions of the study is that the present morphology of Spurn is largely artificial, a product of 19th-century construction works following the breakthroughs in the 1840s'. However, that was scarcely a new conclusion since de Boer had always stated that Spurn's morphology since the 1850s was largely artificial. He had identified the installation of hard sea defences after the breach as the main reason why the spit had not been washed away. In that event, a new spit would have begun to form a little to the west, as he argued had already happened on previous occasions. Another of Pethick's statements that 'Spurn has remained relatively stationary and coherent throughout the past 6,000 years' was much more controversial, and could easily be challenged by historical geographers. Considering too that, in Roman times, the Holderness coast lay several miles to the east of the present one, it would be difficult to see how Spurn, in its present position, could have been attached to the coast to its north.

The new study was widely circulated and publicised, and its principal result was that the policy of letting nature take its course, which had by necessity been adopted by the Trust since its purchase of Spurn in 1960, now apparently had scientific backing. The crumbling of the sea defences could now be seen as a positive benefit since it would allow the neck of the peninsula to 'roll over' as nature intended.

Pethick's theory of the growth and development of the peninsula led indirectly to the loss of two more of the peninsula's historical features. In 1995 the lifeboat house and slipway at the Point were demolished, together with the old military railway jetty. They were demolished because it was thought that they were preventing the sand moving up the south-western side of the peninsula to feed the Narrows further north.

Spurn Bird Observatory

Newcomers to Spurn are often confused by the relationship between the Trust and the Observatory. Of course the two were, and are, distinct entities.

Until 2000, when Spurn Bird Observatory Trust was instituted, the Observatory was run by a sub-committee of the Yorkshire Naturalists' Union (YNU). The Yorkshire Wildlife Trust owns Warren Cottage, which became the headquarters of the Observatory, as well as all the rest of the buildings in the Warren area. The 'annexe' had become part of the Observatory's accommodation from the early 1960s, and other buildings not needed by the Trust were later used by the Observatory for ringing and accommodation. The Trust had representation upon the Observatory Committee and the Observatory was represented on Spurn Management Committee. Generally speaking the relationship was very amicable. Barry Spence, as Trust warden, had no official role with the Observatory, but over the years the committee came to rely upon him for taking bookings, keeping the accommodation in good order, being the most constant attendee at the nightly log, and generally contributing to the smooth running of the Observatory's affairs. Barry had become the YNT's warden of Spurn in 1964, the same year that John Cudworth took over as chairman of the Observatory, and the two men worked closely together for over 35 years.

Spurn Bird Observatory has always been well supported, with a core of regulars who come to stay there almost every weekend, their numbers being augmented by additional birdwatchers who stay in the spring and autumn migration periods. Spurn's importance as a migration route is second to none, and the locals in that corner of Yorkshire have grown used to being 'invaded' at certain times of the year. By the 1970s the 'ornithologists' and 'bird-watchers' had been joined by two new breeds – 'birders' and 'twitchers'. As communications between birders improved they were increasingly willing to travel long distances to see a rarity, and Spurn has always had plenty of those. The spread of car ownership meant that a stay at the Observatory was no longer an essential part of a birder's weekend, and that had a deleterious effect on the number of 'man-nights' at the Observatory by the 1980s. However at the same time birding became more popular so that the 'obs' continued to be very busy at weekends in migration periods. Gillian Granger recorded in her diary of 11 September 1981:

'There are birdwatchers prying everywhere to the wrath of the inhabitants. One person said she has refused to pay her rates till all the birdwatchers are removed.' Since then, with pagers and mobile phones, the numbers of people rushing along the winding roads of South Holderness to Spurn seems to grow every year.

In 1996 the 50th anniversary of Spurn Bird Observatory was celebrated with a barbecue, held in front of the annexe in clear view of the beach. When the Observatory was established in 1946 the sea was quite a distance away and separated by a marsh. (See below.) Now the complex of buildings which were the Observatory's base are all uncomfortably close to the sea. Although various improvements were made regularly to the furniture and fittings, such as the addition of fridge-freezers and carpets in the bedrooms, it was clear to the committee that they were living on borrowed time. Plans needed to be put in hand to move into new premises before they were washed out. In 1998 Spurn Bird Observatory Committee, having been left a substantial legacy by John Weston, a long-time committee member, purchased a wooden bungalow (Kew Villa) and its adjoining field near the church. It is hoped that this building, although at present only large enough to provide accommodation for the Observatory warden, will eventually form the nucleus of a new observatory when funds can be raised.

John Cudworth, chairman of Spurn Bird Observatory since 1963 and a member of the Observatory committee since 1954, retired in 1999. The editors' foreword to *Spurn Wildlife* 9 (the annual report of the Observatory) paid tribute to his years of service to Spurn:

> John pioneered visible migration studies at Spurn from his watch point at the 'narrow neck'. His thousands of hours of meticulous recording form the basis of our present understanding of migration patterns at Spurn.

In 2002 another Spurn stalwart, the Trust's warden, Barry Spence, retired, having been warden for 38 and a half years. To many people Barry was Mr Spurn himself, a familiar figure to all who came to Spurn or had any association with it. As an all-round naturalist Barry's expertise covers birds (he is a qualified ringer), plants (his knowledge of the plants on Spurn approaches that of many more specialised amateur botanists) and of course moths, butterflies and dragonflies. The number of species recorded at Spurn, most of them by Barry, makes it one of the most important sites for Lepidoptera in Yorkshire, and each year the list of new species for the site grows.

The new Spurn Reserves Officer was Andrew Gibson, no newcomer to Spurn, as he had been closely associated with the area since the late 1970s. He took over not only the care of the peninsula and its tenants, and the Trust's other local reserves at Welwick and Skeffling, but also the supervision of the Hebridean sheep flock, which is now a regular part of Spurn's conservation management.

The Wildlife

The Yorkshire Wildlife Trust (as it became in 1984) and Spurn Bird Observatory have, over the years, worked together for the good of Spurn and its wildlife. Many things have threatened Spurn in the last three decades of the 20th century. The colony of Little Terns at the Point gradually diminished in the 1970s. Two pairs had nested at the tip of the peninsula in 1970, but their nests were destroyed when a helicopter landed upon them. Thereafter the odd attempt at nesting was made, but with little success. Fortunately the birds found a more suitable site when they moved northwards to the Lagoons area. Spurn has a remarkable diversity of plants, recorded by one of the peninsula's regulars, Dr Eva Crackles, a visitor to Spurn from the 1940s. The rabbits that kept the grass short and helped to encourage that diversity were the descendants of those who occupied Spurn Warren (near Chalk Bank) and Kilnsea Warren over a period of several hundred years. Sadly, like others in the British Isles, they were devastated by myxomatosis in the 1970s and almost wiped out (though they have made a good come-back in recent years). That had a damaging effect not only upon botanical diversity, but also upon the provision of habitat for ground-nesting birds, and upon the foxes that preyed upon them. Spurn's fragile environment can be easily unbalanced,

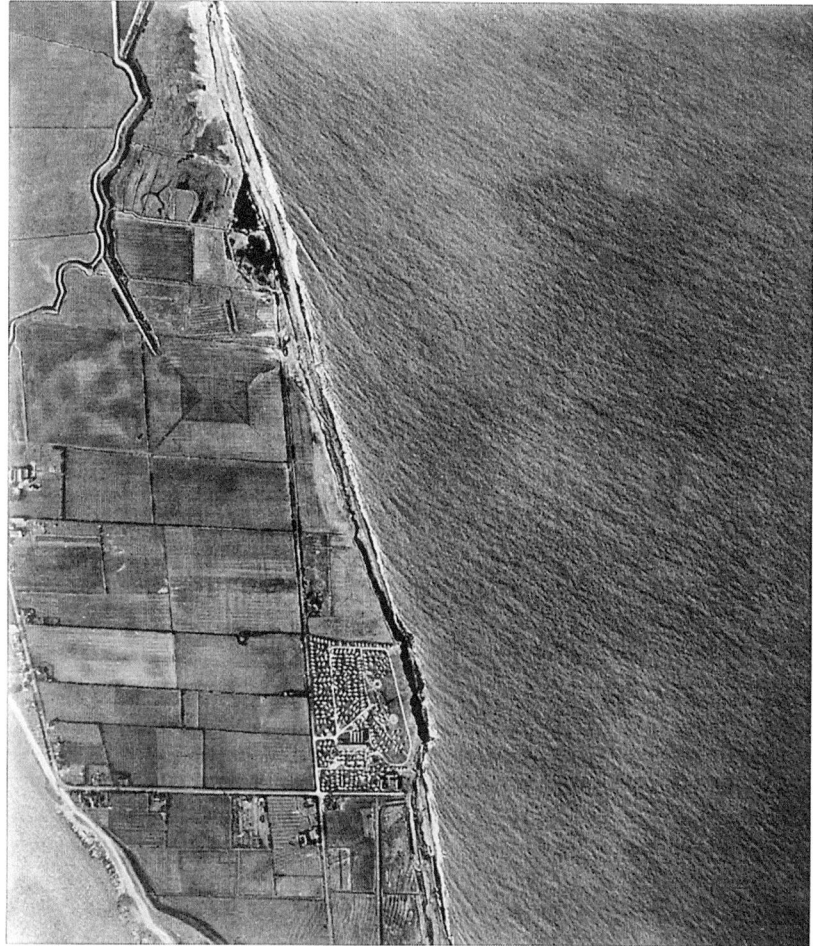

186 *Kilnsea aerial view, March 1976. Much land has been lost since this photograph was taken, and brackish water covers a large part of what now remains in the north. At the top of the picture a corner of Easington Lagoon may be seen. Near to Long Bank the shape of some of the fields depicted on the 1818 strip map of Kilnsea can just be picked out. In Kilnsea itself some relics of the two wars may still be seen. Murray's Post is on the left of the lane, the 9.2-inch gun emplacements are on the camp, and the officers' quarters are still fronting the road to the sea just below them.*

as it is so cut off from the land to its north. Another loss involved an area of land to the immediate east of Warren Cottage, the phragmites marsh, with its rare plant life and pools. By 1977 it had been entirely washed away.

Some plants have flourished, however, and tried to take over: in the late 1970s sea buckthorn was encroaching on the road, making it difficult for car-drivers to see birds, and a team of volunteers, including the Trust's Manpower Services Commission team and Hull University Conservation Corps, began clearing strips of land of about four feet wide on each side. In August 1978 Gillian Granger found Spurn's first yellow horned poppy on the peninsula, a plant that now makes erratic appearances, as do many other rare flowers.

In the 1970s neither the Trust nor the Observatory owned any land north of the gate apart from Clubley's Field, which was part of the land bought from the MoD in 1959. Nevertheless, Kilnsea contained many areas of good habitat for wildlife. Ponds and ditches, pasture fields and good hawthorn hedges were all features to be treasured. Relationships between the wildlife groups and local farmers were generally friendly, though sometimes the interests of agriculture and conservation were in opposition. In 1972 a permanent pond, flanked by mature hawthorns, was grubbed up in the field north of 'Big Hedge', that is, the large hawthorn hedge to the north of Clubley's Field. Land drains were put into that field, which then more or less dried out and became less attractive to birds.

187 *Northern Kilnsea aerial view, June 1976. The long narrow field (which was called Two-acre Marsh and belonged to John Hunton in 1818) appears to be flooded. The island in Easington Lagoon is the site of the ancient burial mound, which was first excavated by Dr H. Bendelack Hewetson in the 1890s, and subsequently by Rod Mackey in the early 1960s and 1996. Material dating from the Neolithic period was found below Iron-Age remains.*

Changeable weather often provided a challenge to the good management of the reserve. The hot summer of 1976, though disastrous for plants, resulted in an excellent year for butterflies and moths. A Clifden nonpareil and two Camberwell beauties were seen. By that time the YWT warden, Barry Spence, was establishing Spurn as an important site for the recording of Lepidotera. Situated on the East Coast, it was visited by many migrant moths.

Oil Slicks

In the 1970s the beaches around Spurn were threatened by oil slicks on several occasions. In October 1970 a large oil slick washed on to the mud flats between the Warren and High Bents in late October, fortunately with few problems for birds. There were others in 1971 but the most serious was in June 1973, when the tanker *Conoco Britannia* grounded on Haile Sand and holed herself on her own anchor. The Humberside Oil Pollution Committee had tugs round her spraying leaked oil with dispersants very promptly, but oil began to come ashore at Spurn the following day. Fortunately no oil came ashore on the mud flats on the Humber side of the peninsula and it was probably the prompt action of the Humberside Oil Pollution Committee that mitigated the effects of the accident, whilst the wind and weather also favoured Spurn. Gillian Granger recorded in her diary in August 1973:

Beacon Lane was a great shock to us – it's been stripped of grass and flowers and is just a wide area of mud and stones ... The sea wall near the camp has been smashed to bits. We met Mrs Tennison in the lane and she told us that it was ripped up by machines used to clear oil from the beach, and the lane had to be cleared and levelled.

In October 1983 another oil slick threatened the area. Gillian's diary recorded: 'I went to the Humber which reeked of oil – no ships or helicopters were there spraying. I then called on Barry, who lamented and expected the worst – 3,000 birds have already died further up river.'

Beacon Ponds, Easington Lagoons and the South Holderness Countryside Society

In 1982 a group of people who had attended a course on natural history tutored by Howard Frost inaugurated a society to help the conservation of South Holderness. The society has grown over the years, and one of its important initiatives has been, with the help of grants, to purchase and/or manage vulnerable areas of land in order to preserve them from development and for wildlife. The members were aware that the land south of Long Bank in Kilnsea was of considerable interest to naturalists. Commemorated in the name of North Marsh Lane (also known as Beacon Lane), the North Marshes on the eastern side of Kilnsea were used for pasture for centuries. In 1818 the marsh was 142 acres, but by 1843 it had been reduced by erosion to 99 acres – a substantial loss that has continued to this day. In the late 19th century lepidopterists recorded moths in 'the Beacon area', and when naturalists visited the area they often walked over that part of northern Kilnsea, which was then agricultural land fringed by sand dunes. The Tennisons, a family who had lived at Northfield Farm since the mid-19th century, were still keeping their cattle on the marsh in the early 1970s.

In the 1970s Easington Lagoon, the body of water created when the new flood bank (New Bank) was built after the 1953 floods, was the largest body of water east of the bank. Kilnsea marsh was turning into an area of small brackish pools fringed with reeds, as the sea encroached on the former

pasture land. As a habitat for birds it was invaluable, and many birdwatchers visited it in preference to Spurn itself. Long Bank and its extension, New Bank, were raised and protected with gabions in the late 1970s, and as a result a deep borrow pit was created to its east (sometimes called Beacon Pond). In August 1977 Gillian Granger explored the area round the pool, and wrote 'it had been a field, but now is becoming a salt marsh – here grow Sea Aster, Marsh Samphire, Saltwort and Sand Spurrey. A digger has gouged out masses of clay from this side of the old reedy pools, which are still beautiful with their fringes of Sea Wormwood.' The gales of 1978 created more saltmarsh habitat and took more land. The Little Terns, which favoured shingle with adjoining dunes for cover, found very suitable habitat here. Unfortunately egg-collectors were still busy in the 1970s. The area also attracted wildfowlers, some who had a legitimate right to be there, some who had not.

Matters were much improved when, in 1980, the YNU took up its old role of protecting Little Terns. The area favoured by the birds was fenced, to the annoyance of some people who considered that their rights to walk unhindered on the beach were being infringed. In fact the area being fenced was owned by the Yorkshire Water Authority. A local Easington birdwatcher, Arthur Piggott, was asked to warden the area on a voluntary basis, and he continued to act as voluntary warden until 1988 when it was decided to employ a full-time seasonal warden. In 1989 the South Holderness Countryside Society bought some marginal land from a local farmer, leased some more from the Environment Agency (which had taken over the powers of the Yorkshire Water Authority), and became the formal 'custodian' of the breeding colony. The society has held ultimate responsibility for the breeding colony ever since, though between 1989 and 1996 the Spurn Heritage Coast Project provided welcome manpower and resources for the Little Terns protection scheme. After the demise of the project the lead in wardening the site was taken by the South Holderness Countryside Society and, since 2001, by the Spurn Bird Observatory. The South Holderness Countryside Society bought more land in the marshes in 1991 and 2000, and that part of Kilnsea is now a protected area, though the sea takes its usual toll every year.

The dunes on the seaward side have now almost gone, and the Beacon Lagoons Nature Reserve Ponds are mainly composed of brackish pools and lagoons. The two lagoons, sometimes known as the North Lagoon (Easington Lagoon) and the South Lagoon (Beacon Pond) have been designated as a Site of Special Scientific Interest (SSSI), because saline lagoons are uncommon along the East Coast. Their value rests upon the fact that they support populations of the rare spiral tasselweed, and a range of invertebrates characteristic of coastal saline lagoons. As the dunes on the seaward side have washed away, the saline lagoons are increasingly threatened and their long-term survival is in doubt. Since they have been designated as a SSSI, European funds may be available to move the banks back in an attempt to recreate the lagoons, a prospect most unwelcome to the people who live in Kilnsea, where flood defence is increasingly difficult to maintain.

Maritime Services on the Point

By the early 1970s life on the Point for the families of the lifeboat crew was getting a little easier, though few people would agree with Mrs Buchan, the coxswain's wife, when she said 'Now our lives are much the same as anybody else's.' The families still lived in the Victorian terrace, with few modern conveniences. 'Years ago it was a much closer community,' said Mrs Buchan. 'You used to meet together for entertainment. Now it's different with TV, radio and record players. We do have bingo together in the community hall once a week.' They also had cars and could leave the Point for shopping and visiting friends. And they were visited, in their turn, by hordes of people in the summer months.

Plans were being made in the early 1970s for a big expansion of rescue services on the East Coast. The increase in numbers of amateur sailors and yachtsmen meant that coastguards' jobs were changing. The Spurn coastguards, who had been located on the Point since the 19th century, had moved out of the Port War Signal Station in the early 1960s, and into a purpose-built tower on Sandy Beaches Caravan Site. In 1971 they decided to move back onto the Point, and to share an observation tower that the British Transport Docks Board was planning to build for the pilots. That seemed a logical development, and a spokesman said:

> Such a vantage point would enable coastguards to keep a closer watch on shipping entering and leaving the estuary. In addition a medium frequency and high frequency radio, [and] a direction-finding installation could be housed at the pilot station from which fast launches could supply ships with pilots.

Lieutenant Commander Grubb of H.M. Coastguards attended a meeting of the management committee and explained that the function of the

188 *Clearing the site for the new houses, 1974. The former military buildings to the left were retained and later used by the Humber Pilots.*

189 *The new houses, 1976. Soon after they were built the houses were found to be poorly designed for the weather on Spurn, and they had to be re-clad.*

station would include the co-ordination of rescue operations, and the directing and co-ordinating of operations to avert threatened oil pollution. Initially, plans were for an independent observation post to be built on the site of a gun pit near the old sergeants' mess. Later it was decided to combine the observation facilities required by both the coastguards and the pilots in the tower by the parade ground, which had already been chosen by the British Transport Docks Board for use as a radar tower.

This was certainly a time of change on the Point, as the RNLI was seeking permission from the Trust to build new houses for the crew. They wanted to build them at the edge of the parade ground on the former battery site, and some hutments still there would need to be demolished. The plan was for the pilots to use the old officers' mess, a range of concrete First World War buildings overlooking the estuary. A new jetty would be built into the river opposite the pilots' base. The lifeboat crew were to be accommodated in four pairs of semi-detached bungalows at the edge of the parade ground. The Trust and the management committee decided that the plans should go ahead:

> having concluded that any detrimental effects for conservation could be limited to not unacceptable levels, and subject to satisfactory agreements being reached with the bodies concerned ... it should be allowed to proceed ... This is one of the most difficult decisions that the Trust and the Management Committee have had to take. The inescapable

significance of Spurn at the mouth of a major estuary has had the most important consequences for the peninsula throughout its history and inevitably these consequences continue to appear and have to be reckoned by the Trust. In many ways this development is one which conflicts with the proper use of the point area as a nature reserve, but the Trust has to bear in mind the considerable power of national and regional bodies directly concerned with the total economy of the country.

Mrs Buchan was not to enjoy the new modern houses herself, as in September 1973 her husband retired after 22 years' service. He was succeeded by Neil Morris, who only stayed for one year. On 16 February 1975 Brian Bevan succeeded as Superintendent Coxswain at the age of twenty-eight. He knew Spurn already, having previously been a member of the Humber Lifeboat for a year in 1969. He had left to move to Bridlington but he and his wife Ann were very happy to return to Spurn and to move into one of the seven new houses, which were two-storey rather than bungalows as first planned, and had been built at a cost of £100,000. The YNT's *Annual Report* for 1975 recorded that:

> New cottages for the lifeboatmen have been finished and are occupied, the pilots' jetty completed, the radar and coastguard tower is almost ready and a navigation beacon erected at the end of the peninsula. ... The lease of the building and areas involved in the pilots' base to the British Transport Docks Board have been completed and progress

made with the others ... The RNLI has for many years rented from the Trust a terrace of houses near the Point to accommodate members of the Spurn lifeboat crew. These buildings have recently been demolished and the site has been levelled in preparation for a car park ... The Trust has been put to minimal expense during these alterations since the RNLI has been prepared to pay for its greatly improved lot.

The Trust considered keeping the old cottages, which could have been modernised and let out for holiday accommodation. The YNT *Report* for 1976 states that there had been:

> long and anxious consideration of possible uses [but] the cost of rendering useable these cottages that the planning authorities would allow to be retained ... [meant] that complete demolition was the only practicable course.

The YNT *Newsletter* of 1976 described the new headquarters for pilots and other facilities on the Point:

> The old officers' mess near the Point has been developed as a waiting stage for pilots and now includes six bedrooms. The old lookout tower has been extensively refurbished and now provides accommodation for both coastguards and pilots and houses radar etc. A new jetty has been built out into the Humber for use by pilot cutters. The local coastguards have closed the co-ordinating station at Flamborough and now concentrate work at the lookout tower. The lighthouse continues to be serviced once a week.

At that time about 150 pilots worked between Spurn and the Humber ports. Not long after they had moved onto the peninsula they must have thought their time there was going to be short. On 11 January 1978 Spurn was cut off by flooding, the road partly swept away, and the pilots had to be taken in a horse box towed by tractor to the Point.

The pilots are still on the Point, but the coastguards have left. In 1989 they moved out of the tower to a new headquarters in Bridlington. An item in the *Hull Daily Mail* of 5 December reads:

> The Spurn coastguard look-out point is up for sale. Offers living or working space, along with a big fourth floor observation room. After its move to

Bridlington the Humber Coastguard has no more need of its part of the block, which also houses the Humber pilots, and so it is being sold off by the Department of the Environment.

Nobody was interested in taking on a floor of the control tower, and in the event it was to have a new use some 10 years later. In 1997 Associated British Ports, which is responsible for all navigation on the Humber, refurbished the pilots' tower to make it the headquarters for a new Vessel Traffic Services Centre. Equipped with highest-quality radar and computerised information systems, the staff working there can monitor all vessel movements to and from the Humber, the Ouse and the Trent. The operations of the Humber pilots are also co-ordinated from the centre. The VTS Centre (Humber) operates round the clock, and is permanently staffed with two master mariners, one being a qualified Humber pilot.

In 1977 a new lifeboat, the *City of Bradford IV*, came to the station. A 54-foot Arun-class boat with a top speed of 18.4 knots, her hull design meant that she could not be launched down a slipway, so that she had to be kept permanently at moorings. As a result the old lifeboat house now became redundant, its only role to be a picturesque sight on the Point, until it was removed in 1995.

Brian Bevan was coxswain of the Humber lifeboat from 1975 until 2001. During that time he was involved in many outstanding rescues and received many bravery awards. Indeed, he was second only to Robert Cross in that respect. Between the end of 1979 and early 1980 three rescues were carried out by the Humber lifeboat, which were to become widely celebrated. The first took place in very bad weather on 30 December, when the Humber lifeboat was informed that a coaster, the *Diana V*, was in distress 74 miles south-east of Spurn. For that mission, which took over 14 hours and involved a return to Grimsby for repairs halfway through, running repairs on the way back to the *Diana V*, and the eventual rescue in force 10 gales of six people using only the light of torches plus a searchlight from the warship HMS *Lindisfarne*, Brian Bevan was awarded the Silver Medal of the RNLI and his crew the institution's 'Thanks on Vellum'.

Only six weeks later, on 14 February, the lifeboat was called out to a Panamanian freighter, the *Revi*. Again gales were blowing and conditions at sea were appalling. The *Revi* was taking in water and the master asked the lifeboat to take two of his crew off. Coxswain Bevan thought this impracticable, given the state of the sea but, after nine attempts to get close, and with violent waves up to 30 feet high, the two crew members were taken aboard. The master had hoped to get the ship into the river but, discovering that the cargo of silver sand was shifting and that there was flooding in the accommodation space, he decided to abandon ship.

The rescue of the two men earlier was nothing compared to that of the master and mate. No less than 24 times the lifeboat went alongside to try to get the men off, with the crew of the lifeboat lashed to the guard-rails, and Coxswain Bevan at the helm. On the last attempt, when it was clear that the *Revi* was sinking, the lifeboat drove into a trough between two waves. The master jumped, and was grabbed by the lifeboat crew and pulled in. Brian Bevan received the RNLI Gold Medal for that rescue, whilst all the crew, who comprised Second Coxswain Dennis Bailey, Mechanic Barry Sayers, Assistant Mechanic Ronald Sayers and Crew

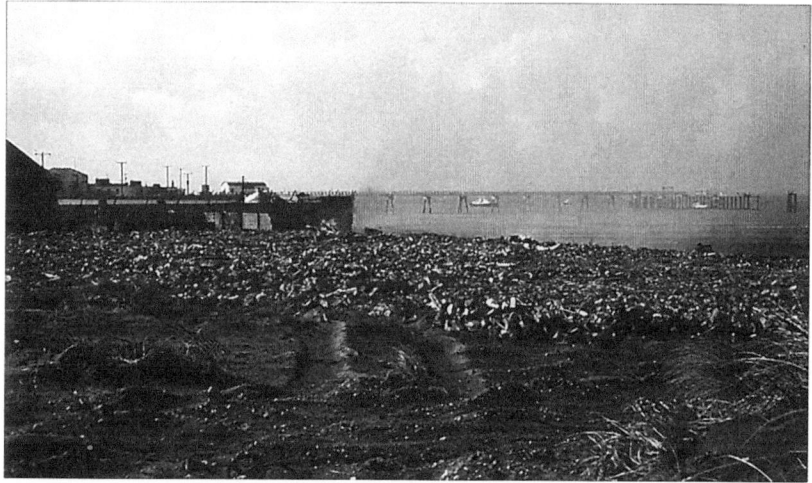

190   *The site of the old cottages, 1976. This became a much-needed car park. Near the Humber it is still (2006) possible to see some of the floor tiles from the coxswain's house, which was of a superior design to those of the crew.*

191   *Building the new jetty, 1975.*

192   *Kilnsea aerial view, July 1977. Considerable evidence of ridge and furrow cultivation may be seen in this photograph. Also visible are the remains of the infantry camp, later a camp for Italian prisoners of war, at Sunny Cliff. The lines of anti-tank blocks stretching from the Humber foreshore to the sea may also be seen.*

Members Michael Storey, Peter Jordan, Sydney Rollinson and Dennis Bailey (Jnr), received the Bronze. The next day the lifeboat was out again, when a Romanian cargo ship, the *Savinesti*, got into difficulties. For that mission, which again took place in appalling conditions and also involved the Wells lifeboat, a Bronze Medal was awarded to Superintendent Coxswain Brian Bevan, with Medal Service certificates for his crew.

In May 1979, whilst a relief crew was left at Spurn, Brian Bevan, his crew and the families went to London to receive their medals. Brian Bevan became the only man ever to receive the RNLI's Gold, Silver and Bronze medals at one presentation. The point was made that:

the leadership and initiative shown by Superintendent Coxswain Bevan was of the highest order and was clearly demonstrated by the confidence his crew showed in him, whilst they were in such great danger themselves on the foredeck with their lives completely in his hands throughout the rescue.

Coxswain Bevan was later to be awarded the Bronze Medal for a rescue which took place in 1982.

In August 1987 the *City of Bradford IV*, having been at Spurn for 10 years, was replaced by a new boat, built for £500,000 from a legacy provided by Kenneth Thelwall and named after him. The naming ceremony took place at the Hull Marina. She was to be replaced in her turn by *The Pride of the Humber*, in 1998.

Under Brian Bevan there was considerable continuity with regard to the crew of the Humber lifeboat. As in the past, sons followed their fathers into the lifeboat service and often acted as auxiliary crew if they were called upon to do so. Spurn coxswains have all known that if a crewman's wife settles down on the Point, then he is likely to stay, often for many years as he and his family grow to love the life and the place. One day off every five days, and one weekend every seven weeks is not everybody's idea of an ideal job. A lifeboatman cannot leave the Point at all when on duty, and he needs engrossing hobbies to pass the time. He cannot accompany his children or his wife to the cinema or to football matches, but he can spend a lot of time with them. Now that the families have good freezers and modern houses the problems of limited access to the shops is not so acute, especially as all the wives have cars. For a night off, the *Crown & Anchor* at Kilnsea or Easington's three pubs are only a few miles away, though the journey back home down a long dark peninsula can be a memorable experience. For the families of the lifeboat crew life on the Point still bears many similarities to the life lived there by their predecessors, though lately they have had to become used to the regular press attention that becomes focused on them from time to time, particularly when the peninsula is having one of its periodic problems with road access. In recent years the provision of state of the art four-wheel-drive vehicles has usually meant that the link with the Point via the beach has been maintained.

Brian Bevan retired in 2001 and was succeeded as Superintendent Coxswain by Bob White, who had been Second Coxswain since 1990 and a member of the crew since 1980. Bob reached the retirement age of 55 in 2003, and was succeeded by Ian Firman, who stayed only a short time. His successor, Dave Steenvoorden, has been a lifeboatman since 1987. He joined the Humber lifeboat in 1990, becoming Second Coxswain in 2001 and Superintendent Coxswain in 2004. Dave is eminently suited to his situation: he loves his job and he loves Spurn, as does his wife Karen. Their twin sons were brought up on Spurn from the age of eight. Dave said:

It's one of those places where if you don't get on, you won't survive ... for the families to live as closely as we do successfully, it's a bit special. The kids play out and its like the old days where you lean over the fence and have a cuppa with your neighbours.

The Lighthouse

From the late 1960s the lifeboat crew was responsible for the daily maintenance of the lighthouse. On the night of 31 October 1985 that job came to an end. Advances in electronic navigational equipment, particularly advanced radar technology, had largely done away with the need for lighthouses. After five and a half centuries of lighthouses on Spurn the light shone out for the last time. The paintwork of the lighthouse is peeling, but given the sturdiness of the building's construction and the ever-deepening erosion of the peninsula, it seems much more likely that the ground will be washed away from underneath it long before it would be likely to tumble into a ruin. Whilst its importance as a landmark and a symbol of the Point remains, it has yet to find a new role. An historic link with the lighthouse keepers of Spurn was broken when their houses in the compound of Smeaton's lighthouse were demolished in 1985, because the wall of the compound on the seaward side was becoming undermined.

The Lightship

Another navigational aid that became redundant in 1985 was the Spurn lightship. Since the 19th century a manned lightship had been moored at the mouth of the river. The Bull lightship was moored on the south-eastern extremity of Bull Sand, and in 1926 the Humber Conservancy Board built a new lightship for the Spurn station, four miles south-east of Spurn lighthouse. She was painted black, and was on station in November 1927, with a crew which consisted of a master, mate, four seamen, a wireless operator and an engineer. They spent a month on duty, after which they were relieved by a duplicate crew. When war broke out the Spurn lightship was moved from the mouth of the river to near Grimsby, and the Bull lightship was moved to Holme Ridge, just off Immingham. Both were moved back to their original stations in June 1945. In the 1950s it was decided that the Bull lightship, built in 1909, needed replacing. The Spurn lightship was painted red and moved to Bull Sand, and a new lightship was placed at the Spurn station in June 1959. Her crew of seven now worked two weeks on board with a week off – a considerable improvement on earlier conditions. By the 1970 plans were being made to replace the manned lightships with catamarans. Bull lightship (the old Spurn lightship) was removed in 1975 and, on 11 December 1985, an unmanned catamaran painted black and yellow, the *East Cardinal*, replaced the Spurn lightship. On 17 December 1986 Spurn lightship left the Humber, having been sold to a Southampton firm. The Spurn lightship, which is moored in Hull Marina is in fact the original one, repainted black and relettered when it was sold to Hull City Council. It can be visited, and houses a display about the history of the Humber lightships.

The Fate of the Forts

Since they were relinquished by the military the Humber forts have had a varied history. Owned by Associated British Ports since 1964, when they were used as sites for weather-monitoring devices and navigational aids, by 1991 their usefulness in this respect had been superseded. They were put up for auction and bought for £37,000 by a 'mystery buyer', which turned out to be an American firm registered in Liechtenstein. There was talk of Bull Sand Fort being modernized and used as a venue for a nightclub, but apparently the plan was to sell bottled water from the underlying spring as a novelty item. Unsurprisingly that venture failed. In 1997 both forts were auctioned again. Haile Sand Fort was sold as a private sea-fishing base and Bull Sand Fort was sold for £21,000 to an Essex-based charity called Streetwise, for conversion to a drug-users' rehabilitation unit. The new owners said that £800,000 would be needed to convert the fort into a unit treating 150 patients at a time in 30-day spells. At the present time (2006), there have been no further developments.

Kilnsea

When the Yorkshire Naturalists' Trust bought the Spurn Peninsula in 1960 all land north of the reserve up to Long Bank was owned and cultivated by local farmers, many of them bearing the familiar names of Clubley and Tennison. Grange Farm, Cliff Farm, Northfield Farm, Southfield Farm and Westmere Farm were still run as mixed farms, as they had been for generations. Like their forebears before them, those with land adjoining the sea saw their acreage shrink yearly. Their land was a diminishing asset in

193 *The Reverend Grenville Heale, Rector, outside St Helen's Church, Kilnsea, March 1995. On the occasion of a coffee morning at Kew Villa, the church was opened for a time, and there was a short service, which may have been the last one to take place there.*

every sense. Perhaps fortunately for them, prospective buyers were on hand by the late 20th century ready and willing to take on marginal land. As a result, over the last 30 years a substantial proportion of the land in Kilnsea has changed hands, mainly being acquired by conservation bodies. When the Tennisons left Northfield Farm in the early 1970s their land was bought by the owners of Sandy Beaches Caravan Site, and the farmhouse was pulled down. When Albert Clubley retired to Easington, Cliff Farm became a private residence. The South Holderness Countryside Society's purchase of land in the Beacon Lagoons area has already been mentioned. In 1993 the Yorkshire Wildlife Trust bought the field south of the *Blue Bell*, a field west of Sunny Cliff in what is now usually known as the 'Triangle', an area of land bounded by the Humber, the road from the *Crown & Anchor* to the *Blue Bell* and the road from the *Blue Bell* as far as the entrance gate to the reserve. The Trust added to that holding in 1995, following the death of Arthur Clubley, when land associated with Southfield Farm came on the market. In 1997 Associated British Ports, apparently unlikely conservationists, bought three fields near Long Bank. That purchase came about as a *quid pro quo*, because ABP wished to buy some land for dock development near Grimsby and were only allowed to do so if they bought land on the other side of the Humber to be used in support of wildlife. Spurn Bird Observatory's purchase of land near the church has already been mentioned. They increased their holding in that area in 2001, when they purchased part of the field adjoining the church. The Wells family, who now run the dairy farm at Westmere (one of only two remaining on the Holderness coast), work quite closely with the conservation bodies and, as in the past, what remains of the fields of Kilnsea are a mixture of pasture and arable.

As the farms have changed hands in the last 30 years so have the residential properties. When properties have come on the market, some have been bought by people who, having had caravans on Sandy Beaches, have decided to settle down in the area. Nowadays very few of the properties are owned by people born in Kilnsea or with close family associations with the area. To an extent this

has changed the nature of the village. It has, however, meant that most of Kilnsea's residents are there by choice, because they love the place. They have accepted that it is a place 'on the edge', presumably a situation that they welcome rather than deplore. When Arthur Clubley died in 1995 and Ernest Tennison died in 1993 those names in the male line died out in Kilnsea, though happily Mrs Audrey Cooper, whose father was a Tennison and mother a Clubley, still lives in the village.

In the last 30 years no totally new dwellings have been built in Kilnsea, though some have been rebuilt on existing properties. Planning permission for new undertakings is fairly hard to come by, because of the eroding nature of the village and the threat of flooding. However, after Blackmoor Farm had a serious fire in December 1990, a new purpose-built 15-bedroom hotel was erected near the site, and opened in August 1991. In 2002, rather surprisingly, an application was made to upgrade the hotel, and provide more bedrooms, as well as a swimming pool and a helipad in order 'to attract Spanish families to the beautiful Spurn area', and apparently to provide short-term accommodation for British expatriates. A partial extension has since been added, though not on the scale envisaged in the planning application.

In July 1993 the last regular service was held in St Helen's Church, the congregation by then having dwindled to two worshippers. The church was deconsecrated and put on the market. Rumours abounded about its possible fate – it was to be taken down brick by brick and moved to the USA, it was to have its roof removed and declared a ruin, it was to be turned into a furniture warehouse. Thankfully none of those things happened. In 1999 it was bought, and is now being sensitively converted into a residence. The external appearance should change very little. The churchyard, which is covered with a succession of spring flowers every year, will remain open for interment of the ashes of Kilnsea residents.

Sandy Beaches Caravan Site continued to flourish, albeit upon a continually diminishing site. Its heyday was perhaps in the 1970s, when foreign holidays were still uncommon. Many of the caravanners did not have cars at that time, and

194 *Gun emplacements and other remains of Godwin Battery on the beach at Kilnsea, 2006.*

Connor & Graham buses were full to bursting on a Friday evening and a late Sunday afternoon. The clubhouse and all the facilities were very well used and there was a flourishing social life, the season being punctuated with festivities, such as the Easter Bonnet parade, the summer procession and so forth.

In 1971 the site was sold to the Skeffington and Schipper families, who stayed for 30 years. The two battery observation posts were taken down in the early 1970s, but much still remained of the military camp. These buildings, or what was left of them, were very popular with the children on the caravan site, and it is a wonder that there were not more accidents. Over the years, because of the hazards they posed, many buildings have been removed, but some of the First World War buildings still remain and are used mainly for storage. The Second World War NAAFI now houses the caravan park's clubhouse. The high cliff where the gun emplacements were located, and where the coastguard tower had been built, was used for touring caravans until the early 1990s but, as the two gun emplacements and the coastguard tower got closer to the edge and subsequently toppled over, the land was lost. Now Kilnsea beach is littered with relics of the old camp. They probably serve to protect the cliffs and have slowed down the erosion here, albeit only temporarily.

The firm of Connor & Graham, whose buses brought so many people to Kilnsea and Spurn over almost seven decades, was sold to East Yorkshire Motor Services in March 1993. The company stressed that they would continue to run services to such villages as Easington and Kilnsea, which were served only by Connor & Graham, but seven weeks later the service to Kilnsea was withdrawn. Carrie Leonard, former doyenne of the little café opposite the *Blue Bell*, had retired from her career on the sea by then, and become a regular visitor to her friend, Pat Stevenson, also retired from the *Crown & Anchor*, but now living next door to the pub. Pat and Carrie were told that to continue their regular contact they would have to use taxis.

Despite their remoteness, Spurn and Kilnsea continue to cast a spell upon people who live there or visit that corner of South Holderness. A small village connected to a three-and-a-half-mile peninsula, surrounded by sky and water, never far away from a reminder of a long and unique history, a key migration route for birds, butterflies and moths, a tourist attraction of an unusual type, an important base for search and rescue, navigation and pilotage services on a major estuary, easily visible on maps of the British Isles, a fragile, vulnerable place with an uncertain future, Kilnsea and Spurn continue to exercise their magic on all those who come to visit this unique and special area or, better still, live there!

Bibliography and Selected Sources

Many sources, too numerous to list, have been consulted in the preparation of this book. Only the principal ones have been listed here. However, a search of current bibliographies will prove fruitful for anyone seeking further information on the area. The East Yorkshire Bibliography is an on-line bibliography hosted by the Brynmor Jones Library, University of Hull at http://library.hull.ac.uk:81/.

The Humber Bibliography, developed and maintained by the Institute of Coastal and Estuarine Studies, is available on-line at http://www.humber-bib.hull.ac.uk/.

A *Bibliography of Spurn and the Lower Humber Estuary* was compiled by Peter Crowther for the Spurn Heritage Coast Project in 1999 and is available on-line at http://www.wilgilsland.co.uk/.

Books and Articles

Allison, K. J., 'Kilnsea' in *Victoria County History: A History of the County of York, East Riding*, Vol. 5: Holderness, Southern Part (O.U.P., 1984), pp. 65-74

Backhouse, J., 'A vanishing Yorkshire village', *Annual Report of the Yorkshire Philosophical Society*, 1908, pp. 49-59

Benfell, Roy, *Spurn Lifeboat Station: the first hundred years* (the author, 1994)

Chislett, Ralph and Ainsworth, G.H., *Birds on the Spurn Peninsula* edited by M. Densley (Peregrine Books, 1996)

Crackles, Eva, *The Flowering Plants of Spurn* (YNU, 1986). Reprinted from the *Naturalist*, April-June 1975 and updated March 1986

Crowther, Jan, 'The ale-houses of Spurn and Kilnsea', *Spurn Wildlife*, no. 3, 1993, pp. 58-62

Crowther, Jan, 'Blue bells and beacons: a Spurn A-Z', *Spurn Wildlife*, no. 13, 2003, pp. 10-15

Crowther, Jan, 'Coxswains of Spurn and their families', *Spurn Wildlife*, no. 11, 2001, pp. 84-7

Crowther, Jan, *Descriptions of East Yorkshire: de la Pryme to Head* (EYLHS, 1992), East Yorkshire Local History Society series, no. 45

Crowther, Jan, *Enclosure Commissioners and Surveyors of the East Riding* (EYLHS, 1986), East Yorkshire Local History Society series, no. 40

Crowther, Jan, ' "Human bones at Kilnsea as coals to Newcastle": the two St. Helen's churches', *Spurn Wildlife*, no. 5, 1995, pp. 71-4

Crowther, Jan, 'The incidence and chronology of parliamentary enclosure' in Neave, Susan and Ellis, Stephen, eds., *An Historical Atlas of East Yorkshire* (Hull U.P., 1996), pp. 66-7

Crowther, Pete, 'Barry Spence, Warden of Spurn National Nature Reserve, 1964-2002', *Spurn Wildlife*, no. 12, 2002, pp. 9-16

Crowther, Pete, 'Ravenser and Ravenser Odd: the early history of Spurn', *Spurn Wildlife*, no. 2, 1992, pp. 51-4

Crowther, Pete, 'Spurn Lighthouse [Centenary], 1895-1995', *Spurn Wildlife*, no. 4, 1994, pp. 60-3

Crowther, Pete, 'When Spurn was an island', *Spurn Wildlife*, no. 7, 1997, pp. 58-62

de Boer, George, *A History of the Spurn Lighthouses* (EYLHS, 1968) East Yorkshire Local History Society series, no. 24

de Boer, George, 'Coastal erosion of Holderness' in Neave, Susan and Ellis, Stephen, eds., *An Historical Atlas of East Yorkshire* (Hull U.P., 1996), pp. 6-7

de Boer, George, 'The history of Spurn Point' in Neave, Susan and Ellis, Stephen, eds., *An Historical Atlas of East Yorkshire* (Hull U.P., 1996), pp. 8-9

de Boer, George, 'Spurn Head: its history and evolution', *Transactions of the Institute of British Geographers*, vol. 34, 1964, pp. 71-89

de Boer, George, 'Spurn Point: erosion and protection after 1849' in Neale, J. and Flenley, J., eds., *The Quaternary in Britain* (Pergamon, 1981), pp. 206-15

Dorman, Jeffrey E., *The Guardians of the Humber: the Humber defences, 1856-1956* (Humberside Leisure Services, 1990)

East Yorkshire Family History Society, *Easington: monumental inscriptions* (EYFHS, 198-?)

East Yorkshire Family History Society, *Skeffling and Kilnsea: monumental inscriptions* (EYFHS, 198-?)

Frost, Howard M., *Sailing the Rails: a new history of Spurn and its military railway* (Spurn Heritage Coast, 2001)

Hartley, Kenneth E. and Frost, Howard M., *The Spurn Head Railway: the history of a unique military line* 3rd ed. (South Holderness Countryside Society, 1988)

Herbert, Barry, *Lifeboats of the Humber* (Hutton Press, 1991)

Jarratt, George A., *Memories of Spurn in the 1880s* (the author, 198-?)

Kendall, Ronald, *Growing up on Spurn Head* (the author, 198-?) Limited ed. of 50. Available in Hull Local Studies Library

Lazenby, Arthur, *The Cobble Stones of Holderness* (the author, 1994)

Malkin, Larry, *et al.*, *Easington in Times Past* by L. Malkin, A. Stothard, and D. Smith (Countryside Publications Ltd., 198-?)

Malkin, Larry, *et al.*, *The School at Spurn Point, 1893-1946*, by L. Malkin, A. Stothard, and D. Smith (Countryside Publications Ltd., 198-?)

Malkin, Larry, *Wavelength Wanderings along the Humber Estuary* (the author, 1992)

Morris, Jeff, *The History of the Humber Lifeboats* (the author, 1988)

Nicholson, J., *The Beacons of East Yorkshire* (privately published, 1887)

Pashby, Brian, *John Cordeaux, Ornithologist* (Spurn Bird Observatory, 1985)

Pethick, J. S., 'The Humber Estuary' in Ellis, Stephen and Crowther, D. R. eds., *Humber Perspectives: a region through the ages* (Hull U.P., 1990)

Pethick, J. S., 'Spurn Heritage Coast Study: final report' (Hull University, 1992) Unpublished

Poulson, George, *The History and Antiquities of the Seigniory of Holderness* (Thomas Topping, 1841)

Pringle, Ada W., *Classic Landforms of the Coast of the East Riding of Yorkshire* (British Geomorphological Research Group, 2003)

Ruddy, Austin J., *British Anti-invasion Defences, 1940-1945* (Historic Military Press, 2003)

Sheppard, J. A., *The Draining of the Marshlands of South Holderness and the Vale of York* (EYLHS, 1966) East Yorkshire Local History Society series, no. 20

Sheppard, Thomas, *The Lost Towns of the Yorkshire Coast* (Mr. Pye Books, 1986) Facsimile reprint of original edition, 1912

Sockett, E.W., 'Yorkshire's early warning system, 1916-1936', *Yorkshire Archaeological Journal*, vol.61, 1989, pp.181-8

Ward, R., *Spurn Head Postal History* (Yorkshire Postal History Society, 1988)

Welton, Michael A., *The Easington Lifeboat, 1913-1933* (the author, 2003)
White, Walter, *A Month in Yorkshire* 5th ed. (Chapman and Hall, 1879)

Newspapers and Periodicals
Holderness Gazette
Hull Daily Mail
The Naturalist
Spurn Bird Observatory *Reports* (from 1991 entitled *Spurn Wildlife*)
Yorkshire Naturalists' Trust (from 1984 the Yorkshire Wildlife Trust) *Annual Reports and Newsletters*
Yorkshire Post
The Zoologist

Manuscript and Primary Sources
Census enumerators' returns for Kilnsea and Easington from 1831 to 1901
Constable papers (DDCC) in East Riding of Yorkshire Archives Office
Electoral rolls
Local directories
Parish records and other sources for Kilnsea and Easington in East Riding of Yorkshire Archives Office

Index

Compiled by Peter A. Crowther

Page references to illustrations and their captions are in *italics*.
Colour plates are referred to by their plate number in **bold**